JEWISH UNIVERSALISMS

THE TAUBER INSTITUTE SERIES
FOR THE STUDY OF EUROPEAN JEWRY

The Tauber Institute Series is dedicated to publishing compelling and innovative approaches to the study of modern European Jewish history, thought, culture, and society. The series features scholarly works related to the Enlightenment, modern Judaism and the struggle for emancipation, the rise of nationalism and the spread of antisemitism, the Holocaust and its aftermath, as well as the contemporary Jewish experience. The series is published under the auspices of the Tauber Institute for the Study of European Jewry—established by a gift to Brandeis University from Dr. Laszlo N. Tauber—and is supported, in part, by the Tauber Foundation and the Valya and Robert Shapiro Endowment.

For the complete list of books that are available in this series, please see https://brandeisuniversitypress.com/series/tauber

Jeremy Fogel
Jewish Universalisms: Mendelssohn, Cohen, and Humanity's Highest Good

Stefan Vogt, Derek Penslar, and Arieh Saposnik, editors
Unacknowledged Kinships: Postcolonial Studies and the Historiography of Zionism

Joseph A. Skloot
First Impressions: Sefer Hasidim and Early Modern Hebrew Printing

*Marat Grinberg
The Soviet Jewish Bookshelf: Jewish Culture and Identity Between the Lines

Susan Martha Kahn
Canine Pioneer: The Extraordinary Life of Rudolphina Menzel

Arthur Green
Defender of the Faithful: The Life and Thought of Rabbi Levi Yitshak of Berdychiv

Gilad Sharvit
Dynamic Repetition: History and Messianism in Modern Jewish Thought

Charles Dellheim
Belonging and Betrayal: How Jews Made the Art World Modern

Yosef Hayim Yerushalmi in Conversation with Sylvie Anne Goldberg
Transmitting Jewish History

Cedric Cohen-Skalli
Don Isaac Abravanel: An Intellectual Biography

Chava Turniansky
Glikl: Memoirs 1691–1719

ChaeRan Y. Freeze
A Jewish Woman of Distinction: The Life and Diaries of Zinaida Poliakova

Dan Rabinowitz
The Lost Library: The Legacy of Vilna's Strashun Library in the Aftermath of the Holocaust

* A Sarnat Library Book

JEWISH UNIVERSALISMS

Mendelssohn, Cohen, and Humanity's Highest Good

JEREMY FOGEL

BRANDEIS UNIVERSITY PRESS

Waltham, Massachusetts

Brandeis University Press

Manufactured in the United States of America
Designed by Rich Hendel
Typeset in Bulmer by Rebecca Evans

This publication was made possible through the generous support of Brandeis University's Bernard G. and Rhoda G. Sarnat Center for the Study of Anti-Jewishness, which aims to promote a deeper understanding of anti-Jewish prejudice, as well as Jewish and non-Jewish responses to this phenomenon, from both a historical and a contemporary perspective.

Library of Congress Cataloging-in-Publication Data
Names: Fogel, Jeremy, 1981– author.
Title: Jewish universalisms : Mendelssohn, Cohen, and humanity's highest good / Jeremy Fogel.
Description: Waltham, Massachusetts : Brandeis University Press, [2023] | Series: Tauber Institute series for the study of European Jewry | Includes bibliographical references and index. | Contents: Introduction: Jewish universalisms—1. The enlightened universalistic devaluation of Judaism—2. Moses Mendelssohn's felicity—3. Universal felicity—4. Hermann Cohen's future—5. Messianic humanity—6. Jewish universalisms. | Summary: "Any version of universalism, pluralistic sensitivities, and post-colonial awareness would need to balance a universalistic perspective with the richness of human diversity. Modern Jewish philosophers who partook in the Enlightenment's universalistic vision and maintained their distinct identity are relevant for current thinking about the balance between universalism and diversity." — Provided by publisher.
Identifiers: LCCN 2023024352 | ISBN 9781684581726 (paperback) | ISBN 9781684581733 (cloth) | ISBN 9781684581740 (ebook)
Subjects: LCSH: Universalism. | Humanity. | Jewish philosophy. | Mendelssohn, Moses, 1729–1786. | Cohen, Hermann, 1842–1918.
Classification: LCC B5802.U65 F64 2023 | DDC 181/.06—dc23/eng/20230607
LC record available at https://lccn.loc.gov/2023024352

5 4 3 2 1

Dedicated to the Blessed Memory

of Amalia Margolin

רבת החסדים והאמת

& of my dearly beloved father,

Daniel Fogel,

who is with me always

Le Plus Beau Tombeau

est le Coeur des Hommes

CONTENTS

INTRODUCTION
Jewish Universalisms

Ours is a global age in which solutions to humanity's critical common problems must be developed from within a universalistic outlook. No one nation, no one ethnicity, no one religious community can, on its own, hope to successfully overcome the urgent existential challenges humanity is facing. Pandemics can't be dealt with only by the Canadians; global warming cannot be solved only by the Catalans; and economic inequality cannot be addressed only by the Buddhists. These challenges, as well as many more on our common horizon that threaten our very survival as a globalized civilization, if not as a species, cannot but be engaged with universally. More than ever, therefore, the twenty-first century seems to be one wherein either we will rise together or fall apart.

Yet the very notion of "universalism," so central to the philosophers of the Enlightenment and so significant to developing a sense of a common fate critically important to us as humans in this day and age, seems at times to have irrevocably fallen from grace. Most notably, the postcolonial perspective on the Enlightenment's universalistic pretenses has uncovered the various ways in which a universalistic discourse has been used to provide a veneer of benevolence to a wide variety of crimes against the very humanity whose common interest it was supposed to uphold.

Of course, the fact a certain discourse was used to justify terrible crimes doesn't necessarily mean that the originators of that discourse would have endorsed them. It seems rather likely that the kind of people who were involved in the crimes of colonialism didn't find it particularly unjustifiable to use lofty-sounding phrases to essentially lie their way through whatever abject horrors they were actually engaged in. It could very well be the case that colonial use of the universalistic language of the Enlightenment is in fact a desecration of what the philosophers themselves had in mind. One could, in other words, ask whether it is fair to blame genuinely universalistic philosophies for the crimes of later political entities malevolently misusing universalistic notions for their particular gain. It was not, after all, Kant who genocidally conquered Namibia or Voltaire who murderously oppressed the Algerians. Can we genuinely ascribe any degree of responsibility to them if later political figures misappropriated or abused their ideas? Should they not be held accountable only for what they themselves understood their ideas to mean?

It does seem at least somewhat unfair to blame a philosopher whose genuinely universalistic thought has been radically misconstrued in order to provide a lofty cover for a nefarious undertaking of any kind. However, things of course become far more ambiguous if the philosopher in question not only developed deeply universalistic ideas (which could arguably be shown to have been misconstrued) but also suggested discriminatory stances; promoted intolerant positions; or expressed, perhaps even developed, racist conceptions and forms of thought. And indeed, this is unfortunately the case for several of the most influential universalists of the Enlightenment.

Still, while frankly nauseating and wholly abhorrent, the racism and bigotry of these figures does not necessarily undermine or taint the importance of the universalistic values they also promoted. It could be the case that people like Voltaire defended deeply important principles even if he himself was unable or unwilling to fully uphold them. We might still argue for the importance of Kant's ideas on eternal global peace while fundamentally rejecting any of his appallingly misguided racist notions about how to differentiate and categorize various human ethnicities. Hume at times expressed racist and antisemitic thoughts.[1] But could other aspects of his writing have still been genuinely aimed at promoting the kind of cosmopolitan spirit that coheres far better with attempts at fundamentally undermining any form of ethnic or religious discrimination?

While these vile, obnoxious, and morally outrageous passages are deeply disappointing, perhaps even devastating to any affection we might as lovers of philosophy carry for these men as human beings, looking at these figures historically, we can still find ways in which the more genuinely enlightened aspects of their thought were significant in developing worldviews we still want to promote. Indeed, philosophers, like most human beings, are complex creatures: their thoughts do not all necessarily cohere; their character and subsequent legacy are at times multifaceted and morally ambivalent.

These tensions reflect an important insight we will delve into in greater depth later on, namely, that a single human being, let alone something as wide and complex as an ancient religious tradition with all its varied sanctified texts and sundry movements, could very well reflect both universalistic values as well as values opposing that very same universalism. Furthermore, the fact that figures like Kant, Hume, and Voltaire can be shown to have at times failed the universalistic values they themselves supposedly promoted already suggests that while the universalistic values we might wish to uphold were central to the philosophers of the Enlightenment, they cannot be reduced solely to the particular formulations they gained in that era. Indeed, if we find it reasonable to judge the Western Enlighteners, for better or worse, according to universalistic principles, then these principles are, at least in our eyes, potentially distinct from their work and personalities. And while these figures might have done much to develop such principles at a given time in European culture, they might not have been their source or for that matter the sole or most exhaustive manifestation of such thinking. This already indicates it would be wrong to think of the Enlightenment's version of this kind of thought as "universalism" itself rather than one of many forms of universalism. It seems to me, therefore, advisable to think in terms of multiple "universalisms."

Forms of universalism arose in Jewish, Christian, and ancient Greek contexts, generating concepts that might very well have in some ways set the intellectual framework for their modern European successors. But, of course, universalism is more universal than just these versions. Other forms of universalism arose completely independently in cultures far away from Paris, Athens, or Jerusalem. So, for example, in the fifth century BCE, during the early years of the Warring States period of Chinese history, Mozi, the founder of Mohism, taught that "'universal' is the means of changing 'discriminating,'" explaining that "if people were to regard others' states as they regard their own state, then who would still mobilise their own state to attack the states of others? They would regard others' [states] as they regard their own . . . it is 'mutual' and 'universal' which gives rise to the world's great benefits."[2]

While there are commonalities between Mohistic universalism and the universalism of the Enlightenment, it would clearly be a mistake to uncritically categorize them as conceptually similar. Each version of universalism ought to be contextualized and analyzed within the context of its own particularities. This is the case even if the problem of particularity is seemingly one that universalism seeks to overcome. Indeed, universalism, one could think, demands that we surpass our particularities in order to join in a grandiose global togetherness, which necessarily supersedes our petty tribal, ethnic, or other parochialisms. But even so, the ways in which this kind of demand is made, the arguments used, and the kind of global togetherness envisioned could all be radically different in differing universalistic visions. In other words, in our quest for universalism, particularities are very much maintained.

Furthermore, it is not only the case that any universalistic philosophy is ipso facto also a particular philosophy but also that the abovementioned less naïve postcolonial gaze on the Enlightenment's universalism uncovers the significance of the hegemonic status of the white, male, and Christian thinkers who articulated it. It was, in other words, not only in and of itself particular but belonged to a particularism sufficiently powerful to assert itself as universal. A common characteristic of the universalisms voiced by hegemonic social groups is the ease with which their particular sensitivities, whether moral, aesthetic, or religious, are presented and imposed as universally valid. Accordingly, universalism tended in the Enlightenment, and arguably continues today, to threaten cultural particularities and has all too often been used by hegemonic powers to legitimize erasing cultural variety.

Any version of universalism relevant to our hopefully more attentive gaze, pluralistic sensitivities, and postcolonial awareness would therefore need to balance the current urgent need for a universalistic perspective with the desire to maintain the richness of human diversity. In this context, thinking of the modern Jewish philosophers who sought to partake in the Enlightenment's universalistic vision, on the one hand, and to maintain their distinct identity as members of a religious minority within Europe, on the other, potentially offers uniquely insightful answers to these questions. Indeed, given these thinkers' sensitivity both to the necessity of a universalistic perspective and to the concern for maintaining diversity, their philosophical efforts are deeply relevant for current thinking about the balance between universalism and diversity.

Jewish Universalisms analyzes the way in which two major such figures, Moses Mendelssohn and Hermann Cohen, formulated their universalisms and dealt with the perceived tension between the universal values characteristic of the Enlightenment and aspects of Judaism often depicted as particularistic and parochial. It seeks to add to the lively scholarly debate on the question of universalism in modern Jewish philosophy by offering a thorough comparative examination of these thinkers and, furthermore, analyzing their worldviews from an innovative axiological perspective, that is, from the perspective of values.[3] As such, its premise is that in order to gain a precise and insightful understanding of how Mendelssohn and Cohen argued for the concordance of Judaism and universalism, one must first analyze the axiological structure embedded in their respective philosophies. One must, in other words, first seek out what they delineated as ultimately valuable and then work out the ways in which that highest good and the method of valuation it sustains are universal. Indeed, as the highest good outlined in Mendelssohn's and Cohen's philosophy is presented as the ultimate aim of Judaism, the universalism of that highest good will be at the heart of their attempt at depicting a universalistic Judaism.

This axiological analysis will enable not only a clearer understanding of these fascinating universalistic interpretations of Judaism but is also helpful in finding ways of developing forms of universalism that respond both to the desire to maintain cultural particularity as well as to the need for a common, global sense of human destiny. In analyzing Mendelssohn's and Cohen's universalisms in terms of their constitutive values, I hope to show how insightful thinking about any form of universalism in terms of its constitutive values is. Such an analysis does not only enable a clear demarcation of the various versions of universalism but also a better understanding of the aspects of any form of universalism we find objectionable and of those of which we approve. In doing so, it reveals the degree to which various forms of universalism can be riddled with inner tensions even if they are casually presented as coherent aspects of a supposedly unified ethos.

Indeed, the term *universalism* is too often left uncritically vague. It is not at all clear that it designates a distinct and crystalized worldview or even a coherent set of values. Even a relatively well-defined universalism, say the "universalism of the Enlightenment," seems to serve, rather, as an umbrella for various ethical principles, such as tolerance, equality of all human beings, or the importance of reason. So while a wide variety of thinkers have universalistic tendencies, *universalism* does not carry the same meaning or reflect the same prioritizations among all of them. In fact, some of these principles may conflict with one another. So, for example, a universalism that strongly upholds reason could conflict with one that focuses on equality. After all, even if all humans are thought of as endowed with reason, they might not all be endowed equally. Whether because nature gifted some individuals with a greater power of reasoning than others or because some cultures are perceived as having a less developed sense of reason than others, reason, even if construed as a universal good, is not necessarily egalitarian. The supposedly universal conception of human beings as all similarly endowed with reason can, furthermore, contrast with toleration: a reasonable agent might refuse to tolerate that which she deems irrational. Understanding these tensions within the Enlightenment's version of universalism is critical. Not only does it again suggest that there is no one single "universalism" but a variety of "universalisms" even within the Enlightenment but also that each version of universalism, whether of the European Enlightenment, of the Jewish tradition, or from other periods and cultures, could be insightfully characterized by the kind of values it promotes.

As mentioned above, a central aspect of these axiological examinations is what any philosopher argues or assumes is the highest good, enabling not only a clearer understanding of the axiological prioritizations within her ethical system but also a more astute delineation of the universalism involved. Indeed, it seems often to be the case that a particular universalism consists in arguing that whatever is thought of as the highest value is, or should be, universally applicable, available, or otherwise made relevant to all. In other words, a universalistic religious or political movement is one according to which the *summum bonum* is, and should be, universally obtainable, if not obtained. Accordingly, as well as evaluating the degree to which each form of universalism prioritizes various universalistic ethical principles, one can also appraise universalisms in terms of their highest good. And the question of the highest good is of course a central question in the field of axiology.

Philosophers tend to suggest a highest human good even if they have very different conceptions of the metaphysical, ontological, or theological status (if applicable) of that highest good. Accordingly, when analyzing the highest good, one must not only find out what the *summum bonum* of a given philosophical system is but also explore the metaphysical, ontological, or theological conceptions within which that highest good gains its validity. Therefore, when looking at Mendelssohn and Cohen, we will seek to delineate their highest value as well as that which enables it to rise in the first place.

Furthermore, our analysis will show that, while Mendelssohn and Cohen suggest radically different notions of the highest good, both share other critical axiological similarities: first, their axiological conceptions are clearly religious in the sense that in both cases the highest value is enabled by God. Second, these highest goods are portrayed as bonded in a deeply meaningful manner to their notions of Judaism. Indeed, in both cases Judaism is portrayed as essentially seeking to promote these highest values. Finally, while different, both of these highest goods share a critical commonality: they are in a deeply meaningful sense universal.

The focus on the highest good raises an issue it is important to address, namely, the contrast between the very notion of *summum bonum* and the non-essentialist sensitivities characteristic of modern axiology and already implicit in the introductory remarks above. Indeed, one major impetus for the rise of axiology in modern philosophy is the post-Kantian skepticism of all things metaphysical, among them structures that served as obvious sources of value for centuries. It is therefore not surprising that Nietzsche, whose work reflects the post-metaphysical crisis in modern philosophy with such great poignancy, gave values such a crucial importance in his writings.[4] In turn, his ideas about values played a very significant role in drawing further attention to the question of value as a critical philosophical problem.[5] And a major aspect of Nietzsche's thinking about values is his characteristic non-essentialism.

As he puts it in what I take to be a seminal phrasing of this position, "only something which has no history can be defined."[6] One can very easily define a square or an even-sided triangle, for example, but any definition claiming to encapsulate the essential meaning of a historical phenomenon (whether Judaism, the practice of punishment, or a particular morality) must necessarily be illusory. Historical phenomena, like practices and ideologies that rise in the lives of actual women and men, let alone values and methods of valuation, demand a different kind of treatment, one that, according to Nietzsche, remains acutely aware that meanings are often reinterpreted and values often revaluated. This treatment is what Nietzsche thinks of as a *genealogy*. Critically to us, Nietzsche's genealogical non-essentialism emphasizes the importance of untangling the seemingly crystalized notion of the Enlightenment's universalism into its various constitutive values, which, as we already saw above, may very well not be as coherent as they are usually assumed to be.

An axiological methodology centered on such a non-essentialist attitude seems to contradict any mode of thought that seeks to establish a notion of the good that is unified, let alone indubitable or objective. However, the fragmentation of the good, or more precisely the emphasis laid in modern axiology on tensions at play between differing methods of valuation or different values, does not of course mean that philosophers themselves have not historically sought to suggest a unified notion of the good. Even if we were to find various tensions in their notion of the good, it would not follow that they did not believe it, mistakenly or not, to be coherent and in some sense monistic. Moreover, the increased awareness of such tensions does not necessarily, in and of itself, mean that a unified notion of the good is impossible, let alone that a particular kind of value cannot be construed as the highest of values. After all, even philosophers who think reigning popular methods of valuation are clearly fragmented or even incoherent could very well themselves still suggest ones that they take in some sense as valid. So, for example, Spinoza famously related our notion of the good to our desires rather than some kind of good in itself, writing that "we neither strive for, nor will, neither want nor desire anything because we judge it to be good; on the contrary, we judge something to be good because we strive for it, will it, want it and desire it."[7] And yet, he himself still also explicitly suggested a highest good, namely, "knowledge and love of God."[8] Nietzsche himself, who deconstructed what he took to be the reigning European notion of the good into conflicting elements, also suggested a rather consistent notion of a highest good throughout his productive life, namely, the development of our vitality and our affirmation of life.[9]

Most importantly to us, both Mendelssohn's and Cohen's thought suggest notions of the highest good. Accordingly, while a non-essentialist axiological methodology provides the discursive tools to analyze axiological tensions, it must still also address the concept that historically might very well have been the most important axiological concept of all: the *summum bonum*, or highest good. In the spirit of Nietzsche's reluctance to define historical phenomena ahistorically, we will delineate the way the very notion of the highest good functions through the particularities of its use in the philosophies of Mendelssohn and Cohen rather than provide an essentialist general definition. Still, in order to better contextualize the term, it is worthwhile to briefly bring to mind several aspects of Plato's and Aristotle's views regarding the *summum bonum* that in many ways have framed the debate throughout much of Western philosophy as well as between Mendelssohn and Cohen.

Plato's idea or form of the good relates not merely to ethical values, but rather to the very possibility of the emergence of value in general. Indeed, having stated in the *Republic* that there is something even more important than justice and the other virtues, Plato writes that "the form of the good is the most important thing to learn about and . . . it's by their relation to it that just things and the others become useful and beneficial."[10] In other words, the good for Plato is the source of value; nothing can be construed as valuable unless it draws its value from it.

Yet, in spite of the centrality of the concept, he famously provided no systematic elucidation of it. Demos suggests this is because of his distrust of the written word and reminds us that Plato is said to have orally discussed the good explicitly with his students.[11] This is not to say Plato does not provide some clarifications in his writings, but these clarifications mostly only illustrate the degree to which his notion of the good is transcendental and ineffable.[12] So, for example, Plato states that the good is not being "but superior to it in rank and power."[13] This establishes the source of value, indeed of being itself, as beyond being, or rather perhaps as a higher form of being. The source of this-worldly value is essentially, therefore, otherworldly. And, furthermore, precisely because of that transcendence, this source cannot be comprehended like other things. As reflected in the allegory of the cave, the good can only be perceived by the few who escape the shadowy world of illusion inside. Accordingly, talking of the good, Socrates tells Glaucon that while it is important to establish that "there is something to be seen," he also warns the young man he will not be able to lead him to it "for you would no longer be seeing an image of what we're describing, but the truth itself."[14]

Socrates does tell us that the point "most necessary to assert of the good" is that "everything that has any notion of it hunts for it and desires to get hold of it and secure it for its very own, caring nothing for anything else."[15] We should therefore "do all things for the sake of what's good," and indeed "the end of all action is what's good."[16] Of course, in contrast to Spinoza's above-mentioned view (a position characteristic of much modern axiological thought),[17] Plato does not see the good as good in virtue of our desiring it. Rather, we desire it because we recognize it as absolutely valuable. Indeed, once it has glimpsed it, the soul's nature is such that it cannot but be attracted to this absolute good and seek to maximize its presence in our lives. And while Plato's descriptions of the good must remain necessarily vague and figurative, it remains clear that, in his eyes, the good life, and indeed any conception of the highest good for human beings, must directly relate to the one universal source of all value that is the form of the good. Plato's highest good, therefore, is one that maximizes the good in our souls and thus in our lives as well.

Aristotle criticizes this Platonic notion of the good, writing that the good "is not something common answering to one Idea."[18] He provides several arguments against the Platonic idea of the good,[19] all leading to a comprehensive refusal to accept that the same form of the good is present in all different kinds of good. However, that does not mean Aristotle himself did not suggest a highest good for human beings; he most explicitly did. Indeed, it is *eudaemonia* that is for Aristotle the highest good.[20] Aristotle argues that eudaemonia, usually translated as "happiness,"[21] is generally perceived to be the highest good as "both the general run of men and people of superior refinement say that it [the highest of all goods achievable by action] is happiness, and identify living well and faring well with being happy."[22] This of course raises the question of what the most exalted happiness is. For Aristotle, it is provided by the contemplative life. Indeed, "if happiness is activity in accordance with excellence," Aristotle writes in his *Nicomachean Ethics*, "it is reasonable that it should be in accordance with the highest excellence; and this will be that of the best thing in us," and as that which guides us "to take thought of things noble and divine" consists of contemplative activity, this activity "will be complete happiness."[23]

Many of the assumptions both Plato and Aristotle share about the highest good, such as it being self-sufficient or the proper end of human action and indeed of human existence, have remained mainstays of the concept of the *summum bonum* throughout the history of Western philosophy. A similarly prominent assumption is that the ultimate source of value in both cases is metaphysical. Indeed, while for Plato there can be no highest good without the transcendental form of the good, for Aristotle, it is the unmoved mover that ensures our actions can have a meaningful end and that a highest good can emerge.[24] As we shall see, all of these conceptions, in particular the metaphysical source of the good, are also clearly recognizable in the philosophies of Mendelssohn and Cohen.

Given the importance of the gulf between Mendelssohn's emphasis on felicity and Cohen's radical non-eudaemonism to our comparative analysis, the most important aspect of Aristotle's and Plato's originative treatment of the highest good for our current concerns is the contrast between Aristotle's emphasis of eudaemonia and Plato's seemingly more transcendentally oriented position, often perceived as being more focused on the metaphysical than the human realm. I have qualified this description of Plato's position because while the almost archetypical dispute between Aristotle's earthlier eudaemonistic emphasis and the cosmic, impersonal, and metaphysical weight of Plato's vision is critical to us, it might still in many ways be factually far less pronounced than its historical reception has made it out to be. While it is beyond the current scope to exhaustively explore why that might be the case,[25] suffice it to note that a central question in the *Republic*, where Plato delves so memorably into the metaphysical aspects of his axiological picture, is whether just people are happier than unjust ones.[26] Still, even if the contrast between Aristotle and Plato tends to be exaggerated, it remains the case that it carried great influence in Western thought and is conceptually helpful to have in mind when comparing Mendelssohn's and Cohen's axiological thinking.[27]

Finally, to further delineate our axiological methodology, an additional concept must be brought to the fore, namely, the notion of revaluation. As mentioned above, Nietzsche's interest in axiology was primarily driven from the metaphysical crisis he so memorably encapsulated as the death of God. This development, Nietzsche thought, was primarily a crisis of values: Nietzsche thought that European morality derived its values from the otherworldly divine realm and that after the death of God, this axiological mechanism has become unsustainable, raising the specter of nihilism. In light of the axiological crisis he identified, Nietzsche claimed that the task of the true philosopher "calls for him to *create values*."[28] He himself sought to undertake with his own philosophy the grandiose task of a creative "revaluation of all values."[29] It is, however, important to keep in mind that the effort of revaluation is not only depicted as an urgent task to be undertaken, but rather as a significant aspect of human history, one undertaken with particular vehemence by philosophers. It is the latter claim that matters to us most as the underlying principle of this study. We do not have to agree with the values Nietzsche promotes, not even necessarily with the results of his genealogical analysis. We take, rather, the methodological assumption that philosophers, modern as well as ancient, tend to engage in revaluative efforts.

By revaluation, I therefore mean any effort of reinterpreting, redefining, or reprioritizing values, as well as suggesting innovative ones.[30] Nietzsche pointed out that such an effort is especially relevant in a clash of cultures as a necessary response, as it were, to what Charles Taylor calls an "identity crisis," an "acute form of disorientation" wherein people "lack a frame or horizon within which things can take on a stable significance, within which life possibilities can be seen as good or meaningful, others as bad or trivial."[31] The rise of a secular age, and the seemingly unprecedented possibility of full and equal access to European culture and society, was such a cultural clash, leading to a potential crisis in identity, which could not but urgently demand a revaluation of Jewish values. Indeed, in light of the enlightened universalistic devaluation of Judaism discussed in the next chapter, an axiological response would naturally involve a revaluation of Judaism. We will keep this, and the importance of revaluation in philosophical projects more generally, in mind throughout this study as we explore Mendelssohn's and Cohen's attempts at arguing for the universal credentials of Jewish values.

Our axiological analysis of both Mendelssohn and Cohen will therefore look at the highest good their philosophies suggest and contextualize it within their respective theo-ontological conceptions. Furthermore, throughout our analysis, we will rely on the analytic discourse enabled by modern axiological thinking to critically assess their methods of valuation, uncovering the prioritizations they suggest as well as the tensions within them. Finally, we will argue, in both cases, that a critical aspect of their methods of valuation is that it enables a universalistic revaluation of Judaism. And while they construe their methods of valuation as essentially Jewish, engaging with their efforts as creative revaluations enables an insightful contextualization of their axiology in their philosophical efforts.

Overview

The first chapter seeks to provide the philosophical and cultural context within which modern universalism arose. While attacks on the perceived parochialism of Judaism were already common in antiquity among both pagan and Christian writers, the universalism characteristic of the philosophers of the Enlightenment cannot be reduced to the universalism ancient critics of Judaism had in mind. The beginning of the chapter therefore focuses on three characteristic aspects of modern universalism, which it argues are common among the major figures of the time: egalitarianism, tolerance, and the ubiquity of reason. Many philosophers of the Enlightenment attacked Judaism for its supposed opposition to all three. Accordingly, they depicted Judaism as hierarchical, exclusivist, and based on superstition. It is further argued that the most poignant thinker in this context is Spinoza, as his work reflects the most acute enlightened universalistic devaluation of Judaism. The general intellectual climate devaluative of Judaism and Spinoza's challenge in particular form the context within which both Mendelssohn and Cohen formulated their positions.

The second chapter analyzes the method of valuation that Mendelssohn's philosophical argumentation reflects and promotes. It argues that Mendelssohn's highest value is eternal felicity (*Glückseligkeit*), which is construed as dependent on the existence of a providential God who ensures human immortality. The chapter explores Mendelssohn's prioritization of felicity, as well as his view of God and immortality, emphasizing in particular how his metaphysical ideas are, according to Mendelssohn's own epistemological thinking, derived from commonsense rather than speculative reason. It then seeks to show how this axiological structure directs his political philosophy by analyzing how the primordial importance Mendelssohn attributed to eternal felicity in his political calculations lies at the heart of his criticism of both Hobbes and Locke on the relation of church and state. The chapter concludes by arguing that while reason is often branded an ultimate value in Mendelssohn's philosophy, he actually holds a rather ambiguous position towards it.

Having established this axiological grounding, the third chapter shows why and how Mendelssohn thought his highest good, that is, eternal human felicity, is accessible to all. This leads to an analysis of the religious pluralism reflected in his thought, as well as of its limitations. The chapter also shows why Mendelssohn not only thought that Judaism does not hamper the universal accessibility of felicity but even encourages it. This leads to a discussion of how the axiological angle reframes Mendelssohn's position vis-à-vis accusations of overly particularistic tendencies inherent in the Jewish heritage, as well as doubts concerning the authenticity of his loyalty to Judaism.

The fourth chapter shifts to an exploration of the axiological structure embedded in Cohen's philosophy. Given the importance of Kantian philosophy to Cohen, it begins with a description of Kant's *summum bonum*. It shows that while Kant criticized happiness as an end for practical reason and thought the good will was the unlimited good, he did also think that happiness could not but be taken into account for the complete good. Cohen, in stark contrast to Mendelssohn, completely rejects happiness as a worthy value, going even further than Kant in this regard. The chapter shows how this anti-eudaemonism is reflected in his depiction of Judaism, which he argues has continually eschewed the quest for happiness. Instead, Cohen suggests the highest good is the messianic future. This future, his religious version of the kingdom of ends, is enabled by a correlation (*Korrelation*) with the unique God, the proper understanding of whom is critical for the infinite messianic task to arise.

The fifth chapter further analyzes the way in which Cohen thought about the value of religion, above and beyond philosophy, and specifically how he delineated the significance of Judaism, which he describes as the primal source of the religion of reason. It then focuses on the ways in which Cohen argued for the universal scope of the morality Judaism seeks to promote. This universalism is emphasized through the all-encompassing reach of the messianic ideal, as well as through notions such as the Noachide laws, or the love of the *rea*. While Cohen is, according to his own principles, committed to the idea that other cultures have developed and advanced the cause of the religion of reason, this chapter shows that, with the notable exception of his highly idealized notion of Germanism, no such culture is unambiguously valued. Furthermore, as Cohen argues that errors in the conception of God lead to the gravest moral offenses, the chapter shows how his demand for a universal Messianism involves moments where intolerance is construed as necessary. The chapter concludes with an analysis of the existential repercussions of Cohen's idealistic revaluation of Judaism and argues that the emphasis on the idea of humanity and the messianic future does not necessary disavow Jewish existential vitality.

The sixth and final chapter compares the universal sensitivities uncovered by our axiological analysis of Cohen and Mendelssohn. It argues that while in both cases Jewish particularism is justified because it serves a highest good that is essentially universal, the different highest goods suggested lead to very different Jewish universalisms; whereas Mendelssohn's promotes egalitarian tolerance, Cohen's is based on reason at the expense of tolerance. This chapter analyzes the different values these universalisms prioritize and shows how they are reflected in the different tonalities of their writings, in particular about Spinoza. It also shows how, while radically different, both Mendelssohn and Cohen argue that their notions of Judaism reflect its original essence. However, while essentialist in their apprehension of Judaism, both philosophers sought to reflect in their conception of the essence of Judaism the dynamism of the interpretative aspect of the Jewish heritage.

While these differing notions of Judaism are similarly universalistic, it is not a matter of comparing the degree to which either Mendelssohn or Cohen upholds universalism. Both strive to be universalistic, but their universalisms are completely different. The conclusion, accordingly, points out that the notion of universalism in and of itself does not mean much. The real question is what the highest good any version of universalism is actually seeking to promote is. Values, this book suggests, are as constitutive of our particular selves as they are of universalism itself.

(1)

THE ENLIGHTENED UNIVERSALISTIC DEVALUATION OF JUDAISM

An Ancient Modern Problem

Within the faith of your fathers itself lies an immense rift that bars your nation from unlimited participation in the public and private benefits of society that put everyone in the state on an equal footing.[1]

THE "SEARCHER FOR LIGHT AND RIGHT" (1782)

The euthanasia of Judaism is pure moral religion, freed from all the ancient statutory teachings, some of which were bound to be retained in Christianity (as a messianic faith). But this division of sects, too, must disappear in time, leading, at least in spirit, to what we call the conclusion of the great drama of religious change on earth (the restoration of all things), when there will be only one shepherd and one flock.[2]

IMMANUEL KANT (1798)

The question, rather, is whether the Jew as such, i.e., the Jew who is himself aware that his own essence obliges him to live in eternal separation from others, is able to receive universal human rights and accord them to others. His religion and way of life commit him to eternal separation: Why? Because they are his essence.[3]

BRUNO BAUER (1843)

The seeming exclusivity of the notion of a chosen people, and the stiff-necked aspiration to maintain a unique religious and cultural heritage, generated controversy for the Jewish people long before the enlightened age of reason, during which the "Searcher for Light and Right" (August Cranz),[4] Kant, and Bauer stated their rather vitriolic accusations. As Jon D. Levenson notes, "pagan authors in antiquity resented what they saw as Jewish exclusiveness and early Christianity often claimed to universalize the Hebrew Bible's supposedly parochial view of the divine covenant, making it available to all the nations of earth."[5]

So, for example, Diodorus Siculus describes, in the first century BCE, how King Antiochus VII Sidetes was advised by his counselors during the siege of Jerusalem to "take the city by storm and to wipe out completely the nation of the Jews, since they alone of all nations avoided dealings with any other people and looked upon all men as their enemies . . . the Jews had made their hatred of mankind into a tradition, and on this account had introduced outlandish laws: not to break bread with any other people, nor to show them any good will at all."[6]

Similarly emphasizing the supposed contrarian character of the Jewish religion, the famed Roman historian Tacitus writes that "to establish his influence over this people for all time, Moses introduced new religious practices, quite opposed to those of all other religions,"[7] adding that "the Jews are extremely loyal toward one another, and always ready to show compassion, but toward every other people they feel only hate and enmity. They sit apart at meals and they sleep apart, and although as a race, they are prone to lust, they abstain from intercourse with foreign women."[8]

Perhaps the most enduringly pertinent ancient example is the apostle Paul, who describes the Jews as "opposing everyone,"[9] and who expounds his universalistic credentials in an oft-quoted passage of his Epistle to the Galatians, stating that "there is no longer Jew or Greek, there is no longer slave nor freeman, there is no longer male nor female; for all of you are one in Christ Jesus. And if you belong to Christ, then you are Abraham's offspring, heir according to the promise."[10]

While Paul, and many other early Christian authors,[11] had clear polemical reasons to claim a universalistic superiority with regards to Judaism, which they sought to diminish as particularistic and parochial, contemporary writing on these issues often still echoes these ancient depictions and their biases.[12] So, for example, in his work on Paul, Alain Badiou not only argues for the apostle's foundational importance to universalism but repeatedly contrasts it to a Judaism uncritically depicted as particularistic. Interestingly, as an atheist, Badiou states that his interest in Paul is not religious,[13] but rather centered on the possibility of a universal teaching; "Paul's unprecedented gesture consists in subtracting truth from the communitarian grasp, be it that of a people, a city, an empire, a territory, or a social class."[14] Yet Badiou's declared detachment from religious concerns does not seem to assuage the degree to which the ancient religious polemic is reflected in his analysis, which recurrently opposes Paul's universalism to Jewish "communitarianism."[15] Badiou characterizes the Jewish discourse as "a discourse of exception" the object of which is "elective belonging, exceptional alliance between God and his people."[16] While he admits his book's subtitle, *The Foundation of Universalism*, is excessive in so far as "real universalism" is already present in Archimedes's theorems, in Greek political practices and tragedies, and even in the Psalms or Ecclesiastes,[17] Badiou construes Paul as exemplarily universalistic because "thought becomes universal only by addressing itself to all others."[18] And this, Badiou explains, is precisely what the apostle to the nations did.[19]

Jon D. Levenson questions the view, held by the early Christian church and later commentators, that Judaism is to Christianity "as exclusiveness is to inclusiveness, closedness to openness, particularism to universalism," and indeed "as bad is to good" and claims that Paul's vision cannot be construed as genuinely universalistic given that whether one is heir to Abraham's particular covenant is still of utmost significance in his eyes. Although Paul "specifies a different rite of passage from that of the Rabbis, like them, he still assumes that whether one is in Israel or not is of supreme importance."[20] Paul does seek to abolish the difference between Jew or Greek, slave and freeman, man and woman, but only insofar as all of them are united in Christ. Rather than abolishing all differences, this founds a new one between those that are in Christ and those that are not. In other words, there is a clearly exclusive theological underpinning to the seeming inclusivity of Paul's thinking. Quoting the words of the Jesus of the Johannine tradition, "No one comes to the father except through me,"[21] Levenson accordingly concludes that Christianity is at least as particularistic as Judaism, as neither affirm a wholly undifferentiated humanity, and that the perception that this is not the case finds it source in confusing the majoritarian character of Western Christianity with a genuinely universal religion.[22]

While our focus is on the modern debate about universalism rather than the ancient one, a first insight suggested even by a brief foray into the latter, and which is critical to the former as well, is that the notion of "universalism" itself is rather muddled and opaque. Indeed it is, prima facie, not exactly clear what the longed-for universalism is supposed to mean. If, say, Christian "universalism" designates the universal reach of Christianity in so far as it is universally the case that anyone must adhere to the particular Christian faith to find salvation, then, as Runesson argues, this form of universalism really means missionary activity.[23] Yet, as Runesson further points out, scholarly analysis of ancient Jewish religion does not merely use the term *particularism* to refer to a lack of missionary activity.[24] It designates, rather, a much wider field encompassing the Jewish attitude towards gentiles.[25] In this discourse, *particularism* is used almost interchangeably with *nationalism*, *exclusivism*, or *communitarianism*, while *Jewish universalism* comes to designate, roughly speaking, an attitude towards gentiles that can be construed as positive.[26]

In order to gain greater precision in evaluating the question of universalism with regards to religions and their sources, Runesson offers a more detailed typology and suggests examining three different theological aspects: the ethnic aspect, which assesses the degree to which the religion in question is identified with an ethnicity and according to which religions can be classified as closed, open, or nonethnic; the aspect of salvation, assessing whether salvation is inclusive or exclusive (i.e., whether it is available to people of other faiths or not); and the aspect of mission, which Runesson suggests can be either a proselytizing, an ethical-religious, or an inward mission. This more precise terminology, Runesson concludes, shows that the simplistic description of ancient Judaism as particularistic and ancient Christianity as universalistic fails to meet the demand of scientific argumentation and instead reflects the theological and ideological bias of the scholars using the terms.[27]

Jon Levenson's and Runesson's arguments, though raised primarily at ancient critics of Judaism and the scholars who study them, do point at assumptions about both Judaism and universalism still held in modernity and reflected in the above quotes by Cranz, Kant, and Bauer.

Though part and parcel of a completely different era, all three still clearly believed that Judaism, whether because of some essential elements in its faith or because of its statutory laws, reflects a particularism that is significantly different from the particularism naturally associated with any other particular religion or movement. As opposed to Christianity, or indeed more relevantly, as opposed to the Enlightenment and its values, it offers no universal scope, carries no universal aspiration, and stands accused of its own social isolation or of focusing exclusively on the destiny, the well-being, and the purpose of one particular people or religious community.

Still, though the Christian heritage of the culture from which the Enlightenment arose did not evaporate overnight and the modern discourse on Jewish particularism can, to some degree, be traced back to more ancient Christian ways of engaging with the issue, modernity in general and the Enlightenment in particular did redefine this debate in profoundly significant ways. Most importantly for us, it redefined the debate by suggesting new characterizations of universalism. We saw above that *universalism* can carry differing, at times even opposite, meanings. This complexity demands a historical contextualization of modern "universalism" and its significance. Indeed, the universal values of the Enlightenment, even when developed by Christian philosophers, cannot be simplistically identified with those championed by Christianity in the centuries before the age of reason, let alone in antiquity. So, for example, ancient Christian universalism includes neither pluralism, in so far as a particular faith must be universally accepted, nor necessarily even tolerance, in so far as the kind of universalism reflected by, say, Paul does not ipso facto involve promoting peaceful coexistence with groups that refuse his particular faith. Yet pluralism and toleration are in fact, as will be shown below, critical to the universalism of several major philosophers of the Enlightenment. And of course, while ancient Christian universalism is based on miraculous revelation, the universalism of the Enlightenment is, generally speaking, based on universally shared reason.

In other words, "universalism" in the centuries relevant to us cannot be characterized in terms of ethnicity, salvation, or missionary activity only, but encompasses rather a variety of notions and values, such as equality, tolerance, and reason. The set of values at hand, as well as their prioritization, might very well differ quite significantly between different movements or philosophers and, accordingly, the elusive and problematic notion of universalism must be elucidated and delineated with regards to each movement or philosopher. But even if its details need to be fleshed out on an almost individual basis, it remains the case that modern universalism differs, and rather significantly, from ancient religious universalism.

It is therefore not surprising that while the three authors quoted above criticize supposed particularistic aspects of the Jewish religion, they cannot be construed as representatives of traditional Christianity and its own claims. To the contrary, their work reflects to some degree a critical attitude towards their own religious heritage as well, even if that critique is at times more nuanced or less bluntly formulated. Thus, Cranz was a deist who, to quote Feiner, "had nothing but contempt for clerical forces, superstition, and religious fanaticism." Cranz saw himself, rather, as fighting "the battle of Enlightenment" and outspokenly argued for religious toleration, including of the Jews.[28]

Though Kant would certainly not have used the term *euthanasia* when writing of Christianity, the moral religion he advocated, based as it is on reason, clearly differs from the traditional religious heritage he had been educated into.[29] While his thought reflects some aspects of Christian morality and is in that sense arguably not wholly secular, Kant clearly felt Christians ought to reframe their faith according to the Enlightenment's values and has accordingly been characterized by major scholars as having had a profoundly secularizing influence.[30] Indeed, the "all-crushing Kant,"[31] as Mendelssohn famously called him, generated a dramatic sense of religious crisis among his contemporaries, a sense of loss poignantly encapsulated by Heinrich von Kleist, who in a letter to his fiancée describes having recently become acquainted with Kant's philosophy and having consequently reached the despairing conclusion that ultimate truths cannot be obtained and that any wisdom gained disappears with death: "If the blade of this thought does not cut your heart," Kleist plaintively writes, "do not laugh at another who feels himself wounded by it in his Holiest inner self. My one highest aim has sunk, and I have no more."[32]

Bauer, as disturbing a tone as he might have used against the Jewish religion, had not only also written against Christian practices he felt were obsolete,[33] but eventually came to explicitly reject Christianity altogether, arguing that Jesus never existed and that religion is nothing but a repressive delusion.[34] As he put it in his *Christianity Unclosed*, which is dedicated to promoting "atheistic Enlightenment":[35] "all good things that religion possesses and grants become evil in the possession of religion."[36] Christianity, he furthermore declares, is nothing but "an independently established expression of a disgust that antiquity found toward itself in the end."[37]

While Bauer's treatment of Christianity might have been particularly belligerent, by the time he wrote his *Christianity Unclosed* (1843), the status of traditional Christianity had been growing increasingly precarious even among less radical thinkers for about two centuries.[38] As McCarthy indicates, in the wake of writings by Reimarus, Lessing, Diderot, Voltaire, and others, "not only the Old Testament's God but also the New Testament's Son of God had become stumbling blocks for reasonable men," adding that "the momentum of Enlightenment philosophy of religion was to reject Christianity and its Christ and to replace them with a universal religion of reason."[39]

These religious and philosophical developments reflected dramatic cultural and political changes that affected both Christians and Jews.[40] Crucially, the delineation of a secular state, the concept of human and civil rights as universal principles, and the prospects of emancipation seemed, prima facie, to offer Jews not only a long-yearned-for relief from centuries of religious intolerance but even a pathway to full participation in modern society.[41] Jewish thinkers who joined the exciting new world of enlightened learning and free thought had therefore perhaps an even greater incentive than their Christian peers in the quest to create a tolerant society based on reason and protective of universal human rights. For these intellectuals, harmonizing the seemingly particular aspects of Judaism with the Enlightenment's proclaimed universalism was not only an apologetic enterprise aimed at proving both to gentiles and to Jews that they could be part of such a society without letting go of their unique religious and cultural heritage but also an integral aspect of their effort to contribute to the rise of this enlightened society.

Therefore, the rise of Enlightenment values and their fervent development in the works of several major European philosophers, coupled with the prospect of an unprecedented emancipation of European Jewry, led to an acute need for the formulation of a synthesis of Judaism and the philosophies and values of the modern era. Indeed, more specifically, it is clear that modern Jewish philosophy could not but concern itself with trying to provide an intellectual framework that would harmonize the perceived universal nature of the values of the enlightened age of reason with several prima facie particularistic aspects of the religious tradition it developed from.

As this book analyzes the ways in which Moses Mendelssohn and Hermann Cohen developed such frameworks in their philosophy, we will begin by looking at the kind of universalistic values the Enlightenment brought to the fore. Indeed, as will be shown extensively throughout our analysis, Mendelssohn and Cohen were not only both deeply concerned with the question of universalism and wholly committed to a philosophy and a Judaism that are universalistic in character, but, while active in very different intellectual climates, both still thought of themselves as part of the Enlightenment tradition. And while universal Enlightenment values (priority of reason, civil and human rights, universal ethics, etc.) are prioritized and emphasized differently in Mendelssohn's and Cohen's distinct methods of valuation, both still very much promoted values recognizable to universalistic Enlightenment thought. In order to better understand these efforts, we will therefore first contextualize the question of universalism in early modernity and explore the intellectual developments that spurred the Enlightenment's demand for universal values. Having sketched the relevant background, we will then look at the enlightened devaluation of Judaism this axiological framework entailed, focusing on Spinoza, who I will be arguing is the central figure in the enlightened and universalistic devaluation of Judaism.

Modernity and Universalism

The beginning and the end of historical periods are of course difficult to pinpoint, and historiographies are varied and diverse. Though useful, such determinations tend to be scaffolds for reflection rather than empirical facts.[42] There is, however, a wide agreement as to the seminal events and developments at the rise of what the West thinks of as modernity.[43] Originating in fourteenth-century Florence, the cultural movement known as the Renaissance, often characterized as marking the end of the Middle Ages, brought the study of ancient Greek and Latin works back to the heart of European cultural life and developed groundbreaking humanistic philosophies as well as artistic and scientific innovations. The invention of the printing press in the mid-fifteenth century enabled ideas to spread faster than ever before and reach a far greater audience.[44] The Reformation, which symbolically began with Luther posting his ninety-five theses on the door of Wittenberg's Castle Church in 1517,[45] put an end to almost a thousand years of religious, cultural, intellectual, and political rule by the Catholic Church.

The Reformation not only eventually enabled the rise of secular states but also encouraged the awakening of European thought from its dogmatic slumbers. Indeed, the reemergence of skepticism on the philosophical scene, which had been spurred on by the rediscovery and publication of Sextus Empiricus's works in the sixteenth century,[46] was significantly amplified when advocates of both the Reformation and the Counter-Reformation borrowed Sextus's skeptical arguments to dismiss the cases of their opponents.[47] Among the great masters in the art of using skeptical arguments in such debates was François Veron, who taught at a Jesuit college in La Flèche. One of his pupils there, René Descartes, was to ground a methodology of doubt that would herald the rise of modern philosophy.[48]

The crumbling of an ancient intellectual world correlates too with the European exploration of the Americas at the end of the fifteenth century. These geographical discoveries shook the intellectual foundations of European culture. After all, if the ancients had missed out on a whole continent, what else could they have omitted? Furthermore, the tales of encounters with peoples deemed uncivilized but moral, the so called "noble savages," raised doubts as to whether only the European could be moral and gave rise to an enduring philosophical fascination with radical cultural differences, as is reflected in the writings of authors such as Montaigne and later Rousseau.[49]

Perhaps most importantly, Copernicus's publication in 1543 of his *De Revolutionibus Orbium Coelestium* shattered an image of the universe that had remained relatively stagnant since the days of Ptolemy and signaled the radical nature of the rise of the scientific revolution. It also, crucially, strongly undermined the absolute literal authority of the Bible. Indeed, the new sciences not only superseded Ptolemy but also contradicted the geocentricism reflected in the Bible.[50] And if in scientific matters human reason is more trustworthy than biblical authority, the leap to moral and philosophical matters is not far away.

Trying to salvage a unified and cohesive notion of universalism from these colossal developments in Western society and thought would be not only beyond the scope of this chapter but, more importantly given the fluid nature of the concept of universalism, probably impossible. However, we will seek to provide a more limited historical contextualization by focusing on the rise of three interrelated notions that are central, in some version or other, to most modern forms of universalism and constitutive of the framework within which the Enlightenment's values arose and bloomed: equality, toleration, and reason, all of which can be shown to emerge from the intellectual revolutions at the heart of European modernity.

THE END OF ARISTOTELIAN HIERARCHIES

The intellectual crisis that occurred in seventeenth-century Europe is often related primarily to the collapse of the Aristotelian scholastic worldview and the rise of the new philosophy and sciences.[51] A particularly dramatic and significant aspect of this revolution was, to refer to Koyré's famous phrasing, the transition from a closed world to an infinite universe. Indeed, according to Aristotelian cosmology and Ptolemaic astronomy, which held sway in Europe until the end of the sixteenth century, the cosmos is spherical, enclosed, and ordered.[52] This fully chartable universe, wherein all things had a distinct place, also had a center, namely, earth, around which the planets and fixed stars moved, embedded in celestial spheres of which Aristotle suggested there was a sum of fifty five.[53] The spheres that made up the Aristotelian universe rotated under the ultimate control of the unmoved mover, who first instigated motion.[54]

Unsurprisingly, the perpetually taxonomic Aristotelian philosophy also suggests this universe can be categorized according to clear hierarchies, of which God is the best and highest being.[55] As Funkenstein puts it, "Aristotle's *nature* is a ladder of *natures*."[56] So, for example, the sphere of the stars, nearest to the unmoved mover in Aristotle's cosmology, is involved in the least movement and accordingly is prioritized as closer to the universal telos than lower spheres.[57] Sublunary nature too, of course, is organized in a hierarchy, which Sedley names "cooperative" in so far as it is structured so that "the lower benefit the higher."[58] So, for example, having inferred that plants exist for the sake of animals, Aristotle writes in his *Politics* that "if nature makes nothing incomplete, and nothing in vain, the inference must be that she has made all animals for the sake of man."[59]

The hierarchical cosmos had profoundly significant political implications. Indeed, the polis was perceived not only as an individual writ large, as is the case notably in Plato's *Republic*,[60] but also as a small small-scale cosmos.[61] The same order that obtained in the cosmos would therefore have to obtain in the body politic as well. Accordingly, the Greek universe,[62] as Ferry points out, was naturally hierarchical in both its cosmology and its politics, and a just Greek polis is one in which human beings function according to their preordained ranks, fulfilling the harmony of set hierarchies and reflecting the order of the cosmos.[63] In other words, the Greek cosmology enabled a clearly aristocratic ethos, according to which, as Aristotle puts it, "from the hour of their birth, some are marked out for subjection, others for rule."[64]

Aristotle's deeply stratified characterization of humanity differentiated not only between natural slaves and rulers but also between men and women, the latter of whom were regarded as naturally inferior,[65] as well as between Greeks and non-Greek people, the latter being relegated, albeit to varying degrees, to the status of slaves.[66] All these hierarchies are presented as beneficial to both parties because they are natural,[67] and as they are natural, they must be good. This of course is the very same good that is reflected by the order of the stratified cosmos.[68] That cosmos, furthermore, could sustain clear hierarchies precisely because it was construed as a closed system, one wherein all things are embedded according to their place or rank. It is critical to keep these crucial aspects of the Aristotelian universe in mind when reflecting on the primordial effects of its collapse.

As mentioned above, the collapse of the Aristotelian cosmos began in earnest with the Copernican Revolution. This tremendous intellectual upheaval, which took the European mind from a geocentric to a heliocentric cosmos, was, as has already been indicated, in and of itself deeply significant in encouraging critical and secularizing modes of thought. But Copernicus's cosmos was still finite, enclosed, and well-ordered.[69] The cosmic Aristotelian hierarchies would only be truly disbanded once the universe became infinite. Indeed, the infinity of the universe entailed ideational consequences as radical, if not even more so, than those the Copernican Revolution had engendered. Lovejoy points at several such revolutionary innovations more "startling and pregnant" even than Copernicus's that gained ground in the sixteenth and became accepted by the seventeenth century:[70] the breaking down of the outer walls of the cosmos and the infinity of the physical universe, and the assumption that the fixed stars are suns like our own and that they are surrounded by planetary systems inhabited by conscious life, as indeed the other planets of our system are.[71] Though several figures had already pointed to such a universe,[72] it was, Lovejoy explains, Giordano Bruno who "must be regarded as the principal representative of the doctrine of the decentralized, infinite and infinitely populous universe," a vision that he preached throughout Western Europe "with the fervor of an evangelist."[73]

It is this vision that brought about, as Koyré puts it, "the destruction of the Cosmos . . . of the conception of the world as a finite, closed, and hierarchically ordered whole," replacing it with an infinite universe "bound together by the identity of its fundamental components and laws, and in which all these components are placed on the same level of being." Human beings, Koyré says, therefore lost not only their place in the world but indeed the world itself and hence "the very framework of [their] thought."[74] The clear hierarchies of the Aristotelian cosmos became irrelevant in a universe where earth was one more planet orbiting one more star, and we were but one rational species among potentially endless others living their lives under any one of the endless suns. Crucially, too, as it had become infinite, this new, disorienting universe had lost its center. And if there is no center and no boundaries, there can be no higher or lower; there can be no clear cosmic hierarchy. As Badiou points out in a different context, "all true universality is devoid of a center."[75]

In short, the infinite universe of the Enlightenment is far less able to sustain the kind of aristocratic ethos that flourished in the Aristotelian one. A new cosmology cannot but underlie a new politics, and it cannot but encourage new values. Specifically, while it seemingly makes sense to deny the highest good to human beings who are born lower on the ranks of an essential cosmic hierarchy, it becomes more difficult to argue for such an exclusion once that hierarchy ceases to be ingrained into the very fabric of the universe.

This is not to say, of course, that this new infinite universe brought to a halt human demarcations of superiority. Human beings seem particularly eager to find ways of generating such demarcations, and indeed, the development of racial theories in modernity, for example, clearly shows that the Aristotelian cosmos is not a necessary prerequisite for hierarchical views of humanity.[76] Frederickson even argues that "paradoxical as it may seem, the rejection of hierarchy as the governing principle of social and political organization, and its replacement by the aspiration for equality *in this world* as well as in the eyes of God, had to occur before racism could come to full flower."[77] But even if racism was developed to maintain power structures and prejudices endangered by the collapse of the hierarchical views that had previously maintained them, it reaffirms that this collapse could at the very least potentially spur the view that no such differentiations were legitimate.

Accordingly, while the universe becoming infinite and the development of the notion of the equality of all people cannot be linked in an exhaustively simplistic causal manner, they are related nonetheless and are not coincidental aspects of the emerging world of the Enlightenment and its philosophers. The infinite universe draws the ideals of universalism in ways in which the closed one did not. It is in this context interesting to note that Thomas Jefferson, who declared that "all men are created equal" at the beginning of the American Revolution,[78] was an enthusiastic admirer of Epicurus, who he referred to as his "master."[79] Epicurus, like other atomist philosophers and as opposed to Aristotle, whose conception historically gained mainstream acceptance, believed in an infinite universe. Tellingly, the first sentence of Jefferson's syllabus of the doctrines of Epicurus states succinctly, "The Universe Eternal. Its parts, great and small, interchangeable."[80]

TOLERATION, THE MORAL OTHER, AND THE COSMOPOLITAN AGE

We mentioned above that the European "discovery" of the Americas and the encounters with its peoples was another significant aspect of the great intellectual crisis that signaled modernity. Perhaps because of the earth-shattering nature of this discovery, as well of course as the impossibility of deriving accurate geographical insights until far more thorough explorations had been undertaken, the European explorers did not immediately realize they had actually stumbled on what would later be referred to as a "New World" that forever changed their conception of the old one.[81] Gradually, the realization dawned that this was indeed a whole new continent,[82] and the accepted geography collapsed just like Ptolemaic astronomy would a few years later. The former, like the latter, encouraged skeptical thought: "I am by no means sure that some land may not be discovered in the future," Montaigne wrote about the discovery of America, "since so many persons, greater than we are, were wrong about this one!"[83]

The New World was not, however, only fascinating geographically, but anthropologically as well. The notion that people in faraway lands who had never even heard of Christianity, let alone converted to it, and lived in what was often described as a "state of nature" still seemed to behave in ways no less moral than Christians and led lives often portrayed as rather blissful proved to be enduringly enthralling to early modern intellectuals.[84] Montaigne is again an exemplary thinker in this context, providing what Conley describes as "perhaps the first and greatest reflections on the impact of the discovery and colonization of the New World upon Europe and early modern consciousness."[85] So in his famous essay "On the Cannibals," while describing peoples who engaged in ritualistic cannibalism of executed enemies, Montaigne seeks to show that Europeans, and the terrible acts engendered by the raging wars of religion, are no less cruel. "There is," he writes, "nothing savage or barbarous about those peoples, but . . . every man calls barbarous anything he is not accustomed to."[86] Montaigne describes a rather idyllic existence of communal living, dance, hunting, exhortations by "prophets" to virtue and duty, and so on.[87]

Their cannibalism, it turns out, is not undertaken for food, but as ultimate revenge, one that is accepted as normative by all involved.[88] Montaigne tells us this, however, not because he is seeking to argue that these cannibalistic practices aren't wrong; he thinks they are. He is, rather, making the far more sophisticatedly egalitarian point that "while judging correctly of their wrong-doings we should be so blind to our own." Indeed, there is more barbarity than that exhibited by the inhabitants of the New World who execute and eat their war prisoners, he continues, in eating men alive; in torturing their living bodies; in feeding them, while still sentient, to dogs and pigs; all of which occurred in his time and "among our fellow citizens and neighbors—and, what is worse, in the name of duty and religion."[89]

Montaigne closes "On the Cannibals" with an almost eerily significant passage describing a visit of three natives who, "unaware of what price in peace and happiness they would have to pay," left the "gentleness of their region to come and see ours." At Rouen, they meet King Charles IX. When asked what amazed them most, they make three points out of which Montaigne remembers two: they ask why all the fully grown, bearded men around the king "consent to obey a boy rather than choosing one of themselves as commander," and secondly, noticing the strong disparity between rich and poor, they found it odd that the emaciated poor "should put up with such injustice and did not take the others by the throat or set fire to their houses."[90] The natives had noticed, in other words, the absurdity of French monarchy and of its overly economically segregated society. Through the eyes of these reasonable and egalitarian "savages," Montaigne already saw the roots of the revolution that was to come two hundred years later.

Montaigne's writings, the many extremely popular accounts of travel and exploration,[91] and the ever more precise and widely read maps, all of which could now, after the spread of printing, be swiftly disseminated, reflected an increasingly interconnected world. The creation of global sea lanes, which enabled a global system of transportation and communication, encouraged a global economy.[92] Accordingly, the sixteenth century saw, as Bentley remarks, the rise of "an age of cross cultural interaction on a previously unprecedented scale," one which "brought almost all of the world's peoples into frequent, intense, and sustained interaction with one another,"[93] heralding a "genuinely global epoch of world history."[94] The emerging "global consciousness" encouraged by these historical developments encouraged a more unified view of humanity and spurred the cosmopolitan ideal, which blossomed in the eighteenth century.[95]

In a polemical poem providing an apology for luxury, Voltaire exults in a globalized economy that brings to a European table a delicious cup of coffee in which Arabian beans are served in Chinese porcelain on a plate of silver from the New World.[96] The worldwide collaboration of individuals and materials that here stirs Voltaire's "cosmopolitan imagination" reflects a more profound cosmopolitanism that, to quote Schlereth, seeks to "transcend chauvinistic national loyalties or parochial prejudices."[97] Voltaire states in a chapter of his *Treatise on Toleration* entitled "On Universal Tolerance" that "we ought to regard every man as our brother" and continues by exclaiming, "What? The Turk, my brother? The Chinaman, my brother? The Jew and the Siamese as well?" before emphatically concluding, "Yes, assuredly, for are we not all children of the same father, and the creatures of the same God?"[98] That same cosmopolitanism is reflected too in his universal history in which, to quote Schlereth again, he promoted a "Copernican revolution in historiography, displacing the Christian European from his comfortable seat at the center of the historical universe."[99] Indeed, Voltaire emphasized the cultural richness of India, Persia, and in particular China, which he suggested was the actual cradle of civilization.[100]

Voltaire's sinophilia was not an innovation. Leibniz, who denied being "one of those impassioned patriots of one country alone" and claimed to work "for the benefit of the whole of mankind, for I consider heaven as my country and all cultivated men as my compatriots,"[101] had been passionately interested in Chinese thought and culture. "Who would have believed," he writes in the preface to *Novissima Sinica*,[102] "that there is on earth a people who, though we are in our view so very advanced in every branch of behavior, still surpass us in comprehending the precepts of civil life?"[103] A similarly admiring view was held by Christian Wolff, who was famously expelled in 1723 from the University of Halle, and indeed Prussia, for having given a lecture in which he praised the profound soundness of Chinese morality and Confucian thought.[104] Given that these Chinese moral teachings were based on reason rather than revelation, Wolff was perceived as heretically arguing that atheists and pagans could be as moral as Christians—a position the theologians at Halle found unacceptable.[105]

"There are great Advantages in travelling," Hume wrote in a letter to John Home, "and nothing serves more to remove Prejudices."[106] However extensively the Enlightenment philosophers travelled physically (which they tended to do),[107] their thought travelled even more widely. Accordingly, describing human beings, Hume sees "a creature, whose thoughts are not limited by any narrow bounds, either of place or time;

who carries his researches into the most distant regions of this globe, and beyond this globe, to the planets and heavenly bodies."[108] These mental voyages, whether to China or the New World, Ancient Egypt or contemporary Persia, made ancient prejudices irrelevant to the new global world. Furthermore, given that many of these societies were not Christian, this made Christian exclusivism itself an untenable prejudice. So with the discovery of the moral other, whether in Confucius or in the Native Americans, the Enlightenment's version of universalism, as opposed to the Christian one, sought a religion that would not deny them salvation.

Perhaps the most poignant expression of this spiritual aspect of the cosmopolitan's worldview is Rousseau's priest of Savoy. In his religious guidance to Emile, the priest bases himself on a noticeably modern, egalitarian, and tolerant worldview according to which "there is not a being in the universe that cannot in some respect be regarded as the common center around which all the others are ordered."[109] He therefore also thinks of human ranks as a dismal spectacle.[110] Aware of the multiplicity of creeds and religions, the priest focuses on the wide human agreements on basic moral laws: "Cast your eyes on all the nations of the world, go through all the histories. Among so many inhuman and bizarre cults, among this prodigious diversity of morals and characters, you will find everywhere the same notions of good and bad."[111] In light of this common human decency, Rousseau's God could not have intended his salvific message to be heard only by one specific people: "He who begins by choosing a single people for himself and proscribing the rest of mankind is not the common Father of men. He who destines the great majority of His creatures to eternal torment is not the clement and good God my reason has shown me."[112] This would show a great cruelty towards all those that did not have the opportunity of hearing that particular salvific message, those in the "still unknown heart of Africa, where no European has ever penetrated up to now"; the wandering hordes of the deepest Tartary who "far from having heard of the Pope, hardly even know the Grand Lama"; those in the "immense continents of America, where whole nations still do not know that peoples from another world have set foot in theirs"; the "thousands of poor slaves" in the harems of Asia; those who died on the "eve of the day that the first missionary arrived" in their country. "If there were only a single man in the whole universe who had never been preached to about Jesus Christ," Rousseau concludes, "the objection would be as strong for that single man as for a quarter of mankind."[113]

It was clear to Rousseau, as it was to most cosmopolites, aware that they shared a world with a bewildering variety of humans whom they nonetheless saw as essentially similar, that a particularistic faith would be unworthy of a truly global God. The age of cosmopolitanism was therefore one of cultural and religious toleration. As long as the basic, natural human morality, shared in Peking, London, or the New World, was alive in the hearts of worshippers, their faith must be considered acceptable if not truthful. "Bear in mind," the priest tells Emile, "that the true duties of religion are independent of the institutions of men; that a just heart is the true temple of the divinity; that in every country and in every sect the sum of the law is to love God above everything and one's neighbor as oneself."[114]

THE RISE OF REASON

The scientific revolution clearly emboldened the confidence put in reason. The groundbreaking new sciences increasingly proved that truth must be discovered through the application of autonomous reasoning rather than through authority. This spirit, it is important to note, was true both of what we think of today as scientific research as well as philosophical thought. These, as Koyré points out, cannot, in the context of the great intellectual revolutions of the sixteenth and seventeenth centuries, be understood separately.[115] Indeed, at the time, the term *natural philosophy*, or even the word *philosophy*, were used for what we currently refer to as *science*. So Newton, in the preface to his *Mathematical Principles of Natural Philosophy*, writes that the "basic problem of philosophy seems to be to discover the forces of nature from the phenomena of motions and then to demonstrate the other phenomena from these forces."[116]

The most striking and historically significant example of this insubordinate autonomy of reason is arguably Descartes, widely perceived as the father of modern philosophy and of course himself, using contemporary terminology, both a philosopher and a scientist.[117] The method of radical doubt his *Meditations on First Philosophy* suggests is one that does away with any and all authority. It assumed, as he put it, that "it was necessary, once in the course of my life, to demolish everything completely and start again right from the foundations if I wanted to establish anything at all in the sciences that was stable and likely to last."[118] In other words, in his quest for certainty, Descartes eradicates all prior knowledge to build anew with bricks that are sound because they are yielded from reason and reason alone. There is in this thought, which was to be foundational to modern philosophy, no trace of the authority of the church, of scripture, of the intellectual heritage of the ancients, or of any previous generation for that matter. None of these remain relevant after the gesture of methodological doubt has done away with all prior knowledge.[119]

Indeed, the radicalism of Descartes's act is such that it can be thought of as an intellectual precursor to the decapitations of prior authority that characterized the French Revolution, during which, as in Descartes's *Meditations*, all authority was erased in order to build a new order based on reason. It also, as Gellner argues, points to a quest for "liberation from dependence on the accidents of a given historic situation."[120] Gellner therefore describes Descartes as a "cognitive Robinson Crusoe" who transcends culture,[121] and adds that this abstraction from culture was shared by Kant and Hume, who also would view the transfer of "cognitive sovereignty to 'custom and example'" as the endorsement of "any old *ancien régime*."[122]

Reason gained supremacy not only in science and philosophy but in religion as well. The enlightened natural religion was based not on revelation, but on reasonable comprehensions all could achieve. As Thomas Paine put it in his *The Age of Reason*, "I do not believe in the creed professed by the Jewish church, by the Roman church, by the Greek church, by the Turkish church, by the Protestant church, nor by any church that I know of. My own mind is my own church."[123] While Paine's formulation is particularly radical, in so far as they sought to retain religion, most enlightened philosophers were not that distant from Paine's position, if at all. After all, what Paine thinks of as the most sublime activity in his mental church is the free exercise of the universally shared reason that he describes as the "choicest gift of God to man."[124] Accordingly, he writes that "it is only by the exercise of reason that man can discover God."[125] Many of the members of the religious enlightenment would similarly agree that reason is a genuine and trustworthy source of religious truths (even if not necessarily the only source). As Funkenstein notes, in the

Enlightenment, "the Christian tenet that 'there is no salvation outside the Church' was matched by the new belief that there is no salvation except through the use of reason."[126]

But reason was not valued solely because it led to religious salvation. Indeed, some of the more radical individuals and groups who refused to believe in any form of religious salvation still remained fervently committed to reason. So, for example, Franciscus Van Den Enden, the deeply egalitarian democrat who famously taught Latin to Spinoza (as well as influencing his early philosophical development) and was ultimately hanged because of his involvement in a republican plot against Louis XIV of France,[127] was described in 1662 by the Danish scholar and scientist Olaus Borch as a Cartesian atheist who denied the sacred mysteries and whose "religion is nothing other than sound reason."[128] A later and particularly extreme example is the "cult of reason," which briefly flourished during the French revolution. In the spirit of dechristianization, this movement rededicated the cathedral of Notre Dame in November 1793 to reason, organizing a public festival involving a live allegory of the goddess of reason and a choir singing the "hymn to reason" in a cathedral where busts of Voltaire, Rousseau, Franklin, and Montesquieu, as well as a torch of liberty on a small Greek altar, had come to replace Christian iconography.[129] While for the followers of the "cult of reason," reason did not necessarily lead to religious beliefs, it still had to replace religion.

Critically, the primacy of reason strengthened the conception of human equality. A critical aspect of the modern scientific revolution was the uniformity of the laws it uncovered. As Koyré puts it, modern science enabled the "substitution of the homogenous and abstract space of Euclidian geometry for the qualitatively differentiated and concrete world-space conception of the pre-Galilean physics."[130] This, of course, could not but emphasize that at all times, in all places, the same laws applied. Considerations of value or of perfection gave way to a universal mathematical exactitude and uniformity. For Newton, Funkenstein explains, space, time, and nature are all homogeneous in all respects, and accordingly "the same forces can act everywhere in the same manner, the same laws of nature can be valid everywhere."[131] Newton's laws, furthermore, offered the thrilling promise of accurately defining the principles of this uniformity.

Inspired by their scientific heroes, philosophers too sought to address humanity with the same universal uniformity. So Spinoza famously declares he "shall consider human actions and appetites just as if it were a question of lines, planes and bodies."[132] When describing his "science of man," which seeks to "explain the principles of human nature," Hume writes that "we must endeavor to render all our principles as universal as possible."[133] The uniformity of nature inspired a quest for both a unified morality for all humanity as well as one for uniform religious principles. Having noted that "there is no sect in geometry," Voltaire suggests a universal religion that would overcome sectarianism, one based on the commonly agreed upon notion that "there is a God, and we must be Just." With this, Voltaire concludes, "we have the universal religion established in all times and among all men."[134]

The enquiry into human nature inspired by the scientific revolution further linked reason and equality by ascribing reason to all human beings. To quote Montaigne, "all men are of the same species, and, in varying degrees, are all furnished with the same conceptual tools and instruments of judgment."[135] So too Hume, Kant, and many other of the philosophers of the Enlightenment assumed that the human mind was identical in all ages and all societies,[136] an identity grounded in reason.

It is, however, critically important to note that the ubiquity of reason, and reason as a value, can also at times strongly conflict with the egalitarian worldview. Indeed, as the passage from Montaigne already indicated, while all people are endowed with reason, they might not be so to the same degree. Whether because nature gifted some individuals with a greater power of reasoning than others or whether because some cultures are perceived as having developed reason less than others, reason, either as a quality all human beings share or as a value that must be prioritized, can find itself in a rather tense relation to equality. It can, furthermore, similarly contrast with toleration. Thus, a reasonable agent might refuse to tolerate that which she deems irrational. This tension within the Enlightenment's version of universalism is critical, and we will return to this issue at some length later on.

To conclude, equality, toleration, and reason are all particularly salient aspects of modern universalism. These conceptions lead to values that can be prioritized differently. In other words, any of the Enlightenment's philosophers might promote some elements and reject others, but in so far as it is possible to suggest a framework within which "universalism" in the modern context finds its meaning, it would seem hard to neglect these basic notions.

These aspects of the modern worldview, furthermore, differentiate modern universalism significantly from the Christian version, which as we saw was explicitly rejected by the modern universalists as inadequate. But, returning to the passages quoted at the beginning of this chapter, one element that did remain was the critique of Judaism as especially particularistic. While a belief in a deity itself was far from unacceptable and in fact often argued for, the notion that it would have focused exclusively on a "chosen," particular people seemed thoroughly absurd to the enlightened philosophers. In so far as Jews maintained their traditional beliefs, these thinkers saw them as negating the essential values modern universalism aspired to. The belief in chosenness seemed to contradict the equality of all people; the Jewish faith was depicted as based on an exclusivistic revelation that does not seem to admit the aspired-for cosmopolitan worldview; and indeed the sanctified Jewish sources were deemed not to show a commitment to reason.

These, then, are the fundamental principles at the heart of the criticisms both Mendelssohn and Cohen sought to respond to. In the case of Mendelssohn, active as he was in the eighteenth-century cosmopolitan republic of letters, there can be no doubt as to the relevance of the historical context delineated above. For Cohen, one must take into account some drastic changes between the intellectual environments of the late eighteenth and the late nineteenth centuries. Cohen's was a time when significant aspects of the Enlightenment's cosmopolitan values had been forsaken for a newly nationalistic spirit. We will examine this critical difference in the historical context of both philosophers in greater length later in the book.[137] Suffice it to say that in spite of the significant epochal difference between the two, as a dedicated Neo-Kantian who sought to restore Kant's universal morality, Cohen explicitly commits himself to the Enlightenment's ideals. He is therefore challenged, as Mendelssohn was, to show they cohere with Judaism and to provide a philosophy that is committed to both.

It is, furthermore, important to keep in mind that while both responded to critiques yielded from the wider intellectual context delineated above, they themselves, out of their own philosophical systems, were also deeply engaged with the universalistic vision that context aspired to. They themselves were inherently part of the context of modern universalism. It is not the case that Mendelssohn and Cohen stepped out of some deeply particularistic bunker into the daylight of universalism. To the contrary, from their perspective, the sanctified Jewish sources are in many ways the sources of that daylight, and the Enlightenment's values are in fact those espoused by Judaism in some essential way. Indeed, Mendelssohn believed that "according to the concepts of true Judaism all the inhabitants of the earth are destined to felicity,"[138] and for Cohen, the prophets "exhorted men to a kind of politics as if they were eighteenth century cosmopolitans."[139]

So while the historical contextualization suggested above provides an important background to the rise of universalism and universalistic values in the Enlightenment, both Mendelssohn and Cohen will seek to provide a genealogy of these values that traces them back to Jewish sources they suggest are at the basis of Western culture. The equality of all human beings, the toleration of the moral other, or, indeed, the quest for world peace might very well relate to modern conceptions, but they are also, both Mendelssohn and Cohen argue, primarily anchored in ancient Jewish notions, such as the descent of humanity from one man created in God's image, the Noahide laws, or prophetic Messianism.

Accordingly, in responding to the enlightened universalistic challenge, they also challenged the way in which it was posed, and while Mendelssohn and Cohen undoubtedly engaged with the dichotomy between universalism and particularism, the systems they suggest to overcome the dichotomy challenge the way in which the dichotomy itself is presented. It is of course the case that many of the critiques of Judaism we have seen above almost assume a supposed tension between universal values and some aspects of the Jewish heritage deemed overly particularistic. Yet, this does not mean Mendelssohn and Cohen shared that assumption. Uncritically agreeing to that would mean reading them through the eyes of their philosophical adversaries. Indeed, many of the philosophers in question (with of course the notable exception of Spinoza) had very little knowledge of these sources, let alone of the way they had been traditionally interpreted. Why accept their interpretation or even their discourse? Whether convincingly or not, it is important to realize Mendelssohn's and Cohen's responses do not seek to solve the tension but rather to show it never was.

Arguably the most acute enlightened universalistic devaluation of Judaism, and therefore also a particularly critical aspect of the kind of philosophical challenge both Mendelssohn and Cohen sought to overcome or dismantle, was not formulated by the French philosophes or by the great German cosmopolitans, whether Leibniz or Kant. It is from within the Jewish people that a particularly devastating devaluation of Judaism arose, one in which the values of Enlightenment universalism are clearly embedded. This challenge, of course, is the one posed by Spinoza. In order to further examine the historical context of Mendelssohn's and Cohen's revaluations, and to make fully explicit the enlightened devaluation of Judaism, we will briefly explore Spinoza's radical and devastating depiction of Judaism and its (lack of) value.

Spinoza's Devaluation of Judaism

Spinoza's life and thought provide some very obvious sacrilegious credentials, perhaps none more evident or dramatic than his particularly severe excommunication at the age of twenty-three and his proud defiance in the face of its backlash. Due to lack of historical evidence, it has remained a mystery what precisely the "abominable heresies" were that brought about this *cherem* in 1656.[140] While we cannot necessarily assume he already held some of the more famous heretical opinions found in works written years later, it is of course possible he did at least already hold some of them.[141] Perhaps the most fascinating clue available is the testimony of the monk Tomas Solano y Robles, who when reporting to the inquisition in Madrid in 1659 about his travels, mentions meeting two excommunicated Jews in Amsterdam: Doctor Prado and "a certain de Espinoza." Prado and de Espinoza told him they were circumcised and had observed the Mosaic law but were expelled from the synagogue because "it appeared to them that the said Law [of the Jews] was not true and that the souls die with the bodies and that there is no God but the philosophical one."[142] At any rate, whatever the exact reasons for Spinoza's early excommunication, it is clear that his full-blown philosophy, based as it is on the identification of God with nature, was perceived as profoundly heretical by both Jews and Christians throughout Europe.

Spinoza's philosophical pantheism posits the beatific knowledge of God as the highest value: "knowledge of God is the Mind's greatest Good; its greatest virtue is to know God."[143] This knowledge is dependent on reason, which Spinoza describes as "the true original text of God's word" and opposes to the "dead letters" of scripture, which "men's wicked conduct could have corrupted."[144] Spinoza's salvation, furthermore, is fundamentally universal. Though the way leading to it "must be hard,"[145] it is open to anyone willing and able to take it: "the greatest good of those who seek virtue is common to all, and can be enjoyed by all equally."[146] Indeed, reason, and the resulting kind of universalism, are foundational principles of Spinoza's philosophy and are, furthermore, at the heart of his critique of Judaism.

While the full exposition of Spinoza's philosophical system is to be found in the *Ethics*, the *Theological-Political Treatise* already contains much of the extremely devaluative consequences of this philosophy for Judaism. Indeed, though much of the most virulently subversive content of the *Theological-Political Treatise* is written, as Leo Strauss put it, between the lines,[147] even the overt text is quite outrageous and openly disputes orthodox views on the meaning of prophecy, of Jewish chosenness, of miracles, of the authorship of the Pentateuch, and so forth. Perhaps most significantly, as Spinoza's God and his notion of true blessedness are sought through universal principles of reason, he judges the value of any text according to its ability to promote these salutary doctrines. The Old and New Testaments, therefore, are only spiritually valuable in so far as they promote such values. If they do not, one might as well be reading "the Koran, or the dramas of the Poets, or even the ordinary Chronicles, with the same attention as the common people usually give to these things."[148] So by disconnecting the bond, previously perceived as necessary, between the highest value, that is, "the knowledge and love of God,"[149] and the canonical Jewish texts, Spinoza opens the possibility of a fundamental devaluation of the most supremely valuable and sanctified Jewish source. That devaluation is, furthermore, based on the fact that the genuine "natural divine law" is "universal, *or* common to all men, for we have deduced it from universal human nature." Accordingly, "faith in historical narratives, no matter how certain that faith may be, cannot give us any knowledge of God."[150]

Spinoza's reliance on passages from the scriptures to make his arguments is not a mere reinterpretation of the Bible. Such interpretations had, after all, been an intrinsic part of the intellectual efforts of previous Jewish philosophers, Maimonides being of course the prime example, and belong to a rich tradition dating back to the sages and even earlier. Spinoza, however, does not merely reinterpret the Jewish scriptures as essentially historical and concerning a particular people at a particular time. He, rather, also relies on this interpretation to radically devalue these canonical texts. His extensive reliance on biblical quotes to do so is not a testament to a lingering sense of authority the Jewish scripture still held in his eyes, but rather a brilliant and deeply subversive exercise in irony. To quote a Dutch proverb Spinoza himself cares to mention: "*geen ketter zonder letter* [there is no heretic without a text]."[151]

Let us now look at that devaluation itself. Spinoza clearly does not believe the Bible to be valuable as a source of truth. "Scripture," he writes, "does not condemn ignorance; it condemns only stubbornness," and faith derived from it "does not expressly demand true dogmatic belief, but only such beliefs as are necessary for obedience."[152] Accordingly, the revelation at Sinai was not about God teaching the Israelites the "absolute attributes of his essence. (He did not reveal any of them at that time)."[153] Rather, it was about drawing them to obedience. Servitude to God is therefore the essence of Judaism for Spinoza. This, however, is not yet necessarily devaluative. Mendelssohn, as we will see in greater depth later on,[154] makes quite similar claims about both the nature of the Sinaitic revelation and the essence of Judaism as obedience to a sanctified revealed legislation without devaluating either that revelation or the Mosaic law.[155] This position does entail, however, that the value of the Old Testament and Judaism depends on the value of the Mosaic law, through which servitude to God is so closely associated in Judaism. Accordingly, in order to make the case for Spinoza as the central figure in the enlightened devaluation of Judaism, we need to delineate what Spinoza thought the value of the obeisance to the sanctified Jewish legislation is. I would like to start by focusing on a passage from the fifth chapter of the *Theological-Political Treatise*, in which Spinoza suggests the following unspiritual political rationale for, and origin of, the Mosaic ceremonial law:

> In order that the people, who were not capable of being their own masters, should hang on the words of its ruler, he [Moses] did not permit these men, accustomed as they were to bondage, to act just as they pleased. For the people could do nothing without being bound at the same time to remember the law, and to carry out commands which depended only on the will of the ruler. For it was not at their own pleasure, but according to a fixed and determinate command of the law, that they were permitted to plow, to sow, to reap. Likewise, they were not permitted to eat anything, to dress, to shave their head or beard, to rejoice, or to do absolutely anything, except according to the orders and commandments prescribed in the laws. This was not all. They were also bound to have on the doorposts, on their hands, and between their eyes, certain signs, which always reminded them of the need for obedience. This, then, was the object of the ceremonies: that men should do nothing by their own decision, but everything according to the command of someone else, and that they should confess, both by constantly repeated actions and by meditations, that they were not their own master in anything, but were completely subjected to someone else's control. From all this it is established, more clearly than by broad daylight, that ceremonies contribute nothing to blessedness, and that those of the Old Testament, indeed, the whole law of Moses, was concerned with nothing but the Hebrew state, and consequently, with nothing but corporeal advantages.[156]

In this particularly daring and outrageous passage, Spinoza describes the ceremonial law hallowed by generations of Jews, who identified it with the very essence of religious life and its most intimate and existentially significant expression, and which he himself posited as the essence of Judaism, as nothing more than a cunningly deceitful and decidedly oppressive political tool. Indeed, Spinoza does not merely describe the lowly political origin of the ceremonial law; he also delves into its psychological effect. Spinoza's conception of the effect of the Halakha is one that reduces those who uphold it to feeble beings whose very ability to make any kind of independent decision whatsoever has been completely jeopardized. In the passage above, he accordingly describes Moses as having systematically stripped the Hebrews of the very ability to act as autonomous agents. While Moses is traditionally depicted as the great liberator of the enslaved Hebrews of Egypt, Spinoza describes his rule as one that succeeded in transforming an external kind of slavery into a much more radical internal slavery.

It is important to note that in the framework of Spinoza's deterministic worldview, freedom consists in acting from within one's own necessity as opposed to being forced to act from outer necessity. Moses, however, compels the Hebrews to act under external authority always and therefore denies their freedom completely. Furthermore, acting freely, from this inner necessity, is for Spinoza the increase of one's "conatus," or that with which we strive to persevere in our being.[157] The religious heritage Moses burdened his people with, the ceremonial law, is therefore detrimental to the increase of the conatus and thus detrimental to the most basic, healthy, affirmative, and vital forces. This is why, in a famous and remarkably prescient remark on the possibility that the Jewish people could regain political sovereignty, he writes this would be possible "if the foundations of their religion did not make their hearts unmanly."[158] Though rather chauvinistically put,[159] the idea here is now clear: if the Jews have not been overly enfeebled by the weakening force that is their ceremonial law, they might be able to "set up their state again."[160]

Though debilitating and weakening, this ceremonial law did at some point in time have a sound political role, namely, maintaining the Hebrew sovereignty. While the sovereignty that, in order to maintain itself, resorted to the kind of theo-political maneuvering reflected by the Jewish ceremonial law clearly does not accord with Spinoza's democratic tendencies, he does admit of its efficiency while it lasted. After that Hebrew sovereignty was lost, however, the debasing ceremonial law, which maintained it, lost any concrete use it might have had. Spinoza's devaluation of Judaism is therefore twofold: First, having exposed the historical origins of the Mosaic law and stripped it of any sanctified aura, he shows how its very structure debilitates and negates the healthy vital forces of those who adhere to it. Second, he argues that even if this inherently enslaving system might have been useful at some point in history, it has since ceased to be so, as whatever purpose it might have had was lost after the demise of the Hebrew political sovereignty. Anyone maintaining a lifestyle based on traditional halakhic Jewish values, therefore, would not only be decreasing his conatus but doing so for no reason whatsoever.

Accordingly, Moses, supposedly the great liberator of the Hebrew people, its most important prophet, is in actual fact an enslaver whose constitution continues to decrease the freedom and conatus of those burdened with the Jewish ceremonial law. Furthermore, the claim of Moses's direct conversations with God is but a ploy to solidify his rather tyrannical power. Indeed, in the beginning of chapter 17 of the *Theological-Political Treatise*, Spinoza tells us of various great leaders who used the illusion of divine legitimacy to further their political power. Though not explicitly put, it is quite obvious that Moses, whom Spinoza discusses right after these other political leaders, is supposed to fit right in.[161] His commandments, which as we saw were no more than a tool for oppression, are therefore falsely sanctioned as divine law. Moses claimed to have encountered God face-to-face as a ruse for ungodly power.[162]

Crucially, it is Spinoza who does in fact encounter God face-to-face. When discussing the very notion of law in the beginning of chapter 3 of the *Theological-Political Treatise*, Spinoza distinguishes between laws dependent on natural necessity and those dependent on human decrees. He goes on to point out that only laws dependent on human decrees should really be thought of as laws, which Spinoza therefore defines as "a principle of living man prescribes to himself or to others for some end." If its end is to render life and the state secure, it is human law; if its purpose is the highest good, that is, true knowledge and love of God, it is divine law. At any rate, as opposed to laws dependent on human decrees, laws dependent on natural necessity cannot be properly thought of as laws since "the word *law* seems to be applied figuratively to natural things."[163] In a letter to George Schuller, Spinoza describes what we usually refer to as laws of nature as the "face of the whole universe."[164] Laws of nature are neither commanded nor ordained; they cannot be transgressed or obeyed,[165] but are simply an aspect of what is; the face of the whole universe. And if the whole universe is God, they are the face of God. It is therefore not Moses who encountered God face-to-face, but Spinoza who does so when he uncovers the workings of the universe. So, while the Mosaic heritage is one of deluded political laws that are oppressive and detrimental to human beatitude and have long ago lost the political use they once might have had, Spinoza teaches the actual, universal divine law leading to the face of God, to a genuine awareness of the divine and to true human blessedness.

Accordingly, Spinoza suggests it is he who presents the path to the universal highest good and opposes the Mosaic path, which far from any good leads to a downtrodden, passive, and worthless kind of particularism. Meanwhile, as Goetschel puts it, theology is expounded as a "non-cognitive but distinctly cultural and political practice of securing social control," which is why the *Theological-Political Treatise* "rejects all the universalist pretenses of historical religions."[166] Spinoza's ideas are accordingly a particularly poignant and acute expression of the enlightened devaluation of Judaism that Mendelssohn's and Cohen's revaluations sought to counter.[167] Keeping in mind Spinoza, as well as the above-delineated wider historical, cultural, and philosophical context within which modern universalism arose, is obviously critical to understanding Mendelssohn's and Cohen's treatment of the issue. As we shall see, most, if not all, the central themes discussed above will be explicitly addressed by both, and indeed, both were deeply concerned with Spinoza in particular.

(2)
MOSES MENDELSSOHN'S FELICITY

Following the axiological methodology mentioned in the introduction, we will begin our inquiry into Mendelssohn's revaluation of Jewish values by looking at the method of valuation his philosophical argumentation reflects and advocates. We will start by exploring the structure that underlies the very possibility of value in his thought, focus on the supreme value it upholds, and analyze how this axiological configuration directs his philosophy. We will then be able to adequately examine in the next chapter universalism and universal valuations in the context of Mendelssohn's philosophy and inquire into the nature of his revaluation of Judaism as well as the resulting axiological tensions.

The Source of Value

Mendelssohn explicitly addresses the way in which he thinks of the source of value in human life, and this axiological position remains consistent in his philosophical work. Because of the importance of this matter to our inquiry, I will quote in full relevant passages from three of his most famous philosophical works. In *Phädon*, which catapulted him to the forefront of Berlin's thriving intellectual scene as the "German Socrates,"[1] Mendelssohn writes that

> If our soul is mortal, then our reason is a dream, which was sent by Jupiter, to deceive us wretched ones; thus virtue lacks all the brilliance, which makes it divine in our eyes. Then the beautiful and the sublime, moral as well as physical, is not an imprint of the divine perfection; (for nothing perishable can grasp the weakest ray of divine perfection); and so we, like the cattle, have been put here to seek food and die. So it will be the same in a few days, whether I have been an ornament or a shame to creation, whether

> I have troubled myself to increase the number of blessed people or the wretched ones . . . man, robbed of the hope for immortality, is the most wretched animal on earth, who, reflecting on his misfortunate situation, must fear death and despair.[2]

There can be no value without the eternity of the soul. Even if there is a God, without life eternal, life has no meaning, beauty is worthless, morality has no value, and reason is illusory. Accordingly, a truly providential God would not create beings that can be completely annihilated. This idea, as we shall see below, is at the heart of Mendelssohn's *Phädon* and remained a mainstay of his thinking. The passage above already suggests, therefore, that the construct that functions as source of value and enables the highest and all other values to emerge is the onto-theological reality of a providential God who ensures the immortality of the beings he created. Indeed, fifteen years after *Phädon*, in *Jerusalem*, Mendelssohn expressively posits this construct as the source of all value. Reflecting on "those fundamental principles on which all religions agree, and without which felicity [Glückseligkeit] is but a dream, and virtue itself ceases to be virtue,"[3] Mendelssohn writes that "without God, providence, and a future life, love of our fellow man is but an innate weakness, and benevolence is little more than a foppery into which we seek to lure one another so that the simpleton will toil while the clever man enjoys himself and has a good laugh at the other's expense."[4]

In *Morning Hours*, published just a year before his death, Mendelssohn again states a similar position regarding the primordial axiological importance of God, providence, and immortality:

> In all honesty, for me, were I to lose the sureness of my conviction about this [God and His attributes], life itself would have no pleasure, and all of my good fortune would give me no joy. With all my heart and soul I confess that I owe my confidence in these truths all the cheer, joy, and happiness that any day may bring to me, and if you have observed that in the adversities of life I retain some calmness of mind, it is simply and solely due to this confidence. Without God, providence, and immortality, all the good things of my life are in my eyes worthless and contemptible, and my existence here on earth seems to me, if I may make use of a well-known and often misused comparison, like wandering all day in wind and

> storm without the consolation of coming at nightfall to the refuge and shelter of a hostel—or as Voltaire says, without this comforting prospect we are all swimming in the deep, constantly struggling against the waves, with no hope of ever reaching the shore.[5]

The idea that without God, providence, and the immortality of the soul there can be no meaning to life, no value to our moral feelings and judgments, and no felicity or happiness, is therefore one that recurs in Mendelssohn's philosophy and the importance of which it would be difficult to overstate. This Mendelssohnian trinity, widely thought at the time to reflect the commonly accepted truths of natural religion,[6] lies at the very heart of his philosophical effort; as the source of all value, it is what directs his thinking and is therefore a constant presence in his writing.

In fact, these principles most probably had been underlying his thought ever since the resolution of the religious crisis he seemed to have experienced as a young man and budding philosopher. Altmann finds an "unmistakable autobiographical ring" in the following passage of Mendelssohn's early *On the Sentiments*,[7] in which Mendelssohn describes a state of crisis and its resolution through the encounter with "genuine philosophy":

> My feet wandered from the blessed path of truth. Like hellish furies, cruel doubts about providence tortured me; indeed, I can confess, without skittishness, that they were doubts about the existence of God, and blessedness of virtue. . . . Thanks be to those true guides who have guided me back to true knowledge and to virtue. Thanks to you, Locke and Wolff! To you, immortal Leibniz! Without your help I would have been lost forever. . . . In my soul, your writings have planted the holy truths on which my happiness [Glückseligkeit] is based; they have inspired me.[8]

While little textual evidence is available about the precise nature of the crisis here described, the logic of its resolution is most likely reflected in the passages quoted above. It would, in other words, have been resolved through the encounter with philosophical ideas that led Mendelssohn to the indubitable reality of God, providence, and immortality, which crucially enabled him to find a way towards felicity. It is important to note, furthermore, that Mendelssohn's early crisis, as the passages in which he iterates his solution to it suggest, did not consist only of doubts concerning the very existence of God, but rather of the dread that if there is not a very particular kind of God, life is not worth living. We shall later look more closely at Mendelssohn's conception of God, but it is already clear that that which makes life worth living, indeed that which enables the emergence of any kind of value, is not merely the existence of a God, but the existence of a perfectly providential one who ensures immortality and therefore human felicity too.

Mendelssohn's axiological position, therefore, is not that God as such is the source of all value. A careful reading of the passages above shows that the source of all value is God only in so far as He enables the possibility of eternal human felicity. A God who would not ensure the beatific immortality of the soul, and famously the God of the Old Testament does not seem to promise such a thing,[9] would be of no positive value to us whatsoever and could certainly not function as a source of value. Without immortality, "the most confused mortal has the power to even revoke the rule of God, and a dagger could cut the bond which connects men to God." In fact, any God that would not ensure immortality would be "not the most-kind God, who takes delight in the felicity of his creatures, but a sadistic being [ein schadenfrohes Wesen]."[10] This critical point is repeated in Mendelssohn's introduction to Ecclesiastes: "the believer in the existence of God and his providence must choose one of these alternatives: either believe that the souls have an afterlife, and that the time of trial for each deed, good or bad, will come; or—God Forbid!—attribute evil and violence to the holy God himself."[11]

The notion that God's very goodness and His very value would be radically undermined were He not to ensure immortality and the felicity that is dependent on it is, it seems to me, very revealing. Clearly, both in tone and in content, such passages radically differ from a wide variety of traditional and arguably more reverential approaches that would never dare put into question the divine glory even if it did not ensure a lasting bliss for human individuals. Calvinism, for example, and its insistence on predestined and unconditional election (notions well rooted in the work of notable Christian theologians from Augustine of Hippo to Thomas Aquinas and others) clearly does not posit the felicity of every individual as a prerequisite to the absolute goodness of God.[12]

While some Jewish sources are at least somewhat nearer to Mendelssohn's position, others do not seem to posit human beings as the axiological center at all.[13] Mendelssohn's position, therefore, cannot be construed as necessary or inherently obvious in the context of the Jewish tradition. Notably, Mendelssohn's emphasis on the critical theological centrality of human beings and their felicity radically differs from Maimonides's view in spite of the fact the Rambam was of course to him a formative influence of profound significance.[14] Gottlieb points out that while "human beings were generally thought by Jewish thinkers to be the crowning purpose of creation," Maimonides offers a "strikingly nonanthropocentric account of the purpose of creation where angels are much more important in the cosmic scheme than human beings."[15]

For Maimonides, in other words, the universe cannot be construed as having been created for human beings or their felicity. As he explicitly puts it in the *Guide for the Perplexed*: "Be not misled in your soul to think that the spheres and the angels have been brought into existence for our sake. For it has explained to us what we are worth: *Behold, the nations are as a drop of bucket* (Isa. 40:150)."[16] More generally, and in accordance with the lesser centrality of humans in Maimonides's worldview, his conception of providence is very different from Mendelssohn's. It is therefore perhaps not accidental that when thanking the philosophical guides who drew him out of the religious crisis discussed above, Mendelssohn mentions Leibniz and Wolff but not Maimonides. It could very well be because, as Gottlieb points out, Mendelssohn sees Leibniz and Wolff as having set providential theism on a robust philosophical basis, while the same can certainly not be said about Maimonides's philosophical project and ideas.[17]

So Mendelssohn's position and the extent to which it radically differs from less human-centered religious axiological structures cannot be taken for granted within the Jewish tradition. Indeed, Mendelssohn, usually a moderate in his positions, takes here a fundamental and uncompromising stance that differs completely from the non-anthropocentric axiological worldviews reflected in Maimonides and Calvin. Value, for Mendelssohn, even the value of divinity itself, is intrinsically related to human beings, and more specifically, to their felicity. So while an absolute onto-theological reality of the divine serves as the source of value, it does so only in so far as God enables the possibility of eternal human felicity. The supreme value, therefore, for Mendelssohn is strictly speaking not God, and certainly not any God, but rather that divinely enabled eternal *human* felicity.

SPHERES OF VALUATION

Looking at Mendelssohn's axiological structure in terms of spheres of valuation and their hierarchization,[18] Mendelssohn's prioritization is clear: the religious eudaemonic sphere, which combines adequate religious beliefs and human happiness, is primordial. Reflecting on the introductory notes about Plato's and Aristotle's axiological positions, we see that Mendelssohn's view carries aspects of both positions: the metaphysical emphasis of Plato and the Aristotelian emphasis on eudaemonia.

This primordial religious-eudaemonic sphere is of course valued above the economic one: "If the endeavor of the so called alchemists were also not in vain, if they actually discovered the secret of refining common ore into gold, their pride would still be forever ridiculous" because, Mendelssohn points out, they would have completely misjudged the purpose of philosophy and the true locus of wisdom. The good life, understood as peace of mind derived from the contemplation of truth, is "a richer source of happiness, than all the economical means that human beings dream up to improve their situation."[19]

As divinely enabled eternal happiness is the most complete, the religious-eudaemonic sphere is also higher than the sensual one and any form of happiness it might procure: "Do you see my friends!" Mendelssohn's Socrates tells his interlocutors in *Phädon*, "how far the man who loves wisdom must distance himself from the senses and their objects, if he wants to grasp what is true felicity to grasp, the All Maximum and Most Perfect being? In this quest for ideas he must close his eyes and ears, and pay no attention to pain and sensual pleasure and if possible, forget his body entirely, in order to focus himself all the more completely on the capacities of his soul and its inner activity."[20] The person who craves luxuries and sensuous pleasure, Mendelssohn writes in the *Bi'ur*, pursues the imaginary beautiful and good "while abandoning the true good."[21]

Of course, the experience of felicity is itself most definitely a pleasant sentiment. But Mendelssohn clarifies that the highest good is not conceived of as such in so far as it is a pleasant sentiment, but rather in so far as felicity is a process of perfection.[22] Indeed, felicity for Mendelssohn is inherently linked to a gradual increase of perfection,[23] and he uses the concepts interchangeably. So, for example, Mendelssohn describes the concept of *Glückseligkeit* as consisting of a "progress to a higher level of perfection."[24] Felicity, then, is not only a pleasant sentiment; it is much more significantly the endless human perfection through which we eternally grow nearer to a maximally perfect being.

Mendelssohn's axiological prioritization, however, goes much further as the religious-eudaemonic sphere goes beyond not only economic and sensual goods, but moral ones as well. In each of the three passages we quoted from the *Phädon*, *Jerusalem*, and *Morning Hours*, Mendelssohn explicitly argues that without the possibility of divinely enabled eternal felicity, morality has no value; without immortality, virtue lacks all of its divine brilliance, and love of humanity would be nothing but a congenital weakness, humanitarianism little more than a chimera. The moral sphere of valuation, Mendelssohn therefore repeatedly claims, would be worthless without the religious-eudaemonic sphere to back it up.

This, it is important to note, does not necessarily mean Mendelssohn thinks felicity trumps morality. Indeed, as felicity and morality are necessarily conjoined in the process of human perfection, a contrast between both is not possible. Felicity means progressing towards perfection, which necessarily involves moral betterment as well. Accordingly, anyone on the path of felicity is ipso facto also on the moral path.[25] Still, the axiological dependence of morality on felicity remains firmly embedded in Mendelssohn's method of valuation.

Finally, as discussed above, even divinity in and of itself would be meaningless without eternal human felicity, a position that not only differs radically from traditional approaches but was also controversial among contemporary philosophers. At the height of the pantheism controversy, Jacobi explicitly cites the passage from *Jerusalem* we quoted above to forcefully attack Mendelssohn for positing God solely as a means rather than an end unto itself.[26] In so doing, Jacobi claims, Mendelssohn turns God into a "dead tool, a dumb force." Jacobi goes as far as unfavorably contrasting this view with Spinoza, who, though mistaken about God's nature, at least had His truth in his soul and truly lived God's love. Jacobi believes Mendelssohn's position entails that were other means available for the ultimate end of our well-being, he would get rid of God "like bulky furniture, which takes space, and of itself is worth nothing."[27]

Jacobi's claim that Mendelssohn would do away with God is mistaken because Mendelssohn's position is that nothing but a providential God can assure our felicity, and he would therefore disagree with assuming the very possibility of reaching our ultimate goal otherwise. But while God is in fact absolutely necessary, Jacobi is correct in raising the issue of God's axiological position; God, as we saw above, would have no value to us were he not to ensure our felicity. It is divinely enabled felicity that makes Him valuable to us, and it's the sphere wherein religion and happiness find their completion that is at the pinnacle of Mendelssohn's axiological hierarchization. The religious-eudaemonic sphere is, therefore, beyond the economic, sensual, moral, and solely religious or theological spheres, and whatever value these lower spheres obtain is directly related to the degree to which they relate to, or advance the attainment of, the highest one.

God, Providence, and Immortality

In order to further understand the onto-theological structure that functions as the source of all value, let us further explore its three components, namely, God, providence, and immortality, which enable the rise of the supreme value, namely, divinely enabled human felicity. We will start by looking at these necessary conditions for the rise of Mendelssohn's felicity before examining its implications.

As the inquiry into God, providence, and immortality will take us into Mendelssohn's metaphysics, it is important to note as a preamble that for Mendelssohn, natural language is rather ill fitted to talk about such matters. In fact, as Freudenthal puts it, natural language, which was formed to engage in everyday matters, necessarily, Mendelssohn believes, turns "metaphorical and unreliable" when applied to the metaphysical realm.[28] This is also the case with regards to inner perceptions; for Mendelssohn, to quote Rosenstock, "language is not a mirror of internal states."[29] Accordingly, subtle and abstruse theological differences, or indeed any of our inner perceptions, including of course religious ones, can be neither adequately expressed nor exhaustively and securely grasped. This vagueness is among the reasons Mendelssohn provides when arguing in *Jerusalem* that it makes no sense to ask for religious oaths.[30] Indeed, Mendelssohn explains that the degree of vagueness involved in any expression of our internal perceptions is such as to make it impossible to define precisely what is meant by the religious language the oath consists of. So it is not just the case that the state has no right to differentiate between religions but also that oaths assume the possibility of rigidly demarcating subtle theological differences in a language necessarily too vague to genuinely and reliably reflect inner perceptions.

The vagueness that characterizes metaphysical language is also the reason why, in the introduction to his prize essay for the Royal Prussian Academy of Sciences, Mendelssohn states that "metaphysical truths are capable, to be sure, of the same certainty but not of the same perspicuity as geometric truths."[31] In the second section, he explains that geometry is expressed by "essential signs," which "agree in their nature and connection with the nature and the connection of the thoughts. Lines are essential signs of the concepts which we have of them, and these lines are placed together in figures in the same manner as the concepts are placed together in our soul."[32] Philosophy, Mendelssohn explains in the third section, has lacked the aid of essential signs, and so "everything in the language of philosophers remains arbitrary. The words and the connections among them contain nothing that would essentially agree with the nature of thoughts and the connections among them." This leads to definitions being "endlessly heaped" on top of one another and gives demonstrative philosophy "the look of vain verbosity." When undertaking the complex task of thinking with arbitrary signs, we must therefore constantly focus on the complex combinations of these arbitrary signs, continuously reminding ourselves what they are supposed to designate. This is a treacherous effort wherein "the slightest inattentiveness makes it possible for thought to lose sight of the subject matter, leaving behind merely empty signs," making the most cogent philosopher "appear to be only playing with words."[33]

Consequently, it is, generally speaking, better not to be overly verbose about theological or metaphysical truths, as too much of our necessarily vague discourse would undermine our ability to grasp it: "Too much talk about a matter does not render it any clearer, but rather obscures whatever faint light of truth there is."[34] Accordingly, Mendelssohn blamed the obscuring vagueness of our language for most of the disagreements between the various philosophical schools, clashes which he was inclined to explain "as mere verbal disputes [Wortstreitigkeiten], or at least as originally springing from verbal disputes."[35]

Mendelssohn therefore had a surprisingly skeptical attitude towards metaphysics; too much of it risks jettisoning the commonsensical acknowledgment of God's existence, which is, as we shall see below, the natural response humans have when confronted with the goodness of creation.[36] It is important to further examine this rather surprising skepticism and the ways in which it leads to an epistemology that trusts common sense more than it does abstract speculative reasoning. Therefore, in order to better understand Mendelssohn's conception of the onto-theological structure that supports his axiological view, we need to find out how his fervent belief in it is not threatened by his metaphysical reluctance.

MENDELSSOHN'S SKEPTICISM OF SKEPTICISM

While Mendelssohn's thinking is often characterized as a relic from precritical dogmatism, there is in fact an underlying skeptical bent to his philosophy. Mendelssohn's skepticism, however, is of a rather complex and subtle form. In fact, in many ways, it is a skepticism of skepticism that leads him to a commonsensical approach.

The ancient skeptics famously sought to dismantle any of the dogmatic schools' claims to knowledge, and, as Diogenes Laertius tells us, "they themselves laid down nothing definitely, not even the laying down of nothing."[37] Indeed, while the academics argued that human beings could not obtain knowledge, Pyrrhonian skepticism dismissed even that claim as dogmatic and contended that while we cannot even know whether it actually is impossible to obtain knowledge, we can convincingly show we do not currently possess it. The quest therefore has to continue, which is why they called themselves "inquirers" (*skeptikoi*).[38]

In order to convincingly expose one's current ignorance, Pyrrho and his followers suggested forms of argumentation that could counteract any attempt at asserting knowledge. This philosophical gesture was supposed to lead to *epoché*, or the suspension of all judgments. *Epoché*, in turn, enables the rise of ataraxia, a deep or unperturbable inner peace.[39] Sextus Empiricus famously illustrates the advent of ataraxia out of *epoché* with the story of the painter Appelles, who, frustrated because of repeated unsuccessful attempts at representing properly the foam at a horse's mouth, gave up and flung the sponge he had been using at the painting, which inadvertently produced the effect of a horse's foam on the picture.[40]

This line of thought seems to raise an urgent ethical problem: What am I to do if I do not know what is that should be done? Pyrrho's approach was to follow established norms and live daily life following the appearances he is aware of and his natural inclinations.[41] In other words, the Pyrrhonist ethical response to skepticism is a commonsensical simplicity.

As mentioned in the first chapter, with the rise of modernity, a significant amount of interest was taken in renewed editions of Sextus Empiricus's works, and their skeptical argumentation was commonly used during both the Reformation and the Counter-Reformation, leading to Descartes's methodological doubt, which heralded the beginning of modern philosophy. Yet Descartes's method of doubt, as radical as it was, was part of a philosophical effort to reestablish knowledge on a firm basis. In that sense, Hume, whose devastating skepticism was essentially aimed at undermining human claims to absolute knowledge, or as Craig puts it, at differentiating the human mind from the mind of God,[42] was even more radical.

As opposed to their classical forbearers, both Descartes and Hume agreed that far from leading to a blissful inner tranquility, doubt was mentally destabilizing.[43] Mendelssohn, of course, agrees with Hume and Descartes; to him, nagging doubts are a form of inner torture, certainly not the pathway to peace. As shown above, it is the firm knowledge that a providential God who ensures the immortality of the soul and therefore also human felicity exists that leads to peace. But if Mendelssohn so eagerly insists that forms of seemingly metaphysical knowledge are necessary for felicity, and indeed tirelessly argues for the truthfulness of this knowledge, what then is Mendelssohn's skepticism?

Mendelssohn is skeptical of precisely the kind of overly abstruse arguments skeptical philosophers have used to attack commonsensical truths that he takes to be simple and self-evident; it is therefore a skepticism of skepticism. His response to the unreliability of speculative thought is reminiscent of ancient skeptical response to the ethical question; just as the ancient skeptics advocated trusting customs in their everyday life,

Mendelssohn argues we should trust custom in thinking. It is therefore commonsense that is the proper guide to human life and thought,[44] and it is by common sense, as we shall see in greater detail later on, that philosophical inquiry needs to orient itself.

Indeed, it is precisely because of overly abstruse thinking, which Mendelssohn characterizes as necessarily untrustworthy, that the unhealthy, mentally destabilizing form of skepticism arises in the first place. In *Jerusalem*, Mendelssohn explicitly differentiates between his position as to the necessary vagueness of metaphysical and theological language and the kinds of destructive skepticism he refuses to be associated with. Indeed, he bluntly characterizes the latter kind as a "disease of the soul" he ardently wishes to cure his fellowman of.[45] Mendelssohn's skepticism of skepticism is not supposed to lead away from the obvious truths of natural religion. To the contrary, it is supposed to warn us that the arguments used to undermine these apodictic commonsensical truths are not only necessarily couched in vague language but also abstrusely speculative and therefore prone to lead a thinker astray. Metaphysicians, therefore, "are not afraid to deny things that it would never occur to common sense to doubt."[46] The idealist, solipsist, Spinozist, and skeptic all deny aspects of reality Mendelssohn finds so elementary that he "cannot believe anyone has ever maintained in earnest the truth of these far-fetched suppositions."[47] If such thinkers did in fact reach such far-fetched realms, it is because they lost track of the touchstone of common sense and followed their speculations to the point of absurdity, missing the simple truths necessary for felicity.

Mendelssohn, therefore, repeatedly makes the point that speculative arguments are far less reliable than commonsensical judgments.[48] Accordingly, he thinks of his own metaphysical arguments as confirmations of simple truths. Their purpose is to clarify rationally what is intuitively clear.[49] In fact, even if they fail at performing that role, the truth of the commonsensical facts they are meant to confirm remains unwavering. It is telling, in this context, that *Morning Hours* opens with a frank admission that the kind of arguments it contains might not be relevant any longer. A tired Mendelssohn, beset with "a certain weakness of the nerves" that gravely hinders intellectual exertion, is aware that "his philosophy is no longer in currency" and that the damage to it "is too far advanced merely to give the wheel a push in order to raise back up that which has been so long trampled beneath our feet."[50]

But even if Mendelssohn doubts his own speculative philosophy, he clearly believes that that which it sets out to prove remains steadfast nonetheless. Indeed, rather than suggesting other truths may emerge from the new philosophy superseding his own, Mendelssohn suggests stronger powers with "the profundity of a Kant" should reestablish the doctrines that Mendelssohn's argument advocates. So even if "the all-crushing Kant" made the kind of speculative arguments Mendelssohn uses to confirm commonsensical truths obsolete, the truths themselves remain as actual as ever.[51] It is just a matter of finding more suitable arguments for their confirmation. To paraphrase Mendelssohn in *Morning Hours*' last lecture, the effort is of finding new paths to truths we hold dear.[52] Whether or not we find these paths, the truths we are seeking to reach remain valid and are, as ever, accessible via the royal road of common sense.[53]

Given Mendelssohn's commonsensical sensitivities, it is not surprising that he repeatedly presents speculative arguments he makes in the *Morning Hours* as commonly accepted. Whether or not these arguments were actually commonly accepted or not, it is clear that this particular rhetorical tool reflects the underlying assumption that commonly accepted arguments are ipso facto more convincing and more probably true. So, for example, in order to reinforce a point made as part of a Wolffian argument against Spinozism,[54] Mendelssohn concludes that "all of this is as clear as day to anyone who looks into the matter, and it is explained in superfluous detail in nearly every decent textbook of ontology."[55] A few pages later, he supports another philosophical claim[56] by stating that "these propositions seem to be already a part of the commonsense view of things."[57] Further examples abound, and again, even if one feels such rather speculative claims cannot genuinely be posited as meaningfully commonsensical,[58] the point remains that Mendelssohn clearly assumes commonsense to be a reliable guide to our philosophical escapades.

Mendelssohn perhaps sums his commonsensical sensitivities best when in the appendix to the third edition of the *Phädon*, he states that "when I see a well-trodden path before me, I don't seek to blaze a new trail."[59] So while he may have gained a reputation as a dogmatic metaphysician, Mendelssohn's skepticism of skepticism makes him, to quote Freudenthal, a "commonsense philosopher" who believed the most important religious truths are simple, self-evident, and commonly obtainable and obtained.[60] Accordingly, Mendelssohn believed common people would often be far more just in their religious beliefs than metaphysicians lost in their overly speculative thinking. This position is reflected in a fascinating passage of Sophie Becker's diary,[61] wherein she writes of a conversation between Mendelssohn and the Duchess Dorothea of Courland, who was telling Mendelssohn that there is in us the feeling of having existed before our births and her ensuing conviction we would therefore continue to exist after our deaths. Mendelssohn, Becker writes, seemed to listen with pleasure and "advised the duchess not to allow herself to be robbed of her natural and warm conviction by any learned babble on immortality."[62]

GOD

Mendelssohn's commonsensical sensitivities lead to a notion of God reflective of characterizations that are widely perceived to be commonly held; "Maximum perfection," "Maximum Good," and "Maximum wisdom" are therefore "inseparable attributes of the All Perfect being, without which nothing can exist."[63] These are the simplest, most commonly held truths reflecting the reality of the divine. To quote Leibniz, "the conception of God which is the most common and the most full of meaning is expressed well enough in the words: God is an absolutely perfect being."[64] The fact of the matter is, Mendelssohn will repeat over and over again, that the reality of such an all-perfect being, all knowing and supremely good, is widely accepted by sincere human beings of all cultures.[65] It is a commonsensical truth that can, but does not have to, be demonstrated by speculative metaphysics.

Indeed, Mendelssohn very much emphasizes that these truths are revealed through the overwhelmingly convincing experience of harmony and beauty in the created world. As we shall see below, such direct and aesthetically driven realizations of the reality of the divine are repeatedly praised by Mendelssohn as more commonsensical and therefore also more reliable and more existentially significant than the more speculative philosophical proofs. This, however, does not mean he does not also repeatedly suggest demonstrative philosophical proofs for the existence of a perfect being.

Mendelssohn, for example, returned throughout his intellectual life to various versions of the ontological proof for the existence of God.[66] It was perhaps most confidently stated in his prize essay, wherein, to put it very shortly, a perfect being exists because it is not impossible for Him to exist. Indeed, Mendelssohn writes that it is impossible for a perfect being to be merely possible and that, furthermore, it is only impossible for that which is self-contradictory to exist. Given that the perfect being contains by definition no limitations, it cannot be self-contradictory.[67] Therefore, as it is not impossible for the perfect being to exist, He has to exist necessarily.

Mendelssohn adds later on that this and the other proofs he suggests in his essay are but a few among many possible proofs.[68] And indeed, he emphasizes the existential supremacy of the more experiential forms of conviction, namely, proofs derived from the beauty and harmony of creation or from the laws of motion or proofs based on the "undeniable" purposes in nature. While they "still lack a great deal for demonstrative certainty," they do reach a very high degree of probability, which "approaches necessity," and, most importantly, possess far greater eloquence, as "by their liveliness they make a much greater impression on the mind, awakening the soul to dynamic decisions and producing the practical conviction that should be our foremost purpose in contemplating divine properties." In a rather striking metaphor, Mendelssohn succinctly expresses their greater existential significance when stating that "the demonstrative kinds of proof are the fortresses that protect a country against enemy attacks. For peaceful inhabitants, however, they are not the most comfortable and pleasant places in which to live." Therefore, unless one has to deal with such attackers, one better focus on knowing the creator from the beauty, order, and purposes embedded in nature, an insight through which one finds "the sweetest comfort, the most refreshing consolation, as well as the very fire and animation of knowledge, that transfers into the capacity to desire and occasions decisions that break out into action."[69]

So even when confidently stating philosophical proofs of God, Mendelssohn cautiously makes clear that the soundness of the truths these proofs are seeking to establish does not depend on the soundness of the arguments. This suggests an underlying assumption that the truths of natural religion are accepted as commonsensical and that the demonstrative prowess of philosophy cannot replace that commonsense. As he puts it before beginning his argumentation, his intention with the essay is not "to convince atheists of the lack of any basis for their opinion, but rather, in the presence of a society of genuine philosophers, to appraise the certainty with which we know the existence of God and his properties rationally."[70]

In *Morning Hours*, Mendelssohn returns to philosophical proofs for God's existence but this time, of course, writes after Kant's critical turn had made such arguments far less convincing to his philosophical milieu. Mendelssohn therefore distances his faith in the principles of natural theology even more explicitly from the proofs he will suggest. As mentioned above, he humbly presents himself as a philosopher on the wane, barely recovering from a weakness of the nerves that for years forbade "any intellectual exertion" and unable to provide the kind of philosophical masterpiece necessary to overcome the crisis in the kind of old-fashioned metaphysics he upholds and argues for.[71] He presents the book as stemming from a pedagogical effort directed at the religious and philosophical education of his son and fully acknowledges that his proofs might not carry the force they once did. Yet, crucially, he remains completely convinced that the truths of natural theology can be proved and, more importantly, that these truths are steadfast. While useful to ward off atheists and skeptics, or to educate boys and develop their philosophical abilities, demonstrative proofs of the existence of God are therefore by no means a necessary requisite to establish God's existence.

In the ontological proof he does suggest in *Morning Hours*, Mendelssohn overcomes Kant's criticism by accepting the proof's lack of actual ontological bearing while arguing for its relevance nonetheless. Indeed, Kant had already attacked the ontological proof in his precritical *The One Possible Basis for a Demonstration of the Existence of God*, explaining it relies on the mistaken positing of existence as a predicate even though existence is not a predicate but rather "the absolute position of the thing." Therefore, in order to demonstrate the existence of a thing, "one seeks not in the concepts of the subject" but rather "in the origin of the knowledge I have of the subject."[72] Mendelssohn, as mentioned, is willing to somewhat concede the point; even if all that the ontological proof shows is that the concept of a perfect being necessarily comes to a rational creature, much has been achieved. As Mendelssohn succinctly put it in a letter to Jacobi, "What I cannot think to be true, does not trouble me with doubt."[73] This suggests, as we shall see below in greater depth, that the human viewpoint is prioritized not only in Mendelssohn's axiology but in his metaphysics as well.

It seems likely that Mendelssohn was attached to the ontological proof in spite of his reservations and his reluctance to posit it as foundational to his religious worldview because in so far as it suggests any God, the ontological argument suggests a perfect God. Perfection, after all, forms one of its premises; the perfection of the posited being is that which makes it impossible for God's existence to be merely contingent. Crucially, God's perfection indicates a "wondrous power" of God's properties, which "are so intimately connected with one another that one has only to presuppose a single property of God in order to deduce from it everything that we are in a position to know about the Supreme Being." Indeed, as without the others, each property would be contradictory, "a single chain of inferences combines all perfections of this fecund being," and Mendelssohn derives, for example, all other properties his theological thinking is sustained by from the supremely perfect will, which "presupposes that most perfect intellect and demands the most perfect might," which itself consists "in the inclination to every possible good and aversion from every possible evil . . . from this follow justice, benevolence and wisdom," all of which lead too to God's infinity, singularity, and so on.[74]

While the properties of God have this wondrous characteristic, and Mendelssohn never ceased believing in them even in his less confident later works, it was also the case throughout his writing on this issue that beyond the notion of perfection, which admittedly does involve a plethora of properties, God remains a mystery. The soul, Mendelssohn's Socrates explains, cannot grasp the essence of the "Maximum Being" in its full extent, as it can never form an "idea of a thing of a superior nature than itself, or form an idea of a thing of higher ability than it possesses itself." It can, however, grasp the possibility of a thing more perfect than it. This "glimmer of a conception" is gained when the soul separates in thought that part that has truth, goodness, and perfection "from deficiency and non-being, with which it is mixed, and comes thereby to a conception of an entity, who is pure being, truth, goodness, and perfection." It is, however, only after death, Mendelssohn adds, that we can hope to behold that "Maximum and Supreme Being," and while we are still among the living, God himself remains beyond our reach, as "it is not allowed that the unholy touch Holiness itself."[75]

So, beyond the existence of God as a perfect being (which, arguably, is already in and of itself quite a lot), not much more can be known about God. In an expression that reflects Mendelssohn's metaphysical caution, his Socrates calls God the "All-knowing but All unknowable being" and refers to the divine as the one level in the chain of being that "thinks but cannot be thought of by others . . . the only one, whose perfection surpasses all finite concepts."[76] It is not, therefore, the exact nature of God in and of itself, but rather the way He affects human life that Mendelssohn mainly concerns himself with. This approach coheres profoundly with Mendelssohn's understanding of existence, which in *Morning Hours* he defines as "the common term for *acting* and *being acted upon*,"[77] and is, at least in his later work, part and parcel of a quasi-Kantian denial of the possibility of uncovering the thing in itself: "When I tell you what effect a thing has or how it can be affected by something, do not ask what it is," he writes, adding,

> "What is this thing in and of itself?" has no good reason to be asked. Philosophers for ages have often been tortured with questions that are in principle unanswerable because they consist of empty words that carry no meaning. Thus the atheists asks, "What is God really?" Show him what God has brought about, show him all the glory of creation and all the beauty and perfection that it contains. Tell him that God has brought all this about and has produced it through His wisdom. Tell him that He preserves and governs all of this according to the laws of His wisdom and His goodness, of which he may find a trace in each mote of dust, in a sunbeam just as much as in himself. But all of this does not satisfy him. He goes on to ask "But what is God Himself?"[78]

So while we cannot fully grasp divinity in and of itself, we are naturally led to posit God's existence when facing His effects both in our soul and in the world. The teleological nature of these effects, moreover, cannot be doubted. We saw above how clearly Mendelssohn posited such considerations as much more existentially significant than more speculative methods. Indeed, even in the less philosophically self-assured tone of his later work, he continues to argue uncompromisingly that these commonsensical methods of knowing God are overwhelmingly convincing. "Nothing," Mendelssohn resolutely states in *To the Friends of Lessing*, "can be more beyond question than that in the visible world that surrounds us, as well as [the invisible world] within ourselves, final causes are realized and purposes are carried out," adding that he "cannot possibly believe any philosopher ever seriously doubted this" and that "one need only open one's eyes and give heed, with even the slightest modicum of attentiveness, to any of nature's works, and one will be completely persuaded of this truth."[79]

Introspection enables us to inquire about the artist who drew in us "the picture of maximum perfection, goodness, wisdom, beauty etc." and realize His existence by reflecting on the effects in our soul of what must be a perfectly good creator.[80] A similar conclusion is reached by admiring the beauty of a sunrise, when in the dazzling splendor of dawn, the reality of the sublime beauty of its creature is apodictically obvious.[81] Whether one reflects, therefore, on the creator of both inner and outer realities and the apodictic good and beauty they contain, one cannot but reach the commonsensical conclusion that it is a perfect God who gave rise to them.

From an axiological perspective, the notion that God is best known through His effects and that a God that would not affect us in any significant way would not exist in a significant sense strengthens the structure at the heart of Mendelssohn's method of valuation; a God that would not affect us in a way we would clearly think of as good would not be a clearly good God. So the notion that God is, in and of Himself, unknowable but can come to be known only through His effects on us further emphasizes that a God who does not affect us providentially by ensuring moral rectification and immortality is of no significance and of no value to us.

PROVIDENCE AND IMMORTALITY

God is for Mendelssohn both the primal cause and absolute goodness.[82] Accordingly, the "ground of actuality is goodness."[83] A critical implication is that His providence is complete. Mendelssohn's Leibnizian God could simply not have created creatures whose happiness He would not have ensured. His providence is therefore expressed primarily in the reality of the best of possible worlds, a world wherein we are directed towards the most supreme good of felicity: "if it is true that an all-good and all-wise being has brought us into existence, then by virtue of His unalterable attributes, he could not have fixed our destiny otherwise than for happiness."[84]

Mendelssohn therefore believed that God created human beings for eternal happiness or felicity.[85] However, not only were humans created to experience felicity, the very universe was created for that experience to be realized: "We can say," Mendelssohn's Socrates explains, "that this universe vast beyond all measure, had been created so that there are reasonable beings, which progress from step to step, gradually increase in perfection, and in this increase may find their felicity." Furthermore, as immortality is absolutely necessary for this gradual increase in perfection and the felicity it reflects, God could not have intended for the beings he created to "stop dead completely still in the middle of their course, not only stand still, but are all at once pushed back into the abyss, and should lose all the fruits of their efforts."[86]

The annihilation of the soul, Mendelssohn argues, goes so deeply against the divine nature that it is only possible as a miracle that God would never bring about; we should fear the sun changing into ice, Mendelssohn's Socrates says, "before we fear an evil act from the self-subsisting Good, annihilation by miracle."[87] In *Morning Hours*, after stating that God must have destined us for happiness, he adds that "if this happiness [Glückseligkeit] cannot come to pass if the human being is not destined to live on eternally, then this annihilation is in direct conflict with God's recognized attributes."[88] We see here that by the time he wrote *Morning Hours*, Mendelssohn still felt, as he had when writing *Phädon*, that God's goodness could not but ensure immortality and, indeed, that immortality is necessary for felicity.

The commonsensical providential God is what ensures the immortality of the soul. Indeed, if immortality is indispensable for the possibility of felicity, and as we have seen for Mendelssohn, it absolutely is, a providential God simply would not have created finite beings. This conception is so deeply rooted in Mendelssohn that he argues not only for human but also for animal immortality. After all, if annihilation so strongly contradicts the very possibility of the rise of felicity and of any genuine good and the grounds of actuality are goodness, why would a providential God create any being, human or otherwise, that cannot achieve some measure of felicity? Though he might perhaps have surmounted the issue by arguing, as was and is still relatively commonly done, that animal mortality is less of a threat to their felicity because of animals' supposed lack of awareness of their own finitude or because of some other explanation for why animals are somehow categorically less valuably sentient,[89] Mendelssohn chooses, as it were, to bite the bullet and has Socrates argue that "the spiritual essence, which animates the beasts, is of infinite duration, and also continues in eternity fulfilling God's intentions," adding that he is very inclined to believe these animals eventually lose their lowly stations and, beckoned by "a sign of the Almighty, will lift themselves aloft into the spheres of spirits."[90]

The direct bond of immortality with the felicity of all beings, as well as the established perfect goodness of God, means that human immortality must be, if not immediately felicitous, at the very least eventually so. In other words, Mendelssohn's perfectly good God would not have created beings that must be sentenced, in whatever circumstances, to eternal damnation. In fact, eternal damnation would completely contradict the necessity of felicity, which for Mendelssohn is, as we have seen, anchored in the very onto-theological setup of the universe. Mendelssohn describes, in *Jerusalem*, a conversation with a friend about this issue. The friend, Mendelssohn reports, agreed Mendelssohn "did not have to fear eternal punishment in hell, for God cannot let any of his creatures suffer unceasing misery. Nor can any creature, by his actions, deserve the punishment of being eternally miserable." As God created human beings for their felicity and gave them laws for that felicity to be realized, it cannot be the case that the violation of these laws would result in eternal misery.[91]

Immortality, sooner for the righteous but eventually for the wicked as well, is therefore a blissful form of being. But what kind of experience could it possibly be? Mendelssohn, for reasons elaborated above, is careful not to venture into overly speculative thinking, and certainly for the living to hypothesize about the exact nature of the afterlife would be rather hazardously speculative. It is therefore not surprising to find that Mendelssohn remains coy about several critical aspects of the afterlife. Though his Socrates is fully convinced that the soul does survive the demise of the body, he cannot, for example, promise his friends that they will meet again: "that the providence of God will also rule over me in the next life, this friends! I state it as confidently, as certainly, as I have ever maintained anything in my life," yet he dares not maintain with absolute certainty that he will there "meet the souls of the departed, whose company is to be preferred to all friendship here below," though he does carry the "all-comforting hope" this too will be the case.[92]

However, it is important to note that the reason for this uncertainty is not in any way because our separate identities will somehow become expunged or that we become part of a wider notion of eternity, as Spinoza's model, for example, would suggest. Mendelssohn in fact argues against Spinoza's immersive pantheism by pointing out that "the consciousness of myself as it is bound up with the complete ignorance of everything that does not fall within the circle of my cognitive power is the most telling proof of my extra-divine substantiality."[93] This substantiality of the individual is be maintained too in the afterlife, wherein, Mendelssohn suggests, we eternally strive as separate beings to increase our proximity to God: "Through the imitation of God one can gradually approach His perfections, and the felicity of spirits exists in this approach; but the path to divine perfection is infinite, and cannot be completely traversed in all eternity."[94] For Mendelssohn, it is critical that death does not involve any annihilation of our distinct identities, which must, in order to enable the felicity a providential God cannot but provide, remain substantial and real.

So, while Mendelssohn is careful not to provide too much detail about what the afterlife is like and,[95] as shown above, refuses to commit, for example, to the possibility of reunification with lost loved ones, he does allow himself to posit some ideas about the nature of that afterlife. In keeping with the commonsensical nature of his philosophizing, the notions brought forward, beyond his insistence on lingering individual substantiality, are those widely found in the Judeo-Christian theological and philosophical traditions, namely, that the blissful afterlife consists in some kind of increasing ability to approach God, to grasp His absolute perfection. The soul, therefore, upon the death of the body, rises above the dust and continues "to contemplate the works of the Creator, and to entertain thoughts about the power of the infinite being." It continues to "strive towards felicity,"[96] and as true felicity consists of grasping "the All Maximum and Most Perfect Being,"[97] it follows that "our continued existence becomes nothing other than an uninterrupted contemplation of the Deity, a heavenly delight, which as little as we grasp it now, rewards the noble sweat of the virtuous with infinite usury."[98]

Again, Mendelssohn does not seek to provide radical new ideas. To paraphrase a sentence quoted above, he sees a well-trodden path and so does not seek to blaze a new trail.[99] Indeed, according to his commonsensical approach, the fact ideas are common is a very compelling reason to accept them. The fact notions of *imitatio Dei* or of a quasi-Platonic grasping of beatific forms are so widespread is, therefore, according to his commonsensical sensitivity, a strong indication of their truth.

The critical importance of Mendelssohn's commonsensical understanding of the afterlife in his method of valuation is strikingly emphasized in Mendelssohn's exploration of the axiological consequences of a merely temporal life, which he finds to be dramatic. Without the afterlife, "the present existence would have to be to highest good . . . which nothing could counterbalance." None of the virtuous values widely prioritized, such as concern for the welfare of children, friends, or the fatherland, could weigh against the all-important present existence. After all, robbed of one's present existence, one would have nothing at all. Why then risk it? asks Mendelssohn. Only if we think of our earthly life as a means to felicity can its value be "brought into comparison with other possessions"; however, as soon as we think we lose our existence with the loss of this life, it ceases to be a means and "becomes the ultimate goal, the final aim of our desires, the highest possession we can strive for, which is sought for, loved, and desired for its own sake, and no possession in the world can come into comparison with it, for it surpasses all other considerations in its importance."[100]

It is interesting to note the degree to which Mendelssohn reaches in these passages, a century earlier, very similar axiological conclusions as Nietzsche. Indeed, both realize that without a providential God and the realm of eternity he underwrites, the source of value could only be our this-worldly existences.[101] While Mendelssohn recoils from the consequences of a purely this-worldly method of valuation, Nietzsche of course very much embraced it. In fact, several of the very individualistic moral consequences of a this-worldly valuation, which he describes as terrifying and destructive, are exactly those Nietzsche promoted.[102]

A further striking expression of the zeal with which Mendelssohn held his intertwined beliefs in providence and immortality is reflected by his review of King Frederick's *Poesies diverses*, which was published in Nicola's weekly *Literaturbriefe.*[103] Mendelssohn makes the point that a king such as Frederick would not want his subjects to merely uncritically praise his work and dares making some critical points himself. Firstly, he finds it to be a pity the work is written in French rather than German. The lacuna in Frederick's work he seems to be more concerned with, however, is the emphasis the king's poetry puts on mortality and the finitude of man.

Mendelssohn here dares criticize a king who, as enlightened as he might have been, was still the despotic head of a regime wherein Jewish emancipation was far from fully realized. This lack of political caution seems to be very uncharacteristic of Mendelssohn, a prudent public intellectual who sought to avoid unnecessary controversy and famed, furthermore, for his acute sense of responsibility as the most significant public Jewish intellectual of his generation.[104] If, therefore, the perennially guarded Mendelssohn dared criticize Frederick the Great, it must be because the latter's work touched upon a subject so grave as to make silence impossible. Such is precisely the question of life eternal.

Indeed, Frederick's verses very much expose a radically different sensitivity: "Your term is short, it is finite / the fate of man from the day of his birth / takes him to the fatal night."[105] "Time submits everything to its law / The Present flees far from me / The future hurries to follow it / Man, your limited term / is but a point in eternity / to be for a moment, is called living."[106] Elsewhere, he writes, "Filled with vanities we swim / between the time that precedes us / and the absorbent eternity / of the future that succeeds us . . . Ceaselessly agitated by yearning / filled with seductive dreams / we lose ourselves in the abyss / such is the fate of our lives."[107]

Frederick's despairing tone in his reflections on human finitude leads to another conclusion that radically contradicts Mendelssohn's view, namely, the cruelty of this "unhappy universe,"[108] wherein nature "seems to enjoy their [human beings'] misfortune / Merit, Dignity, Birth / Nothing exempts from suffering / In our destinies, Evil prevails."[109] The pessimistic tone that Frederick's verses are so obviously imbued with relates to Voltaire, the philosopher with whom the Prussian sovereign was in such a close, if at times turbulent, relationship.[110] Voltaire, who had only a year before the *Poesies Diverses* published his *Candide* and attacked the perceived naivety of Leibniz's theodicy with all the biting might his sarcastic pen and literary genius could muster, is mentioned by Frederick as having earned the one kind of immortality the latter did apparently believe possible, namely, enduring literary fame.[111] Mendelssohn is clearly dismayed at Frederick's high regard for Voltaire, whose opposition to the Leibnizian theodicy so deeply important to him he deeply resented.[112]

Mendelssohn cannot restrain his criticism, arguing that it does not befit a king who sends soldiers to battle to doubt immortality, for if this life is all there is, how could any king possibly ask for its sacrifice? As we saw, it is clear to Mendelssohn that without life eternal, nothing can be more valuable than earthly life itself. So the cautious Mendelssohn could not here tame his profound opposition; Frederick was wrong in denying immortality and providence. Had these been minor issues to him, one imagines Mendelssohn would have let them go by. But they are central aspects of his axiology; without them, felicity is impossible and nothing can be of any value whatsoever. This matter is of such critical importance to Mendelssohn that it is worth disputing even with Frederick the Great himself.

Immortality therefore is crucial, and, as mentioned, without it, a king could not demand of his subjects to sacrifice themselves for the greater good (and soldiers aware of their finitude would rightly refuse to sacrifice themselves), but more importantly, God could not be provident; if human life "is confined between the narrow borders of birth and death," we would have good reason to think "that the fate of man would have been designed by a cause, which would find pleasure in evil."[113] Happily, however, Mendelssohn's commonsensical, providential God ensures the immortality necessary for the rise of the supreme value of felicity.

Glückseligkeit: The Supreme Value of Felicity

Divinely enabled eternal felicity is the supreme value in Mendelssohn's method of valuation. This blissful condition, which, as we saw, is described as an eternal striving to further grasp divine perfection and approach it, is that towards which all our existence should be aimed. As such, it is not surprising to find Mendelssohn arguing that it is primarily felicity philosophy is aimed at. While philosophy "should begin with the examination of external objects . . . with each step that it takes, it should cast a glance back to man, to whose true felicity all its endeavors should be directed."[114] In fact, whatever does not have at least an indirect influence on our felicity we should simply not investigate. This is something Socrates, Mendelssohn explains, understood perfectly well as "the felicity of the human race was his only study."[115]

It is therefore not surprising that Mendelssohn himself writes, in one of his last letters, that "philosophy is meant to make me happier than I would be without it." Mendelssohn insists that philosophy must remain true to this vocation and adds that "I stay with her so long as she is a good companion; when she pulls supercilious, frosty or even sour faces and gets into a bad mood, I leave her alone and play with my children." He, furthermore, accepts that this might be "quite epicurean [ziemlich epikurish]" and that he chooses from philosophical systems that which makes him "happier and better at the same time."[116]

Felicity, the supreme value which allows all other values to rise, is that towards which both our lives and our philosophies ought to be directed. Philosophy itself, the highest accomplishment of reason, is of no value if it does not promote felicity. We shall now explore this critical insight further by taking a more detailed look at how this orientation defines Mendelssohn's political philosophy as well as his position towards reason, both of which reflect his overriding concern with divinely enabled human felicity.

ETERNAL FELICITY AS A POLITICAL DIRECTIVE

The consequences of Mendelssohn positing a divinely enabled human felicity as the source of all value, and hence also as the ultimate value, can clearly be traced in his political philosophy. This is no surprise. Mendelssohn's axiological position in many ways forms the center of gravity of his philosophy, both as the point of departure of his argumentation as well as the point towards which all of his thinking leads. Yet, the degree to which divinely enabled eternal human happiness is that towards which humanity ought to direct itself is particularly obvious in Mendelssohn's political thought. Indeed, as we shall see, Mendelssohn very much agrees with Aristotle that political philosophy is aimed at the human good,[117] and it is clear Mendelssohn directs his at the highest good of human felicity. We shall demonstrate this point by looking at his critique of Hobbes and Locke at the beginning of *Jerusalem*, which, it turns out, is based precisely on the seriousness with which he includes eternal beatitude in his political calculations.

Having introduced the theme of balancing civil with religious authority and power and, significantly, having emphasized the degree to which this issue matters by pointing out that disharmony between them threatens "the noblest treasure of human felicity,"[118] Mendelssohn goes on to discuss the views of Hobbes and Locke on the matter before providing his own. Mendelssohn provides three arguments against Hobbes's Leviathanic insistence on a unitary, absolutist rule of the sovereign in both the civil and religious realms. Firstly, Hobbes's belief that "public welfare would be best served if everything, even our judgment of right or wrong, were made subject to the supreme power of the civil authorities" and that "whatever that authority commands is right" exhibits a kind of tone deafness to the critical importance of liberty. Hobbes, writes Mendelssohn, either "had no taste for civil liberty or wished to see it destroyed rather than have it thus abused." Though Hobbes allows for the free exercise of inward religion or private free thought (a right that, Mendelssohn points out, Hobbes himself made use of more than anybody else), civil authorities were to have the final authority on public creed and outward modes of worship, and, accordingly, "every innovation in church matters without its sanction is not only high treason, but blasphemy as well."[119] In so doing, writes Mendelssohn, Hobbes attempted to avoid collision of public worship, over which civil authority must have complete control, and private religious or philosophical conviction.

Clearly Mendelssohn, as a Jew bent on maintaining the possibility of the public but distinct common prayer essential to his creed, would be more sensitive to this collision than Hobbes was. Hobbes allows for private freedom of religion because "internal faith is in its own nature invisible, and consequently exempted from all humane jurisdiction."[120] Judaism, however, and its manifold halakhic demands, cannot be maintained invisibly.[121] Accordingly, Mendelssohn finds Hobbes to be insensitive to religious liberty. This, however, is not as much a philosophical argument as the expression of different sensitivities. Hobbes, living in a time of great instability, treasured the stability offered by his Leviathan's unified theological-political structure and was willing to sacrifice certain religious liberties. Mendelssohn, whose thought reflects a greater concern with protecting religious minorities, treasures the freedom of maintaining a different public worship.[122] Indeed, Mendelssohn himself notes that "weary of civil strife and by nature inclined toward a quiet, speculative life, he [Hobbes] regarded tranquility and safety, no matter how they were obtained, as the greatest felicity."[123] Incidentally, this quote also suggests that Mendelssohn, who here relates Hobbes's philosophical ideas to axiological dispositions and their psychological and historical contexts, agreed, even if tacitly, to the notion of the precedence of the axiological to the philosophical.

Mendelssohn's second claim against Hobbes is that his theory does not allow for us to ever be genuinely raised out of his pitiful state of nature: "If, there is, in the state of nature, no binding obligation other than that based upon fear and powerlessness, contracts will remain valid only as long as they are supported by fear and powerlessness. Thus, men, by their contracts, will not have come any step closer to their security, and will still find themselves in the primitive state of universal warfare."[124]

In other words, in order for a proper elevation of human beings to be possible, for individuals to withstand violating contracts even if they have the power to do so, might and right must clearly be differentiated and understood as having been heterogeneous notions even in the state of nature. There are two distinct claims in this argument; the first one is about security, the second about remaining in a "primitive state." In fact, not only are these separate claims, but they do not necessarily stand or fall together, and while Hobbes would have to disagree with the first claim, he actually agrees with the second. Firstly, Mendelssohn complains that contracts based on fear and weakness do not bring greater security because if fear and weakness are overcome, the contract will no longer be kept. However, as we shall see below, Hobbes makes it explicit he does not believe we ever fully overcome either the fear of others characteristic of his state of nature or indeed the fear of reverting to such a state itself. Fear, therefore, would be a rather stable basis for a lasting contract.[125]

Furthermore, if Hobbes is right in assuming people really do keep contracts because of a fearsome power structure that keeps them weak relative to itself, then such contracts would indeed bring lasting security if the power of the sovereign were formidable enough to uphold a lasting, overpowering, and sufficiently fearsome presence. This is precisely why

Hobbes argues for his seemingly monstrous Leviathan; only a grand, unified construct could be vastly more powerful than any other agent and would therefore be able to secure the society over which it is sovereign. So while Mendelssohn is concerned fear and powerlessness aren't stable foundations because they do not last, Hobbes disagrees because he very much thinks that fear of others and of the state of nature does last and, indeed, that his formidable Leviathan generates sufficient fear and weakness for a lasting political stability to be sustained. In other words, Mendelssohn's argument that Hobbes does not bring us closer to greater security is only convincing if we disagree with Hobbes's analysis of power structures and relations, but were we to agree with Hobbes, there is nothing in Mendelssohn's argument to make us change our mind.

The second, distinct claim, namely, that Hobbes's philosophy does not really ever elevate us beyond the primitive state of nature, is one Hobbes does not have to disagree with. In fact, he actively points out that humanity remains, to some degree, in its primitive state even after the Leviathan has been set up to keep it from the state of nature. Right after the famous passage in the thirteenth chapter of *Leviathan*, wherein life in the state of nature is memorably described as "solitary, poore, nasty, brutish and short,"[126] Hobbes asks those among his readers who find it strange that "nature should thus dissociate, and render men apt to invade, and destroy one another" to consider how even in a state with laws and public officers charged with preventing and avenging violence, we are careful to be armed or well accompanied when going on a trip; we lock our doors; indeed, we even lock our chests inside the house. What do we then think of our fellow citizens, indeed of members of our household, if this is how we act *after* having overcome the state of nature? If we thusly protect ourselves living in political circumstances where crime is punished, Hobbes asks, would we not be all the more fearful in a state of nature wherein no form of punishment or law enforcement exists? Doesn't a person who takes such precautions, grounded in fear of others, "accuse mankind by his actions, as I do by my words?"[127]

Clearly, therefore, Hobbes is not committed to proving human nature to be lofty or sublime, whether before or after human beings elevated from the state of nature. To the contrary, he explicitly shows we do in fact remain fearful of each other even in far less chaotic circumstances.

Mendelssohn's critique does not point at a weakness in Hobbes's system, but rather to the fact he, as opposed to Hobbes, is very much committed to a loftier notion of human nature. Values are deeply related to our sense of identity, and clearly, Mendelssohn's axiology is intrinsically related to human beings as divinely created and possessing souls yearning for a beatific felicity based on the most sublime contemplations. Mendelssohn is really opposing Hobbes here not because of some rational or logical irregularity in Hobbes's philosophy, but because he is committed to a more sublime image of humanity and its circumstances, an image that points at eternal felicity as a perfectly achievable highest good. Mendelssohn is, furthermore, committed to a wholly good God, who would not have brought about the Hobbesian world wherein we primordially are all at war with each other. The differences reflected in Mendelssohn's second claim therefore are not only in the way human beings are depicted but also in the delineation of the basic underlying onto-theological setup of the world. While in Hobbes's world, human beings merely seek to find respite, Mendelssohn's reality encourages them to seek eternal felicity.

The last argument Mendelssohn suggests against Hobbes is less an expression of differing sensibilities or perspectives and is seemingly more damaging. It is presented as exactly the kind of weakness philosophers seek to point out in their interlocutor's system, namely, a contradiction: if political sovereigns are supposed to rule with a degree of justice because of their commitment to God, why couldn't this commitment be the basis too of every individual's elevation from out of the state of nature?

What is interesting to us here is that this is only a contradiction in so far as Hobbes is serious about the divine. It is an issue of contention as to whether Hobbes was or wasn't religious or even whether he was, for all practical purposes, an atheist.[128] Whatever position one holds about this, clearly Hobbes's religious beliefs, whatever they were, gained a very different status and political weight than Mendelssohn's beliefs gained in his political philosophy. Even though it includes the possibility of a divine presence, Hobbes's system is built on entirely naturalistic grounds. We are to start from human passions, desire, and fears, which condemn us to a political genesis rooted in the state of nature. The elevation is enabled through what Hobbes referred to as "laws of nature," which he defined as "a precept, or general rule, found by Reason, by which a man is forbidden to do that, which is destructive of his life, or taketh away the means of preserving the same."[129] These reasonable precepts are that which, through the understanding that peace and collaboration are the most conducive to overcoming the state of nature and ensuring the preservation of life, lead us to the social pact, laws, covenants, indeed, to what we would consider moral behavior. Hobbes later adds, at the end of the fifteenth chapter, that while we call these "dictates of reason" "laws," we do so improperly, "for they are but Conclusions, or Theoremes concerning what conduceth to the conservation and defence of [men]."[130] If, however, we "consider the same Theoremes, as delivered in the word of God, that by right commandeth all things; then they are properly called lawes."[131]

If Hobbes takes God seriously, then his laws of nature are indeed divinely given "laws." If he does not, this is lip service and perhaps a clear indication, between the lines, that we should think of these "laws" as theorems and therefore do not need to postulate them as God-given but as, rather, yielded from human reason when it soberly faces our own lowly nature.[132]

Hobbes does indeed mention God as ruling over the sovereign. In the eleventh chapter of *Leviathan*, when discussing the case of David and Uriah, Hobbes makes the point that David is committed to the law of nature. His killing of Uriah is an offense not to Uriah, who gave him the right to do what he pleased, but to God "because David was God's subject; and prohibited all iniquitie by the laws of Nature."[133] Mendelssohn seems to have passages like these in mind when making his third argument against Hobbes. Not only is David God's subject, and therefore beholden to Him, but so are we. Why then not construct the social construct from the loftier sources of human servitude to a divine being? Again, this is a problem only if Hobbes is serious about the law of nature as divinely given. If they are just theorems of reason, and the whole way in which his system is fashioned strongly indicates that this is in fact the case, then David is beholden not so much to God as, like everybody else, to the dictates of reason that enable us to overcome the state of nature.

Mendelssohn's problem is therefore once again the fact Hobbes builds a political theory wherein a materialistic notion of power is central while sublime felicity is impossible and divine presence is added almost as an afterthought or perhaps, even worse, as lip service. The most obvious exemplification of the difference here discussed is that while Mendelssohn's political philosophy is based on and aims at what he takes to be the highest good, an eternal divinely enabled felicity, Hobbes explicitly disavows the possibility of attaining that felicity in our earthly lives. Indeed, Hobbes understands felicity completely differently than Mendelssohn. Felicity, he writes in *Leviathan*, is "a continuall progresse of the desire, from one object to another,"[134] or more comprehensively, "Continual Successe in obtaining those things which a man from time to time desireth, that is to say, continual prospering, is that men call felicity."[135] Crucially, Mendelssohn's kind of eternal beatific happiness cannot even be imagined and might therefore be among the inconceivable terms he characterized not as wrong, but as "without meaning; that is to say absurd." The materialistically inclined Hobbes denies the very possibility of the kind of felicity Mendelssohn holds dear: "there is no such thing as perpetual Tranquillity of mind, while we live here; because Life itself is but Motion, and can never be without Desire, nor without Feare, no more than without Sense. What kind of Felicity God hath ordained to them that devoutly honour him, a man shall no sooner know, than enjoy; being joys, that now are as incomprehensible, as the word of School-men, Beatifical Vision, is unintelligible."[136] Elsewhere, he writes that "the felicity of this life, consisteth not in the repose of a mind satisfied. For there is no such *Finis ultimus*, (utmost ayme,) nor *Summum Bonum*, (greatest Good) as is spoken of in the Books of the old Morall Philosophers."[137]

More than just theoretical issues, what is at stake in Mendelssohn's critique of Hobbes is the very orientation of their thought. Mendelssohn prioritizes the religious-eudaemonic sphere and orients his philosophy towards divinely enabled felicity. Hobbes aims not at a lofty highest good but seeks a more restricted political aim, namely, relief from the ever-threatening chaos of the state of nature and its overriding principle of *Bellum omnium contra omnes.*[138] Such a respite would go quite some way to enabling more human contentment. This, however, is not ambitious enough for Mendelssohn, who does of course aim his philosophy at his notion of the highest good. Indeed, felicity, that to which our thought and politics should be directed, is much more than just the Hobbesian possibility of this earthly contentment, and as without it nothing has any value, it needs to orient our political thinking. As we shall now see in his critique of Locke, the overbearing presence of the highest value of divinely enabled eternal felicity is again that which directs his argumentation.

Indeed, having criticized Hobbes's monolithic theological-political structure, one may have expected Mendelssohn to express agreement with Locke's separation of the religious and civil authorities. Mendelssohn, however, whose thinking is often too subtle to be binary, does not agree with Locke. His disagreement, as with Hobbes, is based on the axiological underpinnings of his philosophy.

In his *Letters on Tolerance*, Locke suggests at least three distinct arguments in order to promote religious tolerance and, crucially for Mendelssohn's exposé at the beginning of *Jerusalem*, the separation of civic and ecclesiastic authority. Vernon labels them the argument from the mandate of state, the argument from belief, and the argument from error.[139] According to the argument from mandate, "the civil ruler has no more mandate than others have for the care of souls." Not only was the ruler not granted such a mandate from God, but no such power can be given to him by human beings, as "no one may abdicate responsibility for his own eternal salvation, by adopting a form of faith or worship prescribed to him by another person." The argument from belief holds that the state, with its power of compulsion, simply cannot affect human understanding and belief. As "true and saving religion consists in inward conviction of the mind,"[140] the state's external punishments and rewards, active on the outer plane, cannot be effective in the inner, religious plane. Finally, the argument from error holds that even if rulers could be effective in changing people's minds, given that there is but one true religion and many false ones, the ruler would most likely be imposing a false religion on his people. So by linking the religion of the citizens to the one chosen by their ruler, one unfairly ties their salvation to their ruler's wisdom or lack thereof.

Proast, whose reply to Locke ensured the latter wrote several letters concerning toleration rather than just one, focuses on the argument of belief, claiming that it is the "final argument by which the author endeavors in it to establish his position."[141] Proast makes the claim that one can in fact very much affect people's interior beliefs with external measures. While Proast agrees with Locke that it is absurd to starve, torment, imprison, or kill unbelievers in order to make them Christian,[142] he does believe that if force is used, not instead of reason, but "only to bring men to consider those reasons and arguments which are proper and sufficient to convince them, but which, without being forced, they would not consider," it is legitimate. Indeed, who, Proast asks, would deny that "indirectly and at a distance, it [force] does some service toward the bringing of men to embrace that truth which otherwise, either through carelessness and negligence, they would never acquaint themselves with, or through prejudice they would reject and condemn unheard under the notion of error?"[143]

In his reply, Locke remarks that the argument of belief Proast chooses to focus on is but one among several,[144] and he attacks Proast's position that force can "indirectly and at a distance" encourage proper religious belief. What precisely is the judicious distance? What degree of punishment is acceptable to overcome religiously unacceptable beliefs or behaviors? If force is "indirectly" effective, why not focus on that which is directly effective? Locke's counter argument culminates in asking whether Proast would endorse castration if it turned out it were to "indirectly and at a distance be serviceable towards the salvation of men's souls."[145] Locke, in short, sticks to his guns and to his steadfast position that external interference is both inefficient and inappropriate when it comes to religious conviction. He states, to quote his first letter again, "I can grow rich by a profession I dislike, I can be cured by medicines I view with suspicion, but I cannot be saved by a religion I reject. It is useless for an unbeliever to adopt a certain mode of external behavior, since pleasing God requires faith and inner sincerity."[146]

This is a sentiment with which Mendelssohn clearly agrees, and he almost seems to paraphrase Locke when writing in *Jerusalem* that religion "knows no act without conviction, no work without spirit, no conformity in deed without conformity in the mind. Religious actions without religious thoughts are mere puppetry, not service of God. They themselves must therefore proceed from the spirit, and can neither be purchased by reward nor compelled by punishment."[147] However, like Proast, Mendelssohn does believe that society can promote eternal salvation and "if men *can* promote their eternal felicity by public measures, it should be their natural duty to *do* so, their rational obligation to join forces for this purpose and to enter into social relations."[148] So while Mendelssohn does seem to think some public measures can be useful, he does not, as does Proast, focus on the argument of belief, as he shares Locke's conviction that external measures are ultimately not suitable for dealing with the inner conviction absolutely necessary for religious salvation.

Mendelssohn's critique of Locke really only seriously addresses the argument Proast completely neglects, namely, the argument from mandate. Indeed, having first pointed out, quite characteristically (given his distrust of language), that Locke's solution works perfectly as a verbal distinction but is unsatisfactory nonetheless, Mendelssohn goes on to argue that if the state limits its concern to temporal matters and the church is entrusted with eternal salvation, then clearly the state is "subordinate to religion, and must give way whenever a collision arises." If a citizen would have to choose between loyalty to the ruler at the expense of prison or even death and loyalty to his church at the expense of eternal damnation, clearly the latter, if taken seriously, is more persuasive. Mendelssohn therefore claims that this distinction leads to the position of "Cardinal Bellarmine and the frightful concatenation of his arguments [to the effect] that the head of the church, on behalf of the eternal, ought to be in command over everything temporal, and therefore possesses, at least indirectly, sovereign authority over all goods and minds in the world."[149]

This line of thinking again significantly emphasizes the degree to which Mendelssohn's axiological presuppositions direct his political philosophy. It is because to him eternity is far more serious than anything else that he realizes with such acuteness that leaving responsibility for it solely to religious authority could lead to the collapse of the civil authority responsible for a clearly less meaningful earthly existence. Mendelssohn perhaps disagrees with Hobbes but here shows a Hobbesian concern for the stability of the state, whose secular pillar would come crashing down under the weight of the eternal religious one.

This argument against Locke's model of the separation of church and state leads to a fascinating conclusion wherein Mendelssohn further embeds his sense of the primordial meaning of humanity's eternal life:

> It is, in the strictest sense, neither in keeping with the truth nor advantageous to man's welfare to sever the temporal so neatly from the eternal. At bottom, man will never partake of eternity; his eternality is merely an incessant temporality. His temporality never ends; it is, therefore, an essential part of his permanency and

> inseparable from it. One confuses ideas if one opposes his temporal welfare to his eternal felicity. And this confusion of ideas is not without practical consequences.[150]

This very revealing passage again shows how deeply Mendelssohn's metaphysical and, most importantly, axiological concern with eternal life dictates his philosophy. Mendelssohn takes eternal life so existentially seriously that he overcomes in his thinking what he considers a rather illusory and temporary differentiation between earthly life and eternal life. Both are part and parcel of human existence, which is critical, for without life eternal, human existence, morality, and all of our hopes would have no meaning. Locke therefore perhaps posits a system that might have ensured earthly stability or freedom but fails as it does not sufficiently take divinely enabled human beatitude into account. Mendelssohn, for whom this beatitude is simply the most important thing there is, cannot agree.

So we see that the seriousness with which Mendelssohn takes God, providence, immortality, and their critical axiological importance as enabling of the supreme value of felicity lies behind his disagreements with both Hobbes and Locke. With Hobbes, he refused to compromise on public prayer, was disappointed with the lowly, unspiritual description of man, and crucially did not understand why Hobbes introduces God into his philosophical system as an afterthought rather than as the very premise and base. If God is in the picture, Mendelssohn suggests, he ought to be at its very center philosophically, for that is where God is axiologically to him. With Locke, he makes the point that if one takes human eternal bliss seriously, and Mendelssohn very much does, one has to take it into account politically as well. Indeed, it is not the case that Locke's political theory ignores or contradicts the possibility of salvation; it is rather that it does not prioritize its value quite like Mendelssohn does.[151]

So while we quoted passages above wherein Mendelssohn explicitly describes his prioritization of human felicity and its status as the most supreme value, examining his arguments against Hobbes and Locke further reveals how this conception is reflected less explicitly in other areas of his thinking. The notion that divinely enabled human beatitude is the highest value not only remains constant in his criticism of Hobbes and Locke but also guides his own suggestion for how to best balance civil and religious authorities. While the state should allow individuals the freedom to pursue their own religion, it should ensure, albeit from a distance, that the teachings in question are those leading to felicity. The state, through education if possible and discipline if not, should encourage its citizens' adherence to precisely the same principles true religion should lovingly teach. Both the state and religion are therefore aimed at Mendelssohn's highest good, human felicity.[152]

REASON AS A SUBSERVIENT VALUE

Establishing the onto-theological structure that is the source of all values, and therefore also of the supreme value, in Mendelssohn's thought enables the clarification of his position vis-à-vis reason. Indeed, reason is often carelessly branded an ultimate value in Mendelssohn's philosophy. However, if the ultimate value is really human felicity, reason is only valuable in so far as it enables this. Crucially, it does not always necessarily do so. Reason, therefore, is not quite as valuable to Mendelssohn as many commentators have made it out to be.

In fact, in a crucial passage in *Jerusalem*, Mendelssohn overtly admits that were reason to contradict faith, he would have to side with the latter. Though of course Mendelssohn will dedicate much of the second part of *Jerusalem* to refuting Crantz's claims regarding the contradiction between Mendelssohn's use of reason as reflected in his argument for religious liberty and the seemingly unreasonable and coercive nature of the Mosaic ecclesiastical law, he does, when first bringing it up, honestly write that were he to find such a contradiction between reason and his faith he would have to "bring reason into captivity."[153] In spite of the fact that authority could suppress reason "but not put in fetters," Mendelssohn believes he would be able to "impose silence upon . . . [his] reason," though he adds this would continue to perturb him, "reappear in the most secret recesses of . . . [his] heart," and lead to disquieting doubts that would resolve themselves "into childlike prayers and fervent supplications for illumination."[154] However difficult such a crisis would have been to Mendelssohn, his axiological hierarchization is clear: even for the great modern synthesizer of reason and Judaism, faith remains primordial. True commonsensical faith in the providential God who ensures our immortality and therefore our felicity, whether in the bounds of reason or beyond them, is more directly related to the supreme value than reason is.

All of this of course accords very well with what we wrote above about Mendelssohn's skepticism of skepticism; while many great rationalists were led to destructive skepticism by following their speculations, much simpler and common people, who rely less on the use of reason than on their commonsensical intuitions, are able to gain knowledge of salvific truths and thus, with their seemingly naïve faith, reach felicity. Common sense, Mendelssohn suggests, is in that sense far more reasonable than the far-fetched conclusions reached by the great philosophical masters of reason. Indeed, as mentioned above, the idealist who denies the existence of a material world, the solipsist who denies the existence of all substance other than himself, the Spinozist who thinks of himself as a mere thought in God, and the skeptic who finds everything a matter of uncertainty all reached with their reason these "far fetched suppositions," which Mendelssohn doubts anyone ever "maintained in earnest truth." The remedy for such intellectual misadventures is to "put reason [Vernunft] to test and ascertain whether it is proceeding apace with common sense [gesunden Menschenverstand]." Indeed, "whenever reason falls far behind our common sense, or ever parts company with it entirely, and is thus in danger of falling into error, the philosopher cannot help but distrust reason."[155]

While Mendelssohn here uses the term with a somewhat pejorative connotation, he also uses reason as a completely neutral concept akin the one advanced by Hume when, in the *Treatise of Human Understanding*, he famously explains that "reason is, and ought to be the slave of the passions, and can never pretend to any other office than to serve and obey them."[156] This notion of reason postulates it not as an independent driving force, but rather as a faculty able to weigh how to best implement a driving passion.

The notion of reason as weighing other forces, rather than being one in and of itself, is reflected in one of the most revealing accounts of Mendelssohn's attitude towards these issues, namely, the allegorical dream he describes in the tenth lecture of *Morning Hours*. Delving into the ultimate standing of reason through the description of a dream may seem somewhat ironic, and given Mendelssohn's careful and meticulous nature, it would likely not just be so coincidentally. At any rate,

Mendelssohn describes how he and his young interlocutors were, in the dream, walking on a mountain path guided by both a sturdy Swiss youth "strong of limb but not possessed of the most refined intellect" and a winged woman "with an inward-looking gaze and a dreamy, rapt countenance." When, at a crossroads, the guides each take a different path, a "somewhat elderly matron" approaches the bewildered group and tells them their guides were, respectively, common sense and contemplation and that at times they part company for a short while "often from trivial causes." If travelers are steadfast enough to wait at the crossroads for their return, she tells them, both come back and wait for her to settle the quarrel. Usually, the young man is right, and, in fact, even when he isn't, "his stubbornness makes him unwilling to yield." The old matron then reveals herself to be known on earth as reason, and right before revealing what she is known to be in heaven, she is interrupted by an enraptured crowd that had "gathered around lady Contemplation and were fixed in their intention to drive out both common sense and reason."[157]

Mendelssohn concludes by remarking that whenever speculation carries him too far from the road of common sense, he seeks to reorient himself by looking back towards the point from which the road split and attempts to compare his two guides, common sense and contemplation. "Experience," he concludes, "has taught me that in most cases right is on the side of common sense, so that reason must speak unequivocally on behalf of Lady Speculation if I am to follow her lead and turn my back on common sense."[158]

So, in his telling of the dream, a more neutral notion of reason is advanced, one different than, for example, the rather pejorative one Mendelssohn suggests we have to distrust when it departs from common sense. While in the pejorative sense, reason can pave its own path, in the neutral one, it judges the varying paths paved by common sense, on the one hand, and speculation, on the other.[159] This ambiguity is not related to different periods in Mendelssohn's thought. In fact, the more pejorative conception is implicit at the end of lecture nine of *Morning Hours*, where Mendelssohn suggests reason must be put to test to "ascertain whether it is proceeding apace with common sense" right before the more neutral if not positive function it represents in the dream described in lecture ten.[160]

To make it even more complex, we can note that in lecture 6 in *Morn-*

ing Hours, Mendelssohn's usage suggests a more positive notion still, and he writes that "common sense and reason both flow from a single source; they are one and the same cognitive power." The sole difference is that reason slowly, step by step, makes it to the goal that common sense rushes to "as if with wings."[161] Here then, we find reason and common sense to be as close as ever, separated only by the burdensome and slow process of continual verification that slows reason on its way to truth.

Mendelssohn's ambiguous use of the notion of reason, though fascinating, cannot be fully explored here. Suffice it to say that however Mendelssohn conceptualizes reason in his thinking, whether as an overly speculative abstraction, as a neutral and passive evaluating faculty, or even as a tool with which to demonstrate the truths of common sense, with whom it shares its source, its axiological standing is clearly below felicity. After all, as previously mentioned, philosophy itself is not undertaken for its own sake, but rather for the sake of felicity. Furthermore, insofar as faith and common sense are more reliable guides towards the truth necessary for human felicity, they are prioritized over reason. Reason, therefore, is of a subservient value in Mendelssohn, and its worth, like all else, is derived from its potential for bringing us closer to the divinely enabled felicity that for Mendelssohn is the highest value and enables the rise of all others.

Having established felicity as the supreme value in Mendelssohn's thought, explored its underlying commonsensical onto-theological settings, its implications in political philosophy, and the ensuing assessment of the value of reason, we will now explore Mendelssohn's revaluation of Jewish values in light of this supremely valuable felicity and the axiological tensions that ensue. As we shall see in the next chapter, which is devoted to this revaluation, thinking about Mendelssohn's philosophy through the prism of the axiology that guides it enables one to better understand how it seeks to overcomes the divide between universal and particular values and methods of valuations.

(3)
UNIVERSAL FELICITY

In the previous chapter, we saw that Mendelssohn's axiological position prioritizes felicity as the highest good and that he construes that felicity as dependent on the existence of a providential God who insures our immortality. Having analyzed this axiological inclination and its significance, we are now able to begin providing answers to the questions we set out exploring. We suggested in the introduction that for a philosopher to offer a universalistic outlook, it is primarily that which he conceives of as the highest good that must be universal. Other aspects of his system, while not negligible, are less pertinent in this context. To put it plainly, if that which matters most is universal, it might not be as grave a problem for that which matters less not to be. The question of universalism as it relates to Mendelssohn, therefore, is primarily one that addresses his *summum bonum*. The question with which we must begin our assessment of Mendelssohn's universalism, accordingly, is whether and to what degree his felicity is construed as universal. We will therefore begin by looking at how and why Mendelssohn argues that felicity is indeed accessible to all, before moving on to assessing the kind of axiological tensions this universalistic commitment raises and the ways in which it informs his revaluation of Judaism.

Beatitude for All

Mendelssohn steadfastly believed that the very fabric of the universe is such as to eventually bring every human being to felicity. A providential God would never have generated creatures whose felicity He could not ensure. Felicity is therefore eminently accessible to every human being, and indeed, sooner or later, whether before or after our earthly death, every human being will find it. Universal felicity is, in other words, an integral aspect of Mendelssohn's optimistic theo-ontological conception of reality. And as that felicity is dependent on developing one's awareness of the truths of natural religion and it is God's design for us to find felicity, it is providence itself that guides us to these truths. It is, therefore, not merely the case that every human being can come to know the providential God who ensures immortality, but rather that most human beings almost intuitively do come to know Him.

This concords with Mendelssohn's commonsensical epistemology and the way it relates to the knowledge of God, providence, and immortality. Indeed, these truths are commonsensical precisely because God intends all human beings to become aware of them. Accordingly, the common sense Mendelssohn is thinking about cannot but be universal. In other words, the scope of Mendelssohn's notion of common sense clearly includes all different kinds of peoples and cultures. The "common" in Mendelssohn's "common sense" is all of humanity. This is meaningful and not necessarily the case; one could construe, and many have construed, notions of common sense wherein *common* only designates, say, a common nationality or religion.

The universal commonsensicality of natural religion is, in turn, a critical aspect of Mendelssohn's argument for the truth of the theological principles he tirelessly argues for. This point is particularly emphasized if we take into account the theory of truth underpinning Mendelssohn's commonsensical epistemology. Indeed, Mendelssohn's commonsensical position directly relates to the importance he repeatedly ascribes to probability in our quest for truth. In his early essay on the matter, Mendelssohn explains that among the kinds of knowledge we have to attain, "probability can perhaps be regarded as the most necessary since it is suited to our limited sphere and, in most cases, must take the place of certainty." Its influence on human action, and therefore also on human felicity, says Mendelssohn, has always been evident to philosophers.[1] The importance of probability comes to the fore again in *Morning Hours* and the theory of truth Mendelssohn suggests in it. As Gottlieb points out, Mendelssohn defines truth as agreement "between the various representations of our different sense perceptions as well as agreement between the representations of different subjects, human and animal alike."[2] This differs from the standard correspondence theory of truth, which Mendelssohn characterizes as positing the agreement of words with ideas and of ideas with objects. While the latter theory is "perhaps not incorrect," Mendelssohn takes it to be "unfruitful" as "there is no way to compare ideas with their objects."[3] That is why he suggests a theory of truth according to which, when it comes to knowledge of the external world, the more agreement one finds both between one's various senses and between various human beings, the more certainty one obtains.[4] Accordingly, the more people agree about something, the likelier it is to be true.[5]

Commonsensicality is therefore embedded in Mendelssohn's very theory of truth. This is a critical addition to Mendelssohn's position; without it, the assumption that the opinion of the many is more likely truthful is unjustified. So the more Mendelssohn can argue human beings actually share a common awareness of the existence of God, providence, and immortality, the stronger Mendelssohn's case for their existence according to his own epistemological position. Mendelssohn's vested interest in the universal nature of our knowledge of God, providence, and immortality and hence in the universal nature of the felicity it ensures, therefore stems, as we shall emphasize throughout the chapter, not only from profound humanistic concerns (reflected in a very strong cultural sensitivity, which will be explored below) but also from deep-seated philosophical ones.

Taking into account the importance of probability in the epistemological backing of Mendelssohn's commonsensical philosophy emphasizes the degree of epistemological soundness his position attributes to tradition as a source of knowledge and wisdom. Mendelssohn's commonsensical philosophy reinforces the notion that if many generations of our predecessors held certain truths to be evident or certain customs to be important, it is likely, indeed commonsensical, for these truths and customs to be genuinely valuable. After all, common sense is in no way restricted only to present "commoners," and previous generations certainly fall under the scope of Mendelssohn's "common" sense. The importance of tradition is of course a fundamental aspect of Mendelssohn's valuation of Judaism, and we shall therefore return to it later on in the chapter.

It is, however, important to emphasize that while Mendelssohn certainly does value tradition and what it can offer in terms of maintaining our ability to securely find the principles of natural religion upon which our felicity depends, it is nonetheless critical to him that the awareness of these principles is not dependent on any particular revelation.

Indeed, Mendelssohn, as we shall see, continually emphasizes that the basic tenets of natural religion are common to us all, even if this does not seem to be the case on first sight, precisely because his commonsensical epistemology would be gravely damaged were the beliefs he presents as universally commonsensical to turn out to be but culturally dependent, particular, and local. If one does not agree with Mendelssohn that it is in fact common among all human beings to believe in a providential God and immortality, then these metaphysical postulates would lose what is for him their most important epistemological foothold. Given his take on the problematic nature of metaphysical inquiry, were the power of common sense to be diminished in Mendelssohn's philosophy, a variety of arguments critical to his thinking would be very difficult to maintain. Again, this emphasizes Mendelssohn's philosophical dependence on universal agreement about God, providence, and immortality, which to him must mean universal accessibility to felicity.

The universality of Mendelssohn's depiction of the commonsensical attainment of truthful religious knowledge is beautifully reflected in one of the more famous passages of *To the Friends of Lessing*, wherein Mendelssohn writes of a Greenlander who, confronted with the beauty of a sunrise, is overwhelmed by the sublimity of the God who created it. This commonsensical realization, "easy enough for a child to draw," has for Mendelssohn "the certainty of a geometric axiom or postulate and the overwhelming force of an irrefutable definition." Crucially for us, Mendelssohn adds that it has the "same force as the simple and artless reason of the Psalmist: He who has planted the ear, surely He must hear . . . [Psalm 94:9–11]."[6] The Greenlander and the biblical psalmist both reach the same commonsensical beliefs directly related to felicity, and more importantly, the psalmist's religion is not presented as inherently superior to the Greenlander's. Both reflect the common apodictic human reaction to the obvious presence of a providential God.[7]

The basic salvific beliefs any sincerely minded person can reach are characterized in *Jerusalem* as eternal truths, "which are not subject to time and remain the same for all eternity," and contrasted with "*temporal, historical truths*; things which occurred once and may never occur again; propositions which have become true at one point in time and space through a confluence of causes and effects." What is critical to us here are that those eternal truths "insofar as they are useful for men's salvation and felicity" are taught by God "through creation itself, and its internal relations, which are legible and comprehensible to all men." Indeed, it would be contradictory to think God would have made these indispensable truths dependent on supernatural revelation (as certain historical truths are) because this would entail God "was good enough to reveal to men those truths on which their felicity depends, but not omnipotent, or not good enough to grant them the powers to discover those truths themselves." This would, moreover, make the necessity of supernatural revelation "more universal than revelation itself does. If, therefore, mankind must be corrupt and miserable without revelation, why has the greater part of mankind lived without *true revelation* from time immemorial?"[8]

For Mendelssohn, given that God created us for felicity, it makes no sense that "the two Indies" would have to "wait until it pleases the Europeans to send them a few comforters to bring them a message without which they can . . . live neither virtuously nor happily?"[9] The religious truths necessary for salvation are and have been available to all human beings irrespective of their awareness to any particular revelation, as Mendelssohn's God simply would not have stranded his creations without the ability to realize felicity. This ability, to the contrary, is an essential part of Mendelssohn's conception of human nature. In his correspondence with Abbt, conducted while conceiving and writing *Phädon*, Mendelssohn seeks to assuage his interlocutor's dismay at the distance humanity exhibits from adequately reflecting God by making the case that every human being must have been born with the capacity to mirror the creator and thus experience felicity.[10] And of course, as he repeatedly argues in *Phädon* itself, an omnipotent God would not have created a "phantom of felicity" and could not, therefore, have created human beings lacking the ability to find felicity.[11]

Mendelssohn beatific notion of felicity is, therefore, eminently open to all. The tremendous importance of this salvific inclusivity to him is repeatedly stated explicitly and emphasized by how profoundly interwoven it is with the fabric of his philosophical system and its underlying theological principles. This inclusivity, moreover, also comes to light in an enduring concern to avoid cultural misunderstandings. Indeed, as discussed above, Mendelssohn repeatedly insists that humans from radically different cultures, like the Greenlander or the population of the two Indies, can reach the highest kind of religious insights and felicity without the need for a Judeo-Christian revelation or even an enlightened European education. While this already shows God's care for all human beings, and as such reflects Mendelssohn's theological priorities, it does not in and of itself properly respond to his epistemological concerns. To do that, he must also show that common salvific beliefs are actually commonly held, that in some meaningful sense they have been common throughout human history and throughout current human cultures. Mendelssohn, in other words, is committed to showing that most people do in fact reach these insights. This, in turn, leads him to repeatedly admonish his readers to be more informed and careful in their understanding of foreign ideas and religious symbolism and to repeatedly warn against misinterpreting foreign religions or cultures as idolatrous. His attention to such misinterpretations is reflected in a very particular kind of cultural sensitivity.[12]

A forceful example of this sensitivity appears in *Jerusalem* in the context of Mendelssohn's explanation of the semiotics of both idolatry and what he takes to be cultural insensitivity. Idolatry, Mendelssohn explains, arises when a person confuses the symbol with that which it is meant to symbolize.[13] So, for example, one could come to confuse a statue with the God it is meant to depict or the actual animal with the divine property it was meant to represent and end up, idolatrously, worshipping the statue or the animal. A complementary mechanism can lead to cultural insensitivity. Indeed, just as one can mistake the symbol for the symbolized, one can easily misunderstand foreign symbols, taking them to be idolatrous or just plain ridiculous because one misses the symbolism at play. Accordingly, in *Jerusalem*, Mendelssohn warns his readers that "in judging the religious ideas of a nation that is otherwise still unknown, one must . . . take care not to regard everything from one's own *parochial* point of view, lest one should call idolatry what, in reality, is perhaps only *script*."[14]

In order to illustrate this mechanism, Mendelssohn ask us to imagine a person whom he calls a second "Omhya" visiting the temple of providence in Dessau.[15] The temple of providence, conceived by the educational reformer Johann Basedow,[16] was meant to enable worship in the spirit of a particularly enlightened version of natural religion and was seemingly wholly purified of even the possibility of idolatry. Accordingly, it is described as bare of any pictures or ornaments except for the writing "God, all-wise, all powerful, all good, rewards the good" on a wall.[17] Mendelssohn then suggests that Mai (Omhya's original name), if he knew nothing of the art of writing, would, were he to regard worship at the temple solely from his own point of view, most probably think that these Europeans are involved in the most incongruous kind of idolatry. Mendelssohn imagines Mai reporting to his countrymen upon his return on the religious ideas he encountered and suggests they would all deride and pity the absurd superstition of these people who "have sunk so low as to show divine adoration to black lines on a white surface."[18] In other words, in spite of the fact it might be obvious to Mendelssohn's readers that the writing on the wall represents a non-idolatrous conception of God, even it could be misinterpreted by a foreigner lacking the relevant semiotic awareness as idolatry.

While it is Mai who is here presented as misunderstanding European culture, Mendelssohn is writing about the tendency of European intellectuals and travelers to mistakenly interpret foreign cultures. He is, after all, warning members of a European rather than a Polynesian audience to refrain from cultural misunderstandings. This concern is made explicit in another example Mendelssohn provides soon after the one involving Mai, namely, the European misunderstanding of Brahminic symbolism.

Indeed, Mendelssohn critiques those among his contemporaries who "laugh at the Indian philosophers who say that this universe is borne by elephants, and place the elephants upon a large turtle, and maintain that the latter is upheld by an enormous bear, and that the bear rests on an immense serpent."[19] Basing himself on the work of John Zephaniah Holwell, who had studied in India and was able, according to Mendelssohn, "to see with the eyes of a native Brahmin,"[20] Mendelssohn argues these conceptions have convincingly proved to be symbolic and could therefore refer to sound divine or cosmic attributes. As with Mai's imagined misunderstanding of our script, the European misunderstanding of Indian symbolism turns into a farce that which in actual fact might very well be symbolic depictions of sound cosmological conceptions.

Mendelssohn would of course have had fairly obvious personal reasons to warn his readers from judging foreign religions carelessly. His own religious culture had after all perennially been derided and misunderstood. Indeed, in between Mai and the wise men of India, Mendelssohn explicitly provides an ancient example of such a misunderstanding, telling of how the conquerors of Jerusalem found the cherubim on the Ark of the Covenant and, illiterate as they were in Jewish symbolism, took for idols statues that really were images symbolizing "divine providence and prevailing grace."[21]

But Mendelssohn's concern for avoiding cultural misunderstandings stems not only from his own uncertain status as a Jew at the threshold of European Christian culture or indeed from his well-known humanistic tendencies. Rather, as mentioned above, it stems also from the deeply rooted theological and philosophical positions we have been analyzing, namely, that God could never have created beings whose ultimate felicity He does not ensure, on the one hand, and the related importance of common sense in his epistemology, on the other.

These provide a vested theological and epistemological interest for Mendelssohn's position that much of what one might take to be genuinely radical differences between competing or even seemingly exclusory paths to salvation are but misunderstandings caused either by cultural insensitivity or, as we saw in the previous chapter, by the vague language of metaphysics. An example of the former would be the inability to understand symbolic contents through the perspective of the culture in which it obtains, as with culturally unthoughtful intellectuals misinterpreting the Brahmanic symbolic language. An example of a misunderstanding brought about by the slippery and unwarranted use of highly abstract speculative language would be Jacobi's mischaracterization of Lessing's Spinozism and his misguided conclusion that enlightened philosophy cannot in the final analysis be harmonized with religion. The fact Mendelssohn related the problems of cultural and metaphysical misunderstanding is exemplified by the preamble with which he chose to open *To the Friends of Lessing*. Indeed, Mendelssohn opens the work, wherein he sets out to clear the metaphysical confusions that led to Jacobi's claims about both Lessing and philosophy in general, with a quote about cultural confusion from "Sensus Communis, an Essay on the Freedom of Wit and Humour in a Letter to a Friend" by Anthony Ashley Cooper, the third Earl of Shaftesbury.[22] In the passage, Shaftesbury ponders about the reaction of a native of Ethiopia who was "suddenly transported into Europe, and plac'd either at Paris or Venice at a time of Carnival, when the general face of mankind was disguis'd and almost every creature wore a mask." Once this man realized what was happening, he would, Shaftesbury suggests, rightfully laugh at our rather ridiculous shenanigans. If he were to keep laughing at the unmasked faces of his hosts because he was unaware of the "fair complexion and Common Dress of the Europeans," he would, however, be carrying the jest too far and become ridiculous himself in mistaking "nature for mere art."[23]

Mendelssohn, it seems to me, hints that Jacobi might be right in his criticism of some aspects of Spinozism, which he compares to the mask, but ridiculous in laughing at the face of true philosophy, which does not contradict religion at all. More importantly, however this preamble is best interpreted,[24] it obviously relates Jacobi's mistake to the one Shaftesbury is seeking to describe. The very fact he remembered that particular passage in Shaftesbury further emphasizes the degree to which he is receptive to the critical importance of cultural sensitivity. If we are not careful in our judgments of other cultures, we risk losing track of our common salvific beliefs because of differing cultural masquerades, just as we might risk losing track of these obvious truths because of metaphysical bloviating.

It is therefore critical to Mendelssohn, to whom the belief that God would not have created beings unable to find felicity is absolutely crucial both existentially and philosophically, that the truths necessary for that felicity are universally available and that many seeming differences about them are but the masks of culture and abstract speculation. This, furthermore, is also why it so important to him to repeatedly make the claim that the truths of natural religion preceded in the history of humanity their debasement into idolatry. Indeed, if healthy, commonsensical natural religion is a late achievement of culture, this would mean earlier generations, without access to the progress necessary for realizing these truths, would have been denied felicity. God would then have allowed humans without the ability of finding the truths necessary for their felicity, which Mendelssohn cannot agree to.

Mendelssohn therefore repeatedly depicts idolatry as a late debasement of that which was originally sublime. When, for example, he discusses Pastor Meiners's remarks that the worship of animals was more prevalent than that of humans among the earliest people, he argues this should not lead to the assumption that animal worship was a primitive form of religion from which later forms, including monotheism, arose. To the contrary, Mendelssohn starts by making the point that animals can be an extremely effective symbolic means through which to express certain attributes as, unlike humans, each one possesses "a definite, distinctive character," and he explains that "therefore, at first one sought to indicate and render perceptible through suchlike signs the attributes of what was deemed most worthy of adoration."[25] People would then gradually have mistaken the symbol with the symbolized, which, as mentioned, is the underlying mechanism of idolatry, and ended up worshipping the animals that were meant to be mere symbolic evocations of divine attributes. In other words, just as we confuse the symbol for that which is symbolized in our analysis of foreign religions, so too can this confusion set in after generations and eventually that which once was meant to symbolize God or His attributes becomes sanctified in and of itself. Indeed, given that common sense is thought of as something akin to a healthy reflex of the mind that leads it to spontaneously accept the obvious, it is only natural that in the history of ideas or religion, the original intent reflects this primary and healthy kind of awareness, only for it to be degraded because of unnecessary, subsequent complications and misunderstandings.[26]

Gottlieb indicates that a rather similar mechanism is reflected in the line of reasoning on which Mendelssohn relies to describe the degradation of the Kabbalah.[27] Mendelssohn description is relayed in a fascinating recollection of Mendelssohn's close associate the writer Friedrich Nicolai, who states Mendelssohn thought Kabbalists, unable to be precise in their theological writings because Hebrew offered no sophisticated metaphysical vocabulary to do so, had to rely on "vulgar imagery" instead. When later generations of Kabbalists interpreted literally the "vulgar imagery" meant to be merely metaphorical, the "grossest nonsense" of pantheism ensued.[28]

Positing origins as more enlightened than later developments when thinking about religion, semiotics, and other phenomena is an intrinsic aspect of a wider position of Mendelssohn's regarding history in general, and Jewish history in particular. Indeed, in Judaism too, later developments are often described as degenerations of originally purer or more enlightened beliefs or practices. So, for example, the Mosaic constitution "did not persist long in its erstwhile purity."[29] Already by the time of the prophet Samuel, and because of the people's demand for an earthly king, the unique identity of civil and religious authority was irrevocably breached.

The exalted view of a more ancient, purer Judaism is also reflected in Mendelssohn's argumentation in his correspondence with the leaders of the Jewish community of the Duchy of Mecklenburg-Schwerin about a controversy over Jewish burial practices, which arose when new regulations where put into place after several reported cases in which unconscious people mistakenly diagnosed as dead were buried alive. In order to avoid such incidents, it was decided to oblige a three-day moratorium to ensure the person was indeed irrevocably deceased.[30] This of course contradicted traditional Jewish practice, which seeks to bring the remains to burial as soon as possible. While Mendelssohn appealed to Duke Friedrich to revoke his order, he also proposed to the local rabbis some halakhic solutions, which they strongly opposed. As opposed to the rabbis' intransigence in altering the accepted Jewish practice, Mendelssohn suggested leaving the corpse in a burial cave for three days before burying it and, significantly, argued this was actually nearer to the ancient, original Jewish practice. Mendelssohn here, therefore, as Sorkin puts it, points "to the ancient practice as being truer to the precepts of Judaism, both biblical and rabbinic."[31] In his letter to Emden on the matter, Mendelssohn notes that he does not know "why we departed from the practice of our saintly forebears of blessed memory. They laid their dead to rest in caves and sepulchral chambers, and observed them three days."[32]

Even in a controversy that arose because of a scientific and therefore inherently modern problem, Mendelssohn, while suggesting an innovative approach (and being criticized for doing so by Emden),[33] argues not for innovation but for reverting to ancient practices perceived as having been more enlightened originally. Again, history is not necessarily a refining force; to the contrary, very often some aspects of the ancient past are construed as more enlightened than the present. The emergence of salvific truths and practices certainly does not depend on some communal human progress, a progress that for Mendelssohn is at times wanting in history, as quite often later practices and beliefs are less enlightened than preceding ones.

This nonprogressive way of thinking about history in general is explicitly stated in Mendelssohn's famous characterization of humanity as being in a state of moral fluctuation and the ensuing disagreement with Lessing's conception according to which "one pictures the collective entity of the human race as an individual person and believes that Providence sent it to school here on earth, in order to raise it from childhood to manhood."[34] A humanity perceived to have been childish at one time would presumably have been unable to avail itself at the time of its infancy to the truths necessary for salvation. This would again decisively tie the possibility of felicity to cultural progress, which would then have left such humans born before the necessary cultural maturity bereft of the possibility of finding felicity. A providential God would never have allowed that to happen. The human race, says Mendelssohn, is therefore "in almost every century, child, adult, and old man at the same time, though in different places and regions of the world," and the term *progress* itself can only be applied to "the individual man, who is destined by Providence to spend part of his eternity here on earth."[35]

The religious truths necessary for human felicity therefore have always been available to all. If cultures exhibit mistaken or idolatrous beliefs, it is because these truths were lost, not because these cultures reflect an earlier, less enlightened religious understanding. It is a constitutive aspect of Mendelssohn's theology that God would not have allowed any human, wherever or whenever that human happens to be born, to be left bereft of his or her potential for felicity. The truths God gave to all of humanity are similarly salvific to all generations; they are not only common to the living in all countries, but to their ancestors as well.

MENDELSSOHN'S PLURALISM

In the introduction, we sought to depict the cosmopolitanism characteristic of several seminal figures of early modern thought and of the Enlightenment. The previous section already makes clear that Mendelssohn fits right into that picture. Like Montaigne, Mendelssohn seeks to contextualize seemingly strange notions within a cultural context in which they are not less reasonable than we think ourselves to be. Like Voltaire or Lessing, Mendelssohn does not assume distant cultures are ipso facto inferior. Like Rousseau, his thought reflects a deep concern with the religious salvation of every single human, wherever on the globe that person might have been born. There is, accordingly, an unmistakably tolerant spirit in Mendelssohn's writing. Indeed, beyond tolerance, there is also a certain kind of pluralism.

Prima facie, the notion of pluralism is, in our context, rather anachronistic. After all, the prominent seventeenth- and eighteenth-century debates about religious diversity centered on the weaker notion of tolerance. Locke's *Letter Concerning Toleration*, discussed in the previous chapter, is in this context exemplary. So too is the British Toleration Act, granting freedom of religious worship to dissenting English Protestants, which received royal assent in 1689, the year Locke published his letter.[36] More importantly for our present concerns is the Edict of Toleration issued by the Austrian Emperor Joseph II in 1782, which was the first to grant religious freedom and civil rights to the Jews.[37]

Yet, though part and parcel of the spirit of enlightened philosophy and politics, tolerance still remains a rather negative concept; the word itself indicates a willingness to bear or endure divergence, certainly not the kind of affirmation of difference pluralism would seem to connote. Indeed, as Gray points out, "when we tolerate a practice, a belief or a character trait, we let something be that we judge to be undesirable, false or at least inferior; our toleration expresses the conviction that, *despite* its badness, the object of toleration should be left alone."[38] While arguably more expressively negative than how the term is reflected in Locke's and Mendelssohn's writings, Gray's characterization is very much reflected by the fact that edicts of toleration, such as the one issued by Joseph II, still include some forms of discrimination.[39] Toleration, therefore, is clearly a significantly weaker idea than the notion of pluralism.

Mendelssohn, however, uses the term *toleranz*, or the similar term *Duldung*, very positively.[40] This reflects the fact that his version of religious tolerance actually reaches the higher threshold of what has been widely referred to as pluralism in contemporary religious thought. Huang usefully delineates a generally accepted typology, differentiating between two models of religious pluralism. The first presents different religions as varying parochial expressions of some universal essence. The second regards religions as different in their fundamentals but embraces that difference nonetheless.[41] While Mendelssohn cannot accept the latter model, his toleration is in fact very much a form of pluralism similar to the former.[42]

Indeed, Mendelssohn's commitment to common salvific principles is, as we saw above, an unavoidable derivative of his concept of a providential God who would not have allowed human beings, wherever or whenever they were or are born, to be left bereft of their potential for felicity. It is also an integral part of his commonsensical epistemology and the theory of truth on which it relies; were it not the case that all religions reflect a universal essence, Mendelssohn's commonsensical natural religion would be deprived of its epistemological grounding.

Accordingly, Mendelssohn is committed to the notion that a similar essence is in fact apprehended differently by different religious cultures. Indeed, he positively embraces that pluralism. This pluralistic enthusiasm is reflected forcefully in the passionate call he makes at the end of *Jerusalem*: "Brothers, if you care for true piety, let us not feign agreement where diversity is evidently the plan and purpose of Providence."[43] Mendelssohn here not only warns that a "*union of faiths is not tolerance* . . . it is diametrically opposed to true tolerance,"[44] but makes a far stronger claim. Not only do the variety of faiths genuinely enable their believers to find eternal felicity, but God positively wants there to be such a variety; God, Mendelssohn writes metaphorically, in his wisdom and providence, "has stamped everyone, not without reason, with his own facial features."[45]

Still, as mentioned above, Mendelssohn's pluralism must assume an essential similarity. As such, it is a weaker form of pluralism than, say, the value pluralism famously espoused by Isaiah Berlin, who argued that "there is a plurality of ideals, as there is a plurality of cultures and temperaments," and accordingly that "there is a plurality of values which men can and do seek, and that these values differ."[46] For Berlin, value pluralism essentially contradicts the monistic notion that "there is a single harmony of truths into which everything, if it is genuine, in the end must fit."[47] Contrarily, while Mendelssohn does suggest a plurality of paths, he does not suggest a genuine plurality of values.

Mendelssohn of course very much argues for a common *summum bonum*, namely, divinely enabled human felicity. And while he tirelessly argues all people can reach the truths of natural religion upon which this felicity is based, he is intransigent about the truths themselves. In other words, while Mendelssohn's pluralism accommodates a variety of paths, these paths can only be valid insofar as they reach the same goal: human felicity, which is dependent on a firm belief in God, providence, and immortality. Mendelssohn, for example, suggests the Brahmanic belief system is legitimate but only because he assumes it ultimately reflects the one genuine onto-theology. Thus, while it may, for example, seem polytheistic, it actually is not, or at least not in a way that precludes the commonsensical recognition of a supreme God.[48] Accordingly, the Brahmanic religion also reflects common and reasonable natural religion. But what if there are, as opposed to what Mendelssohn suggests, at least some of the time genuine differences between various religious cultures on the most crucial salvific matters? What happens when a culture shows itself to be idolatrous even after its symbolism has properly been interpreted and understood? Can Mendelssohn accommodate forms of polytheism that do not posit a supreme God beyond all others or that are not otherwise resolved into monotheism from some higher perspective?

While heartfelt, Mendelssohn's pluralism is one that can accommodate difference on the condition that these differences can be downgraded to what he thinks of as nonessential doctrines. He cannot, in other words, accept a model of pluralism that embraces essential differences. Indeed, when the difference in the varying view is deemed essential, Mendelssohn becomes somewhat less tolerant. A first example is the case of atheism. In *Jerusalem*, Mendelssohn plainly suggests atheism cannot genuinely be tolerated: "The state, to be sure, is to see to it from afar that no doctrines are propagated which are inconsistent with the public welfare; doctrines which, like atheism and Epicureanism, undermine the foundation on which the felicity of social life is based."[49] Mendelssohn is not, of course, thinking here of violent action, but whatever measure the state is supposed to take "from afar," these are measures meant to put the atheistic and Epicurean doctrines beyond the threshold of acceptability.[50]

In fact, Mendelssohn repeatedly makes the case that atheism takes one beyond the borders of common sense. Indeed, while Mendelssohn often uses the term *Gemeinsinn* to refer to that which is commonly translated as "common sense," he also uses interchangeably the terms *Bon-Sens* or *gesunde Menschenverstand*.[51] Given the latter term, literally translated as "healthy human understanding," it is not accidental that when differentiating his own position as to the necessary vagueness of metaphysical and theological language from the kinds of destructive skepticism that put into doubt the truths of natural religion and that he therefore categorically refuses to be associated with, he bluntly characterizes the latter kind of thinking as "that disease of the soul" he ardently wishes to cure his fellow man of.[52] The "diseased" skeptic cannot rely on his "gesunde Menschenverstand" and thus positions himself beyond the discursive limits Mendelssohn assumes are "common."

It is also why, in his prize essay, Mendelssohn brings forth arguments for the existence of God while making explicit they will not convince atheists.[53] The idea is that philosophical arguments for the existence of God will only be convincing to "healthy minded" individuals who have not lost touch with common sense. This does not only again indicate that Mendelssohn felt that the demonstrative prowess of philosophy cannot replace common sense as our guide to religious beliefs but also that atheist lack common sense.

The lack of tolerance towards atheism certainly limits Mendelssohn's pluralism but was rather common during the Enlightenment. After all, even Locke himself, in his letter on toleration, explicitly states that atheism cannot be tolerated.[54] Furthermore, the very moniker *atheist* was more of an insult than a description of an actual philosophical position in eighteenth-century philosophy.[55] Still, a genuine atheist would not consider the term an insult, nor presumably would a genuine polytheist or animal worshiper consider these appellations insulting in spite of their pejorative connotations in Mendelssohn's writing. As mentioned, he could not accept their beliefs as equally legitimate. Mendelssohn does allow for the possibility that animal worship is not idolatry but only because he assumes the animals in question are symbols of the one true God. But were a people or a tribe to genuinely worship an animal, it would be idolatrous and presumably beyond the providential desire for plurality. After all, when describing diversity as "evidently the plan and purpose of providence,"[56] Mendelssohn certainly would not include diverse forms of idolatrous worship. Though idolaters too will end up finding felicity, they cannot do so while they are in the grips of their mistake. Their mistaken beliefs, therefore, induce suffering and unhappiness, or in other words, precisely that which Mendelssohn's providential God does not have in mind for us. And indeed, in a letter to Naphtali Herz Homberg, he argues that even if ritual law lost its usefulness as a kind of "script or sign language," it would remain necessary as a unifying bond, and he adds that this union "will have to be preserved by the plan of providence as long as polytheism, anthropomorphism, and religious usurpation dominate the world."[57] It is therefore clear that forms of religion that are genuinely polytheistic or anthropomorphic are not part of the desirable plurality of religions mentioned at the end of *Jerusalem*. They are something to be actively combatted.

Still, the most poignant tension in Mendelssohn's pluralism is not his difficulties with atheism and idolatry, both of which would have been widely dismissed by most if not all members of the religious Enlightenment. It is, rather, his deeply ambivalent perception of Christianity that seems to undermine his pluralism most. After all, the Brahmins and animal worshippers are almost theoretical constructs in Mendelssohn's writing. It is of course heartening that he expresses a certain sensitivity to such distant cultures and beliefs, but it is not a sensitivity he would have had to put to test in his actual cultural surroundings. The genuine diversity he is confronted with most directly is of course one that cannot but include the Christian faith. Indeed, when making his appeal for diversity at the end of *Jerusalem*, he plainly must have included Christianity; he is, after all, replying to Christian critics and writing for what he knew was mainly a Christian audience.

And yet Mendelssohn repeatedly describes Christianity as at least partly obstructing the path to human felicity. There is of course a rather blunt treatment of Catholicism: "the frightful concatenation" of Cardinal Bellarmine's arguments to the effect that "all secular realms are indirectly subject to the domination of the spiritual monarch, and must take their orders from him" is presented as obviously and dangerously mistaken. Mendelssohn counters the Lockean notion that the state should let go of its ill-perceived mandate for the spiritual well-being of its citizens not with a *reductio ad absurdum*, but with what he takes to be a similarly conclusive *reductio ad Catholicum*. There can be no reasonable doubt that the cardinal's work, though ingenious, is anything but a collection of "sophisms [Trugschlüssen]."[58] He therefore assumes that any philosophy that validates such conclusions cannot but be deeply mistaken.

Mendelssohn, furthermore, unabashedly writes in *Jerusalem* the phrase "hypocrisy or Jesuitry,"[59] implying the identity of both terms. Further misgivings towards the Jesuits are reflected in the letter to Naphtali Herz Homberg quoted above, wherein he writes his friend that "we should obstinately oppose the Jesuitical trickery that, with every appearance of friendliness, asks for union and, at bottom, only intends to tempt us to cross over to the other side."[60]

Yet, such qualms about Catholicism are also reliably within the bounds of eighteenth-century Enlightenment Protestant discourse. Moreover, the criticism of Bellarmine's notions of papal spiritual authority are more of a political concern than one relating to the core religious dogmas of the Christian faith. Indeed, in clearly opposing those ideas, Mendelssohn again follows the lead of Locke, who explicitly puts not only atheists, as we saw above, beyond the scope of toleration, but Catholics as well.[61] Furthermore, the Jesuits were widely perceived in intellectual circles as pretending to engage with Enlightenment discourse only to undermine it and had since the late sixteenth and early seventeenth centuries developed throughout Protestant Europe a reputation as the "shock troops of the Counter Reformation."[62] Mendelssohn's view of Catholicism would not in any way be perceived as intolerant in a Protestant intellectual environment still scarred by the terrible violence and persecution the Catholic battle against the Reformation involved.[63]

The critique of Christianity expressed by Mendelssohn, however, is one that cannot be explained away as merely part of a widespread fear of papal authority or of the supposed anti-Protestant and anti-Enlightenment efforts of the Jesuit order. These are criticisms and objections that seem to broach the core religious dogmas of the Christian faith, dogmas shared by both Catholics and Protestants. Many of them can be found in Mendelssohn's response to the Lavater affair. In fact, they are already reflected in the conversations leading up to it. Lavater fervently hoped to convert Mendelssohn to Christianity and through this conversion bring about the conversion of all Jews, eventually leading to a millennial kingdom of Christ on earth.[64] He thought he might be able to attract Mendelssohn to Christianity because of the latter's generous praise of the moral character of Jesus. Yet a closer look at Mendelssohn's praise of Christ shows the degree to which it was qualified. Mendelssohn did indeed praise the moral character of Jesus but added that he sincerely believes Jesus himself never presumed to be divine. Indeed, Mendelssohn says that he would have had to deny all respect to a Socrates, and presumably anybody else, who would proclaim himself "a divine person or a mediator between God and men, let alone the only mediator."[65] So Mendelssohn's "philosophical respect" is one that does not respect at all those aspects of the Christian story that make of Jesus the founder of a religion rather than a particularly morally approvable figure. Altmann points out that the widespread perception of Jewish acrimonious abuse towards Jesus might have contributed to giving Mendelssohn's rather modest admission the "aura of a great promise" in Lavater's wishful eyes.[66] Yet, whatever the roots of Lavater's misplaced hopes, clearly Mendelssohn expressly disregards any compromise on the status of Jesus. It is not the case that Jesus could be, in some way, divine for Christians only or might perhaps be a divine person who nonetheless does not cancel Jewish obligation to their own ceremonial law. Mendelssohn, to rephrase what we quoted above, lacks all respect for any such claims.

Further severe objections are to be found in various writings Mendelssohn produced in reaction to Lavater's public demand, put in the introduction to the latter's publication of sections of Charles Bonnet's *Palingenesis* (which Lavater published as *Investigation of the Proofs for Christianity*). Mendelssohn either refutes Bonnet's arguments for Christianity or does "what Socrates would have done if he had read this work and found it irrefutable."[67] Given that Mendelssohn clearly was not convinced by Bonnet's arguments and had no intention whatsoever of forsaking his ancestral faith, he faced the prospect of having to publicly engage in a religious battle he had nothing to gain from. Though private conversations and correspondence showed Mendelssohn was angered by Lavater's actions and deeply perturbed by the predicament they had put him in,[68] he was eventually able to curb his annoyance and reply with an eloquent open letter written in a relatively warm and polite tone. Still, in his response, Mendelssohn resolutely refuses to accept Lavater's offensive challenge and reproaches the Swiss theologian for having publicly declared it in the first place, reminding him that assurances had been given to the effect that their conversations about religious issues, which Mendelssohn only reluctantly agreed to partake in, would remain private.[69]

Mendelssohn further explains he had, after many years of study, decided "completely in favor of *my* religion" and that he regards "the religion of my father as the *true* one." He also emphasizes that he shall abide by the principles of his religion "as long as my entire soul does not assume another nature" and that his remoteness from Lavater's religion has not decreased since their conversations. Having explained his reasons for avoiding all religious disputes, he adds that according to Judaism, he is under no obligation to convert anyone and that those who abide by the Noahide law, a "religion of nature and reason," are called "*virtuous men of other nations*, and they are the children of eternal bliss [ewigen Seligkeit]."[70]

When he finally turns to address Bonnet's arguments directly, Mendelssohn starts by claiming he has read better defenses of the same religion by his German countrymen, concluding more generally that "when it is a matter of philosophical principles, the German rarely needs to borrow from his neighbors."[71] In doing so, Mendelssohn immediately disarms Lavater's either/or equation; if Bonnet's argument are not the best defense of Christianity, their soundness is presumably unrelated to its truth. In other words, Mendelssohn could, were he thusly engaged, undermine Bonnet's argument without necessarily undermining Christian belief. Furthermore, Mendelssohn makes this point while emphasizing the aspect of his identity he shares with the German members of the Enlightenment. Mendelssohn does, however, allude to more destructive counter arguments in the letter's last paragraph, wherein he mentions he would say more against Bonnet's book if Lavater insisted and publish, in spite of his great reluctance to do so, "*Counter-Reflections* containing my thoughts about Mr. Bonnet's book and the case that he defends."[72]

So Mendelssohn made clear, both in his conversation with Lavater and in his public response to Lavater's challenge, that he categorically disavows Jesus's divine nature and adds that he adheres to Judaism not only because he was born into it but also because, upon further investigation, he found it to be true. The counter reflections mentioned at the end of his response to Lavater, which did in fact remain unpublished until 1845, contain several further arguments against the viability of the Christian faith that leave even less doubt as to Mendelssohn's low perception of it.

Indeed, though his "Counter-Reflections to Bonnet's *Palingenesis*" reflects gracious appreciation of the "wisest, most venerable men" who speak of the Christian faith with great conviction and won over "the most rational portion of the human race to their side,"[73] it very quickly veers to a far less generous tone. The teachers of Christianity, says Mendelssohn, only *seem* to assure eternal felicity to the whole human race. In actual fact, they threaten with eternal damnation all such people who do not accept their particular historical testimony. "This idea," Mendelssohn bluntly writes, "is repugnant" and turns the Christian faith into a "burden that presses human reason to the ground."[74]

Mendelssohn goes on to describe several of the Christian faith's central dogmas, such as a triune God consisting of three distinct persons, original sin, and the notion of a divine human being who dies on the cross for the sins of humanity. He also mentions Jesus's resurrection, his descent into hell, his ascension to heaven, and so on. These beliefs, which he characterizes as thoroughly irrational, lack the commonality of what Mendelssohn takes to be the universally accepted principles of the religion of reason and yet are in Christianity, Mendelssohn writes, "intimately connected with the assurance of eternal felicity."[75] Christianity, in so far as it hangs on to these dogmas, is therefore, like atheism, below the threshold of the common "healthy human understanding" and indeed, like polytheism, harmful to the salvific vision of universal felicity for all.[76]

Mendelssohn's criticism, though robust and rather uncompromising, might perhaps be less adverse than it prima facie seems if we accept Freudenthal's view that Mendelssohn believed idolatry to be necessarily part of human religion. Basing his analysis on the Mendelssohnian notion that idolatry arises "when the symbol itself is considered as sacred and not only what it stands for,"[77] Freudenthal argues that "the human condition is inseparably intertwined with sign-use and therefore also with idolatry to a greater or lesser extent."[78] Pure religion is not available to humans. Our lot is to progress from whatever cruder forms of religiosity we are facing at first to the least idolatrous one. Enlightenment is therefore a permanent task,[79] as permanent as the eternal road towards perfection every human is treading at his or her own particular pace. And, crucially, idolatry is a necessary part of creation, as without it, humanity would lack the lowly station necessary for human beings to rise on the road of perfection on which they find their eternal felicity. As Freudenthal puts it, "without myth and idolatry, there is neither room nor motivation for enlightenment."[80] Furthermore, while Judaism, for reasons which we will look into below, finds its true purpose in defending pure monotheism, it too can at times fall prey to more idolatrous interpretations and practices. "Which friend of truth," Mendelssohn asks in his open letter to Lavater, "can boast of having found his religion to be free of harmful human additions?"[81]

Freudenthal's interpretation would therefore suggest that the irrational theological notions Christianity mistakenly clings to (as well as presumably also the harmful human additions to Judaism) contribute to the providential plan by offering to believers a darkness to enlighten, or in other words, a path of ascendance towards a higher degree of perfection. Yet while Freudenthal's notion of "no religion without idolatry" is fascinating, it does not seem to strengthen the case for Mendelssohn's pluralism. After all, one can hardly imagine Christian readers finding this highly ambiguous valuation of their faith acceptable. While idolatry might be in some sense useful, it clearly still is preferable to have as little of it in one's religion as possible. Presumably, a believer whose path towards perfection begins in a place less dark and obfuscated than others would find it less challenging to overcome the obstacle of idolatry on the path towards perfection. If, for example, Judaism is less prone than Christianity to idolatry (which, as we shall see later on, Mendelssohn clearly believes is the case), would one not be advantaged by being born to it? If so, would it not then be preferable to have less diversity and more enlightened religion?

We shall return to these issues below when appraising Mendelssohn's Jewish values. In the meantime, it is important to take note of another fruitful way of thinking about this problem. This book looks at both Mendelssohn and Cohen from the axiological perspective, a perspective that suggests an interpretive method according to which Mendelssohn's criticism of Christianity could be mitigated and harmonized with his universal and cross-cultural sensitivity. Indeed, if for Mendelssohn nothing matters more than eternal felicity, mistaken theological views are only problematic in so far as they block the path to it. As we have already seen above, Mendelssohn points out to Lavater that, according to Judaism, virtuous men of other nations are "children of eternal bliss."[82] This of course is absolutely critical to Mendelssohn, as it means they have access to the highest human good of eternal felicity. Indeed, in the continuation of the same passage, Mendelssohn explicitly states that erroneous religious opinions are not necessarily harmful as long as they are not "in direct conflict with the felicity of the human race."[83] What is deeply repugnant to Mendelssohn are the aspects of Christianity he feels disallow eternal felicity to those who do not accept its particularistic historical testimony and quaint theological positions. Turning the table on the oft-repeated Christian criticism of Judaism, Mendelssohn attacks it as radically and unjustifiably exclusivistic.

Unitarianism, which affirms the unity of God and that Jesus was an extraordinary human prophetic human being rather than an uncomfortable synthesis of God and man and which is therefore much nearer to the universal common principles of natural religion, is accordingly described by Mendelssohn as far more acceptable than its Trinitarian counterpart. He therefore makes that point that if Unitarians defend the immortality of our souls and the notions of divine reward and punishment, "then certainly not very much rests on the insignificant differences that we accept such things from testimony drawn from the prophets of the Old Testament and the rabbis, whereas they accept such things on testimony drawn from the New Testament."[84] Indeed, given that they agree on the "essential points [wesentlichsten Religionspunkten]" directly related to humanity's eternal felicity, Jews and Unitarians need not "make a fuss over minor points [unwichtige Nebenpunkte]." The disputed points "can remain undecided forever."[85]

The idea that certain theological differences can remain undecided forever is of course precisely the kind of conception that would very much allow for a genuine value pluralism. Yet, it remains the case that Mendelssohn clearly believed certain tenets of Christianity cannot remain undecided if eternal felicity is genuinely to be championed. This would, in turn, suggest a similar attitude towards a wide variety of other religious traditions as well. All humanity has access to felicity and the truths of natural religion upon which it depends, but all humanity must find these truths and not others to access felicity. Beatitude awaits all, but that is not because every single kind of religious belief is beatific; rather, we will eventually all be corrected in our religious mistakes in the eternal process of perfection that cannot but lead us ever closer to the one true God.

The tensions between Mendelssohn's universal aspirations and the limitations of his pluralism are crucial to our analysis, and we will explore them further both in this chapter and in chapter 6 when comparing Mendelssohn's and Cohen's universalisms. It is, however, also important to assuage the concerns these tensions raise by emphasizing the moderation that characterizes Mendelssohn even in his less tolerant moments. His insistence in *Jerusalem* that the church can neither punish nor even excommunicate but must rather lovingly seek to bring back confused souls to their commonsensical bearings suggests that even the intolerable atheists or idolaters must not be made to suffer.[86] While Mendelssohn's pluralism therefore is limited, these limitations do not lead to a politics of violent or coercive intolerance. More importantly, while Mendelssohn's monistic onto-theology is not wholly pluralistic, it does, crucially, remain universal in the scope of its salvific aspirations. In the following section, we will analyze how the universal scope of Mendelssohn's onto-theology and the resulting axiological implications we have been exploring affect his valuation of Judaism.

Revaluating Jewish Values

In order for Mendelssohn to positively revaluate Jewish values and argue for the value of Judaism, he must, given what we wrote about the devaluation of Judaism in the age of Enlightenment, first show that Judaism is neither exclusivistic nor inherently hierarchic. Given his own axiological positions and his positing of felicity as the highest value, this would mean first showing that Judaism does not contradict the notion of universally available felicity and further making the case that Judaism does not posit Jews as in some way nearer to felicity. As we shall see, Mendelssohn not only insistently argues that Judaism does not hamper universal felicity but that it is in many ways instrumental to it. His position on the second question, however, is, as can already be inferred from our analysis of the limitations of his pluralism, less straightforward.

JUDAISM AND UNIVERSAL FELICITY

As discussed in the introduction, Spinoza made a blistering attack on Jewish particularism. A significant piece of evidence he relates to make the case that Judaism does not allow for universal morality, even when its sources seem to uphold universal values, is a controversial passage of Maimonides wherein the latter seems to oppose the possibility that any gentile, even one having lived righteously according to the Noahide laws, would find salvation if the obeisance to these laws is based on the universal principles of reason rather than an acceptance of the supremacy of the particular biblical revelation.[87] Mendelssohn, to whom the notion that Judaism could contradict the universal availability of beatitude would be wholly unacceptable, addressed the very same passage in his correspondence with Rabbi Jacob Emden. Having raised the issue of Maimonides's position with Emden, he received a letter from the rabbi informing him that Maimonides's view is in fact supported by the Talmud. The great Maimonides, Emden therefore suggested, was correct in emphasizing the exclusivist nature of salvation in Judaism.[88] In his frank reply, written the first of January 1773, Mendelssohn writes that Maimonides's words are to him "harder than flint" and asks: "shall all the inhabitants of the earth from east to west, except for us, be cast into a pit of annihilation and be abhorrent to all flesh if they do not believe in the Torah, which was given as an inheritance to the congregation of Jacob alone?"[89] A few lines later, Mendelssohn insinuates that a God who treats his creatures so would be a tyrannical ruler.[90]

Mendelssohn similarly rebukes the notion that Judaism posits itself as a necessary condition to achieve the loftiest human goals in his public response to Lavater, in which he makes the point that if a "*Confucius* or a *Solon* lived among my contemporaries, I could, in accordance with the principles of my religion, love and admire the great man, without hitting on the ridiculous idea of wanting to *convert* a Confucius or a Solon." This "ridiculous idea," widespread in Christian history, is not one Judaism is afflicted by as "the religion of my fathers does not *wish* to be disseminated. We are not supposed to send missions to either of the Indies or to Greenland."[91]

The universal scope of his axiology is, according to Mendelssohn, fully backed by Jewish tradition and perfectly sustainable within a Jewish context. As the following passage from *Jerusalem* eloquently states, for Mendelssohn, "according to the concepts of true Judaism, all the inhabitants of the earth are destined to felicity; and the means of attaining it are as widespread as mankind itself, as charitably dispensed as the means of warding off hunger and other natural needs."[92] Of course, much of *Jerusalem* is dedicated to arguing that Judaism in no way contradicts the notion that every single human can reach felicity. This fundamental Jewish universalism is Mendelssohn's profound response to the critiques that were among the reasons Mendelssohn set out writing the book in the first place. Cranz, for example, asks of Mendelssohn whether he is loyal to a universalistic religious vision of "worshipping the one sole God, observing the divine commandments given through Moses, and gathering all peoples into a single flock under the universal scepter of a Messiah proclaimed by the prophets," or rather to "the particular Jewish ecclesiastical system that comprises all the determinations from both scripture and rabbinic scriptural exegesis, as well as the statutory ecclesiastical laws, which make up the distinctive doctrines that separate the Jews from the faith of every other nation of the world, and from the Christians as well."[93] A system, he adds, wherein deviations were, and to some degree still are, followed by harsh punishment and that is partly to blame for Jews being "estranged and excluded from the privileges of the state, from the benefits of civil life, from enjoying reciprocal human and fraternal duties."[94]

Mendelssohn's reply to these arguments in *Jerusalem* relies both on his differentiation, already mentioned above, of historical and eternal truths, as well as on his famous demarcation of Judaism as based essentially on "divine *legislation* [göttliche *Gesetzgebung*]" rather than "revealed religion [geoffentbarten Religion]."[95] These claims enable him to depict Judaism as a creed that makes no dogmatic demands compromising reason and the universality of the all-important eternal truths necessary for felicity, on the one hand, and to explain why values relating to obedience to a particular divine legislation do not in any way contradict that universalism, on the other.

Indeed, that which was revealed in Sinai was not metaphysical truths about the deity. God did not proclaim, "I am the Eternal, your God, the necessary, independent being, omnipotent and omniscient."[96] The commandments that were revealed are essentially sanctified ceremonial practices, and their particularity does not characterize the salvific beliefs accessible to all. These eternal truths can and must be sought out by all through their own common sense and reason and, if one so chooses, can be anchored in speculative thought as well. Judaism, in other words, is centered on the historical truth of a people bonded to a divine legislation, a teaching that in no way encroaches on the eternal theological truths valid for everyone everywhere. Moreover, the fact Judaism is embodied by a legislation concerned with the behavior of a particular people does not in any way exclude the Jewish people from the universal precepts of the religion of reason, and the different behavior this legislation leads to is part of the legitimate religious and cultural differences one must accept in a tolerant society.

While the Jewish people must therefore exclude themselves in some ways from general social life because of certain practices their obligation towards the historical truth of the revelation at Sinai commits them to, there is no exclusivity in that which matters the most, namely, felicity. While intermarriage or dietary restrictions have some importance,[97] it is an importance that fades when put in the proper perspective, namely, the perspective focused on that which is most valuable and therefore most important. The axiological perspective we have adopted therefore emphasizes the degree to which Mendelssohn solves this aspect of the dilemma; that which is most important to any human being, felicity enabled by the reality of a providential God and immortality, is in no way contradicted or hampered by the Jewish religion or by belonging to the Jewish people.

Mendelssohn does not solve this aspect of the universal/particular dichotomy in a formal or analytic sense; certain ethical propositions are true for some and irrelevant to others, just as certain historical truths are only valid for one people and not for others. A formal analysis of Mendelssohn's solution, one seeking to find a universal form to his ethical thinking, would, in so far as the commitment to a ceremonial law is perceived as being at least also an ethical matter, therefore reveal a frail position. Yet if we think of this problem from the axiological angle, it seems to me his case is much stronger. It indicates that Mendelssohn's position overcomes the formal bifurcation by continually pointing at the universal resolution of the concerns raised by his lack of formal universalism in the commonality of his *summum bonum*. In other words, the universalism of eternal felicity is far more significant to him than the formal coherence of the ethical aspect of his philosophical system. So while Mendelssohn clearly believes certain propositions (like, say, dietary restrictions) are only particularly valid, he will always emphasize that these particular ethical truths serve universal values. They promote the universal good. So while formal or analytical particularism is difficult to justify in terms of philosophical coherence, it can be justified axiologically. Mendelssohn's universalism would therefore not be damaged by his positing of particular truths because of the values these truths are derived from and because they promote a universal axiological position.

In that sense, Mendelssohn's position can be fruitfully contrasted to Kant's radical universalization of ethics. In fact, Mendelssohn's position anticipates significant criticism of Kant's ethical postulates, the supposed pinnacle of ethical universalism. Kant's grand ethical project is precisely to create a formal system of ethics as universal as Newton's science, hoping to recreate the simple and elegant lawfulness of the latter's first principles of motion. What matters to Kant, as will be further explored in the next chapter, is not the particular person or situation, but the general law. The categorical imperative, therefore, "has to do not with the matter of the action and what is to result from it, but with the form and the principle from which the action itself follows."[98] It furthermore abstracts not only from the "matter of the action" but also from any particularities the rational agents involved carry. In his ethical thinking, Kant overlooks the particularities of actual human circumstances, including not only the particularity of the situation at hand but also the particularities of the cultural identities involved.

The aloofness of Kant's ethical postulates already led Hegel to criticize the "empty formalism" of Kant's categorical imperative.[99] Such criticism became even more widespread in the nineteenth century when significant developments in both the social science and philosophy made Kant's famous declaration that "*empirical principles* are not at all fit to be the ground of moral law" and his disregard for the "*special constitution of human nature* or the contingent circumstances in which it is placed" seem rather obsolete.[100] Marxist writers in particular took issue with it. To quote Gramsci, "analyzed realistically, Kant's formula is only applicable to a specific milieu, with that milieu's moral superstitions and barbaric mores; it is a static empty formula into which one can pour any actual historical content."[101] The notion that concrete ethical interactions are necessarily grounded in the particularities of the identities of the participants (whether class, gender, race, etc.) is not only a fundamental aspect of existentialist thought but also characterizes much of late twentieth-century thinking and further distances contemporary thought from Kant's approach. Feminist philosophy in particular brought to bear an important critique of "abstract individualism," which Friedman defines as a conception that considers "individual human beings as social atoms, abstracted from their social contexts, and disregards the role of social relationships and human community in constituting the very identity and nature of individual human beings."[102]

MacIntyre sums up these reflections eloquently when he writes that "I am someone's son or daughter, someone else's cousin or uncle; I am a citizen of this or that city, a member of this or that guild or profession; I belong to this clan, that tribe, this nation. Hence what is good for me has to be the good for one who inhabits these roles." And while MacIntyre characterizes the search for the good as moving forward from these "moral particularities," he warns that there can never be left behind or wholly obliterated. Escaping to a Kantian "realm of entirely universal maxims" is not only illusory, but dangerous, as "when men and women identify what are in fact their partial and particular causes too easily and too completely with the cause of some universal principle, they usually behave worse than they would otherwise do."[103]

Mendelssohn similarly thinks not only that particularism and toleration are not contradictory, but that certain forms of universalism might actually be violent and impossible to cohere with tolerance. Furthermore, and as opposed to Kant, he advocates against abstracting from the particularity of our identity in our ethical life. His philosophy is one that does not seek a universal, formal, and coherent ethical system, but one that, while aimed at a common felicity, is grounded in the particularities of human communities. It is therefore important to note that, whether for good or ill, Mendelssohn's emphasis on the significance of particularism in ethics and his refusal to abstract from it offers a position that, rather than being a pre-Kantian relic, has, with hindsight, turned out to be one embraced and developed by bastions of post-Kantian Western thought.

Mendelssohn, therefore, did not feel his adherence to a particularistic lifestyle and legislation threatened in any way the universalism of human felicity. Accordingly, he forcefully makes the case that Judaism, while particularistic, is not exclusivistic. The second aspect of modern universalism, related to the anti-hierarchical meritocratic ethos, is more complex, and we will be able to discuss it after we have looked at Mendelssohn's depiction of the positive impact of Judaism.

THE VALUE OF JUDAISM

We saw in the previous section that Mendelssohn's Judaism does not hamper in any way his deep-seated conviction of the universal nature of felicity. This, however, is far from sufficient in order to revaluate devaluated Judaism. Indeed, showing that Judaism is not an obstacle to universal felicity does not yet show how it is valuable if at all. In order to positively revaluate Judaism, Mendelssohn would have to meaningfully link it to his axiological prioritization. In other words, in order for Judaism to be valuable, it has to play an important part in the achievement of felicity.

At the heart of Mendelssohn's treatment of the value of Judaism lies the fundamental sense that with the discovery of the kinds of philosophical ideas he was going to develop throughout his life, he found the genuine conception of Judaism as well. We already noted in the previous chapter how Mendelssohn's *On the Sentiments* reflects his gratitude to his earliest philosophical influences, as he felt the exposure to their philosophy reaffirmed in him the optimistic principles of natural religion and "planted the holy truths on which . . . [his] happiness is based."[104] As Altmann puts it, Mendelssohn's "sense of gratitude to Locke, Leibniz and Wolff was all the more sincere because the verities affirmed by them agreed with what he considered to be the essence of Judaism."[105] Indeed, for Mendelssohn, both philosophy and true religion are aimed at the same purpose; just like philosophy ought to be aimed at felicity, so too the final goal of all religions is eternal felicity.[106]

Accordingly, Judaism, which, as mentioned above, Mendelssohn informed Lavater he had long ago concluded to be true,[107] will lead to the very same truths his auspicious encounter with Leibniz and Wolf lead to. Judaism, in other words, when properly understood, leads to the truths of natural religion upon which our eternal felicity is based and, accordingly, to all that Mendelssohn's axiology implies and assumes. And while all true religions are aimed at these truths, Judaism does so in a particularly direct way, markedly more so than Christianity, for example. Christianity, though aimed at the proper supreme value, is hindered by its own lack of philosophical clarity. Indeed, in spite of his ambiguous take on Christianity, Mendelssohn does agree that the "eternal felicity of the human race is indeed the final goal of this religion, as it is of all religion," but he adds, "under what conditions is this felicity offered to me! What fetters for my reason!"[108]

Clearly, Mendelssohn implies that the added theological baggage Christianity is saddled with distances it at least somewhat from the universal path of natural religion, to which Judaism is more directly dedicated. This is a point Mendelssohn reiterates several times, whether in the open letter to Lavater and the "Counter-Reflections" explored above or in his private correspondence with Prince Karl Wilhelm Ferdinand of Braunschweig. When the latter, whose interest was raised by Mendelssohn's response to Lavater, asked his Jewish friend for his genuine position on Christianity, Mendelssohn writes, as he did in the "Counter-Reflections," that some of the Christian theological notions "seem to contradict the primary fundaments of human knowledge."[109] Again, Mendelssohn mentions too the exclusivistic nature of Christianity, which distances it from both Judaism and natural religion: "Since all people must be destined by their creator for eternal felicity, an exclusionary religion [ausschliessende Religion] cannot be the true religion."[110]

Judaism, we saw above, hampers neither the universal scope of salvation nor the universal scope of reason, as its particularistic sanctified law neither excludes gentiles from salvation nor burdens Jews with elaborate theological structures. Accordingly, it is far nearer than Christianity to embracing directly the truths of natural religion. Indeed, and this is where Mendelssohn's characterization of the positive value of Judaism comes in, that very ceremonial law is essentially a constant, living symbolic presence pointing cognition towards the truths accepted, in his mind, by any true adherent of the universal religion of reason. The very essence of Judaism, like the essence of philosophy, is to remind us of the truths upon which our felicity is based.

Judaism performs this critical function through the semiotic wisdom of the "living script" that is its ceremonial law.[111] Mendelssohn's position was that any permanent symbols risk leading to superstition and idolatry while, on the other hand, alphabetic script leads to the no less mistaken focus on speculations as it "displays the symbolic knowledge of things and their relations too openly on the surface; it spares us the effort of penetrating and searching, and creates too wide a division between doctrine and life."[112] The Mosaic ceremonial law both overcomes the gap between doctrine and life, and, to quote Freudenthal, "meaningful, transient acts that disappear after their performance" overcome the danger permanent signs have of leading to idolatry.[113]

Indeed, if Mendelssohn believed that idolatry consists in mistaking the sign for the signified, when sanctity is attributed to the symbol rather than what it is supposed to symbolize, the transience of the ceremonial commandments ensures one can never confuse the fleeting symbol with the eternal truths it symbolizes. The ceremonial law, therefore, functions as an antidote to the dangers of idolatry. Its purpose is to ensure awareness that "the truths useful for the felicity of the nation as well as of each of its individual members were to be utterly removed from all imagery."[114]

The fact that this living script is one of action, especially as it is often undertaken in communal settings, remedies the danger of an overly speculative tradition. The Mosaic ceremonial law impels human beings "to social intercourse, to imitation, and to oral, living instruction."[115] The great maxim of this constitution, Mendelssohn writes, "seems to have been: *Men must be impelled to perform actions and only induced to engage in reflection*."[116] The ceremonial law drives actions that open a space in daily life for the kind of commonsensical contemplation that leads to the truths that enable felicity. This contemplation is commonsensical because the Mosaic ceremonial law encourages social contact and oral communication, and so the truths gained will be those shared with one's congregation, elders, or family, with which one fulfills one's ceremonial duties.

The particular Jewish faith, therefore, is valuable because it actively promotes the eternal truths necessary for felicity. It is a service God demanded through historical revelation from a particular people, but its purpose is universal. Jews, after all, do not only remind themselves of these eternal truths; they remind others as well. Not that this reminder is necessary to a Confucius or a healthy-minded Greenlander, but at the very least, even to them it is not harmful and in no way does it deny their God-given right for fulfillment in religious felicity.

APPRAISING MENDELSSOHN'S JEWISH VALUES

The exploration of the methods of valuation underlying Mendelssohn's revaluation of Jewish values enables a reappraisal of that critically significant aspect of his philosophy. As we shall see, thinking of his effort as guided by its axiological underpinnings enables us to think differently about, and perhaps even solve some of the problems critics have found in, Mendelssohn's argumentation.

As argued in the previous chapter, some of these problems arise because of a certain lack of precision in the depiction of the problem Mendelssohn is trying to solve to start with. Indeed, various commentators emphasize in their description of the intellectual task Mendelssohn faced the attempt to harmonize Judaism and reason. Alfred Jospe explains that in *Jerusalem*, Mendelssohn attempts to "reconcile philosophically what he was able to fuse in his personal life—unquestioning loyalty to the God of Sinai and the philosophical rationalism of his age."[117] Arkush writes that Mendelssohn "did not seek to develop a comprehensive philosophy of Judaism; rather, he endeavored to explain, in general terms, how he was able to combine allegiance to reason with loyalty to the God of Israel."[118]

Yet, as we saw in the previous chapter, reason is only a subservient value in Mendelssohn's philosophy, and he held a far lower opinion of it than many of his enlightened peers. True reason, when guided by common sense, does lead human beings to the truths necessary for their highest good. Yet speculative reason, especially if lacking the orientation of common sense, will more than likely lead one astray. The most crucial aspect of Mendelssohn's revaluation, therefore, does not consist primarily of harmonizing Judaism and reason (though he does indeed try to do that also), but rather harmonizing Judaism and the eternal commonsensical truths that are necessary for eternal felicity and hence also for the emergence of all values. So while Arkush is right in claiming Mendelssohn must show that the Jewish religion "was entirely in harmony with the universally valid principles of natural religion," it is not necessarily also the case Mendelssohn needed, as Arkush also claims, to "demonstrate that the Jewish religion rested on perfectly rational foundations." It just needs to rest on foundations that do not deny the truths that are necessary for felicity, truths which, as we've seen, necessarily entail the universal accessibility of that felicity. In other words, while Arkush argues that "Mendelssohn had to bring Judaism before the bar of reason,"[119] our axiological analysis suggests he primarily sought to bring Judaism before the bar of universal felicity.

This insight enables us to address the debate surrounding the authenticity of Mendelssohn's attachment to Judaism, which some commentators have put into doubt. So, for example, Arkush believes Mendelssohn was not genuine in his defense of Judaism because he did not genuinely believe in the Jewish faith. Mendelssohn was rather an enlightened theist who upheld the veneer of traditionalism for a variety of reasons, such as maintaining the ability to help steer his people towards greater enlightenment.[120] According to Arkush's reading, the halfhearted nature of Mendelssohn's effort is reflected in the weakness of Mendelssohn's argumentation for the inner rationality of Judaism or, indeed, for the historicity of the Sinaitic revelation, arguments that Arkush claims Mendelssohn knew were defective.[121] Arkush also claims Mendelssohn was unsuccessful in the central task of answering Cranz's demand for him to reconcile the enlightened political principles he espoused with the coercive nature of the Mosaic law and its death sentences for blasphemers, Shabbat breakers, and so on. Arkush writes that the arguments Mendelssohn offers are "evasive,"[122] and he argues that Mendelssohn's claim that religious coercion ended with the end of the Jewish sovereignty is based on faulty history, as even in the diaspora Jews did in fact enact punitive measures.[123]

More important than this historical inadequacy, Arkush claims, is its theoretical inadequacy; even if we accept that postexilic Judaism relinquished religious coercion of any kind, it would remain true that the "old, original Judaism had indeed condoned the use of force to compel Jews to obey religious law," and, Arkush adds, "to explain how the existence at any time of such a state of affairs could be reconciled with [Mendelssohn's] rational principles was precisely the task that Cranz had set for Mendelssohn." Arkush therefore concludes that Mendelssohn was unable to show to his own satisfaction "the rationality of the foundations and the original content of the Jewish religion, or to offer an adequate rationale for its theocratic features."[124]

Arkush here does not give sufficient weight, however, to another important argument Mendelssohn makes about the Mosaic law, namely, that at the time of the Mosaic constitution and the direct divine sovereignty at its core, civil and religious authority were, in the exceptional and unique circumstances of the era, united under God's reign, so that blasphemers, for example, were not coerced to obey religious law, which indeed Mendelssohn cannot accept, but civil law,[125] and civil authority can of course compel and punish.[126] In Mendelssohn's own day, of course, given that God ceased functioning as the direct sovereign, this constitution cannot apply to civil life, and we should, therefore, direct our social lives according to the best principles our commonsensical use of reason can muster.

More importantly, however, Mendelssohn's case is not, as Arkush implies, dependent on the ability to fully explain the reasoning behind God's reign. Mendelssohn, it seems to me, does not have to, and would not claim to, fully understand the ways in which God ruled Israel through the Mosaic constitution. Mendelssohn does not even have to prove that God's rule was driven by considerations human rationality could necessarily comprehend. In fact, we saw in the previous chapter that Mendelssohn certainly did not believe God to be fully explicable to us. So as long as the divine rule over the ancient Hebrew sovereignty does not contradict in any way the availability of universal felicity, there is nothing there to threaten the coherence of his case. And indeed, the Mosaic constitution, while applied, did not contradict Mendelssohn's axiological principles even if it is not clear to what degree it was a phenomenon human rationality can exhaustively grasp.

For Mendelssohn, the Mosaic constitution had divine foundations. While these foundations are not necessarily exhausted by human rationality, they do not in any way contradict universal felicity. In fact, while so far unique, the Mosaic constitution will not necessarily always be unique or necessarily always relate solely to the Jews. Indeed, the Mosaic constitution, Mendelssohn tells us, cannot currently be categorized with any other political system, as it has so far existed only once. Critically, however, he adds that "it has disappeared, and only the Omniscient knows among what people and in what century something similar will again be seen."[127] So while the unique Mosaic constitution, wherein the actual providential God is directly sovereign, has so far been unique in the history of the world, it will not always necessarily be unique to the Jews. If ever God were to take charge of a nation again, it could, according to Mendelssohn, be any other nation. This, it seems to me, again very much emphasizes Mendelssohn's underlying point: the Mosaic constitution does not in any way undermine the universality of divine providence and felicity.

More generally, anything related to the particularities of the ancient Hebrew history or of the Jewish sources cannot be perceived as impinging on the universal inclusivity of Mendelssohn's highest good. This would be unbearable to him. As he rather explicitly puts it in his correspondence, "How unspeakably miserable the human fate would be if the eternal felicity of the whole human race were to depend on the interpretation of obscure passages in a book written for a specific people in Asia, a long time ago, in a foreign, now dead language."[128] So whether they can or cannot be fully comprehended, it is clear that God cannot have made universal felicity dependent on the Jewish sources.

Accordingly, thinking about Mendelssohn's project axiologically emphasizes that while he does not have to commit himself or Jewish values to reason, he must be committed to universal felicity, a necessary consequence of the kind of divine providence his whole method of valuation is founded on. This is why, it seems to me, his argument is far more convincing when conceived of as concerning the synthesis of Judaism and axiological universalism rather than Judaism and reason.

I therefore believe there is no sufficient reason to doubt Mendelssohn's attachment to Judaism.[129] Indeed, the notion he would forsake Judaism because aspects of it cannot be reduced to human reason is unconvincing because Mendelssohn is explicitly more committed to Judaism than he is to reason. He is, furthermore, explicitly skeptical about the human ability to fully comprehend God and the way in which He chose to function in the biblical era. Depicting Mendelssohn's task as offering, for example, adequate rationales for the theocratic features of the unique historical moment of divine rule over a people does not adequately address his most pressing concern, which is proving that this historical era in no way contradicts the universality of felicity.

And indeed, as we saw above, he vigorously argues that there is no problem of exclusivity. That aspect of the enlightened demand for universality is robustly maintained by Mendelssohn. While Judaism might be particular, it does not impinge on the ability of every single human being to achieve the single most important thing human beings can hope to achieve: eternal felicity. To the contrary, the historical function of its ceremonial law is reminding Jews as well as gentiles to seek out the truths of natural religion, which enable felicity to arise. Seemingly, therefore, Mendelssohn's universalism reflects and promotes a strong sense of equality.

Yet for that equality to be absolute, a second demand must be met, namely, the abolishment of any sense of inborn hierarchy or superiority. This, it turns out, is more complicated. Indeed, a central aspect of Mendelssohn's positive revaluation of Judaism is, as mentioned, depicting it as enabling a foolproof method of protecting the essential truths of natural religion. If that is the case, however, that must mean that truly observant Jews must be somehow and to some degree better able to reach these eternal truths than a gentile. For if there is absolutely no difference between the Jew and the gentile on this point, Judaism would not in fact function in any meaningful way as protector of true religion. Were that to be the case, why then would Judaism have a positive value? If Judaism matters, it is because it ensures clarity about these important truths. Any person taking part in this crucial task, namely, any Jew, must therefore have greater access to this clarity than, say, a Pythagorean whose system does not offer the same clarity.[130]

Indeed, as we saw above, Mendelssohn certainly thinks of Judaism as being nearer to the truths necessary for felicity than other religions, such as Christianity. Therefore, the more important Judaism is, the more there is a sense in which Jews have privileged access to eternal truths. If, on the other hand, the access to these truths is in no way privileged by the Jewish religion and there is no hierarchy of salvation, then the value of Judaism is completely undermined.

Eisen describes this apparent problem eloquently, asking, "If all truths essential to human happiness are universally accessible, why is the divine legislation given the Jews at all necessary? . . . Conversely, if the 'ceremonial law' really is helpful (let alone indispensable) to the Jews in achieving full knowledge of God, how can Mendelssohn profess the equal opportunity of all human beings to know and serve the deity?" This tension, which Eisen calls "the old problem of chosenness in a new guise," seems to be a genuine problem, in particular if Mendelssohn is indeed genuine about his attachment to Judaism.[131]

The sole unresolved tension in Mendelssohn's universalist revaluation of Judaism remains, therefore, the salvific privilege the ceremonial law provides Judaism. Indeed, though Judaism is not exclusivist, it arguably cannot but be inherently hierarchical to some degree if it has any value. The more value it has, the more Mendelssohn has to be hierarchical, which would then contradict both his pluralistic tendencies and, in a profound sense, the universal scope of the values of his age.

We shall therefore return to this tension in Mendelssohn's revaluation and suggest possible solutions to it in chapter 6 when comparing the axiological tensions lingering in Mendelssohn's and Cohen's efforts. But first of course we need to similarly analyze Herman Cohen's philosophy from the perspective of its method of valuation. Indeed, having analyzed the structure of Mendelssohn's axiological position and the way it is reflected in various critical aspects of his thought and having looked at the implication of this axiological perspective on the universal scope of his values and view of Judaism, we shall now similarly engage with Hermann Cohen before critically comparing their positions.

(4)
HERMANN COHEN'S FUTURE

We began our inquiry into Mendelssohn in chapter 2 with an analysis of his notion of the highest good, which, as we saw, is centered on a felicity dependent on the existence of God, providence, and immortality. Having examined this axiological position and a variety of its implications, we then moved on, in chapter 3, to look at the kind of universalism this notion of the highest good engenders and how that universalism reframes Mendelssohn's position regarding the particularistic tendencies supposedly inherent in the Jewish heritage as well as how it enables a reevaluation of doubts concerning the authenticity of his loyalty to Judaism. We shall approach Cohen's position in a similar manner. In this chapter, we will delineate Cohen's conception of the highest good and analyze how it guides his thinking about Judaism. In the next chapter, we will assess the universality engendered by this notion of the highest good and analyze how reframing the question of Jewish particularism in light of this axiological framework enables a clearer view of Cohen's position.

Herman Cohen came to prominence as a founding member of the Marburg school of Neo-Kantianism.[1] As will be shown below, there is a significant break from Kant in Cohen's thought, in particular with regards to Kant's axiological position. Yet, even the disagreement described below takes place within a philosophy that sees itself as furthering Kant's critical idealism, to which it therefore remains profoundly related. Therefore, understanding why Cohen chose to negate Kant's axiology is critical in assessing his own philosophy. We will accordingly first look at Kant's axiological position in order to then analyze Cohen's in greater clarity and depth.

Kant's view of the highest good, which in his case might more precisely be referred to as the "complete good,"[2] is particularly important to our inquiry because Kant's position functions as a bridge between Mendelssohn's and Cohen's. Indeed, like Mendelssohn, Kant realized the importance of happiness, but rather than prioritizing it outright, he embedded it in a rather complex axiological conception, the moral leaning of which is echoed in Cohen's work.[3] Accordingly, the profound ethical concern Kant sought to embed in his notion of the complete good will be emphasized in Cohen, albeit at the expense of happiness. While Mendelssohn's highest good focuses on felicity, Kant's *summum bonum*, as we shall see below, rebalances the combination of felicity and moral worth, while Cohen focuses on the moral aspect at the expense of felicity.

Kant's Conception of the *Summum Bonum*

We shall begin by looking at Kant's treatment of the notion of happiness before moving on to see how it forms part of his notion of the complete good. This will in turn help us understand Cohen's position both as it arises from Kantian thought and as it opposes Kant's and Mendelssohn's positions on happiness.[4]

KANT ON HAPPINESS

In his *Critique of Practical Reason*, Kant defines happiness as "a rational being's consciousness of the agreeableness of life as uninterruptedly accompanying his whole existence" and again as "the state of a rational being in the world in the whole of whose existence *everything goes according to his wish and will*."[5] Kant also points out that self-love is the principle that makes happiness "the supreme determining ground of choice" and, more generally, that all material principles (which "place the determining ground of choice in the pleasure or displeasure to be felt in the reality of some object"),[6] as opposed to the formal (according to which "the mere form of a possible giving of universal law through our maxims must constitute the supreme and immediate determining ground of the will"),[7] come under the general principle of self-love or private happiness, which in turn are completely dependent on a sense of pleasure.

Unsurprisingly, Kant very much seeks to distance himself from any view that would value a form of happiness that is derived from pleasure. To quote Cassirer, the value of life as sum of pleasure is, to him, "less than nothing."[8] Kant explains that the obvious divergence of value and pleasure is rendered even in common language, which distinguishes "the *agreeable* [das Angenehme] from the *good* [Guten] and the *disagreeable* [das Unangenehme] from the *evil* [Bösen] and requires that good and evil always be appraised by reason and hence through concepts, which can be universally communicated, not through mere feeling, which is restricted to individual subjects and their receptivity."[9]

Furthermore, echoing the Hobbesian critique of felicity we discussed in chapter 2,[10] Kant argues that the concept of happiness is of such an indeterminate nature that even though we all desire to attain happiness, one can "never say determinately and consistently with himself what he really wishes and wills." The reason for this is that while the actual elements belonging to the concept of happiness are empirical, the idea of happiness demands an "an absolute whole, a maximum of well-being in my present condition and in every future condition."[11] A finite being, Kant argues, however insightful and powerful, could simply not determine what among the vast possibilities of action would in fact lead to happiness. Determining what would actually make us happy, Kant argues, would require omniscience. This explains why happiness is to him "not an ideal of reason, but of imagination."[12] Our indeterminate notion of happiness, as Barney notes, is for Kant both paradoxical and phantasmagoric, as "our inclinations are boundless, conflicting, ever changing and only imperfectly knowable, the perpetual complete satisfaction of all of them is not a genuine possibility." In a Kantian context, happiness, Barney further points out, cannot escape its "hap," nor Glückseligkeit its "Glück."[13]

In the *Groundwork of the Metaphysics of Morals*, Kant suggests another interesting argument for why happiness is not the natural end for human beings: "in a being that has reason and a will, if the proper end of nature were its *preservation*, its *welfare*, in a word its *happiness*," explains Kant, "then nature would have hit upon a very bad arrangement in selecting the reason of the creature to carry out this purpose."[14] Actions leading to happiness, as well as a rule of conduct conducive to it, would be prescribed with greater precision and efficiency by instinct. In other words, were happiness our end, nature would have "taken upon itself the choice not only of ends but also of means and, with wise foresight, would have entrusted them both simply to instinct." It is therefore not surprising to note, Kant remarks, that the "the more a cultivated reason purposely occupies itself with the enjoyment of life and with happiness, so much the further does one get away from true satisfaction."[15] Reason, the faculty Kant of course hallowed and suggested would finally enable an enlightened human emancipation, does not, and was not meant to, aim at happiness.

More importantly than these empirical problems, however, is the principled, categorical, and a priori impossibility of setting happiness as the end of the application of the moral law. Doing so would of course contradict a critical aspect of Kant's deontological moral thinking, namely, that the moral law must be upheld in order to apply its universal legislative form. It is structurally inherent to Kant's moral law that it is applied for its own sake. Therefore, for an action to be thought of as morally good, it is not sufficient that it merely adheres to the moral law; it must, rather, be done for the sake of the moral law.[16] Accordingly, the moral worth of action depends not on the realization of its object, "but merely upon the *principle of volition* in accordance with which the action is done without regard for any object of the faculty of desire."[17]

Indeed, a critical aspect of Kant's moral philosophy, which enables its famed universalism, is that it seeks to answer the moral question (i.e., What ought I to do?) while remaining systematic and unrelated to any empiricism, including crucially the empirical phenomenon of happiness. Kant states in the first critique, "I assume that there really are pure moral laws which determine completely *a priori* (without regard to empirical motives, that is, to happiness) what is and is not to be done, that is, which determine the employment of the freedom of a rational being in general."[18] In the *Groundwork of the Metaphysics of Morals*, he bluntly writes that a philosophy that "mixes these pure principles with empirical ones does not even deserve the name of philosophy . . . much less does it deserve the name of a moral philosophy, since by this very mixture it even infringes upon the purity of morals themselves and proceeds contrary to its own end."[19] A "*doctrine of happiness*," he further points out, is founded entirely on empirical principles. Involving it in reason's quest for universal, a priori moral principles would damage that effort, "just as any empirical admixture to geometrical principles would destroy all mathematical evidence."[20]

Accordingly, given that Kant thinks of reason as "the faculty which secures the unity of the rules of understanding under principles,"[21] reasoned morality seeks to establish principles of a universal legislative form. It is therefore dependent on formal validity and not on the unreliably empirical phenomenon of human happiness. The moral good cannot be dependent on the way it affects human happiness, and accordingly, the moral worth of our conduct cannot be made dependent on happiness. Kant therefore objects to Mendelssohn's view that if our eternal felicity were undermined, the validity of morals would be undermined as well.

HAPPINESS AND THE *Summum Bonum*

As opposed to Mendelssohn, therefore, happiness seems prima facie to find itself very far from Kant's notion of the highest good.[22] And yet, happiness is in fact a central aspect Kant's *summum bonum*. Indeed, it is clear to Kant that it could not be otherwise; in the *Critique of Practical Reason*, Kant writes that "to be happy is necessarily the demand of every rational but finite being and therefore an unavoidable determining ground of its faculty of desire."[23] So while the deontological nature of Kant's system seems to exclude the possibility of thinking of happiness as an end for human action,[24] and while Kant argues, as we saw above, that happiness cannot be that which nature set as a goal for a finite being endowed with reason, he also clearly thinks that it is a factor we must not completely ignore. The problem that arises, therefore, is whether Kant is able to include happiness, which we cannot but yearn for, in his notion of the highest good while maintaining the purity of the moral law, according to which we cannot act in order to find happiness. Kant seeks to overcome this dilemma by suggesting a complex notion of the complete good.

Kant famously wrote that "it is impossible to think of anything at all in the world, or indeed even beyond it, that could be considered good without limitation [ohne Einschränkung], except a good will." It is important to note, however, that this does not mean that there are no other goods, but only that these other goods are dependent on good will for their worth. Indeed, intelligence, for example, can be nefarious if the will that makes use of it is not good. So too "*gifts of fortune*," such as power, riches, honor, and even health, as well as, crucially, "that complete well-being and satisfaction with one's condition called *happiness*," might all be completely worthless or even nefarious "unless a good will is present which corrects the influence of these on the mind and, in so doing, also corrects the whole principle of action and brings it into conformity with universal ends."[25]

As this good will is good not because of what it accomplishes or the fitness it exhibits in attaining some proposed end, Kant argues that "it is good in itself."[26] Accordingly, Kant identifies good will as the "highest good and the condition of every other, even of all demands for happiness" but crucially also states that it may not be the "sole and complete good."[27] Indeed, while the good will is the source of all value and functions as an unconditional good, Kant realizes that in order for his philosophy to offer a complete notion of the *summum bonum*, it must also somehow include happiness given that we cannot but aim for it. In other words, even if the worth of happiness is always conditional on good will, it cannot but be part of what to us is the supreme good.

This problem can also be approached through Kant's thought about duty as opposed to inclination; while one obeys good will out of a sense of duty, one seeks happiness out of inclination. If one acts out of inclination rather than duty, one does not exhibit good will or obey the moral law. And Kant makes it very clear that moral action undertaken out of inclination is not satisfactorily moral. For example, if a shopkeeper prices his wares honestly whether he is selling them to a child or to an experienced customer but does so because he calculates it to be to his own advantage in the long run or because he loves a particular customer, he does not act according to the moral law but out of inclination. The shopkeeper's actions can be termed moral only if they are undertaken out of duty towards the moral law, that is, in order to uphold the universal legislative form of the categorical imperative. Indeed, Kant presents our inclination for happiness as counter to our good will and its quest to uphold moral laws and its duties: "The human being feels within himself a powerful counterweight to all the commands of duty, which reason represents to him as so deserving of the highest respect—the counterweight of his needs and inclinations, the entire satisfaction of which he sums up under the name happiness."[28] Accordingly, as Wood puts it, "happiness must have nothing to do with the motivation of the will, nor with the ends or objects the morally good man sets for himself in obedience to the law."[29] And yet, Kant still insists happiness cannot be axiologically forsaken.

Kant's solution to this conundrum is characteristically subtle. We first must realize that while, in so far as we are sensible beings, happiness cannot but be of primordial consequence to us, it "is not *the only thing* that counts." It is the case that as beings belonging to the sensible, we unavoidably have desires and wants. Accordingly, our reason cannot avoid attending to these matters and seeking happiness. However, a human being is "not so completely an animal as to be indifferent to all that reason says on its own and to use reason merely as a tool for the satisfaction of his needs as a sensible being."[30]

Furthermore, while there is a clear opposition between the principles of happiness and that of morality, pure practical reason "does not require that one should *renounce* claims to happiness but only that as soon as duty is in question one should *take no account* of them."[31] So while one must act out of duty, and while the motivational force of one's actions must be good will and the apodictic respect it commands for the moral law, one can still very much hope to find happiness. Crucially, were we to hope to be worthy of happiness as a result of virtuous action, the tension would be further alleviated. Indeed, and this is critical, one is in fact led by practical reason to allow the desire for happiness as a reward for virtuous action. This is the key to Kant's purified concept of happiness; one cannot seek happiness out of inclination, but our practical reason does inevitably lead us to the desire to gain happiness through virtuous action. Therefore, to quote Bader's succinct phrasing: "while virtue is the supreme and unconditioned good (moral good), happiness is the conditioned good (pathological good), making happiness in accordance with virtue the complete good."[32] This good is complete because it combines happiness, the object of empirical practical reason, with virtue, the object of pure practical reason. Accordingly, as opposed to Mendelssohn's God, who created the universe to enable human felicity, Kant argues that God's ultimate end in creating the world must be thought of as the possibility of a person's worthiness to be happy, which is Kant's *summum bonum*.[33]

Kant's notion of the complete good is, therefore, a dual, or rather dialectic, one.[34] The complete good consists of a correlation between two seemingly distinct principles of Kantian thought: the unconditioned supreme value of good will, which reason cannot but admit as good in itself, and the conditional, empirically derived phenomenon of happiness, which, in our finitude and sensuality, we cannot but be drawn too. Kant believes he can avoid the "impurity" empirical happiness seems to bring to his notion of the highest good by establishing a correlation that dialectically transforms what could be a lowly empirical notion of happiness into a higher one purified by reason. His happiness is, to quote Barney, "systematized by reason out of the raw materials of our inclination."[35] So while the source of all value is good will, the *summum bonum* combines good will with a notion of happiness that is correlated with virtue.

Kant's concept is undoubtedly a sophisticated axiological construct. But for it to carry actual weight, the hope for morally deserved happiness cannot be a mere abstraction. His complete good cannot be only a coherent theoretical construct. It must at the very least be realistically possible as well. And while, in acting according to the categorical imperative, we are presumably doing all we can to bring about a world wherein the correlation of virtue and happiness is maximized, it is ultimately not in our power to ensure it is. The hope for such a correlation involves, in other words, the hope there is a God who providentially maintains it, enabling "happiness distributed in exact proportion to morality," which constitutes the *summum bonum*.[36] Here we find a significant similarity to Mendelssohn's construct: the possibility of the complete good's existing is also for Kant ultimately dependent on a providential God. Unlike Mendelssohn, however, the validity of the moral law, which for Kant is "apodictically certain,"[37] is not determined by the assurance provided by our faith in God and immortality. We act morally because we are duty bound to do so by the moral law that reason uncovers a priori. Furthering this quest of reason, however, does make faith in God morally convincing, if not metaphysically.

Kant therefore famously suggests that God and immortality are "postulates" of practical reason. While his critique of speculative reason revealed that we cannot access the noumenal realm within which God and immortality might obtain, it did also conclude they are at least not impossible. So when the practical use of reason leads, inevitably, to these postulates because of their moral impact, we have, Kant argues, rational reasons for faith. Moral law, therefore, leads "through the concept of the highest good, as the object and final end of pure practical reason, to *religion*."[38]

So we apodictically realize a good will as the source of value and realize moral worth consists of action out of duty for the moral law. Practical reason then leads us to construct a *summum bonum* that is based on the formal requirement to act out of moral duty but, realizing the inevitability of addressing happiness, ends up including a morally purified notion of it, that is, not happiness per se, but a happiness one is morally worthy of. This supreme good must be possible because if it were not, the moral law, which commands us to promote it, would be directed "to empty imaginary ends and must therefore in itself be false."[39] Yet, the moral law is apodictically given. Therefore, as we cannot base the correlation between happiness and moral worth on empirical observation, we are led, out of a necessity of practical reason, to postulate a God that in our immortal lives ensures the realization of that complete good.[40] This, however, Kant repeatedly argues, does not mean I act out of volition for that divine recompense. While the *end* of my action might be to become worthy of happiness, and while I may very well hope for happiness to be in fact meted out according to moral worth, the *motive* of my action must remain the moral law. God and immortality are therefore not "conditions of the moral law but only conditions of the necessary object of a will determined by this law."[41] One acts out of respect for the moral law in order to become worthy of happiness and can rationally hope for a divinely enabled, morally deserved happiness.[42] This hope forms the basis of Kant's rational faith.

Indeed, in a world where not everyone necessarily behaves according to the moral law, morally deserved happiness can only obtain if our reality is ruled by a "*Supreme Reason*, that governs according to moral rules." We are therefore led by practical reason to postulate God and immortality, "two postulates which, according to the principles of pure reason, are inseparable from the obligation which that same reason imposes upon us,"[43] and with these postulates, the possibility of hope arises.[44]

Cohen against Happiness

We saw in the previous chapter that eternal felicity is unabashedly at the very core of Mendelssohn's axiological structure. The passages above show that while Kant very much sought to mitigate the presence of happiness in his concept of the *summum bonum*, he could not forsake it altogether but tied it to morality instead. In clear opposition to Mendelssohn and even to Kant, this section will show how Cohen insistently sought to expunge the very possibility of taking happiness into account in his own axiological structure. The mere hint of eudaemonism, even if linked, as with Kant, to morality, is to him anathema to what our highest values are supposed to be. In this section, we shall begin by looking at how and why Cohen argues against Kant's ideas about happiness and its axiological significance. We shall then see how this opposition to eudaemonism is continually emphasized throughout Cohen's Jewish writings. This will then enable us to delineate the source of value in Cohen's own philosophy, before moving on, towards the end of this chapter and the beginning of the next, to Cohen's own vision of the highest good.[45]

COHEN CONTRA KANT

While Cohen was a leading member of the nineteenth-century German philosophical movement that proclaimed it was time to revert to Kant and to critical philosophy, it was also clear to all involved that it was not a question of arguing for every single one of Kant's positions. The Neo-Kantians were significantly more than mere Kantians. First, these were movements acutely aware of the advances in mathematics and physics, and their members therefore realized the need to revamp Kantian critical idealism and adapt it to recent developments in both science and philosophy. Moreover, the importance they attributed to their version of idealism must be contextualized with problems that were specific to the era. Thus, De Launay notes that the Marburg School of Neo-Kantianism, which Cohen spearheaded, was marked at its origins by its strong opposition both to the encroaching influence of positivism, on the one hand, and panpsychologism, on the other.[46]

Secondly, as we shall see, though of course Kant is a major figure in Cohen's understanding of critical idealism, he argued Kant was but one, albeit central, figure in a wider tradition. De Launey also notes that while known as Neo-Kantianism, it is in a rereading of Plato that Cohen found a foundation for his own conception of critical philosophy.[47] As Poma puts it, for Cohen, Plato had, by way of mathematics, "reached the fundamental discovery of Kantian critical idealism."[48] Indeed, for Cohen, idealism began with Plato,[49] whom Bergman tellingly refers to as Cohen's "revered teacher."[50] It would therefore not be exaggerated, in particular given the importance Platonic thought has for Cohen's axiology, to argue that Cohen could be thought of as a Neo-Platonic philosopher just as much as he was a Neo-Kantian one.

While perpetually enthralled by Kant's philosophy, Cohen was accordingly very far from being a blind follower of the master's footsteps. There is in Cohen, as we shall see, not only a defense of Kant, but at times also a revision and critique of Kant's thought. In the context of the axiological perspective that is here developed, the most immediate concern in terms of Cohen's critique of Kant is the latter's introduction of the notion of happiness, even if highly idealized, in his concept of the complete good.

In his *Kants Begrundung der Ethik*, Cohen enthusiastically expounds many of the Kantian points described above with regards to the profoundly problematic nature of any attempt at postulating happiness as the aim of the practical law. Addressing the "old controversy of the value of the moral principle of happiness [Glückseligkeit],"[51] Cohen, in his exposition of Kant's position on the matter, reviews three interconnected and inevitable conclusions. First, establishing a material ground of determination for the will means establishing the feelings of pleasure and pain as foundational.[52] All who thus proceed reach a *bonum* that does not signify the good, but rather merely well-being, and face a *malum* that does not refer to evil, but merely to "ill-being and woe [Uebel oder Weh]."[53] This leads Cohen to his second point, namely, that establishing the material ground of determination as a foundation for the will is "equivalent to the empirical foundation of morality." The principle of pleasure as motive of volition "rests on the common experience of fluctuating and frequently changing moods," and the good therefore becomes "an empirical concept of human receptivity to pleasure and pain."[54] The good would lose any independence from these phenomena and become, as Kant puts it, a "means to the agreeable," while evil would be "that which is a cause of disagreeableness and of pain."[55] This kind of eudaemonism, Cohen further argues, shows a lack of concern for certainty in our quest to address the fundamental problem of ethics, focusing rather on the "the height of subjectivity; the reaction of transient stimuli that permeate the organism; the expression of a momentary, indeterminate comfort or discomfort, which, however, is not even reliable as a harbinger of future hardship or prosperity."[56] This is the kind of absurd thinking, Cohen writes, that wrongly sets eudaemonism as an ethical principle.

The ensuing third principle again recapitulates the Kantian ideas mentioned above by stating that "the empirical foundation of morality in the feeling of pleasure excludes the foundation of a moral law." Indeed, "the material delusion of pleasure," which characterizes eudaemonism, cannot offer the necessity that is supposed to characterize the law of the will and the "unrestricted and unconditioned ought which we are seeking and which we conceive of as contained in the concept of the pure will." The upholders of such views, Cohen continues, also seem to believe that the "more we are assimilated into the animal kingdom in terms of the motives of our morality, the more universally and thoroughly . . . this morality has been established." This, Cohen adds, shows a fundamental misunderstanding of the concept of ethical reality at the heart of Kant's transcendental method. An ethics that would seek to base itself on some principle of life common to both humanity and animals, which Cohen refers to as a kind of "comparative zoology," would have nothing in common with the Kantian project, which seeks a ground for practical reason different from "the double ratio of matter and pleasure."[57] Quoting a passage from Plato's *Philebus*, in which Socrates argues that pleasure must be perceived as the lowest good even if all the animal kingdom suggest it is the highest,[58] Cohen concludes by stating that "whoever makes pleasure and displeasure the motive of morality, turns reason into instinct, and the noumenon of morality into a member of the animal kingdom."[59]

In order to make sure his readers understand it is not merely base sensual pleasure that is here criticized, Cohen expounds Kant's second theorem of the analytic of pure practical reason, namely, that "all material practical principles as such are, without exception, of one and the same kind and come under the general principle of self-love or one's own happiness,"[60] clarifying that it is all kinds of pleasure, "whether raw or fine, whether sensuous or spiritual,"[61] that fall into this category. Kant's strict distinction between natural and moral law rules out the possibility that practical reason can be derived in any way from human receptivity to feelings, however sublime these feelings might be construed. The notion of connecting the sublime with the physical, which Cohen refers to as "the pride of the naturalistic folly,"[62] cannot generate the necessity we seek for our ethical thinking. In a similar vein, Cohen also develops the Kantian argument we saw above to the effect that were happiness our purpose, it would be attained with greater efficiency by instinct than by reason. There would be, in such a case, as Cohen puts it, "no practical reason, but only the instinct of the practical, which could elucidate the various means [for happiness] more efficiently than all of reason."[63] It is, accordingly, not as a means, but in itself, that we must consider the will to be good.

So we see that Cohen enthusiastically propounds and endorses Kant's critique of happiness as the ground for morality. It seems even that his enthusiasm for that aspect of Kant's treatment of the topic leads him to emphasize it in his interpretation at the expense of the eventual inclusion of happiness in Kant's *summum bonum*.[64] Yet, as we saw above, Kant still did believe that in order for the good to be complete, some form of happiness has to be included in it, which is why he suggested his morally conditioned notion of happiness as the *summum bonum*. In a position that is critical to our analysis, this is a development Cohen strongly opposes. Indeed, already in his early *Kants Begründung der Ethik*, he vehemently criticizes this aspect of Kant's axiological position. As we shall see, this utter and complete rejection of eudaemonism, which goes beyond Kant's reticence with regard to happiness in that it refuses to consider even a morally conditioned version of happiness as part of the complete good, accompanies Cohen's thought all the way into his last works. It is, in fact, a primordial characteristic of his thinking. We shall begin by looking at how Cohen criticizes Kant on this point in his *Kants Begründung der Ethik* before looking at how his virulent anti-eudaemonism remains a mainstay in his thinking.

Cohen's major repudiation of Kant's attempt to salvage happiness as part of his notion of the *summum bonum* is expounded in the third part of *Kants Begründung der Ethik*, which addresses the application of the moral law with regards to the psychological qualities of humanity. As we saw above, he had by this point in the book already robustly expounded the Kantian disregard towards happiness's ethical standing. Yet, in the second chapter of the work's third part, "The Happiness of the Highest Good and the Postulates,"[65] Cohen goes a step further and repudiates Kant's attempt at incorporating happiness, even a morally conditioned version of it, in the highest good.

Kant's inclusion of happiness in the *summum bonum* arose from his attempt to find an appropriate object for practical reason, one that would take into account both the unqualified nature of the value of good will as well as what Kant described as our inevitable concern with happiness. Cohen starts his critique by suggesting happiness is "foreign [ein fremdes]" to the moral law and asks whether there can be any justification in risking the solid and pure formal moral law with such an object, even if construed as psychologically necessary. What is to be gained "if we do not simply objectify the moral law, but rather seek an object that can be adapted to it?" Cohen immediately warns us that "as soon as such an object is specified, the danger of empirical derivation arises," a development that threatens the formalism of the moral law.[66]

This concern leads Cohen to ask rather bluntly, "What on earth made Kant surrender the impregnable fortress of his formalism for the ambiguous, all subjective multiplicity of goods?"[67] A question that he finds particularly perplexing given that Kant himself explicitly noted in his *Critique of Practical Reason* how the ancients had made a similar mistake "by staking their moral investigation entirely on the determination of the concept of the *highest good*, hence the concept of an object that they meant afterwards to make the determining basis of the will in the moral law."[68] Even if virtue is a necessary condition for happiness in Kant's notion of the complete good, it remains a condition and therefore ultimately risks turning the moral law into a means to our pursuit of happiness. It is, in other words, not only "the moral law alone and exclusively, but also worldly happiness which is conceived as an end in itself."[69] Indeed, as it is clear to Cohen that the moral law, in and of itself, offers an object to practical reason that does not depend on the treacherous and fluctuating nature of happiness, he believes that Kant's happiness, even if merely an imaginary "ideal of representation," is unnecessary and harmful in the limitations it imposes on our moral thinking.[70]

So for Cohen the "danger" of Kant's positing of the highest good is that it threatens the independence of the moral law and risks turning it too into a postulate rather than a fundamental and apodictically certain principle.[71] Kant himself notes in his description of the antinomy of practical reason that "the impossibility of the highest good must also prove the falsity of the moral law."[72] As the postulates are that which are meant to solve this antinomy, moral law risks losing its independence and becoming completely conditioned on these postulates. This, for Cohen, is "absolutely incompatible" with Kant's basic ideas,[73] which are fundamentally based on an apodictically certain moral law, conceptually independent of any such postulates.[74] In fact, not only is this position harmful to the moral realm, it does no favors to the divine one either.

Quoting Fichte's "Appeal to the Public against the Charge of Atheism," Cohen describes how the latter, in his "religious clarity,"[75] recognized the aberration of God as the "provider of pleasure."[76]

Cohen therefore resolutely states that for the sake of the "independent, incontestable and unbreakable certainty of the ethical reality, for the sake of the preservation of moral autonomy and the affirmation of the sublimity of the formal moral law," which he characterizes as "fundamental ideas of Kantian ethics," both the postulates and the postulated object of practical reason need to be rejected.[77]

In rejecting the addition of happiness and the postulates, Cohen depicts himself not as swaying from Kant's philosophy, but rather as purifying it. This accords with the way in which he presents *Kants Begründung der Ethik* as the continuation of his efforts for the "restoration [Wiederherstellung] of Kantian philosophy."[78] This means not only formulating answers to objections made towards Kant but also purifying critical philosophy from misjudgments Kant himself made. For Cohen, as we shall elaborate in the next section, Kant's critical philosophy has a coherence and validity that, like scientific theories, are not threatened by mistakes its originator might have made. The principles of Kantianism are true even when Kant himself seems to have diverged from them. Therefore, to quote Fackenheim, "Cohen goes so far as to reject, in the name of Kant' s own ethics and as being inconsistent with that ethics, his entire notion of a *summum bonum*."[79]

In fact, Kant himself, Cohen suggests, was aware that his own theory of the *summum bonum* was, at the very least, less systematically grounded than other aspects of his ethical theory and accordingly downplayed the importance of setting virtuously conditioned happiness as the complete good. Cohen focused on Kant's reply to Garve's objections to make this point.[80] Garve had argued, among other things, that Kant's theory relies on the existence of God and immortality, postulates drawn to enable the meting out of happiness in accordance to virtue, in order to give the moral system "support and stability."[81] In his reply, Kant argues that this "support and stability" for duty is drawn from neither his notion of the complete good nor the postulates it leads reason to. The highest possible good of "universal happiness combined with and in conformity with the purest morality throughout the world" is not the incentive of duty, but the object of practical reason.[82] The will's motives are not "certain objects proposed as ends related to *natural feeling*, but nothing other than the unconditional *law* itself."[83] Kant adds that the concept of duty "in its complete purity is not only incomparably simpler, clearer and, for practical use, more readily grasped and more natural to everyone than any motive derived from happiness, or mixed with it and with regard for it."[84] Accordingly, in a passage Cohen himself quotes, Kant states that "in the question of the *principle* of morals the doctrine of the *highest good*, as the final end of a will determined by this doctrine and conformed with its laws, can be completely passed over and set aside (as episodic)."[85]

Cohen, accordingly, determines that the "error [Irrtum]" of setting this object as an "ideal of imagination" does not damage the fundamental ideas of Kant's ethics.[86] The basic direction of Kant's ethics can be fully maintained without appealing to his misguided and superfluous *summum bonum*. As Wood puts it, Cohen "concluded that the doctrine of the highest good must be completely rejected if Kant's fundamental principles are to be maintained."[87] Indeed, Cohen seeks to emphasize this mistake precisely because its correction serves the furthering of the systematic development of critical philosophy.[88]

This still leaves unanswered the question of why Kant would be making such a mistake, especially since, according to Cohen, he was not only explicitly aware of similar mistakes made in ancient philosophy but also realized the importance of insisting his notion of duty and good will could be construed without relying on his notion of the complete good. It is particularly relevant to us given our comparative interest with Mendelssohn to note in this context that Cohen finds attenuating historical circumstances, as it were, for this mistaken development in Kant's ethical theory in the unbridled Leibnizian optimism that characterized German philosophy in the period preceding Kant's critical revolution.[89] While Kant did largely correct this unwarranted buoyancy through his critique of Leibniz's theodicy and stripped the metaphysical backing of the Leibnizian and Wolffian optimism,[90] he could not completely free himself from the spirit of his time.[91] So while "historically, therefore, a remainder of uneradicated optimism in the postulates can be well understood," it remains the case that in a critically founded ethics, it is an "alien" and harmful motive.[92] As he puts it elsewhere, conjoining the last two points we made about the issue, "we can disregard the fact Kant, in an innermost contradiction with himself, turned God into a 'provider of pleasure,'" adding that this argument is a "mediaeval empty phrase, which does not belong to Kant." Accordingly, it can be uprooted from the principles Kant uncovered even if he was not able to uproot it from his personal thought and remains, in that aspect, "beholden to his generation."[93]

As mentioned above, the opposition to eudaemonism and to the positing of happiness as related to the highest good is embedded throughout Cohen's Jewish writings. We shall now see how Cohen repeatedly seeks, in *Religion of Reason out of the Source of Judaism* as well as in his other writings on Judaism, to characterize that opposition to any form of eudaemonism as an essentially Jewish position.

ANTI-EUDAEMONISM IN COHEN'S JEWISH WRITINGS

In his introduction to the *Jüdische Schriften*, the three tomes of which collect writings from 1867 all the way to those posthumously published in 1918 (a year after Cohen's death in 1917), Rosenzweig notes that Cohen certainly could not repeat Kant's "concession to the sentimental eudaimonism of the time," which expresses itself in postulating God in order to guarantee "the harmony of virtue and felicity, which could not be insured in any other way."[94] Indeed, in some sense, Cohen's Judaism is, in his eyes, more Kantian than Kant; while it includes the insistence on duty and on the purity of ethical action, it avoids Kant's concession to eudaemonism.

In "Internal Connections of Kantian Philosophy to Judaism," Cohen first emphasizes, as he is wont to do, Kant's rejection of happiness. The foremost characteristic of Kant's ethics, Cohen writes, is the rejection of eudaemonism and all its deviations. Kant therefore argues "that all eudaemonistic moral systems are antagonistic to ethics. *Happiness*, no matter what its nuanced form, cannot be the goal of pure will." Crucially, Cohen adds that this fully accords with Jewish philosophy, as "from Saadia to Maimonides and beyond, along the entire arc of Jewish philosophy, happiness is repudiated."

This opposition to the "pleasure principle" is for Cohen not only a "manifestation of the independence and systematic capacity of the Jewish spirit, but also an indication of the consistency of the biblical frame of mind that is manifest here."[95] Indeed, these Jewish thinkers, Cohen writes, continually examine the truthfulness of their thinking in light of the Bible and seek out the Torah itself as the grounding of reason. Moreover, Kant's rejection of happiness as a driving force of the will (if not fully as object of practical reason) and his attempt to establish a logical determining ground based on the general moral law and the notion of duty is also profoundly Jewish. With regards to moral duty, Cohen notes that Kant could have heard that we should not be "volunteers of morality" from a Jewish philosopher or from the Talmud itself before quoting the famous Talmudic dictum attributed to R. Haninah "Greater is he who performs because he has been commanded than one who performs without having been commanded."[96]

Kant, as we saw in the last section, was not able to completely avoid, in one of his "very weakest points,"[97] some nuanced admittance of happiness into his moral thinking. Judaism, as we shall see, does not, which makes it in that respect more purely adherent to the principles of critical philosophy than Kant himself was. In his late "Mahnung des Alters and die Jugend" (1917), Cohen, relying on what he describes as the "prerogative of old age," seeks to express his convictions to the youth and to speak to the young "from the Jewish spirit and heart" as if he "wanted to hand down [his] legacy."[98] Admonishing his readers to "recognize and fulfill [their] spirit with the thought that in the belief in the unique being of God, rests our Jewish idealism, which can in terms of all practical ethical relations compete with purely scientific idealism," he then notes that in light of this belief the psalmist scorns and despises "all goods of the earth and of the heavens." More generally, through this belief, Judaism "has overcome all eudaemonism and rejected earthly feelings of happiness as measure of the value and dignity of human life."[99]

Cohen believes this anti-eudaemonism to have remained essential to Judaism from the Bible to the sages, the medieval Jewish philosophers, and beyond. Accordingly, biblical verses are continually read through the anti-eudaemonistic perspective. Having stated that "opposition to *eudaemonism* is . . . deeply rooted in monotheism," Cohen quotes Ecclesiastes's "Vanity of vanities, all is vanity" and Psalm 73, "Why should I care about the heavens? With the covenant with you I have no desire for the earth."[100] So too Isaiah's "He makes peace and creates evil" reflects monotheism as it "fulfills its opposition to *eudaemonism*." This is because by "evil [Böse]," Cohen understands "ill [Übel],"[101] which he opposes to happiness, and which, as we shall see below in our discussion of suffering, leads to his notion of the highest good. Writing of the famous verse stating that "man doth not live by bread only," Cohen declares that "bread stands here for earthly happiness in general. This saying wards off the idea of eudaemonism."[102] Even in cases where biblical prophecies seem to suggest an earthly happiness, as in Joel's connecting the Last Judgment with the image in which "the mountains shall drop down sweet wine, and the hills shall flow with milk,"[103] Cohen relies on other verses to make the case that "with this external happiness of his own land he connects inwards signs of the messianic future."[104]

A similar interpretation is given to liturgical sources. So, for example, Cohen relates "let my soul be unto all as dust," from the concluding prayer of the *Shemoneh Esreh*, to the Jewish refutation of eudaemonism. "Dust," Cohen writes, "reminds one of the end of all human happiness. 'From Dust you came and dust you shall be.'"[105] More generally, Cohen notes that "in prayer and through prayer the individual is to be turned away from all eudaemonism. Only that which connects human beings with God is to be the content of prayer."[106]

Rabbinic dicta too are repeatedly presented as promoting the notion that happiness is anathema to the possibility of ethics or of a genuine highest good. We saw above how Cohen links Rabbi Haninah's dictum on the virtue of performing out of command to Kant's notion of duty.[107] Elsewhere, Cohen emphasizes rabbinical passages that, he argues, "eliminate any positive or negative eudaemonism from reward as from punishment: 'In the other life there is no eating nor drinking, nor any sensuous enjoyment, but the pious sit with their crowns on their heads and nourish upon the divine splendor.'"[108] So, for example, Resh Lakish's statement to the effect there would no longer be any hell in the messianic age is taken to show an opposition to retributive punishment, which Cohen links to eudaemonism.[109] Indeed, for Cohen, "the positive side of retribution, the reward, belongs to the prohibited land of eudaemonism."[110] More generally, Cohen notes that "suffering as well as bliss in the hereafter were rarely allowed to present a distinct theme of religious imagination in Judaism."[111]

Cohen's insistence on the lack of any kind of eudaemonism in the Jewish conception of immortality is one that is particularly interesting to us in light of Mendelssohn's insistence on the necessity of personal immortality for the possibility of his profoundly eudaemonistic notion of the highest good. As opposed to Mendelssohn's view, Cohen's notion of immortality cannot be related in any way to individual bliss or happiness.[112] In fact, he explicitly notes the nefariously supportive role "the eschatological element in the mythology of all cultures" has had in the "survival of eudaemonia."[113] Indeed, though he writes it is a form of eudaemonism often not recognized as such, he characterizes "the use of the world beyond for reward and punishment" as the "most dangerous variety" of eudaemonism.[114]

For Cohen, as is already clear from the quote above, the idea of immortality of the soul "originates in myth, which in turn is linked with the most primitive notions of man,"[115] not, therefore, with the religion of reason as reflected in Judaism and its sources. Cohen sees in the biblical depiction of the death and burial of originative biblical figures such as Abraham, Sarah, and Joseph a disregard for resurrection. He also notes that "the myth of the netherworld could not contribute to them,"[116] as the concept of the netherworld is based on the gods that inhabit it. Such gods, of course, are denied by monotheism's faith in a unique God. Elaborating on the concept of "thou shalt go to thy fathers," which Cohen takes to mean the "fathers of the national history,"[117] he suggests it is in "the people's soul into which the individual soul enters" and concludes that "*immortality acquires the meaning of the historical living-on of the individual in the historical continuity of his people.*"[118]

Similarly, the image of resurrection relates to the "continuous duration of individual souls in the historical unity of the people."[119] This notion is then universalized through the messianic ideal, about which we will write at length below, which links the individual's soul to the "future development of the human race and consequently of the *development of the human soul.*"[120] Accordingly, "only in the infinite development of the human race toward the ideal spirit of holiness can the individual soul actualize its immortality."[121]

As human beings are individuated through their relation to God, specifically through God's forgiveness of their sins,[122] their constitutive "moral holiness" as the "ideal of life" has to extend into death. These notions therefore illuminate "the horizon of another life."[123] For Cohen, the individual is not "tied exclusively to the organism" and is therefore not fully terminated with the decay of the organism.[124] Individuality is rather most genuinely tied with the spirit of holiness, a wholly moral idea that denotes the "task and, therefore, the motive power of holiness."[125] Referring to a verse in Ecclesiastes, "The dust returneth to the earth . . . and the spirit returneth unto God who gave it," Cohen writes that this return to God can be perceived of as a "return home" to the foundational principle of our individuality as moral beings.[126] The spirit's return to God reflects the actualization of immortality in the messianic ideal through what Cohen refers to as "the infinite continuation of the correlation of man and God."[127] Beyond these highly abstract delineations, Cohen believes the Jewish tradition rightly and self-consciously chose to remain relatively coy about the meaning of immortality, which "belongs to God's secrets."[128]

While Cohen claims Judaism has often been presented as inferior because of its supposed "lack of any tenet of immortality," the Jewish sources do maintain a form of immortality, but one that is "strictly within the ethical context, as circumscribed by the correlation between God and human beings."[129] Accordingly, pointing at Yehuda Halevi, Bahyia, and Maimonides to make his case, he claims that in "the history of Jewish religious philosophy the two motivations of mythical-mystical immortality, namely, the union with God and the meticulous execution of retribution, are in most cases rejected."[130]

Indeed, Maimonides in particular was, according to Cohen, a critical figure in ensuring no lingering eudaemonism remained in the Jewish perception of immortality. Cohen argues that Maimonides "replaces eudaemonia with self-perfection; and self-perfection he equates with 'drawing close to God' (התקרבות)."[131] This nearness to God, which Cohen repeatedly relates to Psalm 73:28, wherein the proximity of God is termed a person's "goodly portion,"[132] transforms the intellectually elitist, noetic, and eudaemonistic immorality characteristic of Aristotle to one that is thoroughly embedded in the ethical.[133] And while even Cohen must admit Maimonides's emphasis on cogitation seems rather Aristotelian and that one might gain the "not groundless impression, considering certain passages in Maimonides' writings, that Life Eternal even for him is vouchsafed purely for the theoretician," he adds that Maimonides's principle of self-perfection "is of such central importance that it must have systematically transformed Aristotelianism even in this controversial issue."[134]

More generally, Cohen's reading of Maimonides's philosophy has at its heart the supposed anti-eudaemonic character of the latter's thinking. An obvious problem is that while, on the one hand, Maimonides is widely perceived to be the most notable of all medieval Aristotelian Jewish thinkers, on the other hand, Aristotle's axiological thinking is not only thoroughly eudaemonistic but also foundational to eudaemonism throughout the history of Western philosophy.[135]

Cohen suggests some reasons why Maimonides could be perceived as more Aristotelian than he actually was. Given the intellectual climate in which Maimonides was active, in particularly the canonic status of Aristotelian thought within Medieval Arabic philosophy, it is clear to Cohen that Maimonides's "routine adoption of Aristotelian terminology" does not "remotely indicate Maimonides' inner methodological dependence on Aristotle nor his agreement with Aristotelianism."[136] Accordingly, Cohen claims Maimonides generally preferred maintaining "the impression of tacit agreement with him." This was not necessarily because Maimonides felt genuinely obligated to Aristotle's philosophy "but also out of literary considerations in order to keep all sorts of critics and opponents at bay." However, Cohen further remarks, there can be no doubt about Maimonides anti-eudaemonistic tendencies; "regarding the entire question of the relationship between Maimonides and Aristotle, it is therefore of utmost importance to note: Maimonides opposes, contends with, and replaces the doctrine of eudaemonia."[137]

Cohen's argument relates to an issue we will delve into at depth in the next section; Maimonides's philosophy is centered, like Plato's and Cohen's own thinking but pointedly unlike Aristotle, on a good that exists beyond nature and being and yet can be ethically correlated to humanity. Plato's idea of the good is in this sense far nearer to the Jewish God than Aristotle's unmoved mover. Maimonides therefore, Cohen argues, substitutes his ethically laden notion of self-perfection for eudaemonia.[138] This is why Maimonides restricts the possibility of positive knowledge of God to actional attributes. In doing so, Cohen writes, Maimonides "pinpoints and limits the concept of a divine attribute to an ethical attribute, thus identifying the concept of God with the ethical concept of God."[139]

Finally, drawing this survey to Cohen's own era in the history of Judaism, we see that Cohen once again bases his critique of Zionism on anti-eudaemonism. Rosenzweig famously tells of a conversation in which Cohen accuses him of having a far too "tolerant" attitude towards Zionism. As Rosenzweig seeks to defend his stance, Cohen interrupts him and, toning down his voice to a "thundering whisper," states condemningly, "those fellows want to be happy!"[140] We shall return later to why precisely Zionism is in "contradiction to the messianic ideal,"[141] but it is clear that Cohen saw a profound eudaemonistic element in Zionism that, given all that we have seen above, would have been fundamentally unacceptable to him.

To summarize, any religion that claims for itself the mantle of reason cannot be, for Cohen, related to eudaemonism in any way. Judaism, which, as we shall see, Cohen characterizes as the primordial source of the religion of reason, is depicted as robustly opposed to binding the highest values to self-interested eudaemonism in any shape or form. The biblical, liturgical, and Jewish philosophical sources are all interpreted and depicted as anti-eudaemonistic through and through, and Zionism, in contrast, is condemned precisely because it is characterized as eudaemonistic.

Cohen's anti-eudaemonism, however, does not necessarily demand the abolishment of all positive states of mind. So, for example, Cohen emphasizes the significance of joy, lauding the "pure joy [Freude] of knowledge and inquiry," which overshadows all material and spiritual suffering.[142] He also emphasizes the significance of the joy of the Sabbath and Jewish festivals, which is perceived as a religious duty.[143] When "peace of the soul [Seelenfriede]" is attained, there manifests, too, a "contentment [Zufriedenheit]," which Cohen characterizes as a religious virtue in so far as "it is concerned with the acknowledgment of God's providence and rule over the world," before adding that "in face of contentment all the assaults of eudaemonism are shattered."[144] These descriptions, however, inevitably relate such emotions not to the fulfillment of any form of self-interest, but rather to selfless dedication and to the fulfillment of messianic ideals. So joy of study relates to the profoundly moral and selfless Jewish historical mission (which we will analyze in the next chapter);[145] the joy of the Sabbath relates to the freedom of all human beings;[146] and the joy of the festivals relate not to Bacchanalian delight in lust but is rather "defined by the shared joy of the stranger and the poor man,"[147] and it remains connected to the joy of the study of the Torah and as such distinct from both "sensual frenzy" as well as "aesthetic delusions."[148] Contentment, too, as we shall see below, relates to a peace that cannot be attained by the individual unless it is secured for the world.[149]

So Cohen seeks to comprehensively eradicate from his system any notion of eudaemonism without necessarily positing himself against all forms of blissfulness. Rather, he sets out to expunge any self-interest, whether bodily or spiritual, from his axiological picture. Indeed, eudaemonism relates not only to sensual pleasures or material benefit but also, as we saw above, to intellectual or spiritual self-interest or pleasure. He strongly criticizes the traces of such self-interest in Kant's notion of happiness and sought to show that Judaism, as well as his notions of joy and contentment, successfully avoid it.

Having analyzed Cohen anti-eudaemonism in both his general writings as well as the more Jewish ones, we are now in a position to focus on that which Cohen suggest does in fact function as a suitable source of value as well as that which he posits as the supreme value.

Cohen's Unique Source of Value

Our analysis of Cohen's interpretation of Maimonides indicates his enthusiasm for what he characterized as Maimonides's insistence on a Platonic source of value rather than the Aristotelian one. It is no surprise that in advocating for this interpretation, Cohen, whose interpretations of Jewish sources clearly reflect his philosophical positions, is here revealing his own thinking about the matter.[150] Like Plato's, Cohen's source of value is beyond nature and sensible reality. In Cohen's case, however, it is not the idea of the good but rather the unique God monotheism introduced to humanity that functions as source of value.

As Rosenzweig puts it his introduction to Cohen's collected Jewish writings, the postulate of God "served only as an ornament in Kant's ethics, and not as a structurally necessary part of the edifice," while Cohen's divine idea is the "keystone [Schlußtein]," a keystone without which "the entire vault of the system would collapse."[151] This echoes Cohen's own phrasing in his *Der Begriff der Religion*, wherein he describes the idea of God as the "keystone [Schlußtein] of his *Ethik des Reinen Willens*."[152] Accordingly, in this section we will seek to analyze how Cohen's unique God functions as the "keystone" to not only his ethical thinking but his axiological structure as well. In this section, we will focus on Cohen's conception of God before analyzing how it functions as the source of value through the notion of moral correlation with human beings. This will enable us to understand why the messianic future is posited by Cohen as the highest value.

COHEN'S UNIQUE GOD

According to Cohen, it is God's uniqueness, and not his oneness, that is to be posited as the "content of monotheism."[153] It is the absolute incomparability of God that must be primarily acknowledged in our engagement with the divine being. God's oneness, one the other hand, is merely a dismissal of polytheism, which as such does not yet suggest the innovative concept of God monotheism introduced. To quote Levinas's elegant formulation, "monotheism is not an arithmetic of the divine."[154] Monotheism does not merely point out there is one God as opposed to two or five; it addresses, rather, the categorical uniqueness of the one unique God. Accordingly, the unique God at the heart of monotheism does not merely stand opposed to the plurality of polytheism but also against the polytheistic perception of the relation between the gods and the universe. The incomparability of the monotheistic God, Cohen notes, "points as much to nature as to every other concept of God."[155]

The critical difference between oneness and uniqueness explains, according to Cohen, the biblical usage of a plural form of God's appellation, *Elohim*, juxtaposed with singular forms of adjectives and verbs. While one might be tempted to explain the plural form of *Elohim* as a remnant of polytheism the biblical sources did not clear out, Cohen suggests it is precisely because the central point of the monotheistic conception of God is uniqueness rather than oneness that a plural form was maintained and combined with singular adjectives and verbs: "the preservation of the plural form testifies to the vigor of the new thought, which simply took no offense at all at the plural form."[156] The oneness of God was so obvious to the religious consciousness that gave birth to monotheism, Cohen suggests, that it chose to maintain this grammatical discordance in order to express God's uniqueness, which it rightly understood to be the center of gravity of its theological innovation.

The starkness of God's incomparability is reflected in Cohen's interpretation of Isaiah 40:25, "There is none like unto Thee," which he suggests indicates a negation of being for that which is not God. Indeed, being cannot be ascribed both to God and to the world. The incomparability of God is such that his being cannot be compared to ours, and there is therefore "only *one* kind of being, only one unique being: God is the unique being," in comparison to which "all other being vanishes and becomes nothing."[157] Monotheism as understood by Cohen leads to the conclusion that besides God there is nothing to which genuine being can be ascribed: "Cosmos and nature are negated."[158] Accordingly, Cohen introduces the distinction between "being [Sein]" and "existence [Dasein]" in order to differentiate divine being from natural existence. While the former denotes the non-sensible true being approached by reason, the latter refers to that which is attested by the senses.[159] God's unique being is, furthermore, also "opposed" to time, and accordingly "God's being also excludes change."[160]

It is firstly important to note that Cohen makes these claims in the very first chapter of his *Religion of Reason*. This already indicates that, structurally, this is meant to function as the "keystone" of the whole work. God is the fundamental idea, the "first principle,"[161] from which Cohen begins his exploration. We saw above that Kant begins his *Critique of Practical Reason* with the apodictic fact of the supremacy of good will, which led his enquiry into the *summum bonum*. Similarly, Cohen begins his *Religion of Reason* by presenting as fact the unique monotheistic God, which, as will be shown below, will back his own depiction of the highest good.

It is also important to note the parallels between this notion of God and Cohen's interpretation of the Platonic idea, an interpretation of which was at the heart of Cohen's burgeoning idealistic philosophical system. Indeed, while Cohen's later religious work goes beyond the limits of his previously purely philosophical enterprise,[162] his notion of God still very much reflects his earlier treatment of Plato's philosophy. In his "Platons Ideenlehere und die Mathematik," published in 1878, Cohen notes and lauds the development of the notion of a unique being held by the Eleatics in opposition to the Heraclitean position of flux and becoming.[163] He then notes another advancement in the atomism of Democritus, who conceived of the Eleatic notion of being as a non-sensible void and in doing so converted the Eleatic notion of being into idealism.[164] While of course Cohen is virulently against atomism in so far as it promotes an eudaemonistic ethics,[165] he believed its version of materialism was less distant from critical idealism than from spiritualism and did enthuse over Democritus's innovative establishment of a non-sensible void as being. Plato's own notion of being, similarly, is non-sensible and wholly beyond the becoming of material existence. The contrast between the flux of becoming, existence, and the unique being beyond it is therefore a theme Cohen recognizes in ancient Greek philosophy and that is, as we saw above, very much present in his depiction of the unique God.

Furthermore, a central aspect of Cohen's treatment of Plato, at least from 1878 onwards, is the notion that in Platonic philosophy, or at least in the most fruitful interpretation of it, "the idea itself is thought of as hypothesis."[166] Plato, Cohen writes, thought mathematical thinking was characterized by the fact it originates with a hypothesis. This method, which consists of "supposing to have found what is searched, and then by the consequences and their combination, find it again,"[167] is, for Cohen, eminently fruitful in philosophical thinking and is perceived by Cohen as having been crucial in the history of modern Western thought. The Renaissance, he writes in his *Logik der Reinen Erkenntnis*, "is primarily the rebirth of Plato." Furthermore, the scientists who heralded the modern era, whether Copernicus, Kepler, or Newton, all relied on Plato in so far as "the most profound and fruitful methodological instrument used by the astronomers who worked on the new conception of the world was the hypothesis."[168]

Crucially, Cohen suggests Plato's innovation steered the path towards the kind of idealistic philosophy Kant, as well as Cohen himself, was developing. The Platonic hypothesis, which, in his introduction to Lange's *History of Materialism*, Cohen equates to Kant's notion of the a priori,[169] enables a non-sensible originative principle that maintains the purity of thought. Interpreting Platonic ideas as hypotheses, Cohen ascribes to Plato the crucial idealistic step of pointing at thought as producing its own contents. Indeed, declining both the ontological or psychological interpretation of the idea,[170] Cohen focuses on the epistemological and suggests that in reflecting on the mathematical method, Plato identified the a priori in sensibility.[171] In other words, Plato had identified what would eventually be known as transcendental idealism. The hypothesis, literally to "put under," or *grundlegung* as Cohen puts it,[172] sets the ground of knowledge on purely ideal sources.[173]

It is highly important to keep in mind Cohen's enthusiasm for the hypothesis in order to understand his own methodology, which posits ideas and principles before finding their confirmation in the fruitfulness of their application. Critically, in this context, in *Religion of Reason*, Cohen identifies God, as well as other "fundamental ideas," as "*first principles*, which have the touchstone of their correctness in their fruitfulness."[174] The idea of God is therefore presented as a hypothesis upon which Cohen's whole system stands. Cohen does not seek to prove God's existence, nor does he argue for it, but rather, approaching God as a fundamental idea, he seeks to expound its validity in the productivity revealed by its application. Cohen, in other words, begins with God as a first principle or hypothesis and seeks to show how that philosophical genesis enables a significant, insightful, and ultimately convincing comprehension of human reality.

There are, furthermore, clear commonalities between Plato's idea of the good and Cohen's depiction of the prophet's conception of the unique God. God, like the idea of the good, is transcendent and forms the ground of ethical knowledge: "where the philosopher designates the idea of the good as 'highest knowledge,' i.e. the knowledge ethics, the prophets speaks, in the same sense of the one God as the Holy One, i.e. as the God of morality."[175] Indeed, Cohen's God, as we shall see later on, and Plato's idea of the good are both "beyond being."[176]

Still, it remains nonetheless important to keep in mind that while Cohen's approach to some aspects of divinity does reflect ideas presented in his philosophical undertakings, it is critical to Cohen's own religious thinking that the unique God presented by the religion of reason and the Jewish sources cannot be reduced to purely philosophical conceptualizations. The comparison between the Platonic idea as hypothesis, or even Plato's transcendental idea of the good, and Cohen's unique God is insightful in some ways, but it certainly is not exhaustive. For Cohen, as we saw above and will delineate further in the next chapter, religion adds a dimension to culture that is irreducible to philosophy in and of itself.

In fact, one of the great problems of philosophical thought is, for

Cohen, its perennial tendency to veer into pantheism,[177] a tendency Cohen believes the religion of reason can remedy. The Eleatics, Cohen writes, sought a concept of God in order to explain oneness with regards to the cosmos. Accordingly, though Parmenides himself already recognized the error of uniting being and becoming,[178] the Eleatic notion of the oneness of God "is only an auxiliary concept for the unity of the cosmos, and thus this unity of God and the world is of use only to pantheism." Monotheism, on the other hand, seeks oneness as it relates to God, a notion of oneness that therefore "had to become that uniqueness by virtue of which God's being is distinct from any being of nature."[179] When understood through creation, which is critical as it is through this "immanent relation of being to becoming" that the divine being acquires its positive content, the unique being of God is conceived of as "the fundamental condition for causality" and accordingly as the foundation of the world of becoming.[180] This, however, by no means dissolves the starkness of the differentiation between being and becoming postulated by monotheism, a difference that Cohen states must be thought of as "the difference between *affirmation* and *negation*." While becoming "in so far as it is false being is removed from unique being," it nevertheless must be explained by it given that if God is the unique being, he is the originative principle of becoming.[181]

Crucially, this creation relates not as much to the question of the primeval act, with which mythology is most often concerned, but rather a process through which the constancy of continual change finds its origin in the same originative principle. Cohen thinks the latter aspect of creation is succinctly contained in the Hebrew term חדוש עולם, or "renewal of the world," arguing it makes "creation a matter of *continuity* within which each day is a new beginning."[182]

The differentiation between being and becoming, which maintains the distance erroneously negated by pantheism, does not merely preserve philosophy from the logical contradictions Cohen identifies in its unification of these notions,[183] but more importantly enables the rise of ethics. Indeed, Cohen emphasizes that the most important aspect of the insight that becoming finds its originative ground in the unique being is its ethical contribution. Accordingly, he emphasizes how the notion of creation is increasingly interpreted in the Jewish sources through a distinctly ethical lens. Writing of the abovementioned term חדוש עולם,

Cohen states that the "real cause for the introduction of the concept of renewal rests with the ethical problem."[184] Indeed, if in Greek philosophy the question of creation related to the origin of the cosmos, in monotheism the interest in creation is not exhausted in the primeval moment but rather seeks a constant teleological guidance that is ever renewed. Creation becomes the divine ethical renewal of the world.

Cohen's repeated depictions of pantheism as an ethical disaster is perhaps most acutely expressed, unsurprisingly, in his writings on Spinoza. The attacks Cohen repeatedly and rather vehemently launched at Spinoza were multilayered, relating to personal, Jewish, and moral aspects. We shall address the personal and Jewish aspect of this critique later on,[185] but what matters to us here is the moral aspect, as it will help us further clarify the ethical significance of the uniqueness of Cohen's God and why it necessitates the absolute separation of being from becoming.

It is clear to Cohen that "the supposed absence of any distinction between God and nature compromises the spirit of *ethics* even more than it compromises the spirit of knowledge."[186] For Cohen, Spinoza's absolutely monistic substance does not allow for the critical distance between what is and what ought to be. After all, if nature as God is all there is, perfection is instantiated in our immanent reality as it is. For Cohen, ethics, in and of itself, must seek to approximate the ideal, and while the "inexorable goal of the approximation is the permeation of actuality with the ideal," the "scientific rigor of ethics" demands it maintains "the separation of actuality from the ideal, and generally between the idea and actuality."[187] As this separation collapses in pantheism, there is for Cohen, as it were, an absolute deafness to the ethical in Spinoza's philosophy. Indeed, as Spinoza's concept of divine substance does not relate to the God of ethics, but the God of nature, it contrasts poorly with Plato's formulation of the good, which, as we saw above, Cohen correlates with Maimonides's thinking and relates to a realm beyond the boundaries of sensibility and matter.[188]

So the separateness of the unique God enables the rise of ethics, which collapses in pantheism. There can be no ethics without the idea of the one God. The unique God, as opposed to the unified God-nature of pantheism, enables the rise of ethics in so far as it underlies the ideal realm through which ethical action must be directed. Furthermore, God functions as the guarantor of morality on earth.[189] Indeed, a critical aspect of Cohen's thinking about God[190] is that God promises the perseverance of humanity and therefore also the possibility of the establishment of morality. "The idea of God," Cohen writes, provides the confidence "that morality will become reality on earth."[191] Accordingly, Cohen claims that monotheism establishes the idea of God concurrently with the assurance of the eternal survival of the world for life and the living through the critical divine promise symbolized in the biblical narrative by the rainbow.[192]

Finally, we must therefore approach God as bastion and provider of morality. This is a tendency Cohen firmly identifies throughout the Jewish tradition. So the prophets understood God's teaching only as "the teaching of morality," and while God is the creator of animals as well, He is the "father" of humanity, as He is "the originator of . . . morality."[193] Cohen points at the same insight in the basic precept that we can only know God's essence through "his thirteen attributes, only in his moral attributes . . . and that he therefore is to be conceived only as we conceive of the idea of the Good."[194] It is this critical insight, which relates to the ethical significance of the God idea, that leads monotheism to think of the unique God as provider of purpose to both nature and humanity. Without this purpose, Cohen writes, "the world would have no meaning."[195]

These thoughts emphasize the importance of Cohen's unique God as "keystone" to ethics, and the last quote about the world's meaning begins to address the axiological question we must further explore, namely, how does the unique God relate to our *summum bonum*? If God's unique being is to becoming what affirmation is to negation, should God not only be posited as the source of value but indeed as the sole possible value? Cohen at times seems to make this point, such as at the end of his *Der Begriff der Religion*, when he writes that "only through the separation between God and man can man learn the true overcoming of this world, and not with contempt for it, but through disregard for all goods of this world, all earthly lust for power, as opposed to the only good which is the only being."[196] Yet, it is also clear that thinking of the good only in terms of God in and of itself, without the world and our human reality, does not make sense to Cohen. As Cohen tellingly asks earlier in the same work, "What would become of the good if nature were annihilated, if it would not, in its perpetual existence, constitute the ground upon which the good can grow and thrive forever."[197] Clearly, then, the good demands both God and nature. While the good is not sourced in this world, it must come into it and bring in this world something that is not of this world.

This, however, still does not elucidate Cohen's axiological picture. On the one hand, as explained above, given that the unique being is to becoming what affirmation is to negation, it is clear that any value must be drawn from it. Yet, on the other hand, given that God's very uniqueness radically differentiates his being from the world of becoming, it is not at all clear how Cohen's idea of God can function as the source of value. How is value drawn from a source that is absolutely other? Cohen's concept of correlation is that which enables the formulation of an answer to this question.

CORRELATION

As we saw above, there can be no question Cohen axiologically prioritizes God's unique being over the lesser existence of becoming. Accordingly, the realm of becoming can only aspire to any value if it can be drawn from being. However, it is also the case that the good can only come into being if the perpetual ground of existence obtains; that is, the good must involve both being and existence. While Cohen demarcated the uniqueness of God as monotheism's "content [inhalt]" in his *Religion of Reason*,[198] he writes at the beginning of the third chapter of his *Begriff der Religion* that monotheism's "essential content [Hauptinhalt]" is "not as much God as man, or more precisely, not God in and of himself, but rather only in correlation with men, just as in virtue of correlation, the issue is not man alone, but always man in correlation with God."[199] While God's being cannot but be axiologically prioritized over natural becoming, and clearly being is the source of any value in becoming, the highest good must be one that somehow involves both, which is precisely what Cohen's notion of correlation, the "fundamental relation of religion,"[200] seeks to achieve.

As already mentioned, the problem is precisely how this interaction between the incomparable realms of being and becoming can occur in such a way as to enable lives lived in becoming to draw value from unique being. It is helpful to begin thinking of correlation on the basis of what we saw above about the notion of creation. Creation is critical to Cohen as it conveys the positive content in Cohen's depiction of the unique God and of His being. Cohen's notion of creation, however, does not depict a simple interaction between being and becoming but rather an ideal grounding of the latter in the former; the origination of becoming in being must be thought of in terms of logical dependence. Were one to think of it materialistically and in terms of emanation, one would be acknowledging material immanence and veer into pantheism.[201] Yet, if we do not realize God as creator, then the distinctness drawn between being and becoming would also collapse, as "nature itself would be God,"[202] and so again pantheism would be reached.

Cohen's solution seeks to avoid both pitfalls; God, as an ideal concept, underlies a worldly reality that is logically dependent on it. Given the emphasis his critical idealism perennially places on the ethical and that "the essence of man is dependent on the knowledge of morality,"[203] it is accordingly most important that in its function as logical ground, idealized being provides a realm of ethical certainty that must inform ours. In the same manner in which we conceive of the unique being as the presupposition for becoming, so too it must also be the "precondition for the knowledge of morals."[204]

It is that logical and preeminently ethical grounding of becoming in being that sets the stage for correlation. Indeed, correlation cannot relate to simply assuming the possibility of communication issued by God to human beings, as that would make God "participate in man—and man in God, [which] assaults the uniqueness of God's being." Correlation, rather, must focus on the logical grounding of becoming in being, which maintains the latter's uniqueness. Accordingly, therefore, revelation is not a matter of God revealing Himself or communicating directly, but rather *"revelation is the creation of reason."*[205] Revelation can only be thought of as occurring through human reason, as it is reason that enables human beings to grasp the non-sensible. We are once again speaking of that part of us that Plato, Kant, and Cohen always insist makes humans particular: "Revelation is the sign of reason, which is not animal sensuality but comes from God and connects with God."[206] Accordingly, "revelation itself can only be thought of as the revelation to reason,"[207] and, critically, "man, as rational being, is the correlate to the God of revelation."[208] The upshot is Cohen's crucial solution to this problem: the correlation of the divine spirit to the human, writes Cohen, "has an unavoidable consequence a kind of identity of logical reason in both."[209] While the religion of reason teaches us the absolute uniqueness of God and his total incomparability, reason is the sole means by which to find a correlation with that unique God. Accordingly, it is a relation that is enabled by, as Wolfson puts it, "the very reason that preserves their difference."[210]

So while "uniqueness excludes any *mediation* between God and natural existence,"[211] human beings are correlated with God in reason, through which logic is accessible to us in the realm of becoming in spite of the fact that it reflects the reality of being. Correlation therefore reflects the logical dependency of all creation on the unique God but still, Cohen argues, "averts unification."[212] As Cohen continually emphasizes the ethical understanding of creation and of the underpinning of becoming by being, the logic reflected by correlation is primarily a moral one. And given that in terms of value, there can be no doubt as to the primacy of being to becoming, axiologically speaking, this correlation to the unique being is that through which value can come to be thought of as relating to the world of becoming.

In order for this correlation to gain its true significance, we need Cohen's clarification as to its content. As indicated above, Cohen's interpretation of revelation suggests that the identity of logical reason in humans and in the unique being, enabling correlation, is reflected in the teachings of Sinai and of the prophets. In many ways, therefore, the content of that correlative revelation is the content of Cohen's religion of reason and the philosophical and religious thinking it involves; it is his ethical monotheism and the messianic future it is aimed at.

HERMANN COHEN'S FUTURE

As described above, both being and becoming are necessary for the good to arise, and more specifically, the good is meaningful only if God and humanity, the basic concepts of religion, are introduced: "What the good is, God will reveal," Cohen writes, before proclaiming that good to be, for humanity as well as for God, humanity and humanity only.[213] The messianic realization of one humanity correlated to the one God is the highest good and the essence of prophetic Judaism for Cohen. Indeed, the Jewish conception of God reaches its highest perfection with the idea of the Messiah.[214] While this idea, like all ideas, grew out of specific historical circumstances, it quickly overcame the narrow bounds of a particular political longing relating to a particular political situation. Accordingly, even though the Messiah rose out as the scion of the house of David, which would restore the Israelite state to its former glory, the religious principles inherent to Judaism soon turned a patriotic yearning into a universal moral idea. The Messiah was demythologized from a person to gain its full sublimity as a symbol of universal peace, "the ethical humanity of future history."[215]

This "confederation of humanity [Staatenbund der Menschheit]," which is "mankind's messianic future,"[216] draws us to the messianic task. Indeed, while future oriented, the messianic task demands actual political action to bring it about in the present.[217] This task is the ultimate demand of bringing humanity together in a peace enabled by a common awareness of the uniqueness of God. The messianic task, therefore, calls on us to obey correlation and maximize holiness by including all of humanity in the sphere of our moral concern. It is the ultimate aim of the ethical contents revealed to us by God in spirit through reason. As such, the messianic future is Cohen's highest good. It is the proper aspiration of ethical action and the most profound realization of correlation with the unique being in becoming, the most significant expression of humanity's holy spirit and, accordingly, the "summit [Gipfel]" of monotheism.[218]

It may prima facie seem, given that, as we saw above, any value must be derived from God, that it is correlation itself that would be the highest good. And indeed, nearness to God (and not a dangerously pantheistic union with God), which Cohen equates to his notion of correlation,[219] is presented by the poet of the Psalms, Cohen points out, as humanity's highest good.[220] But were this nearness understood as a form of personal well-being, it would of course carry with it the eudaemonistic tendencies Cohen so profoundly abhors. We saw above that even the highly refined Aristotelean eudaemonism was rejected by Cohen. Accordingly, even if nearness to God primarily consisted of a highly spiritual form of happiness, it would be just as unacceptable. In other words, if nearness to God were a matter of personal satisfaction, even of a wholly spiritual kind, it would involve the kind of self-interest Cohen fundamentally rejects. This nearness cannot, therefore, be substantiated in terms of a form of personal spiritual well-being, but must rather be substantially determined by those "moral concerns, which connect God and man."[221]

Drawing close to God, therefore, is essentially equated to "the moral activity."[222] And as the messianic idea involves all people experiencing nearness to God,[223] it is that unification of humanity that would represent the highest good. Nearness to God accordingly means seeking to draw all people near to God.

Accordingly, peace, which Cohen describes as the "token of the messianic age,"[224] cannot be attained by anyone unless it is attained by all. The individual cannot attain "peace of soul without securing the peace of the world."[225] Messianism, accordingly, "unites humanity with every individual man" in that it ties one's own sense of peace, and the contentment it manifests, to the advent of harmony between all people.[226] Cohen's messianic peace, the "epitome of human life in the spirit of the Bible," which carries all the "meaning, all the value of life,"[227] carries no eudaemonistic significance; it evades any form of self-interest in so far as it inevitably necessitates universal concerns. Cohen's religious contentment, as we saw above, arises not from one's own well-being, but from the messianic justice established on earth. Nearness to God can only be fulfilled if it involves the nearness of all other human beings. Messianism, accordingly, is the ultimate maximization of God's nearness to humanity. As such, it is the final development of both Jewish social ethics as well as of the concept of correlation.[228]

This, then, enables us to tie in Cohen's religious notion of the *summum bonum* with the one he suggested in his early work on Kant. We saw above that in his critique of Kant, Cohen suggests that the ideal of all human beings living as autonomous moral agents in a community of ends suffices as highest good. We here find this idea again, embedded in his Jewish thinking. Cohen makes the affinity of the Kantian depictions of the kingdom of ends with the Jewish messianic era explicit. The "most profound and crystal-clear significance of the *categorical imperative*," Cohen writes, referring to the demand to always treat humans as ends rather than means, "could well be said to course through the very veins of the Jew."[229] More importantly, the perpetual universal peace to which its implementation would, according to Kant, eventually lead was first conceived by the prophets. Accordingly, for Cohen, "Whoever believes in perpetual peace believes in the *messiah*, not in the messiah who purportedly came, but rather in the one who ought to come, and who will come."[230]

The future coming of the Messiah points at a critical aspect of Messianism, namely, that it focuses not on the present or the past, but on the future.[231] The idea of the Messiah "is the hope of the future of humanity," and the future is, for Cohen, a "demand of faith and its most wonderful blossoming."[232] The most profound meaning of prophetic messianic thinking unfolds itself in this vision of a morally ordained and universalistic future. The orientation of Judaism towards that future, furthermore, is related not only to the unique historical vision of prophecy but is also grounded in the eternal divine being guiding it.

Indeed, when commenting on the biblical "I am that I am," Cohen notes that while grammatically it is nearer to "Ich bin, der ich bin" (which, like the English, is in the present tense), the translation in the future tense as "Ich werde sein, der ich sein werde" not only maintains the insight of God as being but strengthens it as it draws it further away from the perceived reality of the present.[233] Being, Cohen writes, "is not restrained to the present, but rather is suspended above it. Present and future are connected in that being of God."[234] And as in that being temporal distinctions are annulled, it is "the future that can best describe this unique being, the truly spiritual, divine being."[235] This insight also guides Cohen's interpretation of the verses "For I am holy" as relating to God and "ye shall be holy" as relating to human beings. This again suggests God's being relates to our future, and Cohen concludes that holiness, for human beings, means a task while "for God it designates being."[236] So, the derivation of value is continually related to a task yet to be fulfilled, drawn from a correlation with a meta-temporal concept of God that draws us to the future.

It is therefore not only a chronological or historical fact that puts Messianism in the future but also one inherently related to Cohen's conception of God. Correlation with a God couched in the future cannot but be future oriented. Therefore, "just as thought turns away from perception and the reality which is represented in it, so the religion of Messianism turns away from the past and the present; A new concept of time is created by the human being in correlation in God: the future."[237]

Critically, in so far as the messianic ideal is in the future, which stands in opposition to the past and the present, it also opposes, Cohen notes, "every previous eudaemonistic sort of historical existence." Accordingly, for Cohen, the "messianic future is the first conscious expression of the opposition to moral values derived only from empirical sensibility." The notion that the center of gravity of Messianism, and the ethics it pursues, is in the future rather than in the past structurally enables it to rise as an ideal. In fact, Cohen refers to the submerging of the past and the present in this future as the "purest idealization."[238] Cohen's highest good therefore coheres with his critique of Kant's *summum bonum* in that it fundamentally evades the trap of eudaemonism. It stems from humanity's correlation with God, which occurs through reason and in a realm that is wholly non-sensible, and maximizes the ethical task of holiness, which is necessarily in the future and as such beyond the empirically constrained realms of the past and the present.

The axiological picture uncovered is therefore as follows: Cohen posits his primordial hypothesis, the unique God, as the source of all value. God's incomparability is such that only God can claim true being. The material world, sensible reality, is merely becoming. Therefore, value, if it is real, must be derived from the unique being. As both communication and emanation would threaten the uniqueness of God's being, Cohen introduces a notion of correlation enabled by reason. However, this correlation in and of itself cannot be the highest good. Were that to be the case, the emphasis would lay on the enjoyment derived from the possibility of our correlation with God, which would therefore be a form of intellectual eudaemonia Cohen recognized in Aristotelianism and condemned. This correlation, rather, is what gives birth in human culture to the grandiose task of raising in becoming as much of the value of being as possible, a task Cohen identifies as messianic. It is therefore the messianic future that forms the highest good for Cohen. The next chapter will further explicate this notion of the highest good before evaluating how it informs Cohen's position on the tensions between universalism and particularism.

(5)
MESSIANIC HUMANITY

The exploration of Cohen's ideas about the uniqueness of God and His relation to humanity through correlation led to the conclusion that the highest good for humanity is posited by Cohen as the messianic future. The messianic ideal is the proper object of our human aspirations; a non-eudaemonistic, future-oriented goal that ultimately upholds and seeks to maximize the morality correlation calls us to implement. While the passages we looked at in this context in the last chapter were mainly from Cohen's Jewish writings, the notion that a morally united humanity is the highest good is already present in Cohen's early work on Kant. Indeed, while rejecting Kant's own depiction of the *summum bonum*, Cohen repeatedly suggests that the Kantian notion of the kingdom of ends is a far more suitable object for practical reason than Kant's eudaemonistically tainted notion of the complete good.

In *Kant's Begründung der Ethik*, Cohen quotes a passage from the *Critique of Pure Judgement* wherein Kant argues that the highest good, possible solely under God's sovereignty, is "the existence of rational beings under moral laws."[1] The caveat of course is that, as we saw, Kant differentiated between the highest good, which relates to goodwill and its categorical derivations, and the complete good, into which he inserted a morally conditioned notion of happiness. Having quoted this passage, Cohen seeks to rid critical philosophy of this caveat, arguing against Kant that the existence of rational beings under moral law needs no axiological supplementation. Cohen makes explicit he means both the highest as well as the complete good when claiming that "the community of autonomous beings is the sole supreme good" and clarifies the statement as follows: "one does not say, this is relevant only for the meaning of the supreme highest good [des obersten höchsten Gutes]: the complete [vollendete] good is hereby too given." For Cohen, the perfection or completion of the highest good is given by the "immovable goals which the maxim itself indicates and upholds."[2] As he states a few paragraphs later, for critical idealism, "the realm of absolute purposes is the highest good," adding that "we can safely dispense with another spur [to the moral law], another ideal."[3] Accordingly, any notion of the supreme good that seeks to posit itself as higher than the autonomous moral community itself is superfluous.[4]

There are clear similarities between a Kantian kingdom of ends and messianic humanity. Both primarily seem to necessitate the inclusion of all human beings within the scope of our highest moral ideas. It is therefore not surprising that in his critique of Kant, Cohen argues for a notion of the highest good that is later reflected in the parallel notion of the messianic ideal in his religious writings. This suggests that ideas drawn from Cohen's Neo-Kantian philosophy are definitely profoundly embedded in Cohen's later religious and Jewish writings even if the language and conceptual framework of the latter cannot be exhausted by philosophical thought. In order for us to explore how Cohen's mature and religious notion of the highest good relates to the Kantian position he had earlier argued for, we need to find out how, if at all, they differ. We need, in other words, to better assess the relation between a Kantian kingdom of ends and the notion of messianic humanity Cohen draws from the sources.

Indeed, as Cohen himself puts it in his analysis of Kant, "if the realm of ends is merely the methodologically justified expression for the kingdom of God, what then remains for the latter by which it can and may differentiate itself from the realm of ends and from the community of moral beings?"[5] The problem of course being that if no such distinction can be made, "the independence and existence of religion in general is put into question."[6] Even if the ethical and religious ideals aim at the same direction, there must be a particular contribution of religion to culture for it to be justified as a distinct realm in human existence. The axiological consequences are crucial; if religion in general, and Judaism in particular, can be reduced to ethics, their value would be gravely exposed. Indeed, were that to be the case, we might simply seek to teach ethics and let go of religion altogether.

The chapter will therefore begin with a discussion of how Cohen's religious writings argue for the distinct importance of religion, in particular vis-à-vis ethics. This exploration, which will focus on the axiological import of religion, will enable us to better understand the unique worth not only of the religious sphere in general but also of Judaism in particular. This, in turn, will enable not only a greater clarification of Cohen's notion of the highest good but also of the particular importance of Judaism in light of the universal ideals Cohen seeks to maintain, which the section after that will focus on. We will then conclude by engaging, in light of this analysis, with Cohen's universal aspirations and the degree to which they are realized in his thought.

Cohen's Religious Axiology

THE UNIQUE VALUE OF RELIGION

In his introduction to *The Religion of Reason*, Cohen succinctly explains that which makes religion irreducible to ethics. Ethics, in its formal universalism, must tear away humanity's individuality, and so "in ethics *the I of man becomes the I of humanity*."[7] Ethics can approach the individual only as a member of humanity, disregarding the individuated self and thus maintaining its obligation to reject both sensuous reality, as well any individual concern or preferentialism, in its quest. In fact, as Cohen puts in a later chapter of *Religion of Reason*, the "dissolution of the individual is the highest triumph of ethics."[8] This ethical point of view, which Cohen characterizes as one of totality, approaches human beings as "He," but fails to do so as "Thou." The method of ethics, Cohen writes, "fails and must fail in regards to the new problem of the Thou."[9]

While Cohen elaborates these ideas in *Religion of Reason*, they clearly stem from his earlier ethical work, in particular the central claim of his *Ethik des Reinen Willens*, namely, that ethics is founded in jurisprudence.[10] Indeed, it is, for Cohen, jurisprudence rather than morality that is the organon of ethics.[11] Accordingly, the realm of law, which is the legal-political realm, is the beating heart of the ethical realm. And, to put it somewhat metaphorically, the state, which primordially functions as disperser of jurisprudential order, must enforce a justice that is blind. It must judge people without seeing them in their inner particularity.[12] Accordingly, while ethics addresses the legal person,[13] it has—Cohen argues in *Religion of Reason*—no regards for particular persons as individuals. Each individual, rather, represents to it "the same symbol of humanity."[14] A primordial and irreducible contribution of religion is therefore to be found in individuation, in the concept of the person not as universal, but as a particular self. Cohen points at the experience of sin as the heart of that particularity. Accordingly, "the discovery of man through *sin* is the source from which every religious development flows."[15]

It is only through the relation with God, who atones for our sin individually, that each person comes to be an individual. While judges, putting into practice the logic of ethics, can declare a person guilty according to the definition of the law, they cannot make pronouncement on the problem of guilt itself. It is religion that is concerned with a person's guilt, and so the problem of guilt therefore draws us to the borders of the ethical and the religious.[16] Indeed, the problem of guilt can only be addressed by religion because it is only in the religious sphere that guilt can be lifted, only in the religious sphere that sin can be atoned. For Cohen, it is Ezekiel who developed this insight; as opposed to the prophets of social morality, who join in the abstracted ethical task and who accordingly focus on social sins that can be atoned by social justice,[17] Ezekiel "establishes sin as the sin of the individual and in that he discovers in sin the individual."[18] This leads Cohen to suggest the individual, sin, and the sin of the individual are "first principles," which, just like the first principle of God we discussed in the previous chapter, find "the touchstone of their correctness in their fruitfulness."[19]

The consequence of sin as the first principle of individuation is that "the individual should unfold himself as I only through sin."[20] Consequently, the path of redemption, which like the messianic ideal is a continual task, is an individuated path. It seeks a reconciliation that "man has to achieve within himself" and that is finally resolved "in the redemption through God."[21] So all three first principles are joined in the process of atonement, by which sin before God leads to redemption before God, leading to the reconciliation of each person with him or herself, which lastly leads to reconciliation of the individuated self with God. Accordingly, the possibility of redemption from sin enables individuation, or in Cohen's words, the "*possibility of self-transformation makes the individual an I*."[22] This transformation is characterized by Cohen as "self-purification," on which atonement depends.[23] The importance of ethical renewal, which, as mentioned in the last chapter,[24] Cohen suggests as an interpretation of creation, comes here to the fore again. The continual task of self-purification and individuation requires the continuality of the possibility of ethical renewal.

The unique God, therefore, presents himself in correlation in an individuating intimacy and is as such conceived as far more than a mere ethical postulate. While Cohen himself admits he described God as the keystone of ethics in his *Ethik des Reinen Willens*, he clarifies in the *Religion of Reason* that these depictions were by no means exhaustive. The ethical meaning of God reflects the abstracted notion of humans characteristic of the ethical realm. In Cohen's words, "as man in ethics is merely an example of humanity, so God is only the guarantor of humanity."[25] The God of religion includes the role attributed to him by ethics. This role too is described in the Jewish sources through God's promise to Noah that humanity would, after the flood, be protected. The biblical revelation of the rainbow therefore accords with the role God played in *Ethik des Reinen Willens*, but in a merely ethical context it addresses human beings as symbols rather than as individuals. Only in religion does the critical covenant with Noah, which is symbolized by the rainbow and ensures the possibility of a messianic future, become a covenant "with the human soul."[26] The soul, Cohen later explains, was introduced by Ezekiel as "the expression for the person and for the individual."[27] So rather than a formal abstracted directive, religion anchors ethical ideas in the innermost core of the self, where they are unveiled through correlation and where they respond to our innermost concerns and aspirations in a way ethics in and of itself is incapable of.

While Cohen ascribes a unique role and value to the religious sphere as a distinct realm in human existence that relates to individuation and the correlation it enables, it does not lead the individual beyond ethics, as, for example, it does in Kierkegaard's thought. Indeed, while for Kierkegaard, Abraham is drawn beyond ethics to the religious realm, in which he must, as a knight of faith, act unethically if divinely ordered to do so,[28] Cohen's conception of the ethical and the religious is far less tense. The same ideals called for by the "scientific" ethical philosophy Cohen toiled over for years, are, as we saw in the previous chapter, called for by the human correlation with God. There is nothing in the religious realm that calls for the individual, who rises to that correlation through the individuating atonement of sin, to contradict principles that could have been drawn from ethics alone. Religion does indeed allow for individuation and does suggest the first principles that enable this individuation, but the ideals it calls the individual to seek are similar to those ethics is aimed at.

More importantly to us, by addressing the individual, religion is able to address the axiological problem Cohen's ethical system left unanswered. As mentioned in the introduction,[29] the ethical and axiological questions differ: they are, What ought to be done? and, What is worthwhile? respectively. We saw that Kant argued that while the sole unconditioned good is spontaneously recognized by reason to be goodwill, his axiological framework upheld a morally conditioned happiness as the most worthwhile object we could envision. In and of itself, that *summum bonum* does not delineate what is to be done, which is the task of ethics as propounded by reason, but it does reinforce our motivation to do that which reason and goodwill suggest. As such, it adds a crucial significance to the ethical; it ties it to our human concerns and motivations.

Kant was swiftly attacked,[30] and has been ever since,[31] by critics and commentators, including, as we have seen, Cohen himself, who felt that his argument that goodwill commands our dutiful respect autonomously and spontaneously was weakened by the seeming necessity of adding happiness to the system even if it must be posited as concurrent to our moral conduct. Indeed, even if Kant genuinely felt the spontaneous respect for duty, goodwill, and the categorical imperative were sufficient to command ethical action, he also makes explicit the realization that something would be lacking if his practical reason did not address our ultimate individual concerns and hopes. It is also understandable why addressing these most profound concerns and hopes leads Kant to his religious postulates: the religious realm adds an axiological backing to the more motivationally fragile spontaneous respect of goodwill. Kant himself might have sought to resist the thought that spontaneous and unconcerned respect for goodwill is not sufficiently anchored in human beings to function autonomously as the driving force of action, but his position on the issue seems at times to be rather ambiguous.

Cohen's mature position about the relation of ethics and religion directly addresses this concern. Ethics does provide the abstracted, nonpersonal, and formal answer to its own query. Furthermore, as discussed above, in Cohen's ethical thinking, God is present as the guarantor of the possibility of morality on earth. But in and of itself, this ethical God does not yet exhaust our axiological yearning, represented by the psalmist yearning for nearness to God. The purely ethical notion of God, who already ensures the possibility that moral realization could obtain, still remains an abstract and dangerously disinterested one if not enriched by the religious realm, within which human beings come to have an individuated relationship with God. The religious realm provides the principles that add to the ethical realm a layer of human meaning without which ethics remains a strictly formal system, one that brings about the "illusion that ethics deals only with law and rule, but never with human actuality."[32]

Furthermore, while Cohen had already set God as guarantor of the realization of ethics in his *Ethic of Pure Will*, in *Religion of Reason*, he suggests that ethics in and of itself must leave the question of our interest in the realization of its aims untreated. This empties ethics even further of its axiological significance; scientific ethics as presented in *Religion of Reason* provides an answer to the ethical realm but certainly does not in and of itself address the axiological one, which must concretely address our immediate human concerns, most crucially, our concrete, human aspiration for ethical goals to be actualized. Kant sought to remedy these problems and the potential lack of motivation they seem to cause by salvaging the motivational factor of happiness, albeit in a morally conditioned manner, and placing it at the apex of his axiological structure. Cohen, as we saw in the previous chapter, strongly criticized this aspect of Kant's moral thought. Having dismissed this Kantian attempt to provide a motivational aspect to the ethical, it is not surprising that Cohen eventually came to explicitly admit a significant lacuna in the ethical sphere and therefore sought to show how religion remedies it. Ethics does lead to the realization of a formally conceived kingdom of ends but lacks the actuality brought to us by our constitutive relation with our fellow humans and with God and the immediacy of the promise God brings to "messianic humanity," namely, that "morality will be established in the human world."[33] In making this promise, which is also a call to action, to the actual individual through the correlation enabled by atonement, religion functions on a plane the concreteness of which eludes the ethical. So ethics does indeed delineate what we ought to act towards, a kingdom of ends, but religion draws us there through the individuated call made by correlation and the hope it allows individuated selves in participating in the actual realization of our messianic *summum bonum*.[34]

The notion of a messianic future is therefore more suitable to Cohen than Kant's *summum bonum* because it is non-eudaemonistic, as opposed to Kant's morally conditioned happiness. Indeed, the messianic future is even more suitable than Kant's kingdom of ends because even if Cohen himself suggested the Kantian kingdom of ends would have been a more appropriate solution than Kant's relapse into eudaemonism, it is still approached merely ethically. As such, though structurally sound, the notion of the kingdom of ends is axiologically disconnected from the individual. Only by thinking of the kingdom of ends as the messianic future promised by the same God that individuates us through His atoning relation to us do we delineate a *summum bonum* that is not only non-eudaemonistic but that also concerns us most intimately and is, furthermore, not merely possible but rather will eventually come to be. It furthermore rises from a realm we are drawn to as individuals; it reflects a nearness to God, a correlation, to which we are called to respond not merely as reasonable beings, but as human individuals.

Religion, therefore, in its approach to human beings, is more encompassing, more direct, more concrete, and therefore more compelling in terms of actual actions than ethics could hope to be on its own. It offers the necessary axiological element, which addresses our individual human motivations and hopes. It furthermore furnishes the actualization, both in terms of God's relation with the individual as well as his promise to messianic humanity, without which ethical thinking would remain an abstract methodology rather than a profoundly personal and intimate call to action. That call to action is for a future that, according to monotheism, God not merely promised Noah would always remain potentially actualizable in a world the destruction of which their covenant made impossible,[35] but one that we will indeed eventually rise to. While both religion and ethics point at the same future, and while systematic ethics is philosophically indispensable, religion provides an absolutely necessary contribution to Cohen's system; it calls the concrete individual to a task it ensures will eventually succeed. Ethics might be worthwhile in and of itself, but it is only within the religious framework that it becomes most concretely worthwhile to the individual.

There is, therefore, at least according to Cohen's mature view as developed in his *Begriff der Religion* and his *Religion of Reason*, a profound intertwining of the religious and the ethical. Both spheres share common ideals, but while ethics expounds them formally, addressing an abstracted human being, religion calls them from within an individuated correlation, providing for an ideal that functions as highest good because it concerns our innermost selves as well as because it is conceived as promised by God. The profound intertwining of ethics and religion also suggests a position that has up to now only been taken tacitly concerning the relation between Cohen's religious and philosophical writings. Indeed, it takes us back to the debate about whether Cohen's late religious work reflects a dramatic shift with his previous, systematic writings and the perennial question commentators have raised about Cohen almost ever since the publication of his *Religion of Reason*, namely, how his later religious and Jewish writings relate to his earlier critical work. Rosenzweig influentially claimed a radical shift in Cohen's later work, arguing that by introducing "the foundational concept [Grundbegriff]" of correlation, Cohen "secured religion's particular form" and went beyond his nineteenth-century philosophical milieu towards and "into the terrain of the philosophical future."[36] Yet, while Rosenzweig arguably had a vested philosophical interest in presenting the late Cohen as a *baal t'shuvah* and enlisting him for his own philosophical and religious agenda, even he cautiously warns that Cohen would not have allowed "this new content to dislodge the supporting pillars of the system."[37] Therefore, Cohen, according to Rosenzweig, might in some significant sense have gone beyond his system without necessarily contradicting it. What was clear to him, however, was that Cohen's late philosophy had ruptured the "charmed circle of idealism" because "he believed in God and [because] his inherited Judaism had become the dominant force in his life."[38]

The notion of some sort of a break was adopted by later commentators as well, such as Bergman, who sees a "radical change" in Cohen's attitude towards Judaism as well as in his general later philosophical orientation.[39] Contrarily, Altmann argues directly against Rosenzweig's account, claiming that though Cohen did indeed work on a new concept of religion,[40] the notion of correlation on which it is based does not contravene his previous philosophy and is in fact "basically a concept of logic,"[41] a "fundamental scientific form of thought."[42] Altmann therefore concludes not only that Cohen sticks to the basic position of his idealism but, even more, that he "toils with all his energy to develop the 'systematic concept of religion.'"[43] Other scholarly contributions to the question of the continuity or break in Cohen's thought seek to overcome a binary position. So, for example, Zank argues, on the one hand, that Rosenzweig might very well have justifiably found in Cohen's late religious work "the very problem which he and others had discovered for themselves as the most burning philosophical issue of the time," namely, the "constitution of concrete subjectivity," and that, furthermore, Cohen sought a solution in the same direction Rosenzweig would, namely, "in the I and Thou of God and Human being."[44] On the other hand, given that Rosenzweig was rather ignorant of Cohen's systematic thought and shaped his views about his late development without even having read the works in question,[45] it is more an implicit statement of Rosenzweig's own philosophical position than an accurate study of Cohen's thought.[46] Zank's own take is that while it might be the case, as Altmann argued, that Cohen's philosophy of religion does break with his system, the tensions that do surface were already present in his systematic thought.[47]

Weiss, who offers a clear and succinct overview of this scholarly debate,[48] also suggests a nonbinary reading. Weiss's interpretation, however, is nonbinary not because it seeks to resolve the tension between the systematic and religious aspects of Cohen's thought. To the contrary, focusing on *Religion of Reason*, Weiss maintains that Cohen's thought "contains features both of a Rosenzweigian break with the system, and of an Altmannian non-break."[49] This, Weiss argues, is not because Cohen is undecidedly torn between his universal system and his Jewish attachments, but rather because in *Religion of Reason* he sought to engage with religious ideas that cannot but be communicated indirectly. The sense of theoretical incoherence hovering over *Religion of Reason* is therefore an unavoidable effects of Cohen's attempt at communicating religious ideas that "require a nonstandard style that presents multiple 'voices' simultaneously, without seeking to reduce them to a theoretical unity."[50]

My axiological analysis aligns itself with nonbinary readings because it shows that while the continuity is significant, there are some significant shifts as well. In terms of continuity, we saw, for example, that the very same anti-eudaemonistic impulse leads both Cohen's earliest work on Kant and his mature ethical thinking and his last works on religion and Judaism. We saw too that the ideals his *Begriff der Religion* and his *Religion of Reason* uphold are not in themselves different than those suggested by his previous work. In this context, as Kluback points out,[51] it is significant to note that in the new preface to the third edition of his *Kants Theorie der Erfahrung*, written shortly before his death, Cohen still maintains the indelible contribution that Kant's philosophy will play in bringing true peace to humanity.[52] There certainly, therefore, is no late disavowal of Kantian ethics at play in Cohen's later religious thought.

The critical addition of his later work, however, is the fundamental contribution religion makes in relating formal ethical structures to the most profound yearnings of the human soul. This aspect of Cohen's writing is indeed a break from the past. There was, therefore, between his *Ethik des Reinen Willens* and his *Begriff der Religion* and *Religion of Reason* a significant shift in exactly the subject of our current discussion, namely, the role and value of religion. In *Ethik des Reinen Willens*, God is subsumed under the ethical, while, as we already saw above, Cohen explains in his *Religion of Reason* that the ethical notion of God his previous work had upheld could not be exhaustive. Indeed, to quote from *Begriff der Religion*, "the God of Religion enriches Ethics, without which it would remain incomplete."[53] The realization of the necessity of religion in order to complete ethics is at the heart of his later religious development.[54]

In the chapters he added to the 1910 edition of *Kants Begrundung der Ethik*, Cohen still very much lauds his own work for having maintained the priority and independence of ethics and criticizes Kant for taking a position that Cohen himself, in his last works, would adopt.[55] Indeed, while methodologically ethics cannot be concerned with the accomplishment of its aims but must act solely from the formal soundness of its own principles, the "disturbing thought" of the reality of the realm of ends still moved Kant. Religion, which is unencumbered by the methodological strictness characteristic of ethics, addresses this concern by anticipating the realm of God in this world.[56] Kant ends up, therefore, Cohen plaintively argues in 1910, transferring human duty from the realm of ethics to that of religion, and this compels Kant to "place the kingdom of God, as the religious state of men, higher than the realm of ends, which means only the moral state of men."[57] At that stage of his thinking, Cohen suggests this is a problematic stance that threatens the independence of the ethical. If human morality, pure methodological ethics, has to acquire this kind of validity from religion, he suggests, it degenerates into heteronomy. Kant, Cohen writes, is here carried away by his idealizing interpretation of Christianity, clashing not only with the fundamental principles of his ethics, but also, in so far as he makes the Christian faith, even if ethically interpreted, in its historical form, into a general human duty.[58]

Cohen finds this turn in Kant's thought to reflect a deep, lingering influence of the pietism of his education. In spite of all ethical autonomy, "religion still remains to him the deepest interior of man, the primordial source of personality and individual moral strength and sentiment." Ethics, as philosophy, is but a "theoretical force," as opposed to the "primal power" that is religion, even if it must be guided by ethics.[59] Cohen suggests his own *Ethik des Reinen Willens* is here methodologically advantageous in so far as it has "integrated the idea of God into the doctrine of ethics, in order to secure the progress of morality in the history of the human race." This, Cohen argues, both undermines skepticism and relieves religion of the primary right to this idea of progress in so far as that progress is linked to the condition "that ethical knowledge be attained, as knowledge, in all normal members of the cultural world."[60] To this end, religion can participate, but it must be guided, whether voluntarily or not, by ethics. So in 1910, Cohen still agreed with his prior position held in *Ethik des Reinen Willens*, which posits religion as a means to advance morality. Indeed, as he had put it very explicitly in his *Ethik*; "religion must be used as a means to prepare for the transmission of Ethics in general culture."[61]

In so far as there is a significant shift in Cohen's thought with regard to religion, it is precisely on this point. Evidently, he still believed when writing the above-quoted passages added to the 1910 edition of *Kants Begründung der Ethik* that the ideal of God had to be interwoven with ethics in order to strike a better balance between the value of religion and the independence of ethics than Kant had. Yet, as we saw above, by the time he wrote his *Begriff der Religion* (1915), and of course *Religion of Reason* as well, it very much seems Cohen had grown far closer to the position he had previously criticized in Kant, one that thinks of religion as the most profoundly individual and compelling sphere of human life and that therefore, in the final analysis, had to be prioritized. Indeed, as we shall see below, he explicitly relates this prioritization to the very same problem of historical actualizing that Cohen claimed had moved Kant to his position.

This suggests the greater weight Cohen attributed to religion occurred sometime after 1910. It is, in this context, relevant to note that Cohen retired from his academic position in Marburg in 1912, moving to Berlin, where he began teaching at the Lehranstalt für die Wissenschaft des Judentums and focused mainly on religious and Jewish writings.[62] It is also the period in which he visited Poland and Russia, where his encounters with Eastern European Jewish communities left a lasting impression.[63] It is only natural that in these years, the elder Jewish thinker reengaged with his faith in ways more explicit and comprehensive than he had done as a professor of Kantian philosophy. This could not but be a fruitful intellectual ground for the significance of Judaism, and of religion in general, to grow in.

Another significant impetus for this late reevaluation of the significance of religion beyond ethics was provided by the theologian Wilhelm Herrmann, who was a colleague of Cohen's at Marburg and criticized his *Ethik* for lacking a sufficiently developed treatment of the actual importance religion has in human experience.[64] Cohen, who acknowledges Herrmann's critique in the preface to the second edition of his *Ethik*, as well as repeatedly in his *Begriff Der Religion*,[65] clearly came to accept Herrmann's point and sought to address it comprehensively in his later religious writings. Indeed, there is much similarity in the ideas Herrmann himself discusses and those Cohen inserted in his own religious thought, primarily perhaps the profound and constitutive significance of religion for the individual.[66] While probably less comprehensively influential than his increasing concern with Judaism, Hermann's criticism must have had some impact on Cohen's later prioritization of religion.

So while there is continuity in various streams of thought (anti-eudaemonism, the ideal nature of the highest good, etc.), there is in Cohen's later work a realization of the priority of the religious realm, the insight religion can be neither reduced to, nor superseded by, ethics, and accordingly an increased awareness that the religious form does not allow itself to be subsumed in the philosophical one. Religion, however, never divorces ethics. As Cohen puts it in his *Begriff der Religion*, ethics remains a "precondition" of religion, "from whose direction it cannot deviate." Religion does not gain, therefore, a full conceptual independence; it gains, rather, a "distinctness [Eigenart]."[67]

The distinctness of religion was not only a conceptual shift but also one that would lead to significant stylistic changes. Indeed, Cohen's *Religion of Reason* as well as several of his Jewish writings, in so far as they are works of religious rather than purely philosophical ethical thinking, could not but break from the approach and form of previous philosophical work. These writings, after all, are engaged in a distinct conceptual space; they deal directly with "the peculiar spiritual form of religion, for which any theoretical attitude is only preparatory."[68] In his study of *Religion of Reason*, Weiss has accordingly argued that Cohen uses forms of indirect communication that characterize the work of those seeking to communicate the "paradoxical nature of religious concepts."[69] This does not mean these religious contents contradict Cohen's ethical thinking but rather that there are aspects of religious thought that cannot be expounded within what Cohen would have thought of as a "scientific" methodology. While ethics does not bear paradoxes, a religion based on an individuating relation to a God whose primordial characteristic is complete difference cannot but be expressed in a multiplicity of voices that together can make explicit what a direct singular voice cannot. Weiss therefore claims that in *Religion of Reason*, Cohen expresses himself both in a philosophical discourse and a uniquely religious style in seeking to express the paradoxical contents philosophy in and of itself cannot treat systematically.

In fact, a paradoxical religious concept is embedded in what we have delineated above as well as in the last chapter as Cohen's *summum bonum*. We characterized Cohen's axiology as essentially future oriented and saw how he thinks of the infinite task towards an ideal as an antidote to the eudaemonistic aspirations that are empirically actualized. Indeed, we saw that precisely in virtue of being located in the future at the end of an infinite task, the messianic future gains the ideal, non-sensible quality Cohen lauded. This would suggest the infinite religious task must remain unaccomplished for it to function as proper *summum bonum*. To remain systematic, Cohen would therefore have to oppose the very possibility of its realization. And yet, as we have seen above, Cohen insists that, as opposed to the ethical ideal, the religious one must be conceived of as one that will be actualized.

This problem, it seems to me, is solved by a religious cutting of what would appear to be a paradoxical Gordian knot.[70] The axiological import is expressed both through the individual heeding the call of correlation for the infinite task towards an ideal, non-eudaemonistic, and non-sensuous future but also in that said import promises the highest value this correlation calls for, messianic humanity, will become actual: "God can assign no task that would be a labor of Sisyphus."[71] While the methodological rigor of ethics demands that it "maintains the separation of actuality from the ideal,"[72] religion establishes its worth by refusing this equation. Cohen expresses this idea in a few compelling lines worth quoting in full:

> Morality will be established in the human world. Against this confidence, no skepticism, no pessimism, no mysticism, no metaphysics, no experience of the world, no knowledge of men, no tragedy, and no comedy can prevail. The distinction between ideal and actuality must not be transferred to the realm of the shadows and receive this kind of eternalization; it will be buried by the Messiah. The virtue of men will still have to tread new ways of unsuspected steepness, but a level of morality will be attained, which will secure the course of human morality.[73]

While the infinite moral task will still have to be pursued in the messianic age, the messianic task itself will eventually come to a concrete historical actualization. In this revealing passage, Cohen establishes the reality of the divine promise as transcending even the possibility of a philosophical counter argument. This extraordinary moment in his thought is one in which the religious seems to supersede the philosophical. In doing so, it opens the way for a *summum bonum* that, while ideal, will nonetheless be realized.

Kierkegaard's *Fear and Trembling* offers an insightful comparison on this point. Indeed, for Kierkegaard too, faith eventually trumps non-contradiction. The knight of faith both fully resigns that to which he had previously committed his whole being while at the very same time remaining absolutely certain God will uphold its actualization; Abraham both completely resigns Isaac while remaining faithful God will keep His promise.[74] The messianic age must be an ideal not yet actualized, and yet it will be actualized. Unlike Kierkegaard's paradox, however, which takes the knight of faith beyond the ethical, Cohen explicitly states in the quote above that the ethical task will still have to be pursued continually even in the messianic age. Yet, while the ethical task will remain infinite, God will not allow a Sisyphean quest for the messianic age itself; it will be actualized in human history.

Finally, the discussion above enables us to formulate Cohen's axiological position in terms of spheres of valuation, as we did with Mendelssohn. Given our analysis in the previous chapter, as well as in this one, it is obvious that anything relating to material, sensuous well-being is relegated not merely to a lower rung, but to a negative one. Furthermore, anything relating to eudaemonism, even if a morally conditioned as with Kant or highly intellectualized as with Aristotle, is similarly dismissed. While for Mendelssohn, the religious-eudaemonistic sphere reigns supreme and provided value to both the religious and ethical spheres, for Cohen the religious sphere is supreme and is entangled with ethics rather than eternal felicity. Indeed, the religious sphere cannot be fully construed as independent from the ethical one, but, as we saw above, it gains a distinctiveness. Yet, in so far as it is distinct, it also gains a certain axiological priority; after all, all first principles Cohen suggests, namely, God, sin, and atonement, as well as correlation and the highest good of the messianic ideal, are eminently religious concepts.

Having discussed the distinctly religious import of Cohen's philosophy, which has enabled an apprehension of the unique value of religion, as well as a wider look at Cohen's axiology in general, we shall now move on to inquire into the value of the Jewish religion specifically.

THE UNIQUE VALUE OF JUDAISM

The particular input of religion, though expounded in Cohen's position as described above through the Jewish sources, does not belong exclusively to these sources, but rather to what Cohen thinks of as the religion of reason, which has been, he thought, primarily, though at least prima facie not necessarily exclusively, manifested in the Jewish sources. In order to better delineate the particular importance of Judaism, therefore, we will here briefly describe how Cohen thought it relates to the religion of reason before focusing on the characteristics of the sources of Judaism and of Jewish history, which makes Judaism particularly important as a proponent of the messianic highest good.

Cohen opens his *Religion of Reason* by lamenting attempts at grasping the concept of religion inductively. The wide variety of phenomena commonly termed religious would make it impossible, Cohen thinks, to inductively reach a common concept of religion. Instead of starting with a vague notion, religion needs first to be anticipated as a "prototype [Vorbild]" or "model [Vorzeichnung]" in a way similar to embryology,[75] where one starts from the completed concept of the organism and then reconstructs its development. Reason, the "source" and "organ of concepts,"[76] is the means by which a concept of religion must be created that is "independent of the descriptions supplied by the history of religion."[77] Seeking to delineate such a concept, Cohen then moves on to the particular import of religion to the concept of human beings, which, as we saw above, lies in the individuation it, as opposed to ethics, is capable of.

We again find here a methodology echoing Cohen's enthusiasm for the Platonic hypothesis. Reason suggests a concept, which, like a hypothesis, is then evaluated in terms of systematic and existential strength. A similar approach is suggested by Cohen for the notion of Judaism. Cohen writes, in a passage that is absolutely fundamental to his approach to Judaism, that "it is impossible to develop a unifying concept of Judaism out of the literary sources unless the concept of Judaism itself is anticipated as an ideal project, in a manner methodologically analogous to the study of the organism."[78] Cohen further writes that while history is "the factor in virtue of which the actuality of Judaism comes to its realization," this factor does not possess "the value of a criterion, a value possessed only by the concept."[79] As Cohen argues that the ideal project of Judaism is messianic humanity, he consistently relies on that concept to delineate that which in the Jewish sources belongs to Judaism and that which is foreign to it. Universal Messianism is, in other words, the criterion of Cohen's Judaism. Accordingly, the entire Jewish history must be interpreted as guiding towards this messianic goal[80]; as Cohen pointedly puts it, "Without the hope for messianic mankind there is for us no Judaism."[81]

Universalism must of course profoundly relate to the religion of reason, as reason is universally shared by all people. "Universality," Cohen writes, "becomes the fundamental condition for the religion of reason." Accordingly, the religion of reason, as a "*general function of human consciousness*," unfolds itself in a wide variety of ways and "cannot be exhausted by any particular people's consciousness."[82] This, it is critical to emphasize, is just as true with regards to Judaism, and Cohen emphatically states that "it would have been an irreparable mistake in our arrangement if we were to limit and confine the religion of reason to the Jewish religion." However, crucially, he does believe that relying on the concept of *source*, Judaism could have a particular significance. Indeed, Judaism, conceived of as an "*original source* [*Urquelle*]" feeds further sources, which then could just as well instantiate the religion of reason. In so far as Judaism is the original source, however, it does have an "undeniable spiritual and psychological advantage."[83] So while all monotheistic religions have a share in the religion of reason, "in regard to *primary origin* [Ursprünglichkeit] this share cannot be compared with that of Judaism."[84] This primary origin, Cohen further states, "is the distinctive mark of creative reason, which makes itself independent of all other charms of consciousness, and which produces a pure pattern."[85]

So Judaism is to Cohen, to quote Poma, a "conceptual idealization,"[86] which Cohen constructs out of its historical sources, but also through which, in a dialectic peculiar to his hermeneutical methodology, the sources are to be interpreted. This notion of Judaism is centered on the universal, messianic future it seeks to uphold, which, in spite of the specificity of the historical circumstances in which it arose, makes its concern universal rather than particular. Furthermore, as Judaism was the originative impulse of the religion of reason in history, it preserves a priority through the purity Cohen suggests this primacy involves, a primacy that makes it the vital foundation of our ethical conceptions. Indeed, based as it is on the idea of the unique God, as the keystone of both ethics and the religion that calls us to the messianic future, Judaism professes fundamental principles that "are the deepest roots of the moral culture, roots that have not withered and that must not wither if the progress of culture is to continue linearly."[87] There can be no ethics without the idea of the one God, and as such, Judaism, Cohen believes, must have a fundamental share in human culture.

So it is not merely the case that the religion of reason, for Cohen, can be recognized in the sources of Judaism; it actually historically stems from these sources and remains profoundly related to them and to their ongoing history and development. We emphasized above how important the historical actualization of the messianic ideal is for Cohen's demarcation of religion's importance. Accordingly, the actualization of religious ideals through Jewish history gains a critical importance as well.[88]

We, therefore, need to now explore how lofty divine ideals come to be actualized in human history through Judaism. Indeed, Jewish history, Cohen writes, "is but an exposition [Darstellung] of the basic essence of our religion." That essence, of course, is the concept of the unique God through which the prophets arrived at the notion of one humanity, the unification of which is the ultimate task of Judaism. It is only this task, Cohen repeatedly suggests, that "justifies and explains" the continued existence of the Jewish people.[89]

As the world-historical messianic task is the reason for the continuation of the distinct Jewish existence in history, Cohen repeatedly points out that only with the beginning of the exile did Judaism genuinely begin to fulfill its worldly destiny. "The unique God," Cohen writes, "has taken our fatherland from us in order to give it back to us in humanity."[90] The religious insights that eventually developed into the messianic task might originally have been established in a state, but it was only through their dispersion among foreign states that these insights could begin to bear their fruit. So, already the split of the ancient Hebrew sovereignty into two kingdoms is to be regarded as "a prelude to the world history of Judaism," signifying that "David's realm is not the proper soul for the world of monotheism."[91] Later on, the prophets understood they lost their fatherland in order for humanity to become their fatherland,[92] and so the destruction of the Jewish state is perceived by Cohen as a "prime example of the theodicy of history."[93] Given that the essential task of Judaism necessarily brought the Jews towards a wide variety of nations, the dispersion of the Jewish people has "long ceased to be exile to us."[94] It is in fact the most profound historical expression of Jewish nearness to God as it is a fundamental aspect of fulfilling the messianic task correlation draws us towards.

The stateless, distinct Jewish nationality is therefore critical to the eventual messianic unification of humanity. The following passage summarizes these notions eloquently:

> For the furtherance of monotheism we must remain a national individuality, because monotheism has stamped upon us an historical

> singularity. And since this national existence is not inhibited by a state of one's own, it is protected against the fate of a materialization of its nationalistic idea. The national peculiarity in its stateless isolation is the symbol for the unity of the confederation of mankind, as the ultimate value of world history. It is the unity of mankind in monotheism and in the morality founded upon it.[95]

The means by which Judaism is to fulfill its task is Jews furthering within the state in which they live the critical idea of monotheism under which humanity can hope to find its eventual peaceful and morally ordained future. This is why Judaism can be a nationality but not a nation. Indeed, the nation is for Cohen identified with the concept of the state.[96] As such, the nation can involve differing nationalities. And Judaism, as a distinct nationality within the nations, is to further in each the eventual peaceful confederation of all states. Accordingly, Zionism is not only, as we saw earlier, eudaemonistically tainted but is also a negation of the genuine world-historical task Jews are called to uphold. It seeks to isolate Jews as a distinct nation rather than enabling the Jewish people to fulfill their messianic task as a nationality within the nations. The future world, wherein a united humanity lives in harmonious correlation with the unique God rather than a particular state of their own, must be the sole true homeland of the Jewish people.[97]

In fact, the world-historical mission of Judaism and the non-eudaemonistic nature that confirms its moral purity correlate in the notion of suffering that gradually gained critical importance for Cohen. The suffering of the Jewish people is presented as the birth pangs of the messianic era. Indeed, the symbolic messianic figure becomes the "ideal image of the man of the future, the image of mankind, as the unity of all peoples" by virtue of his taking the earthly suffering of human beings upon his shoulders, a representation that wards off any illusion of eudaemonism.[98] This messianic suffering is for Cohen the tragic fate of the Jewish people, who suffer vicariously for "the faults and wrongs which still hinder the realization of monotheism."[99] Ultimately, Cohen adds, just as the person of the Messiah was conceived to be the people of Israel itself, so the people of Israel itself must ultimately be idealized to include all of God's servants.[100]

The ultimate morality of Jewish perseverance in history is, therefore, reflected in its knowing martyrdom for the sake of messianic humanity. Israel, as God's servant, is the "sacrificial victim who exposes himself to suffering because of his knowledge of the irreplaceable value of this suffering for the historical welfare of mankind."[101] Chosenness, "Israel's calling to make of the one God the redeemer of mankind," is accordingly far from some kind of eudaemonistically tainted privilege or arrogant self-serving characterization. It is accompanied throughout by the awareness of the necessary loss the Jewish people have had to suffer and the ensuing continuing suffering they have to go through in order to promote the highest good. Cohen, accordingly, identifies as a "basic motif [Grundmotiv]" of Jewish existence a "lament about the inner necessity of our wandering."[102] There is therefore nothing more fundamentally moral than the deeply non-eudaemonistic task of the stateless Jewish people, whom Cohen characterizes as "the historic people of suffering, of suffering for its unique God."[103] This tragic suffering, Cohen further writes, has "the final good as its end, and therefore despises all transitory, eudaemonistic prosperity."[104]

Ultimately, as the election of "the national consciousness was to be substituted for the religious calling," the election of Israel presaged its eventual universalistic fate, namely, its "*elevation into one mankind*."[105] Indeed, from the messianic perspective, Cohen therefore describes Israel's election as an "anomaly" that is resolved in the messianic future.[106]

The unique value of Judaism is therefore directly related to the highest value of a united messianic humanity. Because it carries monotheism in its purest and most primordial form, it must maintain its distinctness in order to protect the purity of its message. In so far as Judaism remains distinct, it does so not out of a eudaemonistic self-interest, but rather out of a profound concern for the messianic era it is committed to in spite of the suffering it continues to face.

Within and Without Messianic Humanity

The scope of Cohen's messianic ideal is, in terms of its applicability, wholly universal. Indeed, the messianic idea, Cohen writes, "signifies the consolation, the confidence and the assurance that not merely the chosen people, but all peoples altogether will at one time live in harmony."[107] Cohen emphasizes the profoundly revolutionary nature of this aspect of the ancient prophetic ideal, in particular in light of the fact it emerged at a time when narrow tribalism and nationalism were the rule.[108] Accordingly, the rise of the concept of humanity that monotheism introduced,[109] and the universal concern with every person it enabled, is characterized by Cohen as a "historical miracle [historische Wunder]."[110] The prophets were engaged in a continual polemic against nationalism, which "in its arrogant shape is the most offensive antithesis to Messianism."[111] Indeed, the prophets were in fact so distant from such kinds of nationalism that even the enemies of Israel were explicitly included in the messianic unification of all of humanity.[112] Accordingly, Isaiah's universalism, Cohen writes, is simply unequalled in all religious or secular world literature.[113]

The prophets were able to conceptualize a meta-national good because, overcoming the narrow, eudaemonistic concerns for their own present national well-being, they saw the future as the locus of the ultimate religious good: "Messianism degrades and despises and destroys the present actuality," emphasizing instead the supersensible actuality of the future.[114] Cohen believed, as explained in the previous chapter, that this revolutionary universalistic conception of the future ensues from the monotheistic God idea.

We shall begin by analyzing some of the fundamental concepts Cohen locates in the Jewish sources, which apply and reflect the universal concept of the human being described above and ensure the universal nature of Jewish morality. We shall then examine how the universal ideals Cohen identifies in Judaism are promoted and developed by non-Jewish sources. We will then move on to a section dedicated to analyzing how in spite of this seeming absolute universalism, or rather because of certain structural elements inherent to it, Cohen ends up suggesting ideas and thoughts that are far from universally tolerant, before concluding this chapter with some reflections on the nature of Cohen's revaluated Judaism.

UNIVERSAL JEWISH MORALITY

Cohen argues that the innovative universal scope of the morality prophetic Judaism reflects goes beyond anything even Plato, in spite of his lauded idealism, was able to muster. Plato's concept of the philosopher king as the highest political good insinuates the perpetuity of the sharp division between those ruled and their rulers, a notion based on a faulty idea of human beings that unjustifiably denies some the ability to partake in moral reason. This, Cohen writes, explains the "practical advantage" of prophecy over Platonism, as the prophets did not thusly discriminate against some human beings.[115] The prophets seek to advance genuinely social, anti-aristocratic politics, and display, accordingly, an "every one, or no one" ethos,[116] which seeks to include every single person in the messianic future they call for.

Cohen takes this comprehensive concept of humanity to be intrinsically related to God. We saw in the previous chapter how he related unified humanity to the unique God. Similarly, the notion of the one unique God entails the equality of all people God created.[117] All people are God's children and are therefore siblings. This remains the case if they do not recognize their common father. As Cohen eloquently puts it, "God is their father, even if they do not want to be his children."[118] So monotheism brings forth not only a concept of a unique God, but with it a concept of humanity that includes all people and naturally leads to a universal morality.

The universal moral concern for both Jews and gentiles is reflected in the notion of "love of neighbor [Nächstenliebe]," which Cohen declares to be the "basic form of monotheistic morality."[119] To Cohen's great frustration, the notion of "love of neighbor" was radically misunderstood by his contemporaries, and he describes the task of correcting the rampant misunderstanding of the Hebrew *rea* as Sisyphean.[120] Indeed, even well-intentioned figures, such as the "venerable" Delitzsch, whose efforts to defend the Talmud from slander Cohen gratefully recognizes, conceived of the Hebrew *rea* as merely referring to members of the same people (*Volksgenosse*).[121] This would of course radically subvert the universal meaning Cohen wants to attribute to the Levitical injunction to "love your neighbor as yourself,"[122] and it would more generally depict Jewish ethics, centered on a narrow delineation of the scope of *rea*, as exclusivist and particularistic. There can be no question for Cohen that *rea* means "fellowman."[123] He relates, in this context, Leviticus 19:18 to later verses in the chapter, namely Leviticus 19:33 and 19:34, that is, "When an alien resides with you in your land, you shall not oppress the alien. The alien who resides with you shall be to you as the citizen among you; you shall love the alien as yourself, for you were aliens in the land of Egypt: I am the Lord your God." This injunction to love foreigners, echoing the call to love the *rea* of a few verses earlier, ensures any misunderstanding of *rea* as relating solely to other Jews must be corrected.[124]

The repeated references to foreigners and the demand to love the other as one would love oneself are for Cohen characteristic of Jewish monotheism, and the biblical demand to love the foreigner is a crucial development in the concept of fellow humans as *rea*.[125] Indeed, it is specifically with regards to foreigners that the commandment to love human beings arose.[126] As this command must, for Cohen, become the "absolute commandment of religion,"[127] there can be no doubting the centrality he thought the notion of the foreigner carries in Jewish religion. Cohen, furthermore, believed it gained its full moral gravitas when developed through the notion of the Noachide. Indeed, Cohen argues that the biblical notion of "foreigner," that is, *ger*, was formalized in the Talmud as the "Noachide."

The Noachide, while not a believer, remains a citizen.[128] The Jewish sources therefore demand of the state, which Cohen saw as an essentially ethical concept, that it realize the stranger's fundamental equality. The institution of the Noachide, Cohen writes, relies on a separation of state and faith, enabling a conception according to which though not faithful, the Noachide is recognized as an equal, and more importantly, as a person in the moral sense [*Sittliche Person*].[129] Indeed, it is not the case that the stranger, approached through the legal category of the Noachide, enjoys civil or political tolerance but rather that, recognized as person in the moral sense, he is equivalent to the Jew. The Mosaic law is, accordingly, in all moral and legal stipulations as valid for the Jew as it is for the Noachide gentile.[130]

The legal formalization of the Noachide is particularly important because it shows the ethical purity of the concept. Indeed, echoing the Kantian demand that moral purity cannot relate to mere inclination and anticipating his own position in the *Ethik des Reinen Willens* that law and the legal science are the factum of ethics,[131] Cohen argues that by legally formalizing the notion of the Noachide, the Jewish religion ensured the ethical soundness of the concept. This, as Hollander explains, reflects again the philological point that *rea* cannot be a matter of "degrees of otherness."[132] Love dependent on nearness would involve loving an expansion of the self rather than loving the other. Accordingly, while in his *Ethik des Reinen Willens*, Cohen lauds patriotism as a dulling of the egotism of the individual, he warns that it too can be a mere expansion of the self.[133] The notion of the Noachide, as a legally entrenched concept of the other, avoids the pitfall of reducing love of others to a particularistic phenomenon dependent on one's personal contact with strangers.[134] Indeed, given that jurisprudence forms the basis of ethics, depicting the neighbor as a legal concept establishes its ethical, and as such universalistic, credentials.

The concept of the Noachide shows not merely that the ethics reflected by the Jewish sources are not narrowly particularistic but in fact that with them a true, universal ethics emerged. The Noachide laws are accordingly also at the heart of Cohen's critique of Spinoza's interpretation of the Mosaic constitution. While Spinoza interpreted the Mosaic law as merely particularly applicable to a certain state and therefore not properly religious in so far as it lacks a universal applicability, Cohen argues that the concept of the Noahide shows Spinoza to have been fundamentally mistaken. Indeed, given that Cohen argued that the Noahide was a citizen even if not a believer, this already counters Spinoza's characterization of the ancient Hebrew state as a narrowly theocratic one. Cohen takes the Noahide to be the concept of an "*adherent of natural religion*," and as such corrective to the notion that revelation came to the Israelites alone. Indeed, it indicates that God revealed himself to Noah before Sinai, meaning that religion was endowed to all nations rather than merely the Hebrew one, which in turn testifies to an "unambiguous universal humanism."[135] Elsewhere, Cohen relates the religious equality of the Noahide to the lack of enthusiasm for proselytism in Judaism; given that the son of Noah precedes the son of Abraham, and as the pious among the people of the world gain full access to religious salvation, conversion is perceived as completely unnecessary.[136]

Cohen further accuses Spinoza of intentionally misreading the passage in Maimonides, which, as we saw in chapter 3, Mendelssohn also grappled with. Cohen argues Spinoza knowingly made use of an incorrect variant reading and ignored the fact Maimonides addresses the question of the Noachide in two further passages wherein he unconditionally attributed blessedness to the Noachide; Cohen further argues that in the passage Spinoza does quote, Maimonides's qualification might be related to the differentiation between the theoretical concept of the Noahide and the political concept of the "*resident sojourner*."[137]

Even so, the central notion of the Noahide cannot be put into doubt by a single late authority, even one as central as Maimonides.

Accordingly, Spinoza's neglect of the centrality of the Noahide in rabbinic literature, as well as of the other passages in Maimonides, in spite of his rabbinic erudition is for Cohen a "psychological enigma,"[138] allowing us to "peer into his soul,"[139] presumably catching a glimpse of what Cohen refers to later on as "the demonic aspect of Spinoza's character."[140] In suppressing the Noahide, Spinoza willfully sought to defame Judaism, obliterating this "astonishing manifestation of the universal idea of natural religion, in the form of the fundamental idea of Jewish monotheism."[141]

Finally, in *Religion of Reason*, Cohen further establishes the primordial centrality of the fellowman by suggesting the central notion of his religious philosophy, correlation, is dependent on approaching the other as fellowman. We remember that ethics, in and of itself, does not address the individuated self and, similarly, that it addresses the other with the neutral objectivity of the He.[142] It is religion that addresses the question of the I, and accordingly it also addresses the question of the Thou. Cohen suggests a theodicy of suffering, namely, that suffering (*Leiden*) is for the sake of compassion (*Mitleid*).[143] Through the suffering of the other, which we cannot ignore, compassion arises and the Thou in humanity is discovered. And it is through discovering the suffering of the Thou that I examine my own suffering and locate, beside the suffering of the body, the suffering engendered by my own moral frailty.[144] This moral frailty is related by Cohen to sin, the redemption from which enables the emergence of the individuated self. This is why the correlation of human beings and God "is in the first place that of man, as fellowman, to God."[145] So the correlation of God and humans, upon which Cohen's notion of religion in general and Judaism in particular rests, is dependent on the discovery, through suffering and compassion, of the fellowman. Accordingly, Cohen characterizes "the epitome of all religion and the ultimate test of the doctrine of God" as the love of the other; it is by loving the other that one shows one loves God.[146]

So we see that for Cohen, the love for the other, for the fellowman, and the realization of the stranger as the Noahide are fundamental aspects of Judaism. In fact, it is Judaism that first enlightened world culture with these true building blocks of universal morality. The importance of these concepts is again emphasized in Cohen's late religious philosophy, wherein the correlation with God is grounded in discovering the Thou in human beings, from which one's own path to individuation commences. The fundamentals of monotheistic religion are therefore delineated through a universal concern for every single human being reflected in the notions of love of neighbor and the Noahide and reflected in the prophetic concept of humanity and finally of course in the universal scope of the messianic ideal. In order to further assess the universal nature of Cohen's interpretation of Judaism, we shall now look at the ways in which he describes non-Jewish contributors to its universal ideal.

UNIVERSAL CONTRIBUTORS

Judaism's purpose is to bring a messianic future to all of humanity. Accordingly, as we saw above, it fosters a universal morality, relying on the notion of love of neighbor and the legal category of the Noahide to do so. The correlation with God at its heart depends, furthermore, on the discovery of the other as Thou. Its morality is, consequently, for Cohen, of a uniquely universal nature. To further explore this universalism, however, we must address another question, namely, the degree to which other religions and cultures contribute to the development and advancement of these universal ideals. After all, even if Jewish Messianism is thoroughly universal in its scope, it would remain rather narrow if only the Jewish sources have historically contributed to it. In such a case, while upholding a universal scope, Cohen's Judaism would exhibit an exceptionalism that might be perceived as undercutting its universal ambitions. The question, therefore, is whether only Judaism contributes to the highest good of the messianic future.

Cohen repeatedly claims that while Judaism is the origin of the messianic ideal and Judaism as such should be thought of as the original religion, it by no means carries this torch exclusively. It spiritually nourished all other forms of monotheism, which also contribute to the fundamental principles of the religion of reason and the moral ideals inherent to it. Though in regard to "primary origin," the share of other monotheistic religions cannot be compared to Judaism, Cohen states he does "try to understand how other monotheistic religions also have their fruitful share in the religion of reason."[147]

With regards to Islam, these efforts are arguably not very comprehensive. Though the claim that Cohen does not mention the contribution of Islamic sources to the development of the religion of reason is strictly speaking exaggerated,[148] it is the case that it gains no systematic or even independent enquiry. Mostly, Cohen mentions Islam together with Christianity in order to make general, sweeping claims about both faiths' function in the history of monotheism. So Christians philosophized for their religion as "Arabs philosophized for Islam, and Jews for the Bible,"[149] or Jewish dogmatists developed their wisdom in thorough and critical communication with the Greeks, Islam, and Christianity.[150] Cohen also repeatedly emphasizes that medieval Jewish philosophers granted both Christianity and Islam "the merit of spreading monotheism among the peoples of the world."[151] In "Was Einigt die Konfessionen?," he adds that these philosophers realized also that this dissemination involved a "deepening" of monotheism and that "they lived in the Arab world, and created their philosophy of religion in the most intimate connection with that of the Muslims."[152]

Occasionally, there are slightly more developed references, such as with regards to the question of the attributes of God. In "Religion and Sittlichkeit," Cohen mentions how through the connection with Islamic philosophy, the question of the attributes of God became the basic problem of medieval religious speculation,[153] and in *Religion of Reason* he writes that through the concept of "negative attributes," the "philosophical speculation that consciously tried to develop the share of monotheism in reason out of the logic of principles" became the fundamental problem, thereby establishing a "community between religion and philosophy."[154] While this does suggest Cohen thought Islamic philosophy contributed significantly to clarifying the principles of monotheism, he does qualify the influence it might have had, writing that "the Jewish philosophy of the Middle Ages does not grow so much out of Islam as out of the original monotheism," adding that the exceptionally intimate relation between them can be explained "by the kinship that exists between the mother and daughter religion."[155]

It is perhaps therefore not surprising that in his essay on Maimonides, where one might have expected more on the relevant Muslim philosophical traditions, the treatment of Muslim philosophers is rather insignificant. Indeed, Cohen references Muslim philosophers mainly to contrast their positions with Maimonides's, such as, for example, Maimonides's hopeful vision as opposed to al-Razi's pessimism.[156]

So while in principle Cohen is committed to the notion that Islam and Muslim philosophers are part of the development of monotheism, the ways in which this contribution has actually been made remain unexplored. This might just be a case of scholarly caution; given the degree of ignorance Cohen perceives in the treatment of Judaism by some of the most important Christian philosophers, including first and foremost Kant, he might have been wary of making claims he lacked the expertise to back up. Still, it remains the case that, as we saw above, the influence of Muslim philosophers on their Jewish peers is at least somewhat minimized, and more generally Islam, and its presumed contribution to messianic humanity, remains largely ignored in Cohen's writings.

Christianity, obviously, gains a far more comprehensive and profound exploration in Cohen's writings, though it too is in the final analysis ambiguously valued. In his earlier period, where, as we saw above, ethics was often prioritized at the expense of religion, Cohen emphasized the concurrence of Judaism and Protestant Christianity, arguing that the ethical vision he propounded and ascribed to Judaism was fully shared by the Protestant church. So, for example, while he was being considered for his academic appointment at Marburg, Lange reportedly asked Cohen whether they differed with regards to Christianity, to which Cohen answered there was no real difference "because what you call Christianity—I call prophetic Judaism."[157] A similarly harmonizing spirit is reflected in "Ein Bekenntnis in der Judenfrage," which Cohen published in 1880 in response to the virulently nationalistic historian Heinrich von Treitschke's "Ein Wort über unser Judenthum," in which the latter attacked Heinrich Graetz's "fanatical wrath against the 'arch enemy' of Christianity" and "deadly hatred" towards the most sublime Germans from Luther to Goethe and Fichte. Treitschke, furthermore, takes offense at the notion that the "nation of Kant was really educated by the Jews only" and justifies popular antisemitic agitation, writing that "the instinct of the masses has indeed recognized the severe danger,"[158] the danger of a Judaism he repeatedly characterizes as foreign to the German national spirit.[159]

In his response, Cohen does not merely defend the loyalty of Jews to their German fatherland but seeks to show the religious fellowship that unites both Judaism and Protestant Christianity in their common ethical quest. Cohen writes that he cannot locate a difference between the "scientific concept of religion of Israelite Monotheism and Protestant Christianity."[160] So while both creeds could very well have some differences in terms of their sources and history, they both seek to transmit the same philosophically attainable concept of religion. It is significant, in this context, that Cohen makes this remark after having quoted a passage from Kant's "Toward Perpetual Peace," wherein Kant states that while there can be different religious books and different means to promote religion, "there can be only one single *religion* holding for all human beings and in all times."[161] Both Judaism and Protestant monotheism, Cohen implies, who share "the Pentateuch, the prophets, and the psalms,"[162] aim at that unified "scientific" concept of religion.

This profoundly significant similarity then leads Cohen to another question, namely, the meaning of the historical phenomenon of Christianity. His answer suggests a genuine, independent contribution of Christianity to ethics and the "inviolable sanctuary of the Kantian doctrine," namely, the "the humanization of the divine," without which the foundation of the moral imperative, the derivation of the moral law from the concept of law-giving reason, and the character of autonomy would all appear to be "incomprehensible." Crucially, Cohen then adds that this aspect of Christianity is part of the legacy of all modern Jews, whether they know it or not. However, it is theirs with no need for them to confess the gospel of the son of God as they seek to preserve that aspect of the ancient prophetic God that cannot be humanized.[163]

An argument could be made that these claims were made in exceedingly apologetic situations, wherein other judgments brought to bear on Christianity would be detrimental to Cohen himself or to the Jewish community he was seeking to defend. It would, after all, have been ill-advised to write to Lange that they differ on Christianity while being unprecedentedly considered, as a Jew, for a post at Marburg, especially in light of the suspicion Lange's colleagues had towards a Jewish professor of philosophy at a Protestant university.[164] Similarly, it would have been ill-advised to write anything but positively about Christianity when defending the possibility of Jewish integration in a Christian society. So too, when Cohen sought to prove the religious legitimacy of Christianity from a Jewish perspective in "Die Nachstenliebe im Talmud" (1888), writing that "if the Talmud knew Christianity, it must acknowledge it fulfils the seven Noachidic conditions" and making the case that as such it must not be considered idolatry but rather an intrinsic part of the universally valid moral quest the Talmud itself seeks to uphold,[165] he is literally taking part in a trial wherein he is called to prove that the Talmud does not reflect a particularistic system of morality. Accordingly, as Palmer puts it, he is here making "an enormous effort to prove the Talmud to be the source of the precept of universal charity as having developed out of concern for the stranger."[166] So, like Mendelssohn before him, Cohen obviously had to be extremely careful in what kinds of opinions he expressed on the issue.

Still, Cohen would continue emphasizing the kinship of Judaism and Protestantism till the end of his life. It is telling, for example, that when discussing Maimonides's emphasis on ethics, which as we saw was the cornerstone of Cohen's interpretation of the latter's thought, Cohen describes him as the "standard bearer of Protestantism in Mediaeval Judaism."[167] More significantly still, Cohen would continue to emphasize certain uniquely Christian contributions to the religion of reason, doing so even in the book dedicated to how Christianity can be construed out of the Jewish sources. So, for example, when establishing the importance of suffering to his concept of religion in *Religion of Reason* and the theodicy through which suffering is explained through the need for compassion, Cohen states that from this point of view, the "deepest meaning of Christianity, too, becomes intelligible."[168]

So, on the one hand, Cohen could claim, as he did in "Die Liebe Zur Religion," not to "underestimate the share of Christianity, and especially Protestantism, in the continuance of moral culture."[169] On the other hand, however, even this statement is rather ambiguous, coming as it does right after Cohen remarks that "we know that the basic principles of our religion are the deepest roots of moral culture, roots that have not withered and that must not wither if the progress of culture is to continue linearly."[170] So while Cohen might not "underestimate" Christianity's contribution, he still sees it as clearly inferior to the originating contribution of Judaism. In fact, as Erlewine points out, Cohen's treatment of the matter suggest an attempt at positioning Judaism at the heart of Western civilization and, significantly, doing so at the expense of Christianity.[171]

There is, in fact, in Cohen's work, besides the above-described respect for Christianity, several arguments explicitly pointing out its inferiority.

So, for example, while Cohen's ethical monotheism posits a thoroughly ethical notion of immortality, polytheism "assumes immorality to mean only deification."[172] This deification is an idea that has been subsequently taken over by Christianity. It therefore betrays the basic notion of monotheism, namely, the uniqueness and absolute incomparability of God. The notion of the Trinity therefore "falls away" from pure monotheism as it suggests the exaggerated claim that "man should possess eternal and therefore true being."[173]

Erlewine indicates that this problem in Christianity is related, in Cohen's thought, to the Christian adoption of the very same Greek ontology that, as we saw above, tended to lead to pantheism.[174] Indeed, lacking the clear differentiation between God's unique being and natural existence that Cohen ascribed to biblical ontology, the Greeks either veered to pantheism or to mediating concepts like the Logos, which "must inevitably become a second God."[175] Christianity, when basing itself on these notions, ends up with befuddled concepts that mistakenly propose a mediating being or person between God and nature, offering illusions, such as possible deification or human eternity. It also leads to the possibility of Christ as a plastic image of God, which Cohen refers to as nothing less than a "contradiction of monotheism" given the stringent biblical interdiction of image worship and insistence on the incomparability of God.[176] The image, Cohen writes, has to be a likeness, but with regards to God, "there can be no likeness."[177]

Cohen criticizes too the sacrament of Holy Communion, as the transubstantiation involved in the transformation of the wafer into the body of Christ, even if understood symbolically, "would nevertheless be and remain the depiction of an action in God's being."[178] This contrasts poorly with Jewish symbolic observances, which are meant to call to mind God's commandments and the ethical task they seek to promote. So the Christian ritual too is based on a mistaken metaphysics, one that addresses the being of God rather than approaching the unique God through His ethical attributes, as Judaism does and as is reflected in its ritual observances. Similarly, the prophets realized that, in spite of the fact that the entire classical world was attached to it, sacrifice as a ritual reflected paganism and the "root of idol worship." Yet, in the very same paragraph, Cohen describes sacrifice as the "foundation of Christianity."[179]

And while Cohen suggests in the introduction of *Religion of Reason* that suffering and the compassion it gives rise to are the most profound meaning of Christianity,[180] he also, in his depiction of the righteous suffering of the Jews, takes even that meaning away from Christianity. As Erlewine puts it, "the Jews appropriate the mantle of the Christ, as Cohen depicts them as the ones who suffer vicariously for others."[181] In fact, as Erlewine further points out, the Jesus Cohen suggests accords with the religion of reason is de-Hellenized and returned to the Jewish people, where he becomes an exemplar of morality, who, realizing his all-too-human limitations in bringing redemption, realizes also the impossibility of redemption without God.[182]

Accordingly, the deified figure of Christ compares poorly with the Jewish messianic vision. The Messiah brings a representation of human suffering and with it a concept of world history that is ethical and beyond eudaemonism. But in its "*Christological* interpretation," the representation of human suffering becomes also "the representative vicar of guilt."[183] As only God can take guilt upon Himself, this is a distortion that illusorily seeks to relieve human beings of their consciousness of guilt, which is not permitted. Were a person thusly relieved, the continual process of individuation through the divine atonement of sin could not occur. So while in Christology, the Messiah cannot be the human ideal, the Jewish Messiah brings with the dark shadow of the suffering he represents "the most shining light upon the history of mankind."[184] Therefore, while Cohen does not "underestimate" the Christian contribution to Western civilization, he does find some serious flaws in its most basic tenets and clearly believes that contribution to be significantly less than the Jewish one.

Finally, to conclude this section, two more contributors, Greece and Germany, which are unified in their philosophical legacy, need to be discussed. Indeed, in his exploration of the cultural forces leading to the eventual messianic peace, Cohen often emphasizes as critical the "scientific" establishment of ethics. For Cohen, this is largely the heritage of ancient Greece, Plato in particular, which finds its pinnacle in modern Germany with Kantian ethics at the forefront.

Cohen's interpretation of Plato's ideas as hypotheses is, as we saw in the previous chapter,[185] at the heart of his philosophical approach and, indeed, of the Marburg school of Neo-Kantianism he founded. Cohen explains that Plato himself, as we also have seen, came to these ideas through prior developments in Greek thought, which further accentuates the Greek contribution beyond Plato. Cohen, furthermore, continually emphasized the ethical significance of the Platonic doctrine, wherein the *anhypotheton*, the non-hypothesis underlying all other hypotheses, is the form of the good. Accordingly, the great revolutionary insight that philosophy is essentially concerned with ethics is ascribed by Cohen to Socrates. Before Socrates, philosophers were just as much mathematicians and researchers of nature. With Socrates, Cohen writes, "ethics, as the doctrine of man, becomes the center of philosophy. And it is only with this center that philosophy gains its independence and peculiarity and at once also its unity."[186] By applying the doctrine of ideas, that is, hypotheses, to this newly defined discipline, Plato launched humanity on the path towards what would eventually culminate in "scientific" ethics, the pinnacle of which is Kant's doctrine.

Cohen therefore characterizes Plato, along with the prophets, as the "two most important sources of modern culture as a whole";[187] they are both the "spiritual leaders [Geistesführer] of humankind," and both are necessary "to bring the goal of the social ideal within our grasp."[188] Indeed, as important as human compassion is, it is not, Cohen thinks, a substitute for the kind of ethical knowledge the "divine [göttliche] Plato" began developing, and, accordingly, "without philosophy, suffering will not cease among human beings."[189]

So again, on the one hand, we have a robust and unique contribution to the universal messianic future. On the other hand, like with Christianity, Greece, as will be shown below, in the final analysis compares rather poorly with Judaism. As we saw in the last chapter, as opposed to monotheism and its insistence on the uniqueness of God, Greek thought lacks the means of protecting itself from degenerating into pantheism. Moreover, as we saw above, Plato's doctrine of the human being, with its strongly aristocratic and exclusivist bent, is inferior to the prophetic one, which reflects a genuine concern for the downtrodden and the poor. It is, in fact, Cohen claims, not Plato who developed the idea of the human being within the doctrine of ideas, but significantly, a Jew, namely, Philo.[190]

Plato, moreover, functioned in a political environment, wherein the tribal basis of the city-state hampered, Cohen argues, the rise of genuine universalism.[191] Indeed, polytheism might occasionally honor the stranger as a guest, but the stranger remains the barbarian, and the ideal person must be of one's own people. It is only through the unique God, who loves the barbarian and nations hostile to Israel as much as Israel itself, that people's horizons widen. It is, accordingly, Jewish Messianism, and not Greek culture, that enables humanity to reach for genuine cosmopolitanism.[192]

Finally, while Cohen idealizes the national spirit of Israel in the prophetic ideals it gave birth to, he does not similarly essentialize Greece to Plato's ethics. In fact, Cohen often emphasizes the mythical and pagan aspects of Greek culture, which are inevitably depicted as inferior to Judaism. Indeed, Greek myth remains anchored in the past and does not give rise to history "as the idea of the future of mankind under the guidance of God,"[193] a point reflected with particular clarity in the myth of the golden age.[194] Elsewhere, Cohen decries the Greek misunderstanding of the notion of guilt. As we saw above, the origination of the individual in religion occurs by means of guilt, yet Greek mythology misunderstands guilt because according to its notion of it, "man is not an individual, but rather the offspring of his ancestors."[195] Cohen locates this notion as primordial to tragedy, the task of which is, accordingly, to redeem human beings from their inherited guilt. Cohen writes that the Bible too struggles with this mythological misunderstanding of guilt but believes it frees itself from it through the notion of God's love.[196] And while he does believe later tragedies reflect a clearer awareness of the matter, he still does not believe they were able to fully reflect the individuation of the I, which the proper religious understanding of guilt enables.[197]

The Greek contribution, while exemplary, is presented as part of a legacy that carries deeply problematic aspects. A contribution that is, however, most unambiguously valued by Cohen, apart from Judaism, is of course the one provided by Germanism. Cohen, as Derrida points out, belongs to a German tradition according to which "the German holds an absolutely privileged relation to the Greek," which "no other European people is supposed to share."[198] Indeed, Germanism does not merely inherit the Greek heritage; it fulfils the highest and most sublime aspects of Greece by the fruition of philosophical ethics in German idealism. Cohen's highly idealized notion of Germanism is based not only on Plato and the Greek philosophical spirit but also, as a Protestant culture, on the heritage of the prophets, and as such it overcomes the limitations that plagued Greece. The German spirit is for Cohen, accordingly, "the spirit of classical humanity and true cosmopolitanism."[199]

While Cohen's unbridled German enthusiasm cannot but be perceived as tragically tainted by the dramatic events unfolding in the years after his death, it is important to note it was not a hopelessly naïve patriotic adherence. Cohen was well aware that empirical Germany left much to be desired and was far from reliably actualizing a Kantian universal and cosmopolitan ethics. He was, after all, only to deeply aware of raging antisemitism, the intellectual expressions of which he inevitably had to argue against and combat throughout his life.[200] His Germanism is an ideal construct of what Germany could be and should aspire to be. As Schwarzschild points out, to conflate that ideal notion with the actual, empirical Germany, Cohen would have had to be "blind and insensitive to the historical realities that surrounded and even impinged so painfully on his own life."[201] His idealized concept, Schwarzschild explains, is a normative construction that "far from being identical with, in fact constantly opposes and challenges" empirical Germany.[202]

Schwarzschild himself, however, paraphrasing Kant, describes as follows the relation of critical idealism with history and idealization: "history without idealization is blind, and idealization without history is empty."[203] So it is not the case that Cohen thinks this idealization of Germany would be on the same footing as the idealization of any other nation. The effort of idealization might have to be undertaken with regard to all nations, but clearly Cohen believes Germany's history suggests it is, at the very least, a uniquely suitable candidate for idealization. Indeed, Cohen's Germanism remains also a historical phenomenon the history of which can be told as a kind of theodicy of reason wherein the Reformation places Germany "at the center of world history,"[204] and Kant provides the final confirmation of its centrality by delineating the theoretical means for universal peace. Though guided by an idealized Germanism, actual Germany does have a critical mission in empirical history. Accordingly, Cohen believed German victory in the First World War to be critical. Indeed, writing during the war, he claims that without a willingness to acknowledge "German pre-eminence in all foundations of intellectual and spiritual live," there can be no adequate basis for real international understanding, and that "Germanism must become the center of a confederation of states which will establish world peace and within it the genuine foundation of a cultural world."[205]

One of the more astonishing aspects of the tremendous emphasis Cohen laid on the German spirit and its historical significance is the notion that Jews everywhere "have duties of piety towards Germany; for it is the motherland of [their] soul, in so far as [their] religion is [their] soul."[206] Crucially, it is the German spirit through which the messianic ideal was reinvigorated in Judaism. As we saw in chapter 2, Mendelssohn abandoned what for Cohen is the pinnacle of Judaism, messianic progress. While this does not necessarily mean Mendelssohn abandons all forms of Messianism,[207] his remains a position Cohen strongly disavows. Still, Cohen shows understanding towards what he takes to be a grave mistake in so far as Mendelssohn's view reflects an attempt at warding off the notion that Christianity is a step forwards from Judaism, and Cohen blames the narrowing and obscuring of the Jewish outlook at the time on the effects of the ghetto and the fear of persecution. Indeed, it is Herder who restored to the Jews their most precious spiritual possession, namely, the Messiah of their prophet, which he found again through the concept of humanity in German ethics.[208]

The invigorating force of Germanism has been and continues to be, for Cohen, absolutely critical in the quest for the messianic humanity he calls for. Along with Judaism, Germanism is a contributor that can be constructed as an unambiguous idealized force for universal peace. German Jews are, accordingly, in an "exceptionally favorable position." Not only are they in a prime position to realize how the German spirit has elevated their own Judaism; their German Judaism has, in turn, had an incomparable influence on the religious spirit of the Jews of the world. Their spiritual life is enriched by the sense of religious communion reflected in the religious transfiguration and confirmation of their patriotic sense of belonging: "our souls resonate evenly and harmoniously in our German Patriotism and our religious consciousness."[209]

To conclude, while Cohen's thought would imply contributions by all monotheistic religions to his universal ideals, those of Islam are not elaborated in any meaningful manner and indeed are often minimized.

Christianity does make some significant contributions, but it too is far from unambiguously valued. Greece begot the philosophical tradition without which human suffering will not end, but Cohen does not seem willing to suggest an ideational concept of Greece focused solely on that aspect of its culture. Greece remains, in his eyes, too enmeshed in its lesser mythical aspects. So, among the allies of Judaism in its quest for universal messianic peace, Germany is clearly prioritized. Indeed, it is this Germanism that reinvigorated the dormant messianic ideal in Jewish thought. Having looked at the cultural forces pushing towards messianic peace, to complete this aspect of the exploration of Cohen's universalism, we shall now explore the treatment of those forces Cohen believes hinder it.

MORALLY REQUIRED INTOLERANCE

As we saw in the first part of this section, Cohen emphasizes the primordial status of the commandment to love the other in Jewish tradition and developed an ethics based not only on the Kantian categorical imperative but also on compassion for the suffering for every actual human being. We then analyzed how, according to his ideas, some non-Jewish religious and cultural forces are part of the messianic task sourced in Judaism. We did, also, however, note the ambiguous nature of Cohen's treatment of the Christian, Islamic, and Greek contributions. Still, ambiguously or not, these can be classified as within the umbrella of the messianic task. The question now raised is how Cohen deals with cultural forces he classifies as lacking the messianic impulse or even hindering or opposing it.

Some passages seem to exclude that possibility. Cohen writes, for example, that "every people and every state has its own particular world-historical task towards the messianic ideal."[210] Elsewhere, he states that "one should certainly love every religion, one should love religion as such. Religion is in every form the testimony of the moral spirit, the divine spirit within humankind," adding that "science and education expand our horizons and exhort us to this appreciative sympathy towards all cultural religions. This sympathy is itself the most infallible sign of genuine religiosity and humanity."[211] Yet, as we shall see below, there most definitely are peoples who do not contribute to the messianic ideal. Furthermore, with regards to the importance of loving religion "in any form," it is important to keep in mind that, as with many other concepts, "religion" for Cohen is not merely a descriptive concept of empirical phenomena that manifest similar characteristics or some other degree of similarity. It is rather an idealized concept that only very few empirical "religions" instantiate. *Religion*, as Cohen uses the term, is more of a normative than a descriptive term. And indeed, Cohen clearly eliminates many of the phenomena modern scholars might refer to as *religion* from passing that idealized and normative threshold.

So, for example, in his *Begriff der Religion*, while discussing the deeply problematic nature of developing inductively a vague notion of religion, Cohen criticizes approaches that focus on the commonality of the cult (*Kultus*), stating that the cult cannot serve as a distinguishing criterion as it confounds the peoples in a mistaken "harmony," and so the "Indians, the Chinese, the Egyptians, the Babylonians, the Greek and the Israelites, are all united in the notion of the cult by that same concept of religion which for the history of religion remains an unresolved problem."[212] As opposed to Mendelssohn, who as we saw toiled to emphasize the congruence of the Indian and Chinese religions with the universal natural religion, Cohen finds such associations to be confusing and even demeaning to the proper concept of religion. For Cohen, Chinese, Indian, Babylonian, or Greek cults cannot be thought of as "religion," and accordingly, the idea that all "religions" ought to be loved is strongly qualified by his own far more restrictive concept of what actually can be thought of as "religion." So while Mendelssohn toiled to prove the unity of humanity, Cohen here explicitly does not, instead excluding whole cultures from a legitimate stake in his religion of reason.[213]

The stakes of this exclusion could not be higher. As monotheism is perceived by Cohen to be critical for the promotion of a morally conditioned messianic future, contrasting perceptions must be eradicated. As Cohen puts it in *Religion of Reason*, if monotheism "is the only salvation for mankind, then there is no escape from the fact that idol worship and all kinds of magic must be destroyed. Tolerance is a principle that cannot be valid for the origin, setting up and establishment of monotheism." What is at stake is the "being or non-being of the moral universe," Cohen continues, before writing that such errors in people's concepts of God "are the greatest afflictions of man, and perhaps the cause of the greatest suffering which men bring upon themselves again and again. Moral offenses have their deepest origin in these fundamental notions of men about God."[214]

These are critically important passages. Religion is ipso facto related to morality, as we saw above, and here Cohen draws a rather startling conclusion: Theological mistakes are no mere semantic confusion or mistaken but innocuous notions. They are the root for the gravest moral mistakes as well. Idolatry therefore immediately becomes more than a religious problem; it is also an urgently moral one. While one may think, as Mendelssohn did, that responding to religious mistakes is best done lovingly, through encouragement and education, Cohen is far more drastic. The moral degeneracy of idolatry must be eradicated. This leads Cohen to a variety of pronouncements that, while written in a vitriolic manner characteristic of much German writing of Cohen's era, are still rather unsavory to more tolerant and pluralistic sensitivities.

Indeed, given the moral degeneracy attributed to polytheism or idolatry, Cohen suggests in uncompromising terms that they must be absolutely destroyed. This "relentless necessity" is an integral aspect of the "true understanding of monotheism," an understanding Cohen describes as lacking if "one believes one is able to detect even a trace of intolerance, of fanaticism and misanthropy in this holy zeal against the Gods," as "these suspicions merely disclose that one's own heart is not completely filled with the unique God and with the necessity of his unique being."[215]

Perhaps even more disturbingly, Cohen explains this is not merely a battle of ideas, but rather one involving human deaths. When it comes to the destruction of false worship, he writes, "there can be no pity and no regard for men." The love of God "roots out all quietism" as worship of false Gods must be "annihilated from the earth," and there is no "higher spiritual authority that could release men from this fundamental duty."[216] Accordingly, to the prophets, whose task was to creatively form "the history of the spirit," "tolerance had to be an alien, a disturbing point of view." Ensuring there can be no misunderstanding of his position here, Cohen adds that "to be sure, men had to be sacrificed for this purpose, men from their own people no less than from other peoples."[217]

We will return to the telling remark considering the "sacrifice" of Israelites as well as idolaters from other peoples below. At this juncture, it is important to emphasize the radical difference between Cohen's and

Mendelssohn's tones with regards to idolatry and, more importantly, idolaters. This significant difference, which as we shall see in the next chapter is based on dissimilarities in the very structure of their philosophical efforts, is at any rate stark and obvious. While Mendelssohn sought to combat idolatry, as Freudenthal points out, he remained very coy about describing actual idolaters.[218] While he explained the right of the ancient Israelite nation to punish because of its unique Mosaic constitution, which combined the religious and the civil authorities, religion qua religion would not be allowed to punish, much less kill. Finally, Mendelssohn sought to downplay executions carried out by the ancient Hebrew state's civil-religious authority, emphasizing instead its leniency.[219] Cohen, on the contrary, vocally supports clearly aggressive and murderous religious activity. And while he does suggest the "destruction of idolatrous people" involves a logic that "cannot hold its own before pure ethics," he still believes it to be a God-commanded part of the mission "monotheism imposed on humanity."[220]

Though perhaps less dramatic than those calling for holy war and annihilation of idolatrous people, especially compared to the more culturally sensitive Mendelssohn, who writes about foreigners mainly to highlight the ignorance Western culture is capable of, Cohen is far less concerned with not disparaging the spiritual or intellectual adequacy of foreigners from distant cultures. So when denouncing an empirical or historicist approach to religion rather than one drawn from philosophy and seeking an idealized concept (an effort that in this quote Cohen relates to Greece), Cohen makes his point by plaintively writing of thinkers who prefer to "follow the tracks of religion among the savages of America, rather than in Plato, Aeschylus, and Pindar."[221] Though it has thankfully become generally speaking distasteful to write of native peoples as "savages," the distasteful use of the word is of course not exclusively Cohen's. These are terms widely used in his intellectual environment. What is, however, more relevant to our comparison with Mendelssohn is that there is no doubt for Cohen that the native people of America are, at the very least, less religiously enlightened than Plato. This of course is in complete opposite to Mendelssohn's repeated insistence that foreign cultures, even those that seem idolatrous at first sight, are in all likelihood just as enlightened as Mendelssohn's peers would like to think themselves to be.

A similar assumption is reflected in a passage towards the end of his "Der Nächste," where Cohen regrets the lack of "vital science" in the academic biblical research of his time, which he argues begins on a profoundly mistaken footing because it does not recognize the intellectual and linguistic continuity between the Bible and the rabbinic tradition. A mistake that Cohen, for whom this continuity was an essential aspect of his idealized hermeneutics of the Jewish sources, clearly thinks his reading of the Bible does not make. Criticizing these researchers, he writes bitterly that "Bedouins are supposed to make it easier to understand what a visceral Hebrew word of thought [Gedankenwort] means than the homogenous development it obtained in the 'Oral Tradition.'"[222] As with the passage we looked at above, the problem here is not as much with the claim Cohen seeks to make. It might very well be the case that it is more hermeneutically interesting, for any variety of reasons, to seek the spirit of the ancient biblical texts in its rabbinic or Midrashic interpretation or development than to seek to interpret them through the supposed empirical similarity of the Bedouin and the figures described in the Bible. But the way Cohen words his claim makes it obvious that it is highly likely the Bedouin's religiosity would not reflect biblical concepts, or indeed, those of what Cohen thought of as the religion of reason. Cohen's tone, while perhaps somewhat typical of his time, remains again comparatively far less culturally sensitive than Mendelssohn's.

We shall return to a more profound exploration of this difference between Mendelssohn and Cohen in the next chapter as part of a more general comparative effort. To conclude this section and move to the following one, one more comment about Cohen's less tolerant writings is necessary. We saw above that when describing the prophets' holy war against idolatry, Cohen noted "men had to be sacrificed for this purpose, men from their own people no less than from other peoples."[223] This clearly suggest that the Jewish people are by no means spared in the holy war against idolatry and, indeed, that empirical Jews are by no means necessarily the holders of Cohen's idealized Judaism. Of course, not all of the empirical sources belong to Cohen's idealized Judaism. As we've already seen, he most definitely characterizes some aspects of the biblical tale to be more mythological and as such less expressive of his religion of reason and its universal messianic yearning.

That is not to say that Cohen does not clearly prioritize the Jewish sources over others. This can be ascribed to the highly idealized notion of Judaism his "hermeneutics of optimization" leads to.[224] But presumably, had the Jewish sources not offered anything particularly suitable for such an effort, Cohen could have just as well developed an idealized concept of another faith or nation. So, on the one hand, the idealized concept, in and of itself, is beyond the particularities of peoplehood as "monotheism claims that not every people may have its own peculiar God, but that there is *one* God for all peoples, as there is one mathematics for all peoples."[225] In the case of mathematics, however, Cohen writes that "the immortal works of mathematics itself influence other peoples at all times, so that the preservation of the nation of its origin is not necessary" and concludes with the following critical passage: "Monotheism, however, did not come to a final close in the Bible, as did the Greek spirit in its various works. Monotheism required a continuous development *beyond the Bible*, which could not be entrusted to those peoples who did not produce the ancient Bible."[226] So while Cohen's religion is a highly idealized concept, and so too is his notion of Judaism, actual empirical Jewish history, as well as the history of Jewish spiritual development, does reflect the idealized concept of religion and of Judaism that Cohen develops.

The criterion of the idealized concept therefore enables Cohen to separate authentically Jewish passages in the sources from passages construed as not authentically Jewish. And indeed, when Cohen criticizes passages in the Bible as mythological, he describes them as stemming from sources foreign to the Jewish people. In other words, that which is in the sources but falls outside of Cohen's criterion of Judaism is often depicted as foreign to empirical Judaism rather than as merely an aspect of empirical Judaism that is less concordant with his idealized concept. So, for example, while the prophets are essentially Jewish, the legend of the fall and the origin of the myth of resurrection are depicted as having originated in Persia.[227]

So Cohen is clear on the critical importance of the empirical Jewish people in upholding this idealized Judaism, for whose flourishing actual Jews are critical. But that idealized Judaism itself is clearly not shared by all of the Jewish people. Therefore, in redefining Judaism as a messianic religion of reason, Cohen, to some degree or another, creates a gap between empirical Judaism and his concept of it. The next, concluding section of this chapter will look at some of the consequences of this gap.

COHEN'S REVALUATED JUDAISM

The highly idealized concept of Judaism delineated in Cohen's writing puts it at the very forefront of a messianic religion of reason whose task is to bring the reign of morality to all people in a universal messianic age. The crucial ethical force that is Judaism explains the universal necessity of its endurance. This, then, is Cohen's answer to Spinoza's devaluation: the distinct survival of Judaism is essential as it promotes the messianic ideal on which the future of humanity depends.

This revaluated Judaism sheds some aspects, which to Cohen might have been merely empirical or historical, but to other Jews had critical existential and religious significance. Cohen's idealized and hence also abstracted Judaism was almost immediately criticized as being existentially alienated and lacking critical aspects of Jewish religious life. Martin Buber, for example, was an early critic of this highly idealized version of Judaism and of the Jewish God Cohen suggests. While not mentioning Cohen by name, his "The Holy Way," written just a few months after Cohen's death, seems to be directly aimed at Cohen's view. Buber starts by denouncing the "occidental dualism that sanctions the splitting of man's being into two realms," namely, the "truth of the spirit," on the one hand, and "the reality of life," on the other. This, he writes, compares unfavorably with "the most precious heritage of classical Judaism: its disposition toward realization," the meaning of which is that "true human life is conceived to be a life lived in the presence of God." Crucially, Buber then provides what seems to be a thinly veiled reference to Cohen, writing that "for Judaism, God is not a Kantian idea but an elementally present spiritual reality—neither something conceived by pure reason nor something postulated by practical reason, but emanating from the immediacy of existence as such."[228] Indeed, this criticism echoes Buber's earlier "Begriffe und Wirklichkeit," which was directly addressed to Cohen and sought to answer Cohen's antagonism towards Zionism. There too, Buber's critique is based on his view that Cohen's thought on the matter related to nothing but concepts while that which truly matters is actuality.

The abstracted and ethically subsumed religiosity Cohen offered seemed distant and alienated to a new generation of Jewish thinkers who focused their creative efforts on a vital, vibrant, and existentially potent Judaism. Cohen's Judaism, as opposed to, for example, the Judaism reflected in Buber's life-affirming Hassidic masters or his passionate Zionism, seemed rather remote. This is something Cohen himself was aware of, and he wrote in a letter from Naples to Rabbi Leo Munk, "My fate is a very particular kind. If there are people who bring the sacrificio del intelleto [sacrifice of the intellect, *sic*], I bring the one of del sentimento [sacrifice of the feelings/emotions]. You know the degree to which I am bonded in the deepest emotions of my heart and the deepest feelings of my spirit to the inner life of our religion, but here too abstraction is my fate."[229] When discussing this quote and the ways in which it reflects Cohen's transformation of a living God to a philosophical idea, Samuel Hugo Bergson also tells Rosenzweig's famous story of how Cohen supposedly shed a tear after an old man, who had listened attentively to Cohen's idea of God as developed through his ethics, asked the great philosopher, "but where is the *Bore Olam*, the creator of the world?"[230]

The distance between Cohen's idealized Judaism and the empirical forms of Judaism might be why he states, in "Die Nächstenliebe im Talmud," that he cannot be thought of as a "believing Jew [gläubigen Juden] in the usual sense [in dem gewöhnlichen Sinne]."[231] While these words were written in 1888, a relatively early stage of Cohen's development, in particular with regard to Judaism, and Cohen in his later years might very well have wanted to emphasize the authenticity of his version of Judaism, they are telling nonetheless. Indeed, they seem to anticipate the kinds of criticism mentioned above, which view Cohen's idealized Judaism as estranged from the faith familiar to, and valued by, generations of Jews before him as of course as many of his contemporaries.

It seems, however, that Cohen himself realized in the later, more religious, and more Jewish writings the need to reassert some of the living relevancy of a Judaism he had taken to the edge of abstraction. Indeed, the turn to the individuating force of religion that, as we saw above, is at the heart of his later religious writings, precisely addresses the existential concerns his later critics found underdeveloped. In pursuing and developing this aspect of his thought, Cohen might very well have anticipated that criticism itself and sought to remedy it in his last works. Writing of

Neo-Kantianism more generally, Gordon argues that "the relationship between neo-Kantianism and existentialism was often as much dialectical as it was oppositional."[232] More specifically, Cohen's turn to the individual seems to bring him closer to the existentialist Jewish philosophers who followed him, and indeed, even if Rosenzweig exaggerated Cohen's break from systematicity, he might still have correctly perceived a greater existential emphasis.

One further obviously significant expression of this realization is Cohen's evolving treatment of the ritualistic law. We saw how Spinoza's devaluation of Judaism originates with a total devaluation of the ritual law. We saw too how Mendelssohn diligently sought to defend the universal value and significance of the ritual law, which he presented as an antidote to idolatry. Cohen, however, is in his earlier writings ambiguous at best about the importance of the Halakha.

On the one hand, Cohen does argue that ritual legislation does not conflict with ethics but is meant rather to be its "vehicle."[233] Accordingly, in his "Die Nächstenliebe im Talmud," Cohen seeks to emphasize the degree to which the Talmud seeks to shift the emphasis from ritualistic law to morality.[234] The sages, Cohen suggests, sought to do so out of a realization that pure ethical thought cannot be made fully explicit if it remains linked to religiously motivated acts. These, after all, are aimed at religious salvation, not the respect of the moral law as such. This predicament, Cohen then continues, explains the "force of the apostles against the curse of the law," adding that

> it is not only the clarity of conscience which suffers its doubts and distresses under the weight of the ritual law, but also firmness and certainty in the conflicts of social intercourse. Here lies a difficulty for every religion inasmuch as they conceive of man as a believer in their own kingdom of God. This general religious difficulty is greater for the Talmud, because it had to try and establish as divine Justice the connivances and reprisals which the legal doctrine did not easily avoid, so that the concept of man appears to be more disguised and obscured.[235]

This passage not only reflects Cohen's ambiguity with regard to ritual law but also his early position with regard to the undeniably priority of ethics over religion. As we saw above, this is a position that shifted in his later writings. This invites the question of whether his position regarding the Jewish law also evolved in his later works. And indeed, while some of the ambiguity still lingers, his treatment of the matter in his *Religion of Reason* is far more charitable.

On the one hand, Cohen now fully endorses the moral nature of the law, writing that "the only goal of the law is moral perfection" and that "God's law does not contradict the autonomy of the moral will."[236] However, he does also describe some profound problems with the historical, empirical manifestation of the law. So while some laws might have been developed in order to ward off idolatry, it might be the case other laws "have their basis in mythological prejudices, or are the result of concessions to them."[237] Another problem arises because of the relation of the emerging Jewish religion and the basic constitution of the ancient state. The purity of the moral law could have been endangered because "political considerations of only relative value, particularly those of a social and political character, can assume the force of law."[238] In a similar vein, Cohen writes that the needs of the cult and the laws derived from it intertwine with pure moral laws or that primitive and incomplete hygienic measures too were appropriated by religious law. So, for example, practical medical and hygienic considerations are related by Cohen to the dietary laws.[239]

This tension is resolved by the now-familiar reminder of the difference between empirical reality, that is, the historical origins of the ritualistic laws, and its idealized version, namely, the law's significance within the religion of reason Cohen constructs out of the sources. While historically the ritual laws might have had a rather earthly genealogy and significance, Cohen's idealized law is wholly dedicated to morality. Indeed, Cohen explicitly equates the kingdom of God, the kingdom of law, and the kingdom of morality.[240] This law is then presented as englobing all of human life because it seeks, ideally, a full dedication to the moral life. Accordingly, "as no single action can be withdrawn from the unity of life, in the same way no action can be excluded from the law."[241] This, however, draws us back from idealized legalization to actual lived experience. Cohen, therefore, must here explain in greater precision how his idealization is actually expressed in daily life.

Cohen suggests a very flexible position about which actual laws one must obey. So, for example, while it is critical to humanity as a whole that the particular ceremonial law ensures the survival of Judaism and its monotheism, it is not the case that all halakhic obligations held by previous generations must be currently met. In so far as the isolation of Israel and the continuation of the religion of Jewish monotheism are at stake, these are bound to the "continuation of the law in accordance with its general concept—not to the particular laws." Cohen recognizes this attitude as an essentially Jewish one given that the Talmud already changed various biblical laws.[242] Still, his own delineation of what, in the final analysis, is absolutely necessary for the survival of Jewish monotheism is not very extensive: "the law, even if it were to be adhered to only on the holidays, and even, for some or for many, only on the day of Atonement, is a bulwark against levelling pure monotheism."[243]

Whether he is selective in the commandments one must obey or not, the crucial point for us here is that Cohen adds a poignant existential aspect to the law, writing that isolation does not exhaust the law's meaning; rather, "this cannot be grasped in its entire profundity by any outsider—inherent in the law, in its many forms and usages, is a positive force that stimulates, inspires, fortifies, and deepens religious feelings."[244] Cohen later adds that "whoever has not experienced for himself the life under this yoke of the laws will never understand that this yoke is borne as a ladder to heaven."[245]

Cohen here shows precisely the kind of existential sensitivities later critics deemed to have been lacking in his thought. While his depiction of Judaism certainly is focused on the conceptual and the ideal, passages such as these suggest Cohen might have been, in his old age, more attuned to the existential concern of the old Jew seeking his familiar Judaism than Rosenzweig's story seems to imply he had been in Marburg.[246] At the very least, it indicates that the familiar, existential aspects of Judaism do not contradict Cohen's theoretical perspective. Accordingly, to quote Liebeschütz, "in his last phase Cohen had a more sympathetic understanding for the concrete features in Jewish life."[247]

So while Cohen's revaluation of Judaism emphasizes its ideational necessity for messianic humanity, it does not disavow the existential vitality critics have found lacking in his work. Indeed, even if his concept of Judaism, at times, does not emphasize a familiar religious vitality, it certainly does not deny the existential necessity of a lived religious experience. To the contrary, it allows for both that lived experience and the theoretical and moral imperatives Cohen toiled more explicitly over.

We saw in chapter 3 that Mendelssohn's commitment to Judaism was put in doubt. While Cohen's Judaism is pronounced in a manner that makes it difficult to think of him as a universalistic deist, we saw above that the Jewishness of his Judaism, that is, the nearness of his idealized construct to the lived experience of actual Jews, whether justifiable in light of the existentialist tones in his later writings or not, was found lacking. Both kinds of criticisms suggest that in seeking to revaluate Judaism, Mendelssohn and Cohen also redefined it. We will discuss the ways in which they sought to authoritatively establish their Judaism in the next, concluding chapter as part of a comprehensive comparison of Mendelssohn's and Cohen's revaluations.

(6)
JEWISH UNIVERSALISMS

Competing Highest Values

The analyses of the axiological structures embedded in Mendelssohn's and Cohen's philosophies undertaken mainly in chapters 2 and 4, respectively, uncovered a stark contrast. While Mendelssohn's philosophy is structured around a religious eudaemonism, Cohen meticulously seeks to avoid any trace of eudaemonism in his own axiological thinking. As opposed to Mendelssohn, Cohen depicts a religious highest good that relates thoroughly to morality rather than happiness. While Mendelssohn's notion of felicity is certainly not construed as amoral, it is most certainly prioritized over morality or even God. Indeed, without felicity, for Mendelssohn, neither reason, nor morality, nor even God can be construed as valuable in and of themselves. However, given the way in which Mendelssohn's world is embedded in goodness itself, the dreadful nihilistic state is avoided; felicity has been generously made available to all and will be obtained by all sooner or later, ensuring that human life is eminently meaningful and morality justified.

The axiological prioritization of felicity over God and morality, as significant as it may be in exploring the dynamics of Mendelssohn's thought, is therefore attenuated by the absolute optimism of Mendelssohn's onto-theology. While a world ruled by a God who would not ensure providence and immortality would be worthless and lacking in moral standing, Mendelssohn's metaphysics is based on a very different grounding; there is a God that is goodness itself and would never abandon his creation to such a hostile environment. This all-encompassing goodness explains why the process of perfection that Mendelssohn's notion of felicity consists of is holistic, inclusive of the aesthetic, religious, and moral development of human beings. As Mendelssohn famously put it in a seminal phrasing of his profound optimism: "Man's destiny: to seek truth; love beauty; will the good and do the best."[1]

Accordingly, given that pursuing one's own felicity consists of a holistic process of perfection by which we forever grow closer to the perfect God, one cannot be genuinely happy without being moral: "no rational being can promote his true happiness [wahre Glückseligkeit] without becoming a benefactor of the entire creation—so precisely, so inseparably do particular interests and universal interests hang together in the state ordained by God."[2] The notion that Mendelssohn's felicity necessarily involves also the moral development of human beings might have enabled him to argue against Cohen, who sees the polluting trace of self-interest in any form of eudaemonism, that felicity, while experienced by a particular and singular being, does very much promote also the kind of ultimate end Cohen's thought was after. Indeed, describing the process of perfection that our human felicity consists of, Mendelssohn writes that it is "far from canceling the mutual interest of moral entities or even weakening it in the slightest," and that it instead is "the source of universal sympathy [allgemeinen Sympathie], of this brotherhood of spirits . . . which engulfs and entwines each person's own interest and the common interest in such a way that they can no longer be separated without destruction on all sides."[3]

Yet, while Mendelssohn's axiology might perhaps be construed so as to include Cohen's highest good, it is difficult to see how Mendelssohn's highest good could possibly be integrated in Cohen's axiological structure. Indeed, while Mendelssohn's felicity is far from a simplistically hedonistic or narrowly selfish proposition, it still stands in stark, one could even say diametrical, contrast to Cohen's notion of the highest good, which he explicitly sought to purify from any trace of eudaemonism whatsoever.

Prima facie, perhaps some of the starkness of this contrast might be attenuated, in a very Mendelssohnian manner, by ascribing it, at least to some degree, to a semantic difference. Mendelssohn's eudaemonism does after all, very much in the spirit of the original meaning of the term, refer to something like "human flourishing" more than "happiness." Such an effort of mediation would then seek to construe Cohen's critique of happiness as focusing on a more sensual notion of eudaemonism, one based on the thoroughly inferior biological substrate of his religiously individuated notion of the self or one construed, as opposed to Mendelssohn's felicity, as inherently selfish and morally indifferent.

While such semantic and conceptual considerations might carry some weight, they are very far from overcoming the axiological abyss between Mendelssohn and Cohen. Indeed, while Mendelssohn's eudaemonism is necessarily correlated to the development of morality, it still remains deeply concerned with the self. This is clearly reflected in the unequivocal concern for the eternal substantiality of the individual. The destruction of the self, whether because of mortality or because of Spinozistic conceptions of the singular self as in some sense illusory or essentially engulfed in a larger substance, is to Mendelssohn philosophically and indeed existentially inacceptable.[4] In contrast, Cohen's own treatment of immortality seeks to anchor itself in his anti-eudaemonistic ethos, and he therefore refuses to accord that clearly delineated, eternally substantial individuality, which for Mendelssohn is critical for the subsistence of the highest good. Mendelssohn's individualized eudaemonism is, accordingly, focused on the well-being of the singular individual. As such, even if that well-being necessarily involves concern for others, it still cannot but be genuinely different from Cohen's *summum bonum*, which is not only centered on messianic humanity but actively eschews any concern for one's individual well-being, as is, for example, reflected in Cohen's ideas about the profound significance of suffering.

Indeed, Cohen's *summum bonum* is explicitly constructed out of a comprehensive and far-reaching disdain for any position that would reflect a Mendelssohnian concern with individual welfare. As was shown in chapter 4, one of Cohen's most significant criticisms of Kant is directed at Kant's inclusion of happiness in his notion of the complete good. Cohen takes this to be a grave mistake that betrays Kant's own quest for a deontological morality based on an autonomous will freely directed towards the good. Furthermore, Cohen's idealized notion of Judaism is one that is depicted as comprehensively anti-eudaemonistic and accordingly, to quote Rotenstreich, "characterized by opposition to egotism and by a tendency to transcend the horizon of the individual."[5] Cohen's interpretation of the Torah, of the prophetic sources, of rabbinic wisdom, or of the work of the great medieval Jewish philosophers insists again and again on their supposed relinquishment of the quest for individual felicity. This, as we saw in chapter 4, is also at the heart of his criticism of Zionism, depicted as contrasting with Judaism because, supposedly, Zionists yearn for happiness.

Cohen's anti-eudaemonist concept of the highest good is, furthermore, located in the future, which he further argues makes any claim eudaemonism might have on it untenable. And while I suggested Cohen does believe that future will one day come to pass, until it does, it remains an infinite task humans must tirelessly toil for. This infinite task incorporates the ethical mission that a corrected Kantian morality suggests as the highest good, that is, a community of moral, autonomous, and free human beings, but critically includes also the individualized person, which only religion, rather than ethics, can address.

In spite of their competing notions of the highest good, there clearly is a significant similarity in the way in which Mendelssohn's and Cohen's philosophies engage with the problem of universalism. Indeed, in both cases, Jewish particularism is justified because it serves the highest good, and that highest good is construed as essentially universal. For Mendelssohn, all human beings find the greatest value in a felicity that is conditioned on the awareness of the basic truths of natural religion, truths which Judaism is meant to promote and protect from idolatrous impingements. Meanwhile, for Cohen, Judaism historically brought into being the idea of the messianic future, and its historical mission is to promote it. And of course, as the prophets indicated, that future is one in which not just the Jewish people, but all nations will find themselves living in peace under the reign of the religion of reason.

Yet beyond this similarity, our axiological methodology enables us to discern another crucial difference. We saw, in the first chapter, that modern universalism is a loosely defined term that involves the promotion of various values that can be prioritized very differently. Indeed, our analysis throughout emphasized the possibility of axiological fragmentation and the idea that seemingly crystalized notions, say the "Enlightenment" or "universalism," might upon further scrutiny turn out to be far less coherent than what they are made out to be. In light of these insights and of the analysis of Mendelssohn's and Cohen's philosophy undertaken in previous chapters, we can now conclude that the formal similarity, that is, a particularism justified out of universalistic concerns, cloaks a radical difference. As both thinkers interpret Judaism in light of what their philosophy upholds as the highest good, and as their highest goods are radically different, they hold radically different notions of what Judaism is. Similarly, their differing conceptions of the highest good also indicate radically different universalisms, each based on a different set, and a varying prioritization, of universal values. So while particularism is in both cases justified because of its contribution to a universal vision, the essence of that particularism, and the nature of the universalism it is supposed to contribute to, are completely different.

Mendelssohn's Judaism embraces the universal truths upon which felicity depends, truths depicted as commonsensical. It therefore makes no particularly taxing demands on reason. Indeed, like Spinoza, Mendelssohn does not believe the Sinaitic revelation conveyed eternal truths.[6] Yet, unlike Spinoza, for whom salvific truths will be reached only by the very few who are able to develop a very sophisticated metaphysical understanding, Mendelssohn's salvific truths of natural religion are meant to be available to anyone with a healthy mindset. The Judaic law is, accordingly, not aimed at developing speculative reason but is rather meant to remind its practitioners, and those among whom they dwell, of the common truths of natural religion: God's existence, His providence, and our life eternal. Indeed, as we saw at some length, the use of philosophical reasoning is actually hazardous; it can draw us far from common sense into regions of confusion. The Halakha, accordingly, does in Mendelssohn's eyes what Luzzatto suggests his *Mesilat Yesharim* is supposed to do: "Not to teach men what they do not know, but to remind them of what they already know and is very evident to them."[7]

Judaism finds its value, therefore, in contributing to the promotion of the beliefs that human beings need in order to find felicity. Indeed, this would be precisely what any religion would have to focus on: in a world where there is no value whatsoever without the felicity ensured by a providential God whose existence ensures our afterlife, any genuinely meaningful spiritual path must lead to the awareness of these truths and therefore also to felicity.

Furthermore, as that felicity is attained by all human beings, there is nothing exclusivist about Judaism. We will return below to the problem of the advantage procured by the Halakha's salvific effects, but except for this tension, albeit a meaningful one, Mendelssohn does not seek to hierarchize religions, as he tends to assumes they are similarly dedicated to the highest universal good. Critically for our comparison, a religion or culture cannot be construed as superior solely because it is somehow more in line with reason. Rather, all religions are acceptable in so far as they are in line with common sense.[8] The version of universalism Mendelssohn's Judaism and his philosophy are dedicated to promoting is accordingly one that prioritizes the values of egalitarianism, pluralism, and tolerance far more than it does reason.

Cohen's Judaism is, on the other hand, depicted as eminently valuable precisely because it is the historical source and most apt instantiation of the religion of reason. Revelation is essentially correlated to reason. While the prophets were no philosophers,[9] their genius was the ability to incorporate the most sublime insights of reason into a discourse that also invokes the unique contribution of religion. Accordingly, as mentioned above, the messianic task their efforts call for combines both the ethical and the religious realms. This "historical miracle" is not available to all, but only to the monotheistic traditions that grew out of that original source.[10]

Cohen's universalism, accordingly, is based on the universality of reason. But, as has already been indicated in the introduction, the value of reason tends to contrast rather bluntly with those of egalitarianism and tolerance. And Cohen's universalism, based as it is on reason, is not, as we saw in chapter 5, an exception. Not all peoples have succeeded in manifesting the principles of the religion of reason in their religion, or "cult," as Cohen would put it.[11] Therefore, unlike Mendelssohn's continual quest to prove all cultures carry the same truths and thus must be worthwhile, for Cohen, not all cultures manifest the truth of the religion of reason and, accordingly, not all of them are equally valuable. Furthermore, given that for Cohen mistakes in the exercise of reason with regards to God are not merely a philosophical problem, but rather a grave moral one,[12] his Judaism and his philosophy cannot be tolerant of creeds deemed below the threshold of reason. Accepting these cultures would not merely consent to the debasement of reason but also, in Cohen's eyes, to the demeaning of morality and the debasement of humanity. Accordingly, Cohen's version of universalism prioritizes reason far more than it does tolerance, let alone pluralism.

Mendelssohn and Cohen are therefore both concerned with universalism, and both clearly seek to uphold universalism in their Judaism as well as their philosophies. But theirs are radically different universalisms. In fact, the difference is such that the comparative task cannot suggest a qualitative answer to their respective universalisms. In other words, one cannot simply judge who is more universal because universalism for Mendelssohn consists of a different universalistic axiology than it does for Cohen. The comparative analysis, rather, must seek to delineate what these different universalisms mean and what values they uphold and make explicit the different universalistic paths here offered. The next section will offer such an analysis.

Universalisms

The axiological analysis undertaken in this book is not meant to generate an agonistic debate from which either Mendelssohn or Cohen arises as the universalistic champion. Indeed, as mentioned above, given the fact their universalisms are so different, this study suggest one should not necessarily even think of them as competing in quite the same race. Each, rather, pursues his own distinctive universal goal. An axiological analysis enables a clearer understanding of that difference because it is mainly a difference of highest values and an ensuing different prioritization of those values that are shared. Accordingly, framing the comparison by asking who is more universal would be missing the complexity of the matter at hand.

This, however, does not mean arguments cannot be made for which vision is more convincing or better adapted to one's own sensitivities or method of valuation or for which thinker promotes values perceived as particularly relevant to current social realities or sensitivities. Indeed, in so far as we think of previous philosophers as critical in informing our own positions and enriching our own thought, it is inevitable that in comparing the Jewish universalisms of Mendelssohn and Cohen, one finds at least some aspects of either position more attractive. This is particularly relevant if the comparative analysis relates to values, which are profoundly related to deeply engrained desires and preferences and so too constitutive of our sense of identity. As Nietzsche put it in *Beyond Good and Evil*, "A person's valuations reveal something about the *structure* of his soul and what the soul sees as its conditions of life, its genuine needs."[13]

It is of course the case that when comparing any philosophical positions, one can always make arguments about what position is better developed, articulated, and ultimately convincing. But in many ways, the question of agreeing with Mendelssohn or with Cohen with regards to the values their Judaism and philosophy upholds is also necessarily a question that cannot be engaged with impersonally. It relates directly to the kind of person one is and, in so far as one seeks to identify with Judaism, the kind of Judaism one would like to engage with. In order to reflect on both the philosophical merits of the universalisms involved, as well as to clarify that deeply personal axiological choice here offered, we will now assess some critical aspects of the different universalisms suggested by Mendelssohn and Cohen.

MENDELSSOHN'S EGALITARIAN TOLERANCE

Mendelssohn was a staunch defender of a particularly robust version of the Enlightenment's optimistic strain of thought. In the tradition of Leibniz's best of all possible worlds, Mendelssohn's onto-theology is one according to which a providential God ensures our immortality and hence also the possibility of felicity. A crucial aspect of his claim for such a reality is the universal availability of the eternal truths of natural religion, namely, God, providence, and immortality. First, it would be inconceivable that a good God would withhold these truths from any human being, wherever or whenever she was born. Second, Mendelssohn's epistemology, based as it is on common sense and probability, would be gravely damaged if the beliefs he presents as universally commonsensical turned out to be but culturally dependent, particular, and local. If one does not agree with Mendelssohn that it is in fact common among all human beings to believe in a providential God and immortality, then these metaphysical postulates would lose what is for him their most important foothold. Indeed, given his take on the problematic nature of metaphysical inquiry, were the power of common sense to be diminished in Mendelssohn's philosophy, a variety of arguments critical to his thinking would be very difficult to maintain. It is not only Mendelssohn's faith, but his epistemology too, that commits him to the universal availability of eternal truths and the ensuing universal procurement of the highest good.

Mendelssohn's universalism is therefore centered on the equality of human beings and of human cultures in that which matters most, namely, the divinely ensured ability every human being has been endowed with to realize the ultimate goodness of God and embark on a process of self-perfection from which an enduring felicity arises. It is far less concerned with that other popular and universalistic value characteristic of the Enlightenment, namely, reason. Reason, as was discussed in chapter 2, is not unambiguously valued by Mendelssohn. The most direct and unfailing path to understanding salvific eternal truths is common sense, which could be considered a form of reason but is nonetheless demarcated by Mendelssohn from other uses he makes of the concept of reason in his writings. "Common sense" (Gemeinsinn, gesunde Menschenverstand, Bon Sens) is always written about commandingly, "reason" (Vernunft) is not. Furthermore, in Judaism, these truths are promoted not through the use of reason as such, but through a "living script" of acts and behavior that brings to mind salvific ideas that, while simple to realize, can be lost if the proper attention is not brought to them.[14]

More enthusiastic conceptions of reason's potential, such as Spinoza's, are repeatedly designated as untrustworthy. As we saw in chapter 2, human beings seek metaphysical knowledge with words that did not develop to engage with that highly abstracted activity. Words quickly become meaningless when the meanings they seek to contain are overly abstruse. That is why we characterized Mendelssohn as being skeptical of philosophical arguments, even if he did very much enjoy formulating such arguments himself or engaging with arguments developed by other thinkers.[15] Accordingly, opposing Jacobi's depiction of his position, Mendelssohn makes clear that he does not accept being characterized as a "hireling of reason [Vernünftling]."[16] Mendelssohn's distrust of philosophical reasoning and its tendency to conceitedly declare precision in matters where our language makes precision difficult if not impossible is an intrinsic part of the philosophical framework that enables him to construe his egalitarianism as deeply tolerant.

In fact, three related aspects of Mendelssohn's philosophy underlie his tolerant engagement with foreign cultures and religious rites: first, his commonsensical epistemology; second, his tendency to relate philosophical and theological conflicts to semantic battles; and third, his attention to the possibility of misunderstanding foreign symbolism. Indeed, Mendelssohn's commonsensical epistemology necessitates an accepting and open attitude towards foreign cultures and religions. Mendelssohn's belief that natural religion can be grasped by a mechanism akin to a common healthy reflex of the mind is an integral aspect of the optimistic worldview at the heart of his philosophy. He will therefore assume any religion he discusses to be, in the final analysis, in agreement about the essential human salvific principles. Were such an agreement not the case, then, as mentioned above, his claim that these principles are more likely to be truthful because they are commonly agreed upon would be seriously damaged. His commonsensical epistemology depends on there being a common agreement about certain beliefs he takes to be salvific.

In order to make the case such agreements exist even when at first sight it seems they do not, Mendelssohn relies on either his position about the semantic difficulty inherent in abstract thought or on his analysis of the dangers of symbolism. Indeed, when seeming differences arise, Mendelssohn can argue that the debate in question has veered into territory where the different meanings attributed to the abstractions discussed make it highly likely disagreements relate only to the ways words are used. Alternatively, he can make the case, as he often does, that symbols, behaviors, or stories that might look idolatrous turn out not to be so when one does not take literally that which is symbolic or, like actual idolaters, confuse the symbol with that which is symbolized.

These conceptions enable significant flexibility in tolerating other religions and cultures, not, as has previously been indicated, because they are accepted in their ultimate difference, but rather in that they are in the final analysis not different with regards to the most basic and important matters. Indeed, Mendelssohn's conscious reluctance to delineate the core religious principles of both natural religion and Judaism in elaborate theological detail avoids the controversies between what to him are minor details. There is no need to agree on the nature of God in great detail, but we must rather agree that God, in His absolute goodness, could not but ensure our felicity, a proposition he characterizes as obvious to a commonsensical and healthy-minded awareness. Trying to prove or say much more beyond that would only lead to unimportant disagreements about highly abstract notions we cannot talk about with any actual precision. Indeed, overly abstruse theological language is, like philosophical language, misleading.

Mendelssohn's position allows, therefore, for radical differences in the descriptive tools or symbolic framework through which the truths leading to felicity are communicated. And everything but these truths, and the felicity they enable, can be dismantled as an "unessential doctrine."[17] While, again, this is not a pluralism open to all differences, it does strongly minimize the very possibility such differences could actually be genuinely radical. The emphasis is clearly laid on inclusivity. All religions are assumed correct till proven idolatrous. Mendelssohn tends to first rethink our own ignorance and the misunderstandings it can engender before accusing a religion of being wrongheaded. The assumption is that in seas of unclear verbiage, ultimately, we are all roughly speaking about the same God.

This argumentation might be thought to be naïve. Yet many of the points Mendelssohn makes might, even with the hindsight of far more advanced contemporary comparative research, not be wholly exaggerated. So, for example, Mendelssohn's assumption that the tales of Indian cosmology reflect a form of religion that can be construed as common in its ultimate metaphysical principles with his own could certainly be defendable. Many major schools of Indian thought do in fact think of the gods as representatives of various aspects of one underlying principle.[18] Mendelssohn would, one presumes, enthusiastically adopt such readings of Indian religion and argue for the similarity of that underlying principle.[19] Any symbols used to describe that principle could be justified as long as they are not overly confusing, which of course at times they might be.

Mendelssohn is even willing to legitimize a polytheistic pantheon if, that is, one God is depicted as supreme. Indeed, Mendelssohn has a complex judgment of polytheism. While at times he does put it together with clearly nefarious phenomena, such as anthropomorphism and religious usurpation,[20] he does explicitly also suggest that even within polytheistic systems, an ultimate God is present. So, for example, in his commentary on the first of the Ten Commandments, "You shall have no other Gods before me,"[21] Mendelssohn writes that "with respect to all of the theoretical intelligibles . . ., the children of Israel are neither distinguished from, nor possess an advantage over, the rest of the nations. All acknowledge His divinity, may He be exalted; even the worshipers of other gods acknowledge that God Most High possesses the greatest power and absolute ability."[22] Indeed, Mendelssohn writes that "although the nations of the world acknowledge God's existence and power over all matters, they nevertheless also worship other beings,"[23] and he even adds that "the intellect's judgement does not forbid such worship to a descendent of Noah, provided that he does not intend to remove himself from the authority of God Most High."[24]

So while Mendelssohn's pluralism is limited in so far as it cannot accommodate certain very radical differences, it still is rather exceptionally inclusive. While atheism and certain forms of polytheism would be excluded, anything that vaguely resembles his notion of natural religion, including forms of polytheism that posit a supreme God, are acceptable and valid. True, as we explored in chapter 3, he does express some rather acute criticisms of Christianity. But one could, it seems to me, reasonably argue that that criticism was written in moments of bitter turmoil awakened by the likes of Lavater. Mendelssohn's philosophy, furthermore, developed conceptual tools that enable a significant lessening of the importance of that criticism, even if he at times did not rely on these tools to do so.

Another lingering tension in the egalitarian ambition of Mendelssohn's method of valuation is the revealed law the Jews have been chosen to uphold. As we have shown in chapter 3, Mendelssohn's thought does suggest the Jewish people have an advantage other people do not seem to have—a "living script,"[25] the major effect of which is promoting precisely those truths upon which human felicity is based. Accordingly, the more the revealed sanctified law that is the core of Mendelssohn's Judaism is meaningful and valuable, the greater the disparity between the Jewish people and others.

It is often argued that this problem is not, in the final analysis, dealt with satisfactorily by Mendelssohn.[26] But it seems to me there are at least two major arguments that can assuage this concern, if not totally, at least to a significant degree. First, we have suggested throughout this book that the problem of particularism can be alleviated by rethinking the issue while focusing on the highest good or, in the case of Mendelssohn, felicity. Felicity is a progress, a path, and it is the very act of progressing that brings felicity. The Jewish people would have had an advantage if their religion ensures they are nearer to felicity than others. Now, while the halakhic guarantee of maintaining a safe distance from idolatry and remaining focused on the salvific truths does make it in principle more difficult for Jews to fall into the despair of idolatry, felicity is similarly experienced by anyone in progress on the path of perfection. One is, therefore, not necessarily more felicitous by virtue of having attained a certain state or having begun progressing in more favorable circumstances. It is the infinite process that matters. So while the notion of chosenness remains particularistic, it does not contradict the one universal value Mendelssohn is most committed to: felicity.

Second, we should bring back to mind the fascinating comment Mendelssohn makes regarding the possibility that the unique kind of theo-political situation under which the Mosaic constituted arose might obtain again.[27] Having stated that it no longer obtains, he writes that "only the Omniscient knows among what people and in what century something similar will again be seen."[28] This suggests that the kind of revelation at the heart of Judaism is not necessarily only presented to the Jewish people. And if God might choose to reveal other laws to other peoples in the future or provide humanity with different further help to rid itself of idolatry and embrace its felicity, He might also very well have done so in the past. While Mendelssohn does not explicitly mention another Halakha, his position is at the very least compatible with the idea other peoples have been provided with certain cultural, symbolic, or religious apparatuses that contribute to universal felicity.

Indeed, in *Jerusalem*, Mendelssohn writes that when men such as Epicurus, Lucretius, Helvétius, or Hume cast doubt on the simple commonsensical realization of the providential divine presence, "providence again raises up other men among the people who separate prejudice from truth."[29] Again, while not an explicit argument, this at the very least suggests the possibility that the Halakha is not the only means by which God has chosen to protect the truths upon which human felicity depends. If providence raises individuals among the people, Jewish or not, to ensure the beatific truths of natural religion remain obtainable, it might very well have used other means among the nations to maintain and promote the all-important universal accessibility of felicity.

It is, at any rate, impossible to think of Mendelssohn's position as a relapse into a unilateral particularism. The argument we have here suggested shows that such a relapse would not just be a question of Mendelssohn contradicting Enlightenment norms or his humanistic universal sensitivities, but rather of radically subverting the commonsensical epistemology his philosophy is based on and, furthermore, contradicting the crucial beliefs he holds about God's goodness and universal providence, on which his assurance of felicity is based. Again, were God to deny felicity to any human being, He would not be Mendelssohn's best of all possible Gods, and Mendelssohn would accordingly lose his assurance that such a deity would necessarily engage in providence and ensure immortality. Particularism, in other words, contradicts Mendelssohn's *summum bonum* and would completely undermine it.

Mendelssohn is therefore fully committed to a universal concern with the felicity of every single being. His cultural sensitivity, furthermore, enables a universalism that does not crush varying rituals or varying symbolic conceptions of the divine, but construes them all as an essentially common human attempts at grasping the same truths. This commonality, however, is also a limitation; Mendelssohn cannot be shown to be as sensitive towards cultures who are genuinely trespassing the bounds of common sense. Still, Mendelssohn clearly thinks such trespassing is rather rare, and his tone is one of inclusion. We shall now delineate Cohen's very different universalism, which focuses far less on toleration and clearly prioritizes reason instead.

COHEN'S MESSIANIC REASON

There can be no doubt as to the ultimate universalism of the vision that Cohen's thought, in both its ethical and religious aspects, seeks to promote. Following the prophets, Cohen toils for world peace where, following Kant, a conglomerate of states enable an ethical humanity to thrive while also enabling individuals to discover their individuated selves according to the principles of Cohen's religion of reason. This religion of reason is demarcated by ideas and concepts that can be elucidated with scientific precision and can, in principle, be uncovered by all humans in so far as they rely on their reason to do so.[30]

Yet precisely because Cohen's religion of reason can be elucidated with such great precision, Cohen thinks he is able both to accurately locate the developments of these principles and goals in specific historical manifestations and to clearly differentiate religious traditions that are able to uphold his religion of reason from those that cannot. As we saw in the previous chapter, Judaism brought many of the concepts that make up Cohen's religion of reason into history, and while not all of empirical Judaism reflects the religion of reason, Judaism is its closest historical approximation. Furthermore, the fully idealized Judaism that Cohen promotes, which upholds the religion of reason uncovered by Cohen, was enabled by German culture.

So while eminently universal in principle, in practice Cohen's religion of reason is delineated as having emerged with Judaism and as having been, in the modern era, primarily developed by Germanism. Of course, Cohen was not the first to locate the development of reason within particular cultural circumstances. In so doing, he shows himself to be a child of his time and inscribes himself clearly within a tradition of post-Kantian German thought that located Germany as the seat of reason. There is here, more generally, a critical epochal difference between Mendelssohn, who writes at the height of the age of cosmopolitanism, and Cohen, whose thought sprung in the far more nationalistic nineteenth century. It is particularly important to contextualize Cohen with two major figures who similarly combined the Enlightenment's universalistic aspirations with German particularism: Herder and Hegel.

Herder was, as Berlin put it, "the father of the related notions of nationalism, historicism, and the *Volksgeist*."[31] As opposed to the strand of enlightened thought focused on universal reason and the equality of all human beings, he sought to emphasize the singularity of historical periods, civilization, and indeed nations, which he defined essentially as a cultural and linguistic community.[32] This cultural nationalism was by no means xenophobic or parochial. To the contrary, Herder strongly believed in the inherent value of various cultures and that the cultural self-realization of the various nations would strengthen true international cooperation. His ideas in that sense still reflect an eighteenth-century cosmopolitanism. Indeed, while he advocated German cultural unity, he did so for the sake of humanity.[33] He furthermore decried the prioritization of any national group as barbaric and generally espoused pacifistic and pluralistic ideals. Accordingly, as Cassirer points out, while Herder outgrew the intellectual world of the Enlightenment, his thought nonetheless can be seen as one of its "greatest intellectual triumphs."[34] In so far as he did break with his age, however, his ideas, and the emphasis they put on the particular cultural aspects at play in human life, very much set the stage for a later focus on the particular importance of German culture.

A more exclusivistic emphasis was thusly laid by Hegel, for example. As Dussel points out, Hegel clearly laid the axis of history in Europe, writing disturbingly racist and prejudicial passages on other regions of the world and their inhabitants, reflecting in doing so a European sense of superiority common at the beginning of the nineteenth century.[35] Northwestern Europe is construed, in the "moment of development," as the bearer of the spirit, the progress of which marks the heart of Hegel's philosophy.[36] German culture in particular, given that Hegel himself rose within it to unprecedented spiritual heights, is presented in particularly jubilant terms: "The German Spirit is the Spirit of the New World. Its aim is the realization of absolute truth, as the unlimited self-determination of freedom—*that* freedom which has as its own absolute form itself as its purport."[37]

This intellectual patriotism had by Cohen's time become, if possible, even more rampant. The fervency of its presence cannot be reduced merely to philosophical thought. The nineteenth century was an age of competing European national sates seeking military, technological, economic, and indeed imperial superiority.[38] In such an environment, it is not surprising that a more narrowly construed interpretation of Herder's cultural nationalism or Hegel's emphasis on Germany as the seat of reason became increasingly popular. Beyond Herder and Hegel, however, Neo-Kantianism itself was in some ways an integral part of that nationalistic atmosphere. Indeed, Neo-Kantianism was from its very origin tied to German nationalism, and Kant was a figure whose thought and renown was seen as awakening patriotic sentiments.[39]

The nationalism characteristic of Cohen's era, and more particularly the view of Germany as the seat of reason, which thinkers like Hegel had strongly argued for and which was widely acknowledged in his milieu, is, as we have seen, clearly present in Cohen's dealings with contemporary affairs, most notably the First World War, as well as in his depiction of the historical development of reason.[40] While of course other nationalistically inclined philosophers did not include Judaism as an original source of the Germanic religion of reason, and even less as a continued force for the development of a reasoned ethical humanity, Cohen's discourse and its tone is characteristic of his era.[41] These aspects of his philosophy, combined with the above-described precision with which morally superior theologies can be distinguished from morally reprehensible ones, leads to passages that, as we saw in the previous chapter, are rather intolerant.

Such passages are not only fiery, but bellicose, violent, and, at least seemingly, murderous. We looked in some detail at the passage where Cohen states that "idolatry has to be destroyed absolutely" and that "men had to be sacrificed for this purpose."[42] In a later chapter of his *Religion of Reason*, Cohen explains that Deuteronomy "seeks to establish monotheism as the deepest meaning and value of the Jewish people" and that "on the basis of this nationalism, polytheism is to be fought, all idol worship is to be destroyed among one's own people, as well as among all the surrounding peoples. For this goal and purpose Deuteronomy constantly proclaims the extermination of all idol-worshipping peoples as well as the destruction of Israel, except for a remnant."[43] Prima facie, these phrases seem to reflect a willingness to condone, if not encourage, violent holy wars. Though perhaps connotatively less shocking when contextualized in the rather bellicose, perhaps somewhat Wagnerian style many German writers adopted in the late nineteenth and early twentieth centuries, they remain, it seems to me, nonetheless rather disturbing.

Erlewine, however, argues that while Cohen is intolerant towards polytheism, his project envisions the "unfolding of a monotheistic intolerance that is ethical."[44] With regards to these passages, he argues that according to Cohen, the Jewish literary sources themselves "soon recognized that this radical opposition to idolatry and polytheism (i.e., the historical mission of Judaism) is inconsistent with the idea which secures ethics and generates the ideal of humanity (i.e., the unique God) if this opposition is construed as a call to violence against idolaters." Erlewine points at passages in which Cohen emphasizes the love demanded by the Bible for foreigners and the enduring recognition of the humanity even of idolaters. For Erlewine, according to Cohen's interpretation, the significance of this recognition of the idolater's humanity "cannot be overestimated, as it thoroughly permeates Cohen's thought on monotheism."[45]

The claim, then, is that the absolute demand to eradicate polytheism is contrasted with an absolute demand to recognize one's fellowman and the sanctity of humanity and of ethics so deeply embedded in monotheism. Erlewine rightly points out that Cohen himself suggests the Jewish literary sources moderated its originally harsh demand. As Cohen puts it, given that monotheism cannot be fully developed until the "foreigner is . . . recognized as fellowman," when monotheism was further developed, it was "able to correct its own teaching with respect to the strict commandment to destroy idol worship and idolatrous peoples."[46]

Cohen therefore indeed does specifically mention a development abetting the murderous implication of the absolute opposition to polytheism and idolatry. Indeed, more generally, the importance of temporality must be taken into account when exploring Cohen's thought about Judaism. So, for example, Cohen believes an ancient Israeli state might have been justified at some point in history, though he disapproves of it in his own time. Similarly, the physical destruction of idolatry might have been necessary when monotheism was introduced into world history but be illegitimate in later historical stages. Additionally, Erlewine is correct in arguing that the comprehensive ethical construct at the heart of Cohen's philosophy offers a strong rebuttal to a violent combat of idolatry.

However, I would still argue that in depicting Cohen's "ethical intolerance" as one that essentially "eschews all violence,"[47] according to which "violence against the idolater becomes absolutely prohibited as a solution to the problem of polytheism,"[48] Erlewine suggests a position that is far more unambiguous than the one Cohen's own words reflect. This is for two reasons. First, while Cohen indeed believes monotheism developed the most profound ethical notions that encourage a brotherly compassion towards one's *rea*, he provides an interpretation that argues that its inception was somehow intrinsically linked with a historically necessary murderous violence. Second, and perhaps even more importantly, this violence is depicted as not necessarily contradicting the brotherly compassion reflected in the ethics it was violently giving birth to.

To emphasize the first point, it is important to keep in mind the unambiguous language Cohen uses in this context when claiming that the destruction of idolatry was a necessary pursuit that had to be undertaken relentlessly. This venture, he writes, reflects a "holy zeal against the false Gods." Therefore, the worship of the unique God, as quoted in the last chapter, "unavoidably exacts the destruction of false worship.

In this respect there can be no pity and no regard for men." Using a distinctly Hegelian turn of phrase, Cohen writes that we must understand the "*world history of the spirit* from its own principles" in explaining why the prophets could not appeal to tolerance in their quest to "creatively form the history of the spirit." Cohen contextualizes this lack of toleration in the duty to combat polytheism in a "primitive age and the rudeness of its customs." But it remains a necessary "historical duty." And as if the terrible consequences of such a view were not clear enough, Cohen adds a sentence worth quoting again: "To be sure, men had to be sacrificed for this purpose, men from their own people no less than from other peoples."[49]

Clearly, Cohen's reading of the Bible, based as it is on his idealized concept of Judaism, is not a fundamentalist or literary interpretation. Indeed, Cohen loathed literal interpretations of the sources,[50] and as we saw in the previous chapter, uses hermeneutical mechanisms to disengage biblical moments he does not seek to promote, such as ascribing certain aspects of the biblical narrative to Persian influence rather than Hebraic origin.[51] No such mechanism is brought to bear on this aspect of the prophetic effort. While aware that one here finds acts in profound tension with ethics, Cohen accepts their historical necessity and therefore ultimately condones them. This is not to say he is calling for people to massacre idolaters. Again, he does mention that that form of zeal was corrected. But the fact he does not seek to relegate that call as somehow unauthentic to the true spirit of the historical wonder that is Hebraic monotheism, as he is wont to do for other biblical notions, shows that avoiding such violence is not a primordial concern of his. Erlwine's depiction of his "ethical intolerance" as unambiguously opposed to violence is therefore too generous a take on a far more ambiguous position. That which is unambiguous is the notion that the origin of monotheism was accompanied by justified murderous violence.

Second, as mentioned, such violence is not necessarily contradicted by the ethics monotheism was giving birth to or indeed necessarily by later developments in the history of monotheism. So, for example, the development that makes of the foreigner a fellowman, which Cohen addressed when stating the commandment to destroy idolatrous people has been rectified, does not seem to mitigate the legitimacy of violence. While Cohen notes that the conceptualization of the foreigner as the fellowman is particularly striking given that "monotheism made the foreigner into fellowman, even without his joining the monotheistic religion,"[52] this does not ipso facto reflect a nonviolent position. Gratuitous violence vis-à-vis the fellowman would clearly be out of the question, but that does not necessarily entail that all forms of violence are unacceptable. In fact, Cohen points out the same recognition of the humanity of foreigners right after having made the above-quoted claim that some have to be sacrificed to rid humanity of idolatry. He writes that while they did kill idolaters, "the advocates of monotheism did not fail to recognize the humanity of men as such."[53] So the recognition of the humanity of my fellowman does not make me necessarily adopt a nonviolent attitude towards that fellowman. It means rather that even when violence must be brought to bear, it can be done while recognizing the other's humanity. Recognizing the idolator as a fellowman, to put it bluntly, does not mean I shouldn't kill him.

One could convincingly argue that this aspect of Cohen's thought is mitigated, if not placated, by the continual emphasis he puts on morality and on the primordial ethical import of religion and of Judaism. While religion cannot in the final analysis be reduced to morality, it remains morality's greatest and most intimate ally. The notions of compassion and love of the stranger and of the fellowman we looked at throughout our analysis of Cohen ensure that the cruelty of religious persecution would fit rather difficultly in Cohen's system. Yet, while Cohen's philosophy does provide a wide variety of conceptual tools with which to expunge such cruelty, he himself did not unambiguously do so. One would have to engage in a critical reconstruction of his thought, rather like the one he himself undertook of Kant's, to avoid these violent aspects of it. Assuming that the primacy of the ethical is the genuine heart of Cohen's philosophy, efforts could be made to create a Cohenian Judaism that approaches these problematic passages very differently. Still, the fact Cohen, in spite of the primordial importance of the ethical in his thought, did not do so himself is very significant for our analysis.

As opposed to Mendelssohn, who seeks to depict the vast majority of theological differences as essentially yielded from semantic and cultural misunderstandings, Cohen is very clear about the abysmal gap between the very rare correct manifestations of the religion of reason and debasing forms of idol worship. This relates to the fact that the epistemology on which his universalism is based is reason rather than common sense and that as opposed to Mendelssohn's emphasis on the vagueness of language, Cohen emphasizes the scientific accuracy of philosophical thought even when brought to bear on religion. As opposed to Mendelssohn's efforts to generate a tolerant universalism that emphasizes equality, Cohen's universalism is intolerant and emphasizes the absolute nature of very specific ethical and theological positions.

This, of course, is not to say that Mendelssohn too would not be intolerant of the ethical aspect of some theological positions. If, for example, a certain culture were to be involved in human sacrifice, one presumes both Mendelssohn and Cohen would be similarly intolerant of it. And indeed, Cohen does repeatedly emphasize the fact monotheism overcame pagan human sacrifice.[54] So their differences in theological tolerance does not necessarily preclude similar forms of ethical intolerance, just as religious pluralism does not necessarily equate ethical pluralism. Still, Mendelssohn's universalism remains more inclusive than Cohen's, whose emphasis on reason does not allow the equalitarian conceptions Mendelssohn's emphasis on common sense enables.

Indeed, I have argued that the tension between the demand for universal reason and an ethic that values all people equally is inherent to the set of values commonly associated with the Enlightenment. This tension is particularly acute in Cohen, whose thought does not resolve the clash between the prioritization of reason, on the one hand, and tolerance or equality, on the other. To the contrary, Cohen condones violence when it is construed as necessary to make all-important reason manifest itself in history. Indeed, we find here a clear echo of the postcolonial critique of Enlightenment discourse mentioned in the introduction. Such criticism often points at how a discourse centered on reason veers into the need to reform, violently if necessary, cultures that fail to uphold a supposedly universal rationality.[55]

This does not necessarily make Cohen less universal than Mendelssohn, but rather differently so. Mendelssohn's universalism is one of tolerance and equality; Cohen's, one of reason. While Cohen's reason does lead to a messianic future where all human beings are equal, the path to this future involves clear demarcations between various cultures and peoples. Furthermore, this different axiological tendency is seen not only in the different values these universalisms reflect but can also be clearly noticed in the ways in which they express their disagreements. Indeed, the difference we are here exploring is reflected in their different tonalities, which we will analyze in the following section.

TONALITIES: THE CASE OF SPINOZA

We emphasized above that values relate to profound and constitutive aspects of our identity. The variance in the values promoted by Mendelssohn and Cohen, in particular with regards to the ways in which they address the critical problem of tolerance, is accordingly not only related to the structure of their philosophical systems as explored above but also to something more personal. Indeed, if axiology cannot but reflect the self, it is clear that Cohen and Mendelssohn are very different kinds of persons. This variance in personality is reflected with great obviousness in the different tones with which they criticize their philosophical opponents. In this section, we will exemplify this difference through their respective writings about Spinoza.

Spinoza, as has been established in the first chapter, haunts the philosophical efforts of both Mendelssohn and Cohen. It is Spinoza who arguably provides the most comprehensive and acute devaluation of Judaism, and it is often explicitly in light of this devaluation that both Mendelssohn and Cohen seek to revaluate their Jewish heritage. Furthermore, for both Cohen and Mendelssohn, Spinoza's philosophy contains elements that are axiologically threatening not only to their Judaism but to their philosophies as well. And yet, the different approaches they exhibit when dealing with him, and critically also the tones of their writing, are revealingly different.

For Cohen, as we saw in chapter 4, Spinoza's philosophy is plagued by profound mistakes that cannot but lead its followers astray both morally and religiously. Indeed, the separateness of the unique God from the world of becoming is a critical, constitutive aspect of Cohen's system. It is that which enables the separation of the actual and the ideal and hence also the rise of ethics. There could simply not be a more fundamental principle to Cohen's construct. Yet it is precisely that principle that Spinoza's philosophy undermines with its unification of God and nature and the ensuing radically immanent worldview. For Cohen it is not solely the case that Spinoza's philosophy is mistaken in its most basic assumption but also that the unification of God and nature destroys the very possibility of an ethics the kind of which Cohen's philosophy is dedicated to.

Cohen's critique, however, as previously mentioned, is not only moral but Jewish and personal as well. The Jewish angle of his critique seeks to undermine Spinoza's depiction of Judaism, which Cohen claims Spinoza spitefully crafted while willfully ignoring large segments of the Jewish sources. Spinoza, Cohen writes, establishes his entire inquiry into biblical criticism in order to prove that the "*religion* of Judaism founded by Moses set for itself the sole purpose of establishing and preserving the Jewish *state*" and aims at the "destruction of the Jewish concept of religion."[56] By reducing the Mosaic national effort solely to the political, Spinoza completely misses its most enduring contribution to human culture, namely, ethical monotheism. And in so far as he does analyze Mosaic politics, Spinoza, Cohen furthermore argues, completely misses the "social spirit" of the Mosaic political constitution and does not appreciate the "anti-clerical and anti-aristocratic politics of the prophets, which are rooted in socialism."[57] Furthermore, Spinoza ignores the centrality of the notion of the Noachide and misreads Maimonides on the topic. And while Spinoza does show some awareness of the universalism of the prophets, he completely misses the way in which the national state was necessarily connected to it.[58] Putting it more firmly later on, Cohen writes that Spinoza did not have the "faintest clue about the actual founders of Judaism, the prophets";[59] he never understood "prophetic Messianism and its [idea of] the future of humanity."[60]

Spinoza, Cohen argues, created a distorted and falsified depiction of Judaism, which unfortunately gained significant influence among later philosophers. Indeed, while many Christians, including Leibniz and Thomasius, had, Cohen writes, spurned Spinoza, ever since "Lessing and Herder placed Spinoza on a pedestal, he and his *Tractatus* have become the authentic source of biblical and rabbinic Judaism in the modern world." Interestingly, though he writes that Mendelssohn did so "innocently," Cohen believes Mendelssohn too contributed to this erroneous assessment of Judaism.[61] Significant aspect of Spinoza's mischaracterization have therefore misled both Christian and Jewish philosophers. Elsewhere, Cohen explicitly relates Kant's problematic understanding of Judaism to Spinoza as well.[62] All of this, Cohen suggest, is because of "this great enemy who emerged from our midst," who remains "the real accuser of Judaism in the eyes of the Christian world."[63] Indeed, the "demonic spirit of Spinoza" is still "poisoning the atmosphere from within and without."[64]

This phrasing then takes us to the third layer of criticism Cohen makes against Spinoza. It is not merely a matter of correcting his philosophical mistakes, or even his mistakes about Judaism; there are also deeply personal accusations. While Cohen writes in *Spinoza on State and Religion* that he has sought "as much as possible to abstain from judgement on Spinoza's *personal character*," the judgments Cohen found impossible to abstain from are rather vitriolic. So Cohen suggests there is a "demonic aspect" to Spinoza's character,[65] reflects on the possibility of a "diabolical irony" in his interpretation of chosenness,[66] and expresses understanding for the community that had to excommunicate him because of the bitter fate they had so often suffered at the hands of "informers in their midst."[67]

Cohen also suggests that the motives to Spinoza's treatment of Judaism, namely, his grievances towards the Jewish community and political support of Johannes de Witt,[68] make him a biased, unreliable interpreter.[69] He therefore questions the honesty of his motives and suggests Spinoza's depiction of his own people and their religion is akin to intellectual treason. There is, in other words, beyond the philosophical and philological debate, an aggressive ad hominem attack.[70] The hostility aimed at Spinoza was apparently obvious in the seminar in which Cohen formed his polemic against Spinoza. One of its participants, the historian Hans Liebeschütz, describes the degree of animosity raised by any attempt at defending Spinoza as "mysterious."[71]

The virulent antagonism in Cohen's writing on Spinoza echoes intolerance for perceived mistakes his universalism exhibits, and the fury of its tone reflects a personality that does not shy away from conflict when the principles of his understanding of monotheism are attacked. Given that axiology is both philosophical and personal, it is indeed not surprising to find a philosophical and personal intolerance in Cohen's writing. This is not to say that such intolerance is necessarily unjustified, only that it exists. And its ferocity with regards to Spinoza is especially insightful when compared to Mendelssohn's far more generous treatment of the very same figure.

Mendelssohn dwells less on Spinoza's characterization of Judaism, and indeed, as Cohen suggests, his own description of the Mosaic constitution is in some ways drawn from Spinoza's.[72] However, unlike Spinoza and like Cohen, he obviously very much ascribes a religious aspect to that constitution, one reflected in the ceremonial law. Far from being the nefarious, enslaving constraint Spinoza makes it out to be, that law is for Mendelssohn a critical tool in helping to guide humanity towards its highest good of felicity. From this point of view, Mendelssohn's conception of Judaism is as opposed to Spinoza's as Cohen's is.

Furthermore, not only does Mendelssohn disagree with Spinoza on Judaism, like with Cohen, Spinoza's philosophy threatens the fundamental principles upon which his own philosophy is based. Indeed, as we saw in chapters 2 and 3, the continued substantiality of the self is, for Mendelssohn, a crucial component of the salvific truth of natural religion. It is therefore critical to him that we have substantial and distinct identities that cannot be annihilated even after death. But of course, Spinoza's philosophy threatens the substantiality of the individual even before death. If all there is is God or nature, and I exist merely as a modification of God or Nature, I cannot be conceived to exist as a distinct substantive self.[73] Spinoza, in other words, threatens Mendelssohn's philosophy and its highest good no less than he does Cohen's.

The critical importance of Mendelssohn's opposition to Spinoza is dramatically emphasized by how deeply he was affected by the pantheism controversy. Famously, he died because he fell ill after he had, at the end of a bitterly cold Shabbat in Berlin, hurried out of his house to personally carry the manuscript of *To the Friends of Lessing*, which of course addressed the controversy, to his publisher. Agitated as he was, he reportedly left the house without wearing his overcoat, nor had he bothered ordering a carriage.[74] The pantheism controversy, of which Spinoza's supposedly misleading philosophy was at the heart, could clearly not have been more personally disturbing to Mendelssohn.

So, Spinoza's valuation of Judaism contradicts Mendelssohn's, his philosophy clearly threatens the substantiality of the individual at the very core of Mendelssohn's philosophy, and furthermore, Spinoza's thought instigated a scandal that hurt Mendelssohn on a very personal level. Yet, in spite of all this, Mendelssohn was, to quote Guttman, "the first German thinker to try to secure Spinoza his proper place in the history of thought."[75] Furthermore, not only did he suggest ways in which

Spinoza's philosophy could be made palatable to the essential principles of natural religion, but Spinoza also personally remained to Mendelssohn a figure whose nobility of character and philosophical genius was not to be doubted.

First, in his *Dialogues*, his very first publication (1755), Mendelssohn writes that "Spinoza, has participated immensely in the work of bettering philosophy" and that while it was his "unhappy lot" to plunge in "the monstrous abyss" lying between Descartes and Leibniz, this "sacrifice for the intellect . . . deserves to be decorated with flowers. Without him, philosophy would never have been able to extend its borders so far."[76] Thirty years later, Mendelssohn still maintained that early position. While in profound disagreements with some of Spinoza's conclusions, he writes in his *Morning Hours* (1785) that "one rightly admires the intellectual rigor with which Spinoza expounds the fundamental premises of his system and how he binds even its smallest elements together into one geometrically consolidated structure."[77]

Second, Mendelssohn's inclusive philosophical mechanism is brought to bear on Spinoza too. Indeed, given his tendency to think of overly elaborate metaphysical arguments as essentially semantic battles wherein all sides have lost track of what they are actually saying, it is not surprising he makes the case a theist and, to use his expression, a "purified" Spinozist are saying pretty much the same thing.[78] He cannot compromise on the substantiality of the individual but except for this point seeks a common ground even with Spinoza. Furthermore, as opposed to Cohen, who justified Spinoza's excommunication, Mendelssohn explicitly argues that religion should neither excommunicate nor even have the authority to do so.[79] When writing these arguments, it is inconceivable he would not have been thinking too of the most famous excommunicated Jew of the modern era.[80]

Third, the tone with which Mendelssohn handles Spinoza could not be more different than Cohen's. It reflects a profound respect for a man that was to him, as Derrida puts it, "a master, a disputed one, no doubt, but still a master."[81] It maintains, furthermore, the utmost respect for the man's character and that of his followers. So, while discussing the allegations made by Jacobi concerning Lessing's Spinozism, Mendelssohn makes the point that even if his friend had been a Spinozist, it would not have diminished his view of Lessing's genius or character and emphatically makes his point by rhetorically asking, "What do speculative doctrines have to do with human beings? Who would not be overjoyed to count Spinoza himself as his friend, however much of a Spinozist he may have been? Who refuses to admit the truth of Spinoza's genius and noble character?"[82]

So, as with Cohen, there is a symmetry between the inclusivity reflected in Mendelssohn's axiology and the one reflected in the tone of his writing. The axiological contrast between Mendelssohn and Cohen relates to both their philosophies and their personalities. This further reinforces the above-mentioned deeply personal nature of the axiological aspect of a philosopher's worldview. Mendelssohn's and Cohen's values are reflected in their philosophy as they are in the tone with which it is written and the personalities these different tonalities reflect.

Revaluated Judaisms

If Spinoza's philosophy, as was argued in the first chapter, was indeed the most comprehensive enlightened universalistic devaluation of Judaism, this book has argued that both Mendelssohn and Cohen suggest revaluations of Judaism that seek to show how in spite of Spinoza and other thinkers, Judaism is not only valuable but universally so. Indeed, while the highest goods suggested are radically different for Mendelssohn and Cohen, as are the ensuing axiological structures and conceptions of Judaism, in both cases the axiological structure and the Judaism that champions these highest goods are in a critical sense universalistic.

Because universalism is such a clear concern of both Mendelssohn and Cohen, and the devaluative criticism of Judaism perennially depicts it as particularistic, Mendelssohn and Cohen are often depicted as apologists and accordingly as somehow meekly and diffidently pleading their case.[83] This perception is, I would argue, misguided for at least two reasons. First, while Jews were writing from a very difficult political status, assuming their philosophical position to be passive or defensive already implies the ancient trope of Jewish particularism. This, in other words, prejudges their argument as reactive to external universal demands. Yet Mendelssohn and Cohen are explicitly arguing that Judaism is, at least in the ways that truly matter, more universal than Christianity. Indeed, in Cohen's case, Judaism is presented as being the very root of that universalism that it is attacked for lacking. Accordingly, arguing that Jewish thinkers seek to present Judaism as universal solely because Judaism is attacked as particular does not allow for the possibility that Jewish thinkers present Judaism as universalistic because it actually genuinely underlies many of the most important values of the modern universal outlook.

This takes us to the second point. The apologetic effort in philosophy is very far from one that apologizes. The Greek *apologia*, derived from *apologos*, meaning "defense in trial" or "rebuttal of the prosecutor's accusation," is too quickly associated, whether in terms of meaning or even just connotatively, with the contemporary English meaning of *apology* and *apologizing*, as in admission of wrongdoing.[84] It is critical to keep in mind that these varying meanings of the term are radically different.[85] A striking example of that difference is the quintessential philosophical apology, namely, Socrates's. Far from apologizing in the modern sense, Socrates's defense is as defiant a speech as any. The philosopher stands insolently before his jury, damning them just as much as he is defending himself. So, for example, having been found guilty, he begins his second speech, wherein he is supposed to suggest a fitting punishment, by suggesting the proper reward would consist of free meals at the city hall, an honor reserved for Olympic champions.[86] According to Diogenes Laertius, there were more jurors sentencing him to death after his second speech than there had been who found him guilty after the first, reflecting the degree to which this rebellious attitude angered his audience.[87] There are few texts, in other words, that contain quite as much chutzpah as the original philosophical apology.

Similarly, as we have seen throughout our analysis of Mendelssohn and Cohen, far from being a timid reactive effort, their depiction of Judaism is to the contrary as defiant as Socrates's defense. Again, in their apologies, both, as we saw, argue that Judaism rather than Christianity is the more genuinely universalistic religion. While they argue this is the case for very different reasons, and do so in different tones, the fact remains that both are far from apologetic in their Jewish apologies.

The notion that both Mendelssohn and Cohen conceive of their own efforts as proactive depictions of Judaism rather than reactive and defensive efforts is further revealed by the fact they present their revaluated Judaism not as a reinterpreted or reformed Judaism, but rather as the original, authentic Judaism. Indeed, in both cases, their conception of Judaism is intrinsically linked to their distinctly different highest goods, which they present as its essence. So in seeking to prove the value of Judaism, they suggest Judaisms that are essentially different. We will conclude this book with some reflections on how, in both cases, their highest good is presented as the essence of Judaism, an essence that they link to its very historical formation, and on the kind of axiology this reflects.

THE ESSENCE OF JUDAISM

Judaism is for Mendelssohn essentially a divine legislation revealed to a particular people in order to ensure that awareness of the universal salvific truths of natural religion is maintained. For Cohen, its essence is revealed in the messianic future it was always meant to encourage humanity to reach. Though Mendelssohn's more literal interpretative methodology radically differs from Cohen's hermeneutics of idealization, their characterizations of the Jewish religion are presented in both cases as relating to the very core of Judaism rather than as, say, reinterpretations of a phenomenon that might have been radically different.

While non-essentialist sensitivities characterize much of twentieth- and twenty-first-century thought, both Mendelssohn and Cohen are, in this sense, part of a different era. They do not accept the premise that every generation redefines Judaism; rather, they genuinely believed there was, in some sense, an essence that has been present from the very beginning and has been transmitted ever since. And while a non-essentialist perspective has enabled us to analyze their axiological leanings, and from that perspective their revaluations are highly creative enterprises, they themselves did not share that perspective.

Accordingly, in making their philosophical claims, they seek to make historical claims as well. So the essence of Judaism for Mendelssohn begins with the Sinaitic revelation, during which it was already clear that Judaism is a legislative revelation aimed at directing the people towards their God-sanctioned felicity.[88] For Cohen, Messianism is already contained in the notion of the unique God, and the prophets, who are for him the genuine founders of Judaism, unfolded the monotheistic insight into a messianic vision that forms the highest value human beings can aspire to.[89] While Cohen's philosophy, in so far as it sets itself on a course towards a messianic future, is far more concerned with progress than Mendelssohn's and therefore recognizes later cultural forces that have promoted and developed that original messianic insight, that insight still remains essentially identified with the primary origin of Judaism. Accordingly, "*prophetism*," which is reflected "in [Judaism's] *ethical teaching*, in its *universalism*, in its *humanism*," is not only recognized as the "value of Judaism" and posited at the heart of what Cohen describes as "our inherited, our *messianic optimism*"; it is also the "eternal essence [ewigen Wesen] of our religion itself."[90]

This is not to say, however, that Mendelssohn or Cohen held a static view of that essence. Indeed, in different ways, both philosophers sought to reflect in their Jewish thought the dynamism of the interpretative aspect of the Jewish heritage. Though for Mendelssohn the ceremonial laws were unchanging, they themselves encourage, in the social activity their fulfilment demands, a continued, living, interpretative effort. Critically, this, in fact, is a demand inherent to the "basic outlines of ancient, original Judaism."[91] The doctrines and laws of that ancient original Judaism were "entrusted to living, spiritual instruction, which can keep pace with all changes of time and circumstances."[92] Therefore, as Goetschel points out, Mendelssohn sought to rescue "the creative aspect of tradition through a semiotic interpretation of the function of the ceremonial law," emphasizing the "vital and creative potential of ceremonial law as an ever-renewing resource that keeps tradition alive and functioning."[93]

Similarly, for Cohen, the dialectical relation of the idealized concept of Judaism yielded from reason, and the historical sources that anticipate that concept as well as the practices meant to protect it, demands a continual interpretative effort of the latter in light of the former. The effort ensures that, as Poma puts it, "Judaism cannot be reduced to a static or repetitive preservation of tradition."[94] This dialectical dynamism is reflected also in the dynamic nature of the messianic task Judaism calls for. While Cohen strongly resisted the historicistic interpretations of Judaism by positing an unchanging messianic ideal as its goal and pinnacle, that ideal still needs to be applied to the living reality of history. The messianic task, after all, demands actual, empirical action.

So both philosophers conceive of Judaism as a tradition that is interpretative, dynamic, and vibrant. Yet, these characteristics are presented as inherent to its original concept. Whether it relates to the very nature of the ceremonial law or to the concept of the unique God and the messianic ideal that ensues, Jewish dynamism relates in both cases to what they thought of as the essence of Judaism. And that essence, whether at

Sinai or in the prophetic discourse, is conceived as having been delineated at the very origin of Judaism.[95]

To further emphasize the difference between a way of thinking about values that makes no essentialist assumptions and that has no role in preserving that "essence" and one that does, it is helpful to think, as Geuss does, of the crucial distinction between the Nietzschean concept of "genealogy" and the related one of "pedigree." Genealogy, as practiced by Nietzsche, does not seek out a single origin of absolute value. Indeed, in the case of complex phenomena like religions or a given morality, it tends to assume there will not be a single origin, but rather a wide variety of sources. Nietzsche's genealogy, therefore, did not seek to link value to a particular origin, let alone an ancestral chain of heritage. Contrarily, the purpose of a "pedigree" is highlighting the value of an object by linking it directly to its origin, an origin perceived as having some sort of absolute value. Moreover, each step in the pedigree either preserves or increases the value of the object as it is held by figures of worth.[96] Both Mendelssohn's and Cohen's efforts very much reflect such pedigree thinking, wherein the value of Judaism is linked to its origin. Indeed, this aspect of their philosophies reflects ancestral forms of Jewish thought. In explaining his conception of a pedigree, Geuss chooses an example from ancient Greek literature,[97] but, of course, there are plenty of biblical passages emphasizing the degree to which pedigrees are significant in ancient Hebraic forms of valuation. Most obviously, the religion of the Israelites is continually related to Abraham, Isaac, and Jacob. Generations are carefully noted, and the faith of the Hebrews, therefore, is continually presented as part of a linkage leading directly to the covenant of God with Abraham. As this covenant is perceived to hold absolute value, the pedigree is emphasized to enable the transition of that value through the generations.

Mendelssohn and Cohen show this form of pedigree thinking is not only deeply embedded in ancient Jewish sources but remains a very important part of modern Jewish thought as well. It relates, in turn, to an essentialist approach to Judaism and to essentialist attempts at capturing its core, a core supposedly transmitted from ancient generations onwards. Once again, therefore, while their highest values are very different, this is another way in which their axiological assumptions are remarkably similar.

Indeed, while Mendelssohn's felicity is fundamentally different from Cohen's non-eudaemonic messianic future, both are universal in aspiration and both are presented as the very core of Judaism and, indeed, as its purpose. Judaism therefore, to both Mendelssohn and Cohen, has always carried universal values. These were not imposed from the outside with modernity. To the contrary, it is finally with modernity that the outside world headed the ancient call to incorporate the universal values Judaism has always sought to promote.

Mendelssohn and Cohen's faith therefore reflects a universal Jewish optimism. As opposed to the pessimistic notion that values cannot apply to this world, both robustly argue that value can arise in the human realm. Both also argue that the highest values are universal in scope (even if, as we saw above, differently so). Furthermore, the delineation, application, and promotion of these values is what Judaism really is about and what it really always was meant to be about.

These efforts are complex, and the arguments used reflect tensions that cannot necessarily always be resolved. Indeed, the tensions uncovered in our axiological analysis might arguably not always make for the most coherent philosophy. Such tensions, however, might also be inevitable aspects of actual human lives. And axiology is not only about making speculative philosophy cohere; it is also, and perhaps mainly, about lived philosophy, about our lives, our identities, the goals we set for ourselves and that in which we find meaning.

Whether one finds either Mendelssohn's or Cohen's universal optimism convincing, or indeed whether one remains convinced by neither, there is much in these grand efforts to inspire contemporary Jews to reflect on the meaning of their human and Jewish values. It is often said that glorious failures are more important than measly victories. I do not know whether Mendelssohn's or Cohen's argumentations can be, in the final analysis, perceived as victories. But even so, these efforts are certainly worthy of our continued attention and study. Even when torn at the seams, their philosophy reflects a stiff-necked aspiration to creatively engage with their tradition. Jacob became Israel, the Bible tells us, when he wrestled with an angel. Mendelssohn's and Cohen's Judaism reflect such a struggle. It seems to me that even if we do not agree with the result, we cannot but be inspired by the effort. This effort, as analyzed in this book, suggests the critical importance of struggling to clarify our axiological orientation, even if it is one that we conceive of as inherited. Perhaps it would be fitting to encapsulate that particular spirit in a paraphrase that echoes both the transformation of Jacob into Israel and Socrates's defiant apology and suggest a motto yielded from both and reflected with great eloquence in Mendelssohn's and Cohen's efforts: an unexamined Judaism is not worth living.

CONCLUSION

Universalism, I hope to have shown in this book, is not a unified concept. It means different things for Mendelssohn than it does for Cohen, and indeed, it probably carries just as singular a meaning in the philosophies of other thinkers, whether Jewish or not, who have dealt with this question. I have also argued throughout that a particularly useful way to assess what precisely any particular universalistic worldview consists of is by seeking to clarify the values at its heart.

We saw too that many central universalistic values stand in inherent tension with each other, for example, reason and equality. These tensions might just be an aspect of life that cannot be made to cohere. Indeed, each one of us might just have to balance competing values according to our own axiological hierarchies and prioritizations. But making these values explicit is necessary in order to develop a robust worldview.

A further insight enabled by the analysis of such axiological tensions is that tensions habitually depicted as reflecting an abysmal contrast between the Enlightenment and Judaism could very well be interior to the Enlightenment, or to Judaism, or indeed to both. Just as the Enlightenment's emphasis on equality and tolerance can clash with its own emphasis on reason, so too can Judaism itself have both particular and universal elements within its own sources. Crystalizing such wide concepts, whether the "Enlightenment" or "Judaism," risks masking complexities of which it is important to remain aware.

In our globalized society, the question of universalism has become even more ubiquitous than it was in Mendelssohn's or Cohen's time. Yet the values of our universalism, indeed its very meaning, tend to be ill defined and vague. Intellectuals, public figures, and protesters of both the left and the right attack "globalization." Do both sides mean the same thing? What precisely is it in "globalization" that people are against? Wouldn't the very same people find aspects of "globalization" that they are for?

In the introduction, I suggested that Moses Mendelssohn's and Hermann Cohen's philosophies offer particularly interesting case studies of universalistic perspectives because both were members of a religious minority seeking to delineate universalisms that do not erase their distinct identities. A second reason their case is interesting is the degree to which they differ from each other. First, it seems to me that any universalism that could be relevant today must take that minoritarian perspective into account. Such a perspective, however, is in and of itself not enough. The second point, Mendelssohn's and Cohen's differences, namely, Mendelssohn's felicity and his egalitarian pluralism vs Cohen's intransigently universal reason and its messianic promise, show how varied even such minoritarian, in this case modern Jewish, universalisms can be.

Indeed, given the variety of meanings universalism can gain, the question of whether Mendelssohn or Cohen is more "universalistic" is rather moot. One can, however, very much prefer either version of it. For what it's worth, looking back at these giants, I find that Mendelssohn shows impressive cultural sensitivity and a genuine concern for the kind of humane tolerance and compassion I think we are currently in dire need of. And while I find much in Cohen's attempt at construing a Jewish and universalistic philosophy profoundly inspiring, in particular his insistence on the constitutive role of the prophetic moral voice (which is in various forms of contemporary Judaism too often secondary to halakhic concerns), his intolerance is at times appalling. Perhaps that aspect of his work is less dissonant if contextualized historically. After all, claiming Jewish primacy in a cultural milieu that was increasingly demeaning of Jewish culture and religion is far less jarring than doing so in other circumstances. Still, either way, my circumstances aren't quite his. Having taught Cohen in Tel Aviv for a decade now, I find what might arguably have been courageously apologetic in early twentieth-century German comes across as chauvinistic and deeply problematic in contemporary Hebrew. It seems to me desirable that whatever forms of Jewish universalism we develop in our own time should seek to avoid such pitfalls, whatever language they end up being translated into. And realizing what precisely the values we seek to promote are while reflecting on tensions between them and on their proper prioritization is critical for not repeating such mistakes in our own attempts at formulating universalistic worldviews.

It is, then, critical for contemporary universalistic thought to make its values and their prioritization explicit. As mentioned above, there is, it seems to me, no real question as to whether our reality will be universalistic and global. The question, rather, is which values will be prioritized in our universalism. Indeed, universalism in and of itself does not mean much. The real question is what the highest good that any version of universalism is actually seeking to promote is. Values are as constitutive of our particular selves as they are to universalism itself.

ACKNOWLEDGMENTS

Professor Ron Margolin has been a bastion of support throughout the many years I have been working on the research that formed the basis of this book. While he has now been relieved of his responsibilities as supervisor for a few years, he will remain my teacher for as long as I can learn. I am forever grateful for all of his countless efforts. Ron and his wife, Amalia, hosted me for many joyful and warm Shabbat dinners. Amalia, whose strength of character and dignity were deeply inspiring, was always incredibly kind and encouraging to me. The sadness of her passing is endless, and for the little it is worth, I am honored to dedicate this book to her.

I would like to thank everybody at the Ofakim program and, in particular, its coordinator, Noa Israeli, who patiently put up with me. I would also like to thank the faculty at the Department of Jewish Philosophy at Tel Aviv University. Professor Ishay Rosen-Zvi's and Professor Yuval Jobani's guidance at critical junctures has been particularly invaluable.

The team at the Mandel Institute was very supportive in the many months of writing, and I would like to thank Dr. Elie Gottlieb and Yael Hess for their encouragement and patience. Dr. Ruth Calderon at Alma, Tel Aviv's lighthouse of Hebrew Culture, is an endless well of positive energy I am ever grateful for as well.

I am grateful to the Posen Foundation for generously supporting my research. I also received grants from the Neuberger and Nadav Foundations and was supported at the outset with a Fainaru loan.

Some passages in the introduction were published in "The Anti-Christ and the Anti-Moses: Nietzsche, Spinoza and the Possibility of Sacrilegious Beatitude," *Comparative and Continental Philosophy*, 2018. Several sections of chapter 2 appear in "Scepticism of Scepticism: On Mendelssohn's Philosophy of Common Sense," *Melilah: Manchester Journal of Jewish Studies*, 2016, and passages from chapters 3 and 6 appear in "A Polynesian, a Jew, and a Hindu Walk into Jerusalem: On

Mendelssohn's Religious Universalism," *The Journal of Jewish Thought and Philosophy*, 2020.

Everyone at Brandeis University Press has been incredibly generous with their advice and support. I would like to thank Professor Jehuda Reinharz for his generosity and guidance, the amazing Sylvia Fried and Professor Eugene Sheppard for their encouragement and goodwill, and Anthony Lipscomb for his patient and meticulous work. I am also very grateful to Benjamin Woollard for his outstanding editorial work.

My friends are my tribe, and without their continued support, I would never have had the strength to make this book happen. I therefore owe a great debt of gratitude to (in no particular order) my great alchemical Rabbi John, Gilad, Einalem, Itses, Adi, Carmeli, Uri, Shanses, Barik, Guya, Tuval, Nugi, Christopher, Adam, Falou, Jach, Daniels, Ariel, Louis, Ido, Anselm, Linoy, and so many more. Finally, I would like to thank my beloved grandmother for being my sister; my mother for her infinite love; my brothers, Jacky, Jimmy, and Michael for keeping me in check; and all members of my little family for somehow more or less keeping it together.

My father, a wandering and wondering Jew, always sought to guide our perspectives to wider horizons. His presence reflected a unique and genuinely universalistic spirit, which he expressed with kaleidoscopic humor and endless creative energy. I will never quite stop missing him. This book is therefore also dedicated to his memory, which to me very much remains a continued and living blessing.

NOTES

INTRODUCTION

1. For particularly salient examples, see, respectively, Voltaire 1878, 6; Kant 2007, 93; Hume 2012, 86; Hume 2007, 94.

2. Mozi 2010, 147–49.

3. While philosophy has always been deeply concerned with values and it would arguably be difficult to find a major philosopher whose work does not include attempts at addressing, tacitly or explicitly, the question of values, in the late nineteenth century, a field in philosophical thought solely dedicated to the analysis of values began to emerge. Known as value theory or axiology, its raison d'être was the understanding that the ethical question, What ought to be done? is related to yet significantly distinct from the axiological one, What is or is not valuable? and that philosophical enquiry would gain from asking these questions distinctly (Findlay 1970, 3–4). This demarcation was perhaps most famously expressed by G. E. Moore in his preface to *Principia Ethica*, in which he states that moral philosophers almost always confuse the axiological question, which he formulated as, "What kind of things ought to exist for their own sakes?" with the ethical one, namely, "What kind of actions ought we to perform?" (Moore 1922, viii).

4. Deleuze, for example, describes Nietzsche's most general philosophical project as "the introduction of the concepts of sense and value into philosophy" and writes that "with Nietzsche, we must begin from the fact that the philosophy of values as envisaged and established by him is the true realization of critique and the only way in which a total critique can be realized" (Deleuze 2006, 1).

5. According to Heidegger, though it became customary in the nineteenth century to "think in values," only as a consequence of Nietzsche's writings did talk of values become "popular" (Heidegger 2002, 169).

6. Nietzsche 1994, 57.

7. Spinoza 1985a, 500.

8. Spinoza 2016b, 128.

9. Indeed, for Nietzsche life itself must dictate our values, and in turn, our values must affirm life. Nietzsche ultimately sees himself as a yes-sayer and his work as yes-saying. See Nietzsche 2008, 157. In *Ecce Homo*, he accordingly contrasts the "ultimate, most joyous, most wantonly extravagant Yes to life," which

is "the highest insight" as well as "the deepest" in the attitude of "Christians and other nihilists" (Nietzsche 1967, 272). His own prophetic hero, Zarathustra, is, furthermore, described as "the eternal Yes to all things" (Nietzsche 1967, 306; see also Geuss 1999, 105).

10. Plato 1997d, 505a, 1125.

11. Demos 1937, 245.

12. Ibid., 261.

13. Plato 1997d, 509b, 1130.

14. Ibid., 533a, 204.

15. Plato 1997c, 20d, 408.

16. Plato 1997b, 499d, 844.

17. This Copernican revolution in our understanding of values, which precedes Kant's by almost a century (and was already suggested before Spinoza by Hobbes; see Hobbes 1958, 41), shifts the focus of our thinking about values from properties inherent to whatever it is we consider to be valuable, or indeed from the properties of some notion of the good as such, to properties of our psychology. Approaching the notion of value through our desires or will or interest, and the ensuing evaluative inclinations, has remained widely accepted ever since. Von Ehrenfels, for example, establishes, in his *System der Werttheorie*, desire as the primary value-fundamental (see Findlay 1970, 35; see also Köhler 1938, 62). Perry, in his *General Theory of Value*, suggests construing the meaning of value in terms of interest. Though there are various differences between the thinkers mentioned above and others who think of values in terms of desire or interest, it is clear that all of them shift the study of the good from the metaphysical or ontological plain to the human one. Critically, if the study of values becomes the study of our needs, of our desires, of our will, of what became identified with modernity as constitutive elements of the self, it becomes a crucial aspect of any attempt at self-knowledge. Here again, Nietzsche's axiological thinking is very insightful. As values, for him, reflect "something about the structure of [a person's] soul and what the soul sees as its conditions of life, its genuine needs" (Nietzsche 2002, 164), they are often at the foundation of our philosophical perspectives. In turn, philosophical thought itself reflects a certain axiological orientation. Accordingly, Nietzsche thinks that the method of valuation is in a sense prior to its philosophical elucidation. Crucially, this leads to an innovative ability to interpret philosophies from the perspective of values. Indeed, as the axiological analysis of the self is so pertinent and insightful, the axiological angle becomes a pertinent and insightful hermeneutical tool in appraising philosophical ideas, promoting an interpretation that functions, to quote Foot, "by underlying desires" (Foot 1994, 5).

18. Aristotle 1993b, 1096b26, 1773.

19. Jacquette finds in a remarkably laden short passage of the *Nicomachean Ethics* wherein Aristotle critiques the Platonic good (in book 1, §6) seven distinct arguments. For his description of each, see Jacquette 1998, 302–18.

20. This, as Shields points out, is because it answers several criteria Aristotle himself sets: "it is (i) superordinate to all other human goods; (ii) sought for itself; (iii) sought for nothing beyond itself; (iv) something whose possession renders a life perfected or complete (teleion); and, finally, (v) something the possession of which renders life self-sufficient or lacking in nothing (autarkes)" (Shields 2015, 84).

21. Helmreich 2014, 398–99.

22. Aristotle 1993b, 1095a16–19, 1730.

23. Ibid., 1177a18, 1860.

24. See Aristotle 1993a, 1072a20–1072b31, 1694.

25. For more on why Plato's position might be less aloof than it is often made out to be, see Rowe 2007. Rowe argues against the common sharp differentiation between the Socratic quest for the good that is "the good of each of us, our happiness" and the form of the good as introduced in the *Republic* as "some sort of impersonal, or non-personal, good which, even as it serves somehow as the object of human striving, also shaped and gives meaning, if not existence, to the world as a whole," and he suggests a position that integrates both perspectives (Rowe 2007, 124–25).

26. Plato 1997d, 352d, 996.

27. Indeed, as we shall see later on, Cohen explicitly echoes this debate in his thinking (see chapter 4 of this volume). It is, in this context, interesting to point out Rowe's suggestion that the approach focusing on Plato's more metaphysical aspects has "strong Kantian allegiances" (Rowe 2007, 125, n. 3).

28. Nietzsche 2002, 105 (emphasis original).

29. Nietzsche 2005, 11; or Nietzsche 1967, 144.

30. Though both Nietzsche and Charles Taylor suggest such reinterpretations cannot be produced *ex nihilo*, without, as Joas puts it, "any reference to the cultural repertoire" (see Joas 2000, 139; and Nietzsche 1994, 70).

31. C. Taylor 1989, 27–28.

1. THE ENLIGHTENED UNIVERSALISTIC DEVALUATION OF JUDAISM

1. In Mendelssohn 2011, 63; German text in Mendelssohn 1971–, 8:83.

2. Kant 1979a, 95.

3. Bauer 1843, 19 (my translation). Throughout the book, standard translations were used when available. In the remaining cases, unless otherwise indicated, translations are my own.

4. August Friedrich Cranz (1737–1801), a self-styled second Voltaire, admitted in a treatise written in 1798 that he was behind the anonymously published *The Searching for Light and Right* in a letter to Herr Moses Mendelssohn occasioned by his remarkable preface for Manasseh Ben Israel. Cranz sought to make the pamphlet, which spurred Mendelssohn to write his *Jerusalem*, appear to have been written by the celebrated Viennese writer Joseph von Sonnenfels. According to Altmann, Cranz did so because he realized that, given his dubious reputation, a work appearing under his name would carry far less weight. It also would have obliged him to first submit it to the censorship Frederick the Great had put him under. In addition, as he admired Mendelssohn and was on good terms with friends of his, he might have wanted to avoid challenging him openly. See Altmann 1973, 511–12.

5. J. D. Levenson 1996, 143.

6. Quoted in Schäfer 1997, 22.

7. Quoted in Stern 1980, 2:25.

8. Ibid., 26. Schäfer argues that through passages such as these, wherein he clearly adopts common ancient motives of Jewish impiety and misanthropy, Tacitus bequeathed these notions to Western civilization. See Schäfer 1997, 33.

9. 1 Thessalonians 2:15. Throughout the book, quotes from both the Old and the New Testament are from the New Revised Standard Version.

10. Galatians 3:28.

11. So, for example, Justin Martyr, in his dialogue with Trypho, explains to his Jewish conversant that God "shows every race of man that which is always and in all places just, and every type of man knows that adultery, fornication, murder, and so on are evil" (Justin Martyr 2003, 144), implying that the particularistic ways of the people who "even did violence to Christ Himself" (Justin Martyr 2003, 145) are morally and spiritually worthless. For more on Justin Martyr's attitude towards the Jewish people, see Rokéah 2002. For more on early Christian anti-Jewish attitudes generally, see Ruether 1997 and M. S. Taylor 1995.

12. Similarly, as Schäfer points out, many, if not most, studies of ancient pagan hostility towards Jews "start with the methodological premise that the unique religious, cultural and social characteristics of Judaism itself are the cause of what later becomes known as 'anti-semitism.'" (Schäfer 1997, 6). In doing so, he adds, these scholars risk confusing cause with pretext and "finding the Jews themselves guilty of what happened to them" (Schäfer 1997, 8).

13. Badiou 2003, 1.

14. Ibid., 5.

15. Ibid., 29.

16. Ibid., 41, 56.

17. Ibid., 107.

18. Ibid., 109.

19. Ibid., 95.

20. J. D. Levenson 1996, 165–66.

21. John 14.6.

22. J. D. Levenson 1996, 166–67. These thoughts relate to an interesting aspect of Assman's somewhat controversial ideas about what he termed the "Mosaic distinction." According to Assman, the crucial shift from polytheism to monotheism is the emergence of a distinction between true and false religion, the proclamation of "a truth that does not stand in a complementary relationship to other truths, but consigns all traditional or rival truths to the realm of falsehood" (Assman 2010, 3). This development of an exclusivist notion of religious truth ipso facto brings a "new form of hatred into the world: hatred for pagans, heretics, idolaters and their temples, rites and gods" (Assman 2010, 16). While Assman believes this form of highly particularistic hatred characterizes all monotheistic religions, the potential for violence is far greater, he argues, with Christianity and Islam than with Judaism: "whereas the Jewish people's belief in its own election requires that it exclude itself, the Christian obligation to evangelize and the Muslim obligation to compel submission require that they both exclude the Other. . . . Only in this form does monotheism's inherent potential for exclusion explode into violence" (Assman 2010, 18; see also Erlewine 2014, 275). In other words, according to this perspective, the universalistic ambition of Christianity and Islam is precisely that which makes them potentially more violent than Judaism and its particularistic effort to differentiate itself from its surroundings. While it is not certain Judaism never proselytized (see n. 24 of this chapter), Assman's arguments emphasize the degree to which "universalism" as such does not necessarily imply a loftier moral standing than any form of particularism. There have been, and probably still are, forms of universalism more intolerant or cruel than the particularisms they claim to resolve.

23. Runesson 2000, 56.

24. This, of course, is in and of itself a problematic assumption. The question of whether Judaism has always avoided active proselytizing is by no means settled. Indeed, some researchers depict an active ancient Jewish mission. See, for example, Georgi 1986 or Feldman 1992.

25. Runesson 2000, 57.

26. Ibid., 59. It is important to note that even in this context, the legitimacy of particularism, and particularistic concerns, cannot be detached from social power structures. It is, as Brett writes, ethically important when dealing with these complex issues "to take asymmetries of power into account" (Brett 1996, 20). Boyarin, for example, does so when he remarks that ethnocentrism can be

ethically appropriate "when the cultural identity is that of a minority, embattled or, at any rate, non-hegemonic" (Boyarin 1994, 256). As Brett puts it, "what is ethical cannot be decided independently of the social and economic power of those concerned" (Brett 1996, 17).

27. Runesson 2000, 70–71.

28. Feiner 2011, 153–54.

29. For an analysis of the ways in which Kant's religion is significantly distanced from the kind of Christian traditions he would have been educated into, in particular with regards to the highest good, see Insole 2016.

30. So Funkenstein argues that while Kant was not the most radical philosopher of the Enlightenment, his "relentless endeavor to emancipate metaphysics and science from its theological baggage, and to develop an ethical theory in which human beings are their own supreme law-givers, was the most systematic and complex" (Funkenstein 1986, 346–47).

31. Mendelssohn 2012a, 3; 1971–, 3.2:3.

32. Kleist to Wilhelmine von Zenge, March 22, 1801, in Kleist 1923, 351. For a comprehensive exploration of Kleist's reading of Kant, see Mehigan 2011. This very same passage is quoted by Nietzsche in his "Schopenhauer as Educator," the third of his *Untimely Meditations*, when describing how post-Kantian thought risked a "despair of truth" (Nietzsche 2007, 141).

33. See Katz 1980, 169.

34. See Landry 2011, 1.

35. Bauer 2002, 1. Bauer contrasts this strand of the Enlightenment to the religious Enlightenment, which he characterized as "limited and fearful" (Bauer 2002, 13).

36. Bauer 2002, 31.

37. Ibid., 80.

38. Jonathan Israel argues that up to around 1650, "western civilization was based on a largely shared core of faith, tradition, and authority. By contrast, after 1650, everything, no matter how fundamental or deeply rooted, was questioned in light of philosophical reason" (Israel 2002, 3).

39. McCarthy 1986, ix–x.

40. Indeed, the transformation of Jewish communities these historical developments brought about ended up being, as Katz indicates, even more dramatic than their effects on Christian society, at least with regards to Western Europe. See Katz 1973, 1–3.

41. This does not mean, however, that the centuries preceding Jewish emancipation were quite as dark and cruel as members of the Enlightenment often suggested they were. For a critical questioning of the starkness with which these periods tend to be contrasted, see Baron 1928.

42. See Meyer 1975, 21, 26–27; or Bentley 1996, 749.

43. I am here glossing over the historiographical distinction between the "early modern" and "modern" periods. For more on this distinction and the difficulties it involves, see Starn 2002. For reflections on its meaning in the context of Jewish as well as European history, see Ruderman 2000, 207–26.

44. Accordingly, Francis Bacon famously categorized "the art of printing, gunpowder and the nautical compass" as discoveries that "have changed the face and condition of things all over the globe . . . so that no empire or sect or star seems to have exercised a greater power and influence on human affairs than those mechanical things" (Bacon 2000, 100; see also Eisenstein 1980, 3–4). For a characterization of the effects of the invention of the printing press on the emergence of an early modern Jewish culture, see Ruderman 2011, 99–125.

45. Some historians have cast doubts on whether Luther actually nailed his ninety-five theses to the door of Castle Church. Iserloh, for example, argues that the posting of the theses was a legend constructed by the German Lutheran reformer Philip Melanchthon. See Iserloh 1968, 68–73.

46. Popkin 1979, xvi, 19.

47. Ibid., xvi–xvii, 1–4.

48. Ibid., 173.

49. The term *noble savage* was first coined by Marc Lescarbot, a French ethnographer. As opposed to common beliefs, it was neither developed nor even used by either Montaigne or Rousseau (see Ellingson 2001, xv, 1–4). Ellingson also problematizes both the meaning and importance usually attributed to this concept (2001, 4–8). Still, as will be shown in greater depth below, both French writers were critical in incorporating depictions of foreign cultures in arguments for pluralism and toleration.

50. So, for example, Joshua famously asks for the sun to stand still (Joshua 10:12). Tellingly, Spinoza relied on the astronomical misunderstanding this passage seems to reflect in order to make wider skeptical points about the ignorance of the prophets and the misinterpreting of natural phenomena as miracles. See Spinoza 2016, 164–65.

51. See, for example, Israel 2002, 14; Koyré 1957, 1–2; or Grant 1984, 5.

52. Indeed, the Greek word *kosmos* had in the Homeric poems primarily the sense of "order" and aesthetic proportionate harmony. Herodotus used it to refer to a well-ordered state. It was only later that, according to Aetius, Pythagoras applied the word *kosmos* to the "sum of the whole . . . because of the order it displayed" (Wright 2013, 3).

53. Wright 2013, 151.

54. Ibid., 178–79.

55. Sedley 1991, 179–80.

56. Funkenstein 1986, 36.

57. Wright 2013, 179.

58. Sedley 1991, 196.

59. Aristotle 1993c, 1256b20, 1993–1994.

60. See Plato 1997d, 368d–369b, 1007–1008.

61. Wright 2013, 56.

62. It is important to note that while the Aristotelian and Ptolemaic conceptions are those that were adopted in medieval Europe, some of the Greek philosophers, notably the atomists, did believe in an infinite universe. While they were rejected by the main trends of Greek thought, their writings did, as we shall see below, inspire several of the revolutionary cosmological ideas of early modernity. See Koyré 1957, 2.

63. Ferry 1990, 20.

64. Aristotle 1993c, 1254a23, 1990.

65. Ibid., 1254b10–15, 1990.

66. See Heath 2008, 245.

67. So Aristotle describes some as having been "intended by nature to be governed" (1993c, 1265b25, 1994) and claims that for those who are "by nature" slaves, unable as they would be to master themselves, slavery is "expedient and right" (1993c, 1255a1, 1991).

68. A telling example of Aristotle explicitly amalgamating the order of the cosmos and of politics can be found in a passage of his *Metaphysics*, wherein he discusses the good of the cosmic order and argues that "all things are ordered together somehow, but not all alike—both fishes and fowls and plants; and the world is not such that one thing has nothing to do with another, but they are connected" (Aristotle 1993a, 1075a15, 1699). He then goes on to compare this structure to a household containing both freemen and slaves (1993a, 1075a19, 1699). The whole passage is concluded with a quote from Homer: "The rule of many is not good; let there be one ruler" (1993a, 1076a3, 1670), affirming again that a hierarchical order applies to the cosmos as well as to the well-governed army, household, and state. See also Wright 2013, 70.

69. Koyré 1957, 30.

70. Lovejoy 1978, 110.

71. Ibid., 108.

72. Notably, Nicholas of Cusa described a centerless universe that, while not explicitly infinite, was not finite either. Most importantly, he also rejected a hierarchical universe. See Koyré 1957, 12–20.

73. Lovejoy 1978, 116. Bruno enthusiastically revived the cosmological ideas of atomism, specifically, the infinitist Epicurean doctrine immortalized by Lucretius. See Johnson and Wilson 2007, 133.

74. Koyré 1957, 2.

75. Badiou 2003, 19.

76. Frederickson, for example, argues that while various forms of xenophobia and tribalism were rife in antiquity and religiously motivated hatred and discrimination abounded then as it did in the Middle Ages, the specificity of a conception of inferiority based on innate characteristics began to emerge in early prototypical forms in the fourteenth and fifteenth centuries (such as the continued ill treatment of conversos in Spain because of their Jewish "blood") and was spurred on by the rampant slavery that Europeans carried to the New World in the sixteenth and seventeenth centuries. However, it only gained its full scope when it was developed "scientifically" in the eighteenth and nineteenth centuries (when the modern concept of "race" as fundamentally diverse human types differentiated by specific physical characteristics emerged), maintaining its terrifying prominence well into the twentieth century with Nazism, the Jim Crow laws, and the South African apartheid regime (see Frederickson 2002, 5–6, 29–33, 51–58). Accordingly, "racism" is indeed widely agreed to be modern. Even when, against the mainstream view, some researchers argue that aspects of ancient xenophobia can be thought of as racist in some sense, they tend not to argue against the scholarly consensus that the concept of race is modern. So for example, Isaac is willing to refer to a Greco-Roman "proto-racism" but agrees that "scientific racism" was a product of the nineteenth century (Isaac 2006, 1).

77. Frederickson 2002, 47.

78. It is a sad fact of history, however, that in spite of Jefferson's seemingly egalitarian ideology and pronouncements, including various condemnations of the slave trade and of slavery, he held racist views and owned, bought, and sold human beings. For more on Jefferson and slavery, see W. Cohen 1969; and Magnis 1999.

79. Jefferson to William Short, October 31, 1819, in Jefferson 1950, 765. See also Holowchak 2012.

80. Jefferson 1950, 766. Interestingly, Epicurus was also far more egalitarian than Aristotle, accepting women and slaves to his school. See Wider 1986, 50.

81. Famously, Columbus thought he had discovered another part of Asia. See Zerubavel 1992, 4–5.

82. Indeed, piece by piece, this comprehension grew as explorers came back with new and different Information to assimilate, gradually obtaining an increasingly accurate picture. For more on the gradual discovery of America, see Zerubavel 1992, 36–66.

83. Montaigne 1991a, 229.

84. See, for example, Montaigne 1991a, 232.

85. Conley 2005, 74.

86. Montaigne 1991a, 231.

87. Ibid., 234.

88. Ibid., 235. Montaigne adds that the natives ended up foregoing their tradition, switching instead to the Portuguese executory revenge, as they deemed it more severe.

89. Ibid., 235–36.

90. Ibid., 240–41.

91. Literature that, as Schlereth puts it, "provided a continual reminder for the educated of Europe that only forty days' journey from their shores lived people without benefit of kings, the Christian religion, or a rigid social hierarchy—and people seemingly happy in spite of, or perhaps because of, these conditions" (Schlereth 1977, 22).

92. Richards 2003, 1–2.

93. Bentley 2007, 21–22.

94. Bentley 1996, 769.

95. See Richards 2003, 2.

96. Voltaire 1829, 404–5.

97. Ibid., xi; Schlereth 1977, 100.

98. Voltaire 2000, 89. While Voltaire is often remembered as one of the most important eighteenth-century proponents of toleration, it is important to keep in mind, in our context in particular, the abject racism already mentioned in the introduction, as well as the disparaging and hostile, if not frankly antisemitic, attitude reflected in his writings on Jews and Judaism, which he thought of as inherently contradictory to all that the Enlightenment represents. For more on the tension between Voltaire's tolerance and his views on the Jewish people, see Sutcliffe 1998.

99. Schlereth 1977, 71.

100. So, for example, writing about China in his *Philosophical Dictionary*, Voltaire states that "4000 years ago, when we could not read, the Chinese knew all the indispensably useful things of which we boast today" (1971, 115) and gives the following advice to his readers: "Let us then, we who were born yesterday, who are descended from the Celts, who have only just cleared the forests of our savage regions, let us leave the Chinese and the Indians peacefully to enjoy their lovely climate and their antiquity" (1971, 114).

101. Leibniz to Peter the Great, 1716, in Leibniz 1951, 596–97.

102. Published in 1697, *Novissima Sinica* was a collection of contemporary writings on China that Leibniz edited, published, and introduced. See Perkins 2004, 43.

103. Leibniz 1994, 47. For a comprehensive study of Leibniz's fascination with Chinese philosophy and culture, see Perkins 2004.

104. See Ching and Oxtoby 1992, 52. The lecture itself, titled "Discourse on the Practical Philosophy of the Chinese," can be found in Ching and Oxtoby 1992, 149–86.

105. See Lach 1953, 563–64. Interestingly, this event is discussed by Voltaire, who warmly commends Wolff's "very fine discourse in praise of Chinese philosophy" and expresses dismay at the "fury of a fool" that led to Wolff's departure (1971, 112–13).

106. Hume to John Home of Ninewells, April 7, 1748, in Hume 1969, 126. In the same letter, Hume declares himself to be a "man of mankind."

107. Schlereth 1977, 2.

108. Hume 1987, 82.

109. Rousseau 1979, 276.

110. Ibid., 278.

111. Ibid., 288.

112. Ibid., 299.

113. Ibid., 304–5.

114. Ibid., 311–12.

115. Koyré 1957, vii.

116. Newton 1999, 382.

117. Indeed, as Janiak points out, Newton "considered Descartes to be his most important predecessor among the myriad natural philosophers of the 17th century" (Janiak 2010, vii).

118. Descartes 1996, 12.

119. As Schopenhauer famously put it, "Descartes is rightly regarded as the father of modern philosophy primarily and generally because he helped the faculty of reason to stand on its feet by teaching men to use their brains in place whereof the Bible, on the one hand, and Aristotle, on the other, had previously served" (Schopenhauer 2000, 3).

120. Gellner 1992, 23.

121. Ibid., 14. It is, in this context, perhaps worth mentioning that the only book Rousseau suggests Emile should read, except for the universal "book of nature," which is "open to all eyes," is *Robinson Crusoe* (Rousseau 1979, 184, 306).

122. Gellner 1992, 23.

123. Paine 1896, 22.

124. Ibid., 44.

125. Ibid., 47.

126. Funkenstein 1986, 357.

127. See Nadler 1999, 103–7.

128. See Israel 2002, 175.

129. See Ben-Amos 1993, 63; and Daston 1994, 182.

130. Koyré 1943, 404.

131. Funkenstein 1986, 90–91.

132. Spinoza 1985a, 492.

133. Hume 1958, 43–44.

134. Voltaire 1971, 374–75.

135. Montaigne 1991b, 53.

136. See Gellner 1992, 29. Still, as mentioned above, many Enlightenment philosophers, including Hume and Kant, did express racist opinions in spite of the universalism their philosophies seem to commit them to.

137. See the section "Universalisms" in chapter 6.

138. Mendelssohn 1983, 94; 1971–, 8:161.

139. Cohen 1995, 242; 1978, 283.

140. Nadler 1999, 120.

141. It is likely he already held some of the opinions that later surfaced in his *Theological-Political Treatise* but had not yet developed anything nearing the systematic philosophical structure that would characterize his *Ethics*. See Nadler 1999, 132–33; and Revah 1959, 37.

142. See Revah 1959, 64. It seems to me quite poignant that in this source Tomas Solano y Robles describes Spinoza as a "good philosopher [buen Filosofo]." After all, in his few conversations with Spinoza, he apparently heard heresies that to a seventeenth-century Catholic must have been simply harrowing. Even so, it seems that even just a few moments shared with Spinoza could not but make a rather lasting philosophical impression.

143. Spinoza 1985a, 559.

144. Spinoza 2016b, 275.

145. Spinoza 1985a, 617.

146. Ibid., 564. It is significant, however, that while in principle, this greatest good can be enjoyed by all equally, Spinoza claims his universalistic salvation is in practice only found very rarely (see Spinoza 1985a, 617). In other words, as will be argued later in the book, this suggest that while presented as commensurate, reason and equality might actually not be, and while presented as universal, the ideal of reason might actually turn out to be rather particularistic in so far as it is ultimately only truly realized by a very few.

147. Strauss 1988, 24.

148. Spinoza 2016b, 150.

149. Ibid., 128.

150. Ibid., 129.

151. Ibid., 264. The critical difference between the purpose of Spinoza's

rationalist reading of the Bible and the purpose of Maimonides's is too often mitigated. While both offer what can be construed as rationalist readings of the sources, Spinoza certainly does not partake in the same hermeneutical project; his rationalist devaluation is in fact the complete opposite of Maimonides's rational revaluation of the Bible. It is therefore not surprising that Spinoza thinks Maimonides's effort thoroughly misguided. "Nothing," he writes when discussing it, "seems to me more ridiculous" (Spinoza 2016b, 82).

152. Spinoza 2016b, 267.

153. Ibid., 270.

154. See "Judaism and Universal Felicity" in chapter 3.

155. See, for example, Mendelssohn 1983, 97; 1971–, 8:164.

156. Spinoza 2016b, 146.

157. See Spinoza 1985a, 498.

158. Spinoza 2016b, 124.

159. The original Latin word, *effoeminarent*, is here rendered as "making their hearts unmanly" but would be more literally translated as "feminized" or "made effeminate." For more on the significance of the Latin wording, see Gullan-Whur 1998, 15–16.

160. Spinoza 2016b, 124.

161. Ibid., 300.

162. In thusly condemning Moses, Spinoza echoes the heresies of Daniel Ribera, who, with Dr. de Prado, might have played a significant role in encouraging Spinoza's own disenchantment with Judaism. Ribera held that Moses was nothing but a "great sorcerer [grande feiticeiro]" and argued that his acts against the followers of the golden calf, as well as all the precepts he had ordained, were intended to promote and protect his and his brother Aaron's economic interests (Revah 1964, 402). Such themes are in fact rather near to ideas Spinoza himself suggests in chapter 17 of the *Theological-Political Treatise* and elsewhere.

163. Spinoza 2016b, 126–27.

164. Spinoza to George H. Schuller, July 29, 1675, in 2016a, 439. For more on infinite modes, laws of nature, and the face of the whole universe, see Yovel 1991, 88.

165. See Spinoza 1985b, 142–43.

166. Goetschel 2004, 10.

167. Of course, the kind of Judaism Spinoza sought to devaluate is the traditional orthodox or halakhic kind. Other forms of Jewish existence can be perceived as having been valued, if not promoted or even originated by, the great heretic. It is in this context not accidental that he was perceived as a hero by many trailblazing secular or otherwise rebellious Jews of later generations (see,

for example, Maimon 2018, 197; or Heine 2007, 50–51), or indeed, as a precursor of Zionist thought cherished by figures such as Hess or Herzl (see Hess 2005, 1; and Margolin 2018, 75–76).

CHAPTER 2

1. See Altmann 1973, 140; or Feiner 2010, 77. While both Altmann and Feiner write that Mendelssohn gained the "German Socrates" moniker, Bourel and Sorkin write that after his *Phädon*, Mendelssohn became known as the "Socrates of Berlin" (see Bourel 2004, 181; Sorkin 2012, xvi). In a short sketch of Mendelssohn's life and character published in 1789, just three years after Mendelssohn's death, as part of an edition of some of Mendelssohn's philosophical work, the writer and theologian Daniel Jenisch suggested Mendelssohn ought to be thought of as the "Socrates of the modern time [Sokrates der neuern Zeit]" (quoted in Mendelssohn 1971–, 23:281). Interestingly, in a short biographical piece published in 1798 and written, in all likelihood, by Isaac D'Israeli (whose son, Benjamin, was to become the British prime minister), we are told that "Germany calls him the Jewish Socrates" (D'Israeli 1798, 39). For more on this piece, including its attribution to D'Israeli, see Ruderman 2000, 284.

2. Mendelssohn 2007, 104; 1971–, 3.1:79–80. See also Freudenthal 2012, 79.

3. Mendelssohn 1983, 63; 1971–, 8:131. Some linguistic attention must be paid to the notion of *Glückseligkeit*, here translated as "felicity." While the term is also at times translated as "happiness," it differs from *Glück*, which would also be rendered as "happiness" though it could also mean "luck" or "good fortune." *Glückseligkeit* combines *Glück*, which reflects the "hap" of "happiness," with *Seligkeit*, "beatitude" or "blessedness." As such, *Glückseligkeit* carries a spiritual connotation that distances it somewhat from the more coincidental connotation of *Glück*, though, unlike *Seligkeit*, it still very much includes earthly well-being. For more on the difference between these terms and the similarity of the term *Glückseligkeit* to *eudaimonia*, see the entry on "Glück, Glückseligkeit, Seligkeit, Wohlfahrt" in Helmreich 2014, 397–402.

4. Mendelssohn 1983, 63; 1971–, 8:131. The notion that morality would become meaningless without its theological backing is a recurrent one, though of course it has also been thoroughly critiqued. Freud, for example, memorably argued in *The Future of an Illusion* that while religion "has contributed much towards the taming of the asocial instincts" (1961, 37), it would be better for humanity to leave "God out altogether and honestly admit the purely human origin of all the regulations and precepts of civilization" (1961, 41). This, according to Freud, would not only enable people to understand that these regulations and precepts were made to serve their interests, but more generally, were human

beings to withdraw "their expectations from the other world and concentrate their liberated energies into their life on earth, they will probably succeed in achieving a state of things in which life will become tolerable for everyone and civilization no longer oppressive to anyone" (1961, 50).

5. Mendelssohn 2012a, 61; 1971–, 3.2:68.

6. So, for example, Christian Wolff, whose influence on Mendelssohn was lasting and profound, demarcated natural religion as, to quote Sorkin, "containing only those truths universally available to reason: the existence of God, his providence and the immortality of the soul" (Sorkin 2012, 7).

7. Altmann 1973, 27.

8. Mendelssohn 1997, 27; 1971–, 1:64–65.

9. As Arkush notes, this perceived problem led many central figures in the German Enlightenment, like Reimarus or Lessing, to draw some very unflattering conclusions as to the lower spiritual development of the Old Testament and the religion it reflects (see Arkush 1999, 34). Still, while ambiguous on the topic and lacking a prominent and explicit promise of eternal life, the Old Testament does carry some notions of immortality. For a succinct summary and discussion of recent scholarly opinions about the question of immortality in the Old Testament, see Routledge 2008.

10. Mendelssohn 2007, 104; 1971–, 3.1:79–80.

11. Mendelssohn 1971–, 14:154, translated in Freudenthal 2012, 78.

12. Calvinism is not only a clear example of a theology wherein God's exaltation is unrelated to His ensuring lasting human bliss, but one significant to Mendelssohn's time and cultural milieu. Indeed, Gorski relates Prussia's rise to preeminence to the Hohenzollen's Calvinism, in particular, the Calvinization of the Prussian Royal Service and the development of a Calvinist elite under Frederick William (1640–1688) and the religious ethos and worldview of Frederick William I (1713–1740), which, to paraphrase Gorski, "was distinctively Calvinist and became distinctively Prussian" (Gorski 2003, 94). Hubatsch notes that Frederick William's pietistic Calvinism "permeated Prussian life." (Hubatsch 1975, 33). While the freethinking and deistically inclined Frederick the Great (1740–1788) did not share his father's religious conviction, he took seriously his public religious responsibilities and continued to foster a Calvinist elite (see Hubatsch 1975, 190, 194–96). Indeed, Fraser speculates that though inclined towards a Voltairean skepticism, Frederick the Great was touched by the Calvinist belief in predestination (which his father had rejected) "in the sense that freedom of human will is an illusion, that we are all tiny and impotent compared to the remorseless workings of Fate, Providence, the will of God, whatever it be called" (Fraser 2001, 58). We will explore the significance of difference between

Mendelssohn's and Frederick's worldviews when looking at Mendelssohn's reaction to the king's poetry later in this chapter (see the section "Providence and Immortality").

13. So Mendelssohn's position accords well with, for example, the Talmudic parable for God's creation of human beings on the sixth day, which tells of a king who first builds a palace, fixes it up, prepares a banquet, and then brings in the guests (see Babylonian Talmud, Mas. Sanhedrin, 38a), or the famous Mishnaic verse stating that everyone is obligated to maintain that "on my account the world was created" (Mishnah, Mas. Sanhedrin, 4:5). It accords far less with the non-anthropocentric stance reflected in the famous rabbinic story of Moses's reaction to Rabbi Akiba's martyrdom. Having witnessed Akiba's impressive discourses on the Mosaic law, Moses asks God to show him Akiba's reward. When God shows him the Roman soldiers "weighing out his [Rabbi Akiba's] flesh at the market-stalls," Moses cries out, "Such Torah, and such a reward!" God responses succinctly and without much regard to human felicity or providential concerns: "Be silent, for such is My decree" (see Babylonian Talmud, Mas. Menachoth, 29b). While this story is told within a rabbinic framework that affirms future individual resurrection and therefore could eschew the notion that human felicity is here ultimately neglected, the tone of God's response to Moses does at least enable an interpretation that does not prioritize human felicity quite as much as Mendelssohn does.

14. Mendelssohn famously stated he owed the curvature of his back to Maimonides, adding too that he felt compensated for his labors. See Altmann 1973, 12.

15. Gottlieb 2011, 17.

16. Maimonides 1963, 2:455 (italics original). For a comparison of Maimonides non-anthropocentrism and Saaida Gaon's far more Mendelssohnian position, see Lamm 1965.

17. See Gottlieb 2011, 10, 17.

18. The notion of "value spheres" was developed by Max Weber, who more generally strongly emphasized the importance of the axiological perspective. Indeed, Weber thought that the very concept of culture "is a value concept" and that "empirical reality becomes 'culture' to us because and insofar as we relate it to value ideas" (Weber 2011, 76). Weber approached values as goals "towards which human behavior may be oriented" (1990, 31) and thought of both actions and value judgments as taking place within the context of value spheres. He identified six such value spheres: religion, the economy, politics, aesthetics, the erotic, and intellectualism (see Weber 1991; and Oakes 2003, 28). Weber here arguably echoes a central theme of the writings of Kierkegaard, namely, that, as he put it, "there are three existence-spheres: the aesthetic, the ethical, the

religious" (Kierkegaard 1988, 476). Value spheres also form an important part of Perry's axiological analysis. In fact, precisely because he sought to provide a general theory of value, Perry draws our attention to the disparate terms used in acts of valuation (*truth*, *goodness*, *legality*, *wealth*, *beauty*, *piety*, etc.), terms which reflect the various spheres of valuation (epistemic, moral, economic, aesthetic, religious, etc.) in which they apply (Perry 1926, 4–9). The concept of spheres of valuation, and their prioritization, is an insightful critical tool with which to think about the changing and conflicting nature of our valuations, one that will be very useful in categorizing varying prioritizations and subtle axiological differences in our analysis.

19. Mendelssohn 1997b, 26; 1971–, 1:63.

20. Mendelssohn 2007, 82; 1971–, 3.1:55. Mendelssohn's Socrates here seems to slightly overstep the mark set by Mendelssohn in later writings. As we shall see later on, Mendelssohn did very strongly believe our eyes and ears can, through their encounter with the beauty and harmony of the world, realize the reality of the divine. This quote does, however, illustrate the superiority of the religious-eudaemonic sphere to the one of bodily pleasure, a position Mendelssohn does maintain throughout his work.

21. Mendelssohn 2011, 209: 1971–, 15.2:23.

22. Mendelssohn 1997e, 151; 1971–, 1:405. In this relatively early passage (1771), Mendelssohn defines perfection as "'the supreme ground of all free actions,' that is to say, 'the highest good'" (Mendelssohn 1997e, 151; 1971–, 1:405). However, he immediately uses the term *Glückseligkeit* to characterize that perfection (see Mendelssohn 1997e, 152; 1971–, 1:406). While, as we have seen above, it is as *Glückseligkeit* rather than perfection that Mendelssohn's highest good is presented in much of his other work, whether roughly contemporaneous to the *Rhapsody* (such as *Phädon*) or later (*Jerusalem*, *Morning Hours*, etc.), throughout his writings, *Glückseligkeit* and *perfection* remain virtually synonymous and hence are used interchangeably.

23. See, for example, Mendelssohn 2007, 135; 1971–, 3.1:114.

24. See Mendelssohn 1997e, 152; 1971–, 1:406. We shall return to Mendelssohn's notion of perfection in this chapter in the section "Providence and Immortality" and in chapter 6.

25. Mendelssohn 1997e, 153; 1971–, 1:407.

26. See Jacobi 1916, 341–42. See also Gottlieb 2011, 65.

27. Jacobi 1916, 342–43.

28. Freudenthal 2012, 11.

29. Rosenstock 2010, 59.

30. Mendelssohn 1983, 66–67; 1971–, 8:134–35.

31. Mendelssohn 1997a, 255; 1971–, 2:272.

32. Mendelssohn 1997a, 264; 1971–, 2:281–82. Mendelssohn adds that in arithmetic and algebra, a few arbitrary signs do have to be learned but "outside these few simple signs and rules for combining them, nothing has been left to convention; everything is determined in the formulas and equations just as in our thoughts" (Mendelssohn 1997a, 265; 1971–, 2:282).

33. Mendelssohn 1997a, 272–73; 1971–, 2:290–91.

34. Mendelssohn 1983, 89; 1971–, 8:156.

35. Mendelssohn 2012a, 92; 1971–, 3.2:104.

36. See, for example, Mendelssohn 2012b, 158.

37. Diogenes Laertius 1925, 2:487.

38. Ibid., 483. See also Burnyeat 1998, 94–95.

39. See Popkin 1979, xv.

40. See Sextus Empiricus 1955, 21. Interestingly, Mendelssohn refers twice to this story, though in the context of La Mettrie's retelling of it. Indeed, the then-notoriously materialist philosopher used it to illustrate the possibility of seemingly ordered creation appearing randomly, a notion that Mendelssohn obviously objects to. See 2012a, 81; 1971–, 3.2:91; and 2012b, 170; 1971–, 3.2:212.

41. See Popkin 1979, xv.

42. Craig 1997, 9–17.

43. Descartes's description in his second meditation of the effects of the doubt cast in the first is one of a panic-laden and dramatic drowning: "It is as if I have fallen unexpectedly into a deep whirlpool which tumbles me around so that I can neither stand on the bottom nor swim up to the top" (Descartes 1996, 16). Hume famously found his questioning led him to "the most deplorable condition imaginable, inviron'd with the deepest darkness, and utterly depriv'd of the use of every member and faculty," a state only remedied by diner with friends and a game of backgammon (Hume 1958, 269).

44. Mendelssohn uses terms such *Bon-Sens* (e.g., 1971–, 3.2:202) or *gesunde Menschenverstand* (e.g., 1971–, 3.2:102) as well as *Gemeinsinn* (e.g., 1971–, 3.2:81–82), which is more literally similar to the English term, when discussing "common sense." See also Gottlieb 2011, 45.

45. Mendelssohn 1983, 67; 1971–, 8:134.

46. Mendelssohn 2012a, 71; 1971–, 3.2:79.

47. Mendelssohn 2012a, 71; 1971–, 3.2:79.

48. Di Giovanni notes the popularity of commonsensical sensitivities among eighteenth-century German neo-Wolffians and relates it to Thomas Reid's school of common-sense realism, which posed itself against Hume's doubt (Di Giovanni 1994, 28–30). Reid claimed that the proper relation of philosophy to common sense was one of "subordination" and that the open war with common sense was hopeless: "In this unequal contest betwixt common sense and philos-

ophy the latter will always come off with both dishonour and loss; nor can she ever prosper until this rivalry is dropped, philosophy gives up encroaching on the territory of common sense, and a cordial friendship is restored; for the fact is that common sense doesn't need philosophy's permission to say what it does, nor does it need philosophy's help. On the other side (if I may be permitted to change the metaphor), philosophy's only root is the principles of common sense; it grows out of them, and draws its nourishment from them; when it is cut off from this root its honours wither, its sap is dried up, it dies and rots" (Reid 1983, 7).

49. Indeed, Mendelssohn compares the immediate and intuitive ability of common sense to judge truth and falsehood to that of taste in judging beauty and ugliness. Therefore, just as an aesthetic taste needs to be refined, so too this sense needs to be "incorporated into our temperament by constant practice and, as it were, transformed into our sweat and blood" (Mendelssohn 1997a, 303; 1971–, 2:325).

50. Mendelssohn 2012a, 3–4; 1971–, 3.2:3–5.

51. Mendelssohn 2012a, 3–4; 1971–, 3.2:3–5. As he put it in *To the Friends Lessing*, "my conviction in the truth of tenets of [natural] religion is not so entirely dependent upon metaphysical arguments that it is compelled to stand or fall with them. One can cause me to have doubts about my arguments, one can show me that in places my reasoning is in error, but yet my conviction remains unshaken" (Mendelssohn 2012b, 157; 1971–, 3.2:197).

52. Mendelssohn 2012b, 129; 1971–, 3.2:148.

53. As Altmann puts it, "If Kant discovered the validity of his beliefs from the aspect of the moral will, Mendelssohn saw his beliefs safeguarded by common sense" (Altmann 1981b, 137).

54. "Each and every property of a thing has a certain breadth and a certain power, or, in other words, it has both extensions and intensity. By the addition of several like featured things, the extension of that feature increases, but not its power" (Mendelssohn 2012a, 97; 1971–, 3.2:110).

55. Mendelssohn 2012a, 97; 1971–, 3.2:110.

56. "That which no thinking being represents in his mind as possible is not in fact possible, and, what is more, that which is not conceived of as actual by any thinking being cannot in fact be actual" (Mendelssohn 2012a, 123; 1971–, 3.2:142).

57. Mendelssohn 2012a, 123; 1971–, 3.2:142.

58. Philosophers' conception of what is commonsensical could of course be rather different than what would be reflected by, say, the beliefs shared by any community larger than the philosopher in question and his immediate circle. Berkeley, for example, emphasized the importance of "the high-road of

plain common sense" (Berkeley 1967, 25). Yet his philosophy seems prima facie anything but commonsensical. Indeed, Thomas Reid, for example, criticized his immaterialism for being as distant from commonsense as Hume's ideas (See Reid 1983, 7–8). Mendelssohn's notion of commonsense too, which, as we shall see later on, is structured as universal in scope, is a construct which might not reflect what genuinely are universally held opinions. This, however, does not diminish in any way the importance of the concept of common sense, as Mendelssohn construed it, to any attempt at understanding his philosophy.

59. Mendelssohn 2007, 147; 1971–, 3.1:131.

60. Freudenthal 2012, 17.

61. Sophie Becker (1754–1789) was a gifted member of a learned and enlightened family and travelled through Germany with the poet Elise von der Recke (1754–1833) during the years 1784–1786. These travels were recorded in her diary, which was posthumously published. See Altmann 1973, 717.

62. Sophie Becker, diary entry, September 29, 1785, in Becker 1884, 191. Translated in Altmann 1973, 721.

63. Mendelssohn 2007, 80; 1971–, 3.1:52.

64. Leibniz 1973, 3.

65. As we shall see in the next chapter, Mendelssohn seeks to show this is the case even if at first sight it does not seem to be. See "Mendelssohn's Pluralism" in chapter 3.

66. This is not to say that the ontological proof is the only kind of argumentation Mendelssohn suggests. Indeed, in most works wherein it is mentioned, he also suggests versions of the cosmological argument, for example. I have chosen to focus on the ontological argument because, as we shall see, among the demonstrative proofs, it is the one he seems to have preferred and will best serve the points we need to make for our discussion. For a more thorough examination of Mendelssohn's proofs for the existence of God, see Altmann 1981b; and Arkush 1994, 37–45.

67. Mendelssohn 1997b, 281–82; 1971–, 2:300–301.

68. Mendelssohn 1997b, 291–92; 1971–, 2:311–12.

69. Mendelssohn 1997b, 292–93; 1971–, 2:312–14.

70. Mendelssohn 1997b, 279; 1971–, 2:297. It is interesting to think of this quote in conjunction with the one given above wherein Mendelssohn describes demonstrative proofs as "fortresses that protect a country against enemy attacks" (Mendelssohn 1997b; 1971–, 2:314). While Mendelssohn's prize essay does not seek to convince atheists, the demonstrative proofs it suggests are nonetheless also presented as protective of religious truths from atheistic attacks. Their use, Mendelssohn seems to suggest, is therefore mainly defensive. The difficulty of converting atheists and skeptics is a recurring theme in Men-

delssohn. These types of positions are repeatedly construed as beyond the limits of our commonsensical agreement. Accordingly, in *Jerusalem*, atheism is, quite exceptionally for Mendelssohn's pluralistic view, not tolerated politically. See Mendelssohn 1983, 62–63; 1971–, 8:131.

71. Mendelssohn 2012a, 3; 1971–, 3.2:3.

72. Kant 1979b, 59. Kant's argument here relates to a traditional objection to the ontological argument, namely, that it derives existence from an idea. See Altmann 1981b, 136. Of course, after his Copernican revolution, Kant rejected any kind of demonstrative metaphysical argument. At the time of *The One Possible Basis for a Demonstration of the Existence of God*, which was published in 1763, the same year as Mendelssohn's and Kant's essays for the academy's prize, Kant did still suggest a kind of ontological proof but for the necessity of existence, which he then suggested should be thought of as divine. Mendelssohn wrote a positive review of the book, which at the time was significant in promoting Kant's philosophical fame. See Walford 1992, lx.

73. Mendelssohn, 1971–, 3.2:203, translated in Jacobi 1994, 353. See also Gottlieb 2011, 91.

74. Mendelssohn 1997a, 279; 1971–, 2:297.

75. Mendelssohn 2007, 82–84; 1971–, 3.1:54–56.

76. Mendelssohn 2007, 123–24; 1971–, 3.1:100–101. He does add, however, that, "to our consolation," we do know enough for "our peace of mind, for our felicity in this life and in the other life" (Mendelssohn 2007; 1971–, 3.1:101).

77. Mendelssohn 2012a, 38; 1971–, 3.2:44.

78. Mendelssohn 2012a, 52; 1971–, 3.2:60. The notion that while divinity in and of itself is unknowable, God can come to be known through His creation and His effects on the world is a mainstay of Western theological thinking. Paul states that "ever since the creation of the world his eternal power and divine nature, invisible though they are, have been understood and seen through the things he has made" (Romans 1:20). A reformulation of that maxim is repeated several times in Augustine's *Confessions*, where it gains critical importance (see, for example, Augustine 1991, 127). Maimonides's negative theology strongly discourages any attempt at applying positive attributes to God's being and must certainly have been part of what Mendelssohn had in mind when cautioning against asking after God's essence. Yet, even Maimonides is somewhat more permissive when it comes to divine action, stating that "every attribute that we predicate of Him is an attribute of action or, if the attribute is intended for the apprehension of His essence and not of His action, it signifies the negation of the privation of the attribute in question" (Maimonides 1963, 1:136). Another relevant example is Leibniz, who also finds it better to be theologically modest, writing that it is sufficient "to have this confidence in God, that he has done

everything for the best and that nothing will be able to injure those who love him." Although a finite mind cannot know the particular reasons that "moved him to choose this order of the universe, to permit sin, to dispense his salutary grace in a certain manner," it is possible "to make some general remarks touching the course of providence in the government of things" (Leibniz 1973, 8).

79. Mendelssohn 2012b, 170; 1971–, 3.2:212.

80. Mendelssohn 2007, 81; 1971–, 3.1:53.

81. Mendelssohn 2012b, 158; 1971–, 3.2:198.

82. Mendelssohn 2012a, 89–90; 1971–, 3.2:102.

83. Mendelssohn 2012a, 83; 1971–, 3.2:155.

84. Mendelssohn 2012a, 63; 1971–, 3.2:70.

85. See Mendelssohn 1983, 123; 1971–, 8:189.

86. Mendelssohn 2007, 135; 1971–, 3.1:114.

87. Mendelssohn 2007, 96; 1971–, 3.1:70.

88. Mendelssohn 2012a, 63; 1971–, 3.2:70.

89. Descartes, for example, argued that animals are automata and lack thought or self-consciousness, and, as Harrison notes, many of his disciples, most notably Malebranche, went a step further, arguing "that if animals are by nature incapable of feeling pain, then God cannot be held responsible for visiting unmerited suffering upon these innocent creatures" (Harrison 1992, 220).

90. Mendelssohn 2007, 132: 1971–, 3.1:110. The fact Mendelssohn does not hold there to be a categorical difference between a providential care for humanity and some benevolent providential plan for animals is significant in the context of the crumbling of the harsh hierarchization of the Aristotelian universe. Mendelssohn, this already suggests, is not particularly keen on an overly hierarchical conception of creation.

91. Mendelssohn 1983, 123; 1971–, 8:188.

92. Mendelssohn 2007, 77; 1971–, 3.1:49; see also 2007, 84; 1971–, 3.1:56, where Socrates states that we will "perhaps" see others near us enjoying eternal felicity. Again, while very confident about the existence of an afterlife, he takes a less assured tone about this important aspect of it. The notion of meeting loved ones in the afterlife is yet again qualified at the end of the first dialogue: "Perhaps the Deity will lead us one day in transfigured friendship into each other's arms" (2007, 101; 1971–, 3.1:77).

93. Mendelssohn 2012a, 104; 1971–, 3.2:118. We will return to Mendelssohn's objections to Spinoza in chapter 6.

94. Mendelssohn 2007, 134; 1971–, 3.1:113.

95. His Socrates therefore refuses to speculate on what forms of purification the wicked will have to undergo or what kind of bliss the blessed will encounter

but remains steadfast in, and content with, the belief he "will exist eternally under Divine care, that His holy and just providence will reign over me in that life as in this, and that my true felicity exists in the beauties and perfections of my spirit" (Mendelssohn 2007, 143; 1971–, 3.1:113).

96. Mendelssohn 2007, 99; 1971–, 3.1:74–75.

97. Mendelssohn 2007, 82; 1971–, 3.1:82.

98. Mendelssohn 2007, 101; 1971–, 3.1:100.

99. Mendelssohn 2007, 147; 1971–, 3.1:131.

100. Mendelssohn 2007, 136–37; 1971–, 3.1:116–17.

101. So Nietzsche decries "all those other-worldly aspirations, alien to the senses, the instincts, to nature, to animals, in short all the ideals which up to now have been hostile to life and have defamed the world" (Nietzsche 1994, 66) and praises instead the "sovereign individual," described as "like only to itself, having freed itself from the morality of custom, an autonomous, supra-ethical individual (because 'autonomous' and 'ethical' are mutually exclusive) . . . a man with his own, independent, enduring will" (37).

102. See Hägglund 2019 for a striking contemporary this-worldly revaluation, one which arguably goes even further than Nietzsche in contradicting Mendelssohn's axiological position. Indeed, in a Nietzschean vein, and in contrast to Mendelssohn, Hägglund argues that "an eternal life is not only unattainable but also undesirable, since it would eliminate the care and passion that animate my life" (2019, 4) and that "far from making my life meaningful, eternity would make it meaningless, since my actions would have no purpose. What I do and what I love can matter to me only because I understand myself as mortal" (4–5). Hägglund, however, goes even further by arguing that even seemingly secular forms of revaluation, like Spinoza's emphasis on immanent eternity at the cost of a commitment to a genuinely finite life (47) or some of Nietzsche's formulations of his notion of amor fati, which embraces all of life's suffering, in essence nullify the fragile, human all too human, struggle against suffering (48). One could further add that just like with Spinoza's longing for eternity—which Hägglund qualifies as religious—Nietzsche's eternal return also harks back to a valuation that seeks eternity to generate meaning (see Fogel 2018, 2). In other words, from Hägglund's perspective, rather than making life meaningful, Mendelssohn's insistence on immortality robs it of any meaning it might have as an end in itself, and he goes beyond Nietzsche in making the further case that even seemingly secular alternatives, like Nietzsche's or Spinoza's, still refuse to genuinely validate the meaning of finite human life in all its fragility.

103. Mendelssohn, 1971–, 5.1:187–99; see also Shavin 2007, 19.

104. See Altmann 1973, 215.

105. "Ton terme est court, ils est borné / Le sort du jour où l'homme est né / L'entraîne vers la nuit fatale" (Frederic Roy de Prusse et Electeur de Brandebourg 1760, 64).

106. "Le tems soumet tout à sa loi / Le présent s'enfuit loin de moi / L'avenir s'empresse à le suivre / Homme, ton terme limité / N'est qu'un point dans l'éternité / Être un moment, s'appelle vivre" (Frederic Roy de Prusse et Electeur de Brandebourg 1760, 68).

107. "Nous nageons pleins de vanité / Entre le temp qui nous précède / Et l'absorbante éternité / De l'avenir qui nous succède . . . Sans cesse agités par l'envie / Pleins de songe séduisant / Nous nous perdons dans le néant / Tel est le sort de notre vie" (Frederic Roy de Prusse et Electeur de Brandebourg 1760, 72).

108. "Ce malheureux Univers" (Frederic Roy de Prusse et Electeur de Brandebourg 1760, 65).

109. "La nature envers eux marâtre / Semble se plaire à leurs malheurs / Mérite, dignité, naissance / Rien n'exempte de la souffrance / Dans nos destins le mal prévaut" (Frederic Roy de Prusse et Electeur de Brandebourg 1760, 15).

110. Frederick admired Voltaire's rebellious nature as well as his literary genius and sense of style and very much shared the philosopher's religious skepticism. His enthusiasm led him to engage with Voltaire in an enthusiastic, if not adoring, correspondence, eventually inviting him for rather outlandishly expensive visits. Indeed, the king, who had undertaken to cover these costs, was rather dismayed at the bill Voltaire saw fit to send him. For more on this fascinating relationship, see Fraser 2001, 45–48, 81–82.

111. Frederic Roy de Prusse et Electeur de Brandebourg 1760, 78.

112. Mendelssohn branded the notion expounded in *Candide* that a more perfect world would be possible as "obvious nonsense . . . utterly ridiculous" (Mendelssohn 1997c, 115; 1971–, 1:360). More generally, Mendelssohn seemed to have carried a lasting distaste for the French philosophes, who, like in Voltaire's case, were close to the materialist and cynical position some of the greatest French writers of his era took, a position radically different than the profoundly optimistic spirituality Mendelssohn's own thought advocated. See Altmann 1973, 30.

113. Mendelssohn 2007, 140; 1971–, 3.1:120.

114. Mendelssohn 2007, 45; 1971–, 3.1:14.

115. Mendelssohn 2007, 55; 1971–, 3.1:25.

116. Translated in Altmann 1973, 718–19; 1971–, 13:333. A rather similar position is indeed explicitly stated by Epicurus: "Vain is the word of a philosopher which does not heal any suffering of man. For just as there is no profit in medicine if it does not expel the diseases of the body, so there is no profit in philosophy either, if it does not expel the suffering of the mind" (Epicurus 1926, 133).

117. Aristotle 1993b, 1094a18–1094b11, 1729–1730.

118. Mendelssohn 1983, 33; 1971–, 8:103.

119. Mendelssohn 1983, 35–36; 1971–, 8:105.

120. Hobbes 1958, 407. Elsewhere, Hobbes writes that the power of the law rules actions only and should not be extended "to the very Thoughts and Consciences of men, by Examination, and Inquisition of what they hold, notwithstanding the Conformity of their Speech and Actions" (1958, 533).

121. Unless of course it has to be maintained in hiding, which is clearly not a situation Mendelssohn would have suggested was either just or necessary.

122. In his study of Hobbes's *Leviathan*, Carl Schmitt addresses the tendency of Jewish philosophers, Spinoza first and foremost, of turning the inner and individual freedom of thought into the form-giving principle, opposing it to Hobbes, for whom public peace and the right of the sovereign were at the forefront. Jewish philosophers, Schmitt therefore claims, inverted Hobbes's conception of the relation between external and internal, public and private into its converse. He further states that "the Jew, Moses Mendelssohn demands that because everyone must become blessed in his own way, it (the Leviathan) concerns itself as little as possible with the inner disposition of an individual" (Schmitt 1996, 61). This trend, Schmitt felt, turns the Leviathan into a ghost of its former self; when the superiority of the inner over the outer is posited, public power and force, even if respected, become "hollow and already dead" (1996, 61). This is why he characterizes Mendelssohn as "endowed with the unerring instinct for the undermining of state power that served to paralyze the alien and to emancipate his own Jewish folk" (1996, 58) and rather tastelessly identifies "castrating a Leviathan that had been full of vitality" as the work of Jewish thinkers (Spinoza, Mendelssohn, and Friedrich Julius Stahl specifically) (1996, 70). While Schmitt might be right in pointing out the particular sensitivity Jewish philosophers would bring to this issue, he is mistaken in his characterization of Mendelssohn's position; Mendelssohn does not seek to expand inner, private freedom of thought at the expense of public peace; he seeks to make freedom of thought and of religious practice an integral part of the outer, public life because he believes it actually enables a greater and more genuine public peace. He does not therefore seek to validate the distinction between inner and outer, but seeks, rather, at least in this context, to overcome it altogether.

123. Mendelssohn 1983, 35; 1971–, 8:104.

124. Mendelssohn 1983, 36–37; 1971–, 8:106.

125. Fear certainly seemed to have been a mainstay of Hobbes's own psychology. He famously wrote that he and fear were born as twins as his birth had been precipitated when his mother heard reports of the approaching Spanish armada (see Martinich 1999, 2). Hobbes also wrote rather boastfully that he had

been "the first of all who fled" to Paris when the situation in England seemed to become dangerous (see Hobbes 1840, 214). Not only, as we shall see below, did Hobbes explicitly write that people keep on fearing each other even when they have overcome the state of nature, but he proudly positioned fear as a guiding drive in his own life (see also Martinich 1999, 357; and Martinich 2003, 30). It is also telling, in this context, that when Hobbes differentiates religion, superstition, and true religion, he does so on the axis of fear, writing that "Feare of power invisible, feigned by the mind, or imagined from tales publiquely allowed, religion; not allowed, superstition. And when the power imagined, is truly such as we imagine, true religion" (Hobbes 1958, 44).

126. Hobbes 1958, 97.

127. Ibid.

128. Hobbes was in his time accused of being an atheist. However, as Martinich points out, *atheism* was in seventeenth-century discourse often a term of abuse hurled at theological opponents and did not necessarily carry its modern meaning, that is, not believing in any deity (Martinich 2003, 19–22). As opposed to most scholars who count Hobbes as a "tepid theist" (Martinich 2003, 1) or, like Curley, an atheist "at least with respect to the personal God of the Judeo-Christian tradition" (Curley 1992, 56), Martinich argues that while Hobbes's views may have been "unstandard," they were not necessarily "unorthodox" (Martinich 2003, 3) and that he in fact was a genuine Christian. Yet even Martinich admits Hobbes might "not have had a strong emotional commitment to religion" (2003, 1). Taking Martinich's admission, as well as the scholarly consensus he seeks to oppose, into account, it seems difficult to argue against Lorberbaum's assertion that Hobbes is far more interested in "the motivating force of religion than in the truth-value of its claims" (Lorberbaum 2007, 90) or to discard Pogson Smith's doubts as to "whether religion ever meant much more than an engine of political order to Hobbes" (Pogson Smith 1958, xi). While Hobbes's religious views remain a mystery that, as Springborg points out, would only befit a philosopher arguing they were "the private views of someone concerned to conform outwardly to what his church required of him" (Springbord 1996, 369), his laissez-faire strongly contrasts with Mendelssohn's urgent sense that without a wholly providential God, nothing can have any value at all and that divinely enabled human felicity needs to remain at all times our focus as the highest political good.

129. Hobbes 1958, 99.

130. Ibid., 122–23.

131. Ibid., 163.

132. I here follow Cooke, who convincingly shows that Hobbes's political theory is backed not by divine interference but by the fear of violent death

prevalent in the state of nature and that his account of obligation relies on self-preservation using the veneer of religious language to make "the law of self-preservation [appear] holy and transcendent" (Cooke 1996, 3). For a comprehensive analysis of the arguments for and against a "sincere" reading of Hobbes's appeal to religious obligation, which similarly to Cooke's analysis opts for the "insincere reading" and the view that Hobbes position cannot be that natural law is God's law, see Forster 2003.

133. Hobbes 1958, 164.

134. Ibid., 75.

135. Ibid., 48.

136. Ibid., 94.

137. Ibid., 75.

138. See ibid., 128.

139. Vernon 2010, xv.

140. Locke 2010a, 7–8.

141. Ibid., 55.

142. Proast 2010, 59.

143. Ibid., 56.

144. Locke 2010b, 71.

145. Ibid., 83.

146. Locke 2010a, 21.

147. Mendelssohn 1983, 44; 1971–, 8:113.

148. Mendelssohn 1983, 38; 1971–, 8:107 (emphasis original). Another interesting similarity between Mendelssohn and Proast is the notion of "distance" in the context of the means used by civil authorities in these matters. Mendelssohn states that "the state, to be sure, is to see to it from afar that no doctrines are propagated which are inconsistent with the public welfare" and, a paragraph later, that "it is only from a distance that the state should take notice of this, and only with wise moderation should it favor even those doctrines upon which its true felicity is based" (Mendelssohn 1983, 62–63; 1971–, 8:130–31).

149. Mendelssohn 1983, 38; 1971–, 8:108.

150. Mendelssohn 1983, 39; 1971–, 8:108.

151. It is important to note that, unlike Hobbes, Locke was clearly a thoroughly religious person and a philosopher whose work is thoroughly religious. Indeed, as has been argued by Wadron with regards to Locke's notion of equality, it is impossible to bracket out the theological dimension from some of his major political ideas (see Waldron 2002, 44). Locke's depiction of the state of nature is far less brutal than Hobbes's mainly because it already involves the realization that humans are all "the workmanship of one omnipotent and infinitely wise Maker; all the servants of one sovereign Master, sent into the

world by His order and about His business." As "they are His property, whose workmanship they are made to last during His, not one another's pleasure," they cannot harm each other and the state of nature, though one of liberty, is not one of license (see Locke 2003, 271). Indeed, as we saw above, Mendelssohn himself expresses gratitude to Locke for his philosophical guidance in overcoming terrifying doubts (Mendelssohn 1997b, 27; 1971–, 1:64–65). The fact the presence of a religious highest good in Mendelssohn trumps not only Hobbes's doubtful religiosity but even Locke's well-established religious sensitivities in terms of existential urgency further reveals the religious nature of his axiological prioritization.

152. Strauss differentiated modern political philosophy from the ancient kind in that the latter was reliably aimed at lofty objectives while the former rejects such positions as unrealistic and seeks to increase the chances of actualization through seeking out more modest aims. This differentiation would put Mendelssohn squarely in the camp of the ancient kind of political philosophy. See Strauss 1989, 39–59.

153. Mendelssohn 1983, 85; 1971–, 8:153.

154. Mendelssohn 1983, 85–86; 1971–, 8:153.

155. Mendelssohn 2012a, 71; 1971–, 3.2:79.

156. Hume 1958, 415.

157. Mendelssohn 2012a, 72–73; 1971–, 3.2:81–82.

158. Mendelssohn 2012a, 72–73; 1971–, 3.2:81–82.

159. Indeed, in his dream, reason (the old matron) does not provide its own claims and offers no road of its own, but rather judges the active forces of common sense and contemplation. As mentioned, Jacobi also suggests, beyond the pejorative sense given in the passage quoted above, a rather similarly neutral concept of reason. In a letter to Jean François Laharpe, a member of the Académie Française, Jacobi writes that reason, considered as a separate entity or as pure reason, appeared "neither as legislative nor as executive but simply as judging, simply as applying given determinations to given objects. Reason is a superb bearer of light; by itself, however, it would neither give light nor move" (quoted in Di Giovanni 1994, 19).

160. Mendelssohn 2012a, 71; 1971–, 3.2:79.

161. Mendelssohn 2012a, 44; 1971–, 3.2:50.

3. UNIVERSAL FELICITY

1. Mendelssohn 1997d, 233; 1971–, 1:149.

2. Gottlieb 2011, 89.

3. Mendelssohn 2012a, 9; 1971–, 3.2:10.

4. See, for example, Mendelssohn 2012a, 74; 1971–, 3.2:83.

5. It is important to clarify that Mendelssohn's position is certainly not that we ought to believe things because they are commonly believed out of pragmatic concerns. Rather, he thought that the commonality of a belief was indicative of its actuality. Though at times Mendelssohn sounds almost like a pragmatist, he explicitly rejected adopting beliefs because they are useful, good, or desirable. See Mendelssohn 2012a, 62; 1971–, 3.2:69–70.

6. Mendelssohn 2012b, 158; 1971–, 3.2:198.

7. By choosing a Greenlander to exemplify his point, Mendelssohn might be implicitly rebuking Maimonides's glaring expression of a far more exclusivistic position at the beginning of his famous parable of the castle, when he states that by "those who are outside the city [within which the palace is located]" he means "the furthermost Turks found in the remote North, the Negroes [sic] found in the remote South, and those who resemble them from among them that are with us in these climes." He adds that these individuals have a status like that of "irrational animals" and do not "have the rank of men" but one "lower than the rank of man but higher than the rank of apes" (Maimonides 1963, 2:618). In this awful passage, Maimonides therefore denies full human status to peoples of extreme climates, let alone the ability to find religious salvation (which is why they are as distant as the parable allows anyone to be from the palace's inner court). For more on Maimonides's position and how it relates to climatic theories widely accepted in medieval thinking, see Melamed 2016, 38. For the specific source of this passage, see Harvey 1991, and for more on the anti-Black sentiment reflected in it, as well as more generally in Maimonides's writings and his surrounding Muslim cultural context, see Goldenberg 2013. See n. 15 in the latter source for more on the translation of the original *al-sūdān* as referring to all Black people, as is here above implied in Pines's outdated formulation.

8. Mendelssohn 1983, 90–94; 1971–, 8:157–61 (italics original).

9. Mendelssohn 1983, 90–94; 1971–, 8:161.

10. See Shavin 2007, 25.

11. Mendelssohn 2007, 135; 1971–, 3.1:115.

12. The term *sensitivity* here is not meant to imply that Mendelssohn's treatment of foreign cultures reflect all the sensitivities that inform our current more critical and postcolonial discourse on the matter. Indeed, with the benefit of hindsight, our hopefully more penetrating eyes can easily locate various aspects of Mendelssohn's treatment that might strain these sensitivities. It is important, however, to also understand Mendelssohn from within his own cultural environment. From that historically contextualized perspective, his sensitivity is comparatively remarkably comprehensive and robust. So, for example, as we shall see, the foreigners Mendelssohn describes in his writings are continually meant to exemplify our ignorance rather than theirs. This cultural humility is

notable for a time when even the greatest self-proclaimed universalist philosophers of the Enlightenment lapsed into prejudice when describing foreign cultures.

13. See Freudenthal 2012, 196. Mendelssohn's theory of idolatry echoes Maimonides's view on the matter, according to which the well-intentioned worship of intermediaries eventually leads to idolatry. For a comparison of their positions, see Kaplan 1988.

14. Mendelssohn 1983, 113; 1971–, 8:179 (emphasis original).

15. Mendelssohn is here making a reference to Mai, whom the British called Omai. Mai was a pacific islander who came back with Captain Cook after the latter's second voyage in the pacific in 1774 before eventually returning to Tahiti in 1777. In his time in Britain, Mai had become a sensation among the local aristocracy, meeting King George and being invited by various patrons to the theater and to their country estates, where he joined society dinners and family outings. Yet, as is clear from his presence in Mendelssohn's *Jerusalem*, Mai's European legacy grew far beyond the personal bonds he made while in England. The first Polynesian ever to have visited Britain also became a popular literary figure and appeared in a wide variety of pamphlets, novels, and poems. So, for example, in 1785, *Omai: or a Trip around the World*, a grand and popular pantomime, was produced at the Covent Garden Theater (Joppien 1979, 81). In 1790, the French theologian Guillaume André René Baston published *Narrations d'Omaï*, a pretend autobiography of Mai, which included ethnographic speculations and suggestions for a utopian society (Charuty 2011, 196). For more on Mai's fascinating story, see McCormick 2013; or Connaughton 2005. For further analysis of this fascinating passage in Mendelssohn's *Jerusalem*, see Fogel 2020.

16. Johan Bernhard Basedow (1724–1790) was among the most influential educational reformers of the Aufklärung. Inspired by Rousseau and others, he developed and promoted an Enlightenment pedagogy, which he had the opportunity of putting into practice when Prince Leopold III Friedrich Franz of Anhalt-Dessau enabled him to open a revolutionary school, the Philantropinum in Dessau in 1774. An integral part of the school's pedagogical philosophy was a strong emphasis on religious tolerance. Basedow invited Roman Catholic, Greek Orthodox, Protestant, Mennonite, Jewish, and Muslim students and sought to emphasize that which their faith had in common (see Laursen 2016, 40). Like Mendelssohn, Basedow's primordial concern was to maintain the crucial common beliefs in God, providence, and immortality (Bleeck 2008, 149), which is why the temple was supposed to bring attention precisely to these beliefs (Bleeck 2008, 149–50). Mendelssohn supported Basedow's efforts, corresponded with the educator (Altmann 1973, 323), and, according to Beck, even helped Jewish children enter the Philantropinum (Beck 1969, 325).

Basedow was notably endorsed by Kant, who described Basedow's pedagogical efforts towards religious tolerance and the schools it engendered as "the greatest phenomenon which has appeared in this century for the improvement of the perfection of humanity" (Kant 2012, 250). For more on Kant's support of Basedow and Basedow's influence on Kant's own ideas for cosmopolitan education, see Cavallar 2014 and Louden 2012.

17. Mendelssohn 1983, 114; 1971–, 8:179.

18. Mendelssohn 1983, 114; 1971–, 8:180.

19. Mendelssohn 1983, 114; 1971–, 8:180. Though he does not mention him specifically, Mendelssohn might very well be referring here to Locke, who does indeed describe, rather sarcastically, the "poor Indian Philosopher" who was led to find an elephant to support earth "and a Tortoise to support his elephant" (Locke 1985, 175).

20. Mendelssohn 1983, 115; 1971–, 8:180. John Zephaniah Holwell spent almost thirty years in India and was at one point governor of the British East India Company in Bengal. He learned Persian and Bengali, and his writings on India were well received by European enlighteners, such as Edmund Burke and Voltaire (Patterson 2017, 24–25). Mendelssohn quotes from the second volume of Holwell's *Interesting Historical Events Relative to the Provinces of Bengal and the Empire of Indostan* (1767), wherein he discusses the "religious tenets of the Gentoos" (Holwell 1767, 1.2:1). Mendelssohn quotes the passage on creation in section 8 of Holwell's book (Holwell 1767, 1:107–9; and Mendelssohn 1983, 115; 1971–, 8:181; see also Altmann 1983, 225). Holwell indeed explains the passage as allegorical in nature, writing that the personages introduced as "actors in the work of that creation were intended by him [the Brahman] to be taken only in a figurative sense, as expressive of the three supreme attributes of the Deity, his power to create, his power to preserve, and his power to change, or destroy" (Holwell 1767, 2:111). Interestingly, Holwell believed that what he called "the original tenets of the Gentoo" contains the truths necessary for salvation (see Patterson 1767, 27), a conclusion Mendelssohn would certainly have very much appreciated.

21. Mendelssohn 1983, 114; 1971–, 8:180.

22. Many years before, when they were first introduced, Lessing had offered Mendelssohn a treatise by Shaftesbury. Beyond the philosophical significance of the preamble Mendelssohn chose, this could therefore also be a tacit personal tribute to the friend whose intellectual and religious reputation Mendelssohn sought to defend with his book. See Altman 1973, 38.

23. Mendelssohn 2012b, 147; 1971–, 3.2:184. The passage Mendelssohn quotes can be found in Cooper 2000, 39.

24. Rosenstock suggests a slightly different interpretation: "Jacobi takes

Lessing's mask—his Spinozism—to be the truth, and he takes Mendelssohn's truth—his faith in God—to be a mask (for his atheism)" (Rosenstock 2012, 201).

25. Mendelssohn 1983, 112–13; 1971–, 8:178.

26. Tellingly, Mendelssohn's account completely and comprehensively contradicts Hume, who claimed that "polytheism or idolatry was, and necessarily must have been, the first and most ancient religion of mankind" and that it would be unlikely "men entertained the principles of pure theism . . . while they were ignorant and barbarous" and "fell into error, as soon as they acquired learning and politeness" (Hume 1976, 26). Hume further writes that "the savage tribes of America, African and Asia are all idolaters. Not a single exception to this rule" (1976, 26–27).

27. Gottlieb 2011, 95.

28. Quoted in Ibid., 94–95.

29. Mendelssohn 1983, 132; 1971–, 8:197.

30. See Feiner 2010, 107–8.

31. Sorkin 1994, 101.

32. Mendelssohn to Emden, June 30, 1772, in Mendelssohn 1971–, 19:159 (translated in Altman 1973, 290).

33. Feiner 2010, 110–11.

34. Mendelssohn 1983, 95–96; 1971–, 8:162.

35. Mendelssohn 1983, 96; 1971–, 8:162–63.

36. Early biographers claimed Locke was involved in forwarding the bill through parliament. However, while he might have been somewhat involved, these claims remain unsubstantiated. See Schwoerer 1990, 544.

37. These rights, however, were still partial. So, for example, Jews could reside permanently in Vienna only if they performed a "useful" service, possessed at least 10,000 gulden, and paid a "Toleranz-Tax" (See O'Brien 1969, 29). Moreover, as the emperor was concerned with what he perceived as Jewish exclusiveness, the edict demanded educational reforms as well as language requirements for Jews, both of which aimed at moderating Jewish cultural separation (O'Brien 1969, 34). While Mendelssohn was weary of the edict, which he suspected might also seek to lure Jews towards Christianity (Altmann 1973, 462), he still appreciated the profound significance of the event and opened his preface to Menashe Ben Israel's *Vindiciae Judaeorum*, published soon after the edict, with a celebratory formulation which, as Altmann notes, is reminiscent of the Shehecheyanu blessing (see Altmann 1973, 464): "Thank all-bountiful providence that it has allowed me, at the end of my days, to live to see this happy point in time in which the rights of man are beginning to be taken to heart in their true extent" (Mendelssohn 2011, 40; 1971–, 8:3).

38. Gray 2007, 29; or to quote Habermas, "We need tolerance only vis-a-vis

worldviews that we consider wrong and vis-a-vis habits that we do not like" (2008b, 23).

39. As Beneke notes, in Britain's mainland colonies, as in Western Europe, the policy of toleration might have relieved religious minorities of some physical punishments and some financial burdens, "but it did not free them from the indignities of prejudice and exclusion. Nor did it make them equal. Those 'tolerated' could still be barred from civil offices, military positions, and university posts" (Beneke 2006, 6).

40. See, for example, Mendelssohn's warning that "a union of faiths is not tolerance [Toleranz]; it is diametrically opposed to true tolerance [wahren Duldung]!" (Mendelssohn 1983, 138; 1971–, 8:203). See also his impassioned call at the end of *Jerusalem* to "pave the way for a happy posterity toward that height of culture, toward that universal tolerance of man [jener allgemeinen Menschenduldung]" (Mendelssohn 1983, 139; 1971–, 8:203). Again, though used in a very enthusiastic fashion by Mendelssohn, the term *Duldung*, like *Toleranz*, carries a connotation of "enduring" or even "suffering" difference.

41. Huang 1995, 127.

42. This model was influentially expressed by Hick, who described his pluralism as "the view that the great world faiths embody different perceptions and conceptions of, and correspondingly different responses to, the Real or the Ultimate from within the major variant cultural ways of being human" (Hick 1985, 36). Accordingly, at the heart of this pluralistic hypothesis lies the thought that "the Real an sich is one but is nevertheless capable of being humanly experienced in a variety of ways" (Hick 1985, 40).

43. Mendelssohn 1983, 138; 1971–, 8:202.

44. Mendelssohn 1983, 138; 1971–, 8:203 (emphasis original).

45. Mendelssohn 1983, 138; 1971–, 8:203. The idea that there is not merely an acceptable, but rather a positive aspect of this pluralism again reflects Hick's position described above (n. 42). Indeed, Hick suggests a reason why this pluralism would contribute to human flourishing when he writes that "by attending to other traditions than one's own one may become aware of other aspects or dimensions of the Real, and of other possibilities of response to the Real, which had not been made effectively available by one's own tradition" (Hicks 1985, 44). Mendelssohn does not provide the reasons God might have had and would certainly argue that Judaism (as well as other traditions) cannot be perceived as lacking the essential aspects of the Real. The point remains, however, that Mendelssohn's pluralism, like Hick's, does not merely tolerate differences but suggests it actually serves a higher purpose. For more on the philosophical context within which Mendelssohn makes this claim, see Altmann 1974, 200; and 1973, 313–14. See also Gottlieb, who seeks to flesh out the divine plan

Mendelssohn is hinting at by claiming that the awareness of religious diversity makes us realize the signs we use to represent God are inadequate and arbitrary. The more we are aware of religious pluralism, therefore, the less we tend to deify our symbols, which, as we saw, is the mechanism underlying idolatry. For Gottlieb, Mendelssohn therefore suggests religious pluralism guards us from idolatry. See Gottlieb 2006, 222.

46. Berlin 2001, 11–12.

47. Ibid., 14.

48. Indeed, Mendelssohn suggests that some forms of polytheism, namely, those that posit a divinity supreme to the other deities, could be acceptable. See, for example, 1971–, 16:186. We shall return to this issue in chapter 6.

49. Mendelssohn 1983, 62–63; 1971–, 8:130–31.

50. As we saw in the previous chapter, he did still refer to himself as "quite Epicurean" (1971–, 13:333). This could indicate the Mendelssohn has an ambivalent conception of Epicureanism or that the term is used with slightly different meanings or connotations.

51. See chapter 2, n. 70.

52. Mendelssohn 1983, 67; 1971–, 8:134.

53. Mendelssohn 1997a, 279; 1971–, 2:297.

54. "Those who deny that there is a Deity are not to be tolerated at all" (Locke 2010a, 37). More generally, as Altmann explains, "in the 17th and 18th centuries atheism was widely considered asocial in character and, hence, a danger to the very existence of the state" (Altmann 1983, 190).

55. See Martinich 2003, 19–22 (see also chapter 2, n. 128).

56. Mendelssohn 1983, 138; 1971–, 8:202.

57. Mendelssohn to Naphtali Herz Homber, September 22, 1783, in Mendelssohn 2011, 124; 1971–, 13:134.

58. Mendelssohn 1983, 38–39; 1971–, 8:108.

59. Mendelssohn 1983, 72; 1971–, 8:139.

60. Mendelssohn to Naphtali Herz Homber, September 22, 1783, in Mendelssohn 2011, 124; 1971–, 13:134.

61. Locke 2010a, 35.

62. Martin 1973, 32.

63. Of course, these remarks do not justify his position or validate his opinions in any way. They merely seek to contextualize them historically.

64. See Altmann 1973, 206–7.

65. Mendelssohn, 1971–, 7:59, translated in Altmann 1973, 204.

66. Altmann 1973, 205.

67. Mendelssohn 2011, 5; 1971–, 7:3.

68. See Altmann 1973, 210–14.

69. Mendelssohn 2011, 6–7; 1971–, 7:7–8.

70. Mendelssohn 2011, 7–9; 1971–, 7:9–11 (emphasis original).

71. Mendelssohn 2011, 14; 1971–, 7:16. Bonnet himself, in fact, took issue with this characterization. In a letter he wrote to Mendelssohn, Bonnet apologizes for Lavater's tactless challenge and ensures Mendelssohn he knew nothing about it. Indeed, he tells Mendelssohn his work was meant for those disbelievers who are born in the Christian church, rather than for Jews (Bonnet to Mendelssohn, January 12, 1770, in Mendelssohn 1971–, 7:307). While embarrassed by Lavater's misguided effort, Bonnet does express concern that readers of Mendelssohn's response might come to believe he had appropriated arguments from other thinkers and cares to emphasize that "plagiarism has always been a horror to me, and I have always set as a duty to recognize what I owe to writers who have preceded me" (Mendelssohn 1971–, 7:308).

72. Mendelssohn 2011, 15; 1971–, 7:17 (emphasis original).

73. Mendelssohn 2011, 16; 1971–, 7:90.

74. Mendelssohn 2011, 16; 1971–, 7:90.

75. Mendelssohn 2011, 18; 1971–, 7:93.

76. See "Judaism and Universal Felicity" in this chapter for how Judaism favorably compares with this description of the Christian faith.

77. Freudenthal 2012, 196.

78. Ibid., 200.

79. Ibid., 190.

80. Ibid., 199.

81. Mendelssohn 2011, 8; 1971–, 7:9.

82. Mendelssohn 2011, 9; 1971–, 7:11.

83. Mendelssohn 2011, 11; 1971–, 7:13.

84. Mendelssohn 2011, 26; 1971–, 7:102.

85. Mendelssohn 2011, 30; 1971–, 7:106.

86. See Mendelssohn 1983, 77–78; 1971–, 8:145–46.

87. See Spinoza 2016b, 151. The version of the Maimonidean text Spinoza addresses appears to be corrupt, making it more exclusivistic than what it was meant to be (see Schwartzchild 1962, 302), though some scholars insist this is not the case (see, for example, Fox 1990, 132–33). At any rate, whether the passage was corrupt or not, Mendelssohn too only knew it in its exclusivistic wording (see Altmann 1973, 217).

88. The letter wherein Emden first expresses his view of this issue to Mendelssohn has been lost (Mendelssohn 2011, 31), but his opinion is expressed in detail in the correspondence nonetheless; having received Mendelssohn's response, Emden replied with an extensive letter explaining in detail the Talmudic legitimacy of Maimonides's position (see Mendelssohn, 1971–, 19:179–83). For a

detailed examination of the back and forth between Mendelssohn and Emden on this issue and the varying interpretations of the rabbinic sources it reflects, see Schonfeld 2010. For further analysis of the Maimonidean passage itself and its reception by Spinoza, Mendelssohn, Emden, and Cohen, see Schwartzschild 1962.

89. Mendelssohn 2011, 32; 1971–, 19:178.

90. Mendelssohn 2011, 33; 1971–, 19:178.

91. Mendelssohn 2011, 10; 1971–, 7:12 (italics original).

92. Mendelssohn 1983, 94; 1971–, 8:161.

93. Mendelssohn 2011, 57; 1971–, 8:77.

94. Mendelssohn 2011, 57, 63; 1971–, 8:77, 83.

95. Mendelssohn 1983, 89–90; 1971–, 8:157 (italics original).

96. Mendelssohn 1983, 97; 1971–, 8:164.

97. Mendelssohn gives both as examples of ways in which Jews cannot participate in common civil life. Mendelssohn 1983, 135; 1971–, 8:200.

98. Kant 1997, 27.

99. See Hegel 2003, 162. For more on what precisely leads Hegel to make this claim, see Sedgwick 2011.

100. Kant 1997, 48 (emphasis original).

101. Gramsci 1975, 3:323.

102. Friedman 1989, 275.

103. MacIntyre 2007, 220–21.

104. Mendelssohn 1997b, 27; 1971–, 1:65.

105. Altman 1973, 28.

106. Mendelssohn 2011, 17; 1971–, 7:91.

107. Mendelssohn 2011, 7; 1971–, 7:7–8.

108. Mendelssohn 2011, 17; 1971–, 7:91.

109. Mendelssohn to Prince Karl Wilhelm Ferdinand of Braunschweig in Mendelssohn 1971–, 7:301.

110. Mendelssohn 1971–, 7:302.

111. Mendelssohn 1983, 102 1971–, 8:169.

112. Mendelssohn 1983, 118; 1971–, 8:184.

113. Freudenthal 2012, 9.

114. Mendelssohn 1983, 119; 1971–, 8:184.

115. Mendelssohn 1983, 119; 1971–, 8:184.

116. Mendelssohn 1983, 118–19; 1971–, 8:184 (emphasis original).

117. A. Jospe 1969, 3

118. Arkush 1999, 29.

119. Ibid., 30–31.

120. See Arkush 1994, 259.

121. Arkush argues that with regards to the revelation of Sinai and the documents reporting it, Mendelssohn "simply fails to address the doubts and concerns of skeptics, with which he was quite well acquainted" (Arkush 1994, 230). However, as Arkush himself points out, Mendelssohn does argue for the reliability of the sacred texts from the consensus of their truth among Jews, Christians, and Muslims (see Arkush 1994, 175; and Mendelssohn 1971–, 7:88), as well as repeating medieval arguments to the effect that unlike other ancient narratives, this one described an event witnessed by the whole nation as opposed to individuals or small groups (Arkush 1994, 174; and Mendelssohn 1971–, 7:324). Discussing such arguments, Arkush claims that "it is simply not possible to believe" that Mendelssohn thought they "could dispel modern doubts concerning the truth of the biblical narrative" (Arkush 1994, 230). This, of course, is a highly speculative claim. While Arkush might find these arguments exceptionally weak, that certainly still is no reason to ascribe that same belief to Mendelssohn. Indeed, it is telling that both arguments here mentioned for the reliability of Judaic revelation reflect Mendelssohn's emphasis on common sense and its epistemological importance. This reinforces the claim they are indeed genuine Mendelssohnian arguments, rather than merely strategic ones. Furthermore, as Raphael Jospe has convincingly pointed out, there are many aspects of Mendelssohn's views on Judaism that were clearly inspired by medieval Jewish philosophers and commentators, so that "the modern Berlin philosopher is in many respects the student of medieval Sepharad" (R. Jospe 2007, 107). Given the pervasiveness of these influences not only with regards to the status of publicly verifiable truths but also regarding the superiority of the Hebrew language, biblical poetry, and oral communication (see R. Jospe 2007, 114–17), there is no reason to think Mendelssohn did not take medieval arguments about the Sinaitic revelation seriously. Arkush further claims it is suspect that Mendelssohn does not give a lot of attention to the matter, especially in *Jerusalem*, where Arkush would have expected it to be developed at greater length (see Arkush 1994, 177). It is important, however, to remember that the gist of the book is about proving that the Sinaitic revelation does not contradict enlightened political principles and values rather that proving that it did occur.

122. Arkush 1999, 32.

123. Arkush quotes Altmann and Yovel, who are similarly skeptical that punitive measures ceased after the loss of political sovereignty, to back up his claim (see Arkush 1999, 37). As Yovel put it in the quoted passage; "Jewish religion was not voluntary in the sense in which modem political theories use this term. It contained an element of coercion, of legal sanction, banning the rebel and subjecting the members of the congregation to rabbinical authority" (Yovel 1998, 198, n. 11). Yovel further claims that the Jewish congregation imposed

within the community "the authority of a religious law and a semi-theocratic government of the kind which Mendelssohn opposed," concluding that "Mendelssohn's words were intended for the non-Jewish world and are flawed with apologetic imprecision" (Yovel 1998, 198, n. 11).

124. Arkush 1999, 37.

125. See Mendelssohn 1983, 130–31; 1971–, 8:195–96.

126. See, for example, Mendelssohn 1983, 57; 1971–, 8:126.

127. Mendelssohn 1983, 131; 1971–, 8:196.

128. Mendelssohn to Prince Karl Wilhelm Ferdinand of Braunschweig in Mendelssohn 1971–, 7:302.

129. Other arguments to that effect are not sufficiently convincing either. Arkush, for example, claims that while life without God, providence, and immorality conjures up, in Mendelssohn's eyes, a "rather chilling visions of a bleak and inhospitable universe," Mendelssohn nowhere suggests that "he would be similarly bereft of hope if biblical revelation were to be discredited," as even if the Bible were the "product of ignorant and superstitious people and recorded no genuine revelation, he would still have possessed all the necessary means of attaining felicity" (Arkush 1999, 42). Yet, Mendelssohn does in fact mention how much he would despair were his particular religion shown to be misguided. Indeed, in the critical passage we quoted in the previous chapter, wherein Mendelssohn admits he would choose faith over reason were they to clash, he is not speaking of a general theistic faith, but specifically of the Jewish one (see Mendelssohn 1983, 85; 1971–, 8:153). Arkush himself addresses this passage but seems not to take it seriously in spite of its intensely personal tone (see Arkush 1994, 257). Similarly, the language Mendelssohn uses is particularly strong when explaining to Lavater his resistance to conversion, which is ruled out as long as his "entire soul does not assume another nature" (Mendelssohn 2011, 8; 1971–, 7:10). The same image is also found in the "Counter-Reflections to Bonnet's *Palingenesis*," wherein he states his "entire soul would have to be altered" (Mendelssohn 2011, 19; 1971–, 7:94), indicating again the degree to which that attachment is perceived as critical. This is not to mention the obligation of the ceremonial law, which he maintained throughout his life and emphatically reiterates at the end of *Jerusalem* (Mendelssohn 1983, 134–35; 1971–, 8:199–200). If Mendelssohn did not believe in the authenticity of the revelation at Sinai, one might have expected him to be far more lenient with the Halakha than this passage, and indeed his daily life, shows him to have been. And while Arkush might be right that for Mendelssohn, Judaism "retained only a limited, instrumental value" (Arkush 1999, 41), that is not because Mendelssohn is not genuinely attached to it, but rather because its value, as the value of any other

thing, whether morality, life itself, or even God, is, as we have seen, derived from the highest value of felicity

130. See Mendelssohn 1983, 117; 1971–, 8:182–83.

131. Eisen 1990, 242.

4. HERMANN COHEN'S FUTURE

1. Cohen's Marburgian Neo-Kantianism was part of a wider return to Kant that began developing after the failed Revolutions of 1848 and is commonly thought to have gained a prominence in the 1860s, which it maintained in various ways until the First World War. Otto Liebmann's influential *Kant und die Epigonen* (1865) and its repeated admonitions for a return to Kant is often depicted as capturing the spirit of the movement in a particularly influential manner. Indeed, it gave rise to the oft-quoted slogan "Back to Kant [Zurück zu Kant]," which has become a kind of scholarly catch phrase used to describe the Neo-Kantian movement (see, for example, Rotenstreich 1996, 86; or Liebeschütz 1960, 10). Interestingly, Liebmann never actually wrote the "Zurück zu Kant" line, but rather repeated again and again the arguably less catchy "Es muß auf Kant zurückgegangen werden" (see Liebman 1912, 214, 216; see also Beiser 2014, 286). Though not associated with a specific slogan, Friedrich Lange's *History of Materialism* (1866) was probably even more significant, as, according to Beiser, "no other work did more to revive Kant's reputation, to place him at the center of German philosophy in the middle of the 19th century" (Beiser 2014, 356). Lange, of course, is particularly important to us as he was the academic patron of Cohen, who succeeded him upon his death as professor of philosophy at Marburg. It is, at any rate, in this intellectual atmosphere of renewed enthusiasm for Kant that Cohen, only twenty-nine, published his *Kants Theorie der Erfahrung* (1871), which was very well received by Lange, among others. For a succinct contextualization of Cohen within the nineteenth-century return to Kant in Germany philosophy, see Holzhey 2005; or Beiser 2014, 465–91.

2. Indeed, Kant distinguishes between the "supreme [das Oberste]" good, which relates to good will, and the "perfect [das Vollendete]" good (see, Kant 2015, 141; 1902–, 5:110), which, as we shall see, includes a morally conditioned happiness. Elsewhere, Kant reiterates that difference using "highest good [das höchste Gut]" versus the "complete [das Ganze]" good (see Kant 1997, 10; 1902–, 4:396). *Das vollständige Gut*, as used, for example, in the *Kritik der Reinen Vernunft*, is also translated as "complete Good" (see Kant 1929, 640; 1902–, 3:527). In order to avoid confusion, while analyzing Kant's position, I will maintain this subtle differentiation and use the terms *complete good* or *summum bonum* (but not *highest good*) to refer to that which in his system parallels that

which in Mendelssohn we simply referred to as the *highest good* or *summum bonum*. Afterwards, once we have established what Kant means by *complete good* or *summum bonum*, I will revert to using *highest good* to refer to it as well in order to simplify comparative analysis and follow scholarly discourse on the matter. Indeed, the differentiations mentioned above serve Kant in his dialectical argumentation about the *summum bonum*, but once the argument has been made, he himself uses *highest good* to refer to what previously was called the "complete good" (see, e.g., Kant 2015, 105).

3. In a further similarity with Mendelssohn, though not strictly speaking dependent upon immortality and the existence of God, Kant's complete good is also closely connected to them. See Aufderheide and Bader 2015, 2.

4. Throughout Kant's treatment of happiness, he most often uses the word *Glückseligkeit* (e.g., in the definitions of happiness referenced in chapter 4, nn. 6 and 7), for which the term *felicity* was used throughout the chapters on Mendelssohn. Still, I will use the term *happiness* rather than *felicity* throughout the chapter. This is done not only in order to follow the standard translations but also to reflect the difference between Kant's happiness and Mendelssohn's felicity, which shall be clarified below.

5. Kant 2015, 20, 100 (emphasis original). He had offered a slightly different wording in his first critique, stating that happiness is "the satisfaction of all our desires, extensively, in respect of their manifoldness, intensively, in respect of their degree, and protensively, in respect of their duration" (Kant 1929, 636).

6. Kant 2015, 20.

7. Ibid., 37.

8. Cassirer 1981, 15.

9. Kant 2015, 50; 1902–, 5:58 (emphasis original). This common linguistic delineation might be one of the reasons Kant later on states that pure morality is clear to common human reason and that only philosophers make it doubtful. See Kant 2015, 124.

10. See "Eternal Felicity as a Political Directive" in chapter 2; and Hobbes 1958, 75.

11. Kant 1997, 28.

12. Ibid., 29.

13. Barney 2015, 162.

14. Kant 1997, 8–9 (italics original).

15. Ibid., 9.

16. Ibid., 3.

17. Ibid., 13 (emphasis original).

18. Kant 1929, 636.

19. Kant 1997, 4.

20. Kant 2015, 75–76 (emphasis original).

21. Kant 1929, 303.

22. It is important, however, to keep in mind that Mendelssohn's highest good of felicity is not merely an empirical phenomenon but rather a spiritual progress towards divine perfection (see chapter 2). Accordingly, many of the criticisms Kant suggests about empirical happiness as the end of our action, or indeed its moral relevance, might perfectly cohere with Mendelssohn's position as well. However, as will be made explicit below, it is not only empirical happiness that Kant himself objects to as validating the moral law, but rather any form of happiness, including the felicity one might deservedly be granted in the afterlife. This, as mentioned above, is where the genuine difference between them lies; for Mendelssohn, without divine providence and felicity, morality cannot be validated, while Kant continually seeks to argue that while we can hope our actions will be rewarded by divine providence, that theological premise cannot be thought of as validating the moral law (see chapter 4, n. 236). Still, there are many fascinating similarities between Mendelssohn and Kant on these issues and the presentation of Kant's thought in this section is certainly not meant to implicitly contrast with Mendelssohn's on all points raised. It is meant, rather, to enable a thorough understanding of Cohen's position, which we will be looking at in the next sections.

23. Kant 2015, 23.

24. Or indeed any end or result the action might lead to, as the categorical imperative "has to do not with the matter of the action and what is to result from it, but with the form and the principle from which the action itself follows; and the essentially good in the action consists in the disposition, let the result be what it may" (Kant 1997, 27).

25. Kant 1997, 7 (emphasis original).

26. Ibid.

27. Ibid., 10.

28. Ibid., 17.

29. Wood 1970, 51.

30. Kant 2015, 52 (italics original).

31. Ibid., 76 (emphasis original).

32. Bader 2015, 183.

33. Kant 2015, 105.

34. See Wood 1970, 7.

35. Barney 2015, 162.

36. Kant 2015, 90.

37. Ibid., 114.

38. Ibid., 104 (emphasis original). Here Kant reverts to using *highest good* for the "complete" or "perfect" good. See Kant 2015, 226, n. 4.

39. Kant 2015, 92.

40. See ibid., 98–100.

41. Kant 2015, 4. For more on the differentiation of an action's motive and its end, see Wood 1970, 46–51.

42. "Do that through which thou becomes worthy to be happy" is therefore given by Kant as the answer to the question, "What ought I to do?" (see Kant 1929, 638).

43. Kant 1929, 638–39 (italics original). In a rather astounding passage at the end of his *Critique of Practical Reason*, Kant—whose first critique showed metaphysics cannot indubitably prove God's existence—goes as far as providing speculations as to why God might have wanted to hide himself from our pure reason and only offer a glimpse of his presence through our practical reason. Indeed, Kant argues that were we able to have direct access to God's existence, were He to stand before us in "awful majesty," we would be compelled to act morally out of the fear awakened by His immediate presence, and therefore, "the moral worth of actions, on which alone in the eyes of supreme wisdom the worth of the person and even that of the world depends, would not exist at all" (Kant 2015, 118). God's immediate revelation would, in other words, make our moral worth, dependent as it is on the autonomous respect of the moral law for its own sake, impossible. Accordingly, for Kant, "the inscrutable wisdom by which we exist is not less worthy of veneration in what it has denied us than in what it has granted us" (Kant 2015, 641).

44. Given the religious nature of these postulates, Kant writes that "only with religion does the hope for happiness first arise" (Kant 2015, 165).

45. Having dialectically established Kant's complete good as the conditioning of happiness to good will or the moral law in the previous section, I will now (as mentioned in chapter 4, n. 4) revert to using the common term *highest good* to refer to Kant's complete good.

46. De Launay 2000, 13.

47. Ibid.

48. Poma 1997, 31. See also Kajon 2012, 136.

49. Cohen 1928, 336. Having made this point, Cohen qualifies the claim but, interestingly, to point out the seeds of idealism had already been sown before Plato. So while "mature" idealism began with Plato, the Eleatics and Democritus had already introduced its "germ [Keim]" (Cohen 1928, 336). We will further discuss the significance of the Eleatics for Cohen in the section "Cohen's Unique God."

50. Bergman 1961, 32.
51. Cohen 2001, 196.
52. Ibid., 197.
53. Ibid. See also Kant 2015, 51.
54. Cohen 2001, 197.
55. See ibid.; and Kant 2015, 50.
56. Cohen 2001, 198.
57. Ibid., 199–200.
58. "But not first place [among the goods], even if all the cattle and horses and the rest of the animals gave testimony [to pleasure being the highest good] by following pleasure. Now, many people accept their testimony, as the seers do that of the birds, and judge that pleasures are most effective in securing the happy life; they even believe that the animal passions are more authoritative witnesses than is the love of argument that is constantly revealed under the guidance of the philosophic muse" (Plato 1997c, 67b, 456).
59. Cohen 2001, 200.
60. Kant 2015, 19.
61. Cohen 2001, 202.
62. Ibid., 205.
63. Ibid., 216.
64. So, for example, in his *Ethik des Reinen Willens*, Cohen describes the "certainty" with which Kant rejects the "principles of happiness and perfection as heteronomous, and leaves nothing to be acknowledged as foundation of the moral law but autonomy" (see Cohen 1981, 342).
65. Cohen 2001, 344.
66. Ibid., 347.
67. Ibid.
68. Kant 2015, 86 (emphasis original). See also Cohen 2001, 347–48.
69. Cohen 2015, 349.
70. Ibid., 351.
71. See ibid., 254, n. 356; and Wood 1970, 27.
72. Kant 2015, 145. See also Cohen 2001, 354.
73. Cohen 2001, 355.
74. Ibid., 359.
75. Ibid., 360.
76. Ibid.; and Fichte 2010, 110. Fichte's "Appeal to the Public" was written in the midst of the atheism dispute. Indeed, following his "On the Ground of Our Belief in a Divine World-Governance," Fichte was attacked for supposedly being an atheist and nihilist, among other things, by the very same Jacobi who starred in the pantheism controversy. The controversy led to Fichte's eventual

resignation of his post at Jena. Most relevant to our present context is how Cohen's argument concurs with the anti-eudaemonism of the one Fichte presents in his appeal and how both differ from Mendelssohn's view. Indeed, Fichte argues that he seeks beatitude, "not as a pleasurable state . . . but rather because a rational being deserves it" (Fichte 2010, 102), a beatitude he primordially relates to the affirmation of the moral world order, which is a "supersensible divine realm that is infinitely superior to all that is transitory" (Fichte 2010, 103). Meanwhile, his opponents are branded "idolatrous and blasphemous" (Fichte 2010, 123), as their "final goal is always pleasure, whether or not they desire it in a coarse fashion or have purified it ever so subtly: pleasure in this life and, if they imagine a continued existence beyond earthly death, pleasure there as well" (Fichte 2010, 110). Accordingly, their eudaemonistic and dogmatic God is the "provider of pleasure" (Fichte 2010, 110) and "dispenser of all happiness," whose plan "at the creation of the world was to produce the greatest possible sum-total of pleasure" (Fichte 2010, 111). For more on the controversy and Jacobi's role in particular, see Di Giovanni 1989. For a collection of texts central to the atheism controversy accompanied by insightful commentary, see Estes and Bowman 2010.

77. Cohen 2001, 361.

78. Ibid., v.

79. Fackenheim 1996, 48.

80. Cohen 2001, 352.

81. Kant 1999b, 282.

82. Ibid.

83. Ibid., 285 (emphasis original).

84. Ibid., 287.

85. Ibid., 282 (emphasis original). See also Cohen 2001, 352.

86. Cohen 2001, 352.

87. Wood 1970, 38.

88. Cohen 2001, 355.

89. Ibid., 353.

90. Ibid., 366–67.

91. Interestingly, Cohen mentions Mendelssohn in this context in the first edition of *Kants Begründung der Ethik* (1877), writing that "the critical geographer" taught these thoughts with "the attitude of a Mendelssohn" (2001, 611). In the second edition (1910), however, the explicit mention of Mendelssohn has been deleted, and Cohen instead writes he will further the historical significance of Kant's ideas in the added fourth part of the work (see 2001, 367).

92. Cohen 2001, 367.

93. Cohen 2021, 139; "Innere Beziehungen der Kantischen Philosophie zum Judentum," in Cohen 1924, 1:293.

94. Rosenzweig 2021, 207; 1924, 32.

95. Cohen 2021, 136; "Innere Beziehungen der Kantischen Philosophie zum Judentum," in Cohen 1924, 1:290 (emphasis original).

96. Cohen 2021, 137; "Innere Beziehungen der Kantischen Philosophie zum Judentum," in Cohen 1924, 1:292; see also Kant 2015, 107; Babylonian Talmud, Mass. Bava Kamma 87a; and Mass. Kiddushin 31a.

97. Cohen 2021, 138; "Innere Beziehungen der Kantischen Philosophie zum Judentum," in Cohen 1924, 1:293.

98. Cohen 1924, 2:184.

99. Ibid. This already indicates the proximity of Judaism, as a unified concept, to Cohen's notion of the religion of reason, which unsurprisingly is similarly anti-eudaemonistic. Indeed, "pleasure and pain cannot be valid as a positive power of religion," Cohen tells us in *The Religion of Reason out of the Sources of Judaism*. They, as well as the instincts, are "blood-witnesses of animal life; reason does not originate in their track." Reason eliminates all "animal selfishness and self-love, all eudaemonism, which recognizes only pleasure as a legitimate criterion, all materialism, which honors only debit and credit and considers give and take as the essence of man." Accordingly, the religion of reason "protests against all the alleged powers of the self, against all those pretended powers of the I, which are rooted in pleasure and pain" (Cohen 1995, 6; 1978, 7).

100. Cohen 1995, 46; 1978, 54.

101. Cohen 1995, 259; 1978, 302.

102. Deuteronomy 8:3; Cohen 1995, 263; 1978, 307.

103. Joel 4:48

104. Cohen 1995, 287; 1978, 334.

105. Cohen 1995, 427–28; 1978, 496.

106. Cohen 1995, 383; 1978, 446.

107. See also Cohen 1995, 323; 1978, 376, where he quotes Pirke Abot 1:3, "Be not like slaves, that minister to the master for the sake of receiving a bounty," in the same spirit.

108. Cohen 1995, 312; 1978, 362.

109. Cohen 1995, 312; 1978, 362.

110. Cohen 1995, 321; 1978, 374.

111. Cohen 2004, 165; "Charakteristik der Ethik Maimunis," in 1924, 3:280.

112. Cohen refused to grant any philosophical warrant to the notion of personal immortality already in his early work on Kant. See Dietrich 1980, 247.

113. Cohen 2004, 163; "Charakteristik der Ethik Maimunis," in 1924, 3:279.

114. Cohen 1995, 311; 1978, 361.

115. Cohen 1995, 296; 1978, 344.

116. Cohen 1995, 300; 1978, 349.

117. Genesis 15:15; Cohen 1995, 307; 1978, 357.

118. Cohen 1995, 301; 1978, 350 (emphasis original).

119. Cohen 1995, 302; 1978, 351.

120. Cohen 1995, 307; 1978, 356 (emphasis original).

121. Cohen 1995, 308; 1978, 358.

122. See "The Unique Value of Religion" in chapter 5.

123. Cohen 1995, 302–3; 1978, 351–52.

124. Cohen 1995, 307; 1978, 357.

125. Cohen 1995, 303; 1978, 352.

126. Cohen 1995, 305; 1978, 354; Ecclesiastes 12:7.

127. Cohen 1995, 337; 1978, 392.

128. Cohen 1995, 313; 1978, 364. The "secretive" nature of immortality is very much reflected in Cohen's nuanced if not paradoxical treatment of it. On the one hand, Cohen explicitly seeks to expunge any possibility of eschatological self-interest in immortality, which would precisely reflect the eudaemonism his treatment of immortality in Judaism seeks to avoid. On the other hand, as Poma points out, Cohen does also posit "the idea of death as the individual's ultimate redemption" (Poma 2005, 428). So, for example, Cohen writes that "life ought to seek peace; it finds it in death. Death is therefore not the actual end of human life but rather its goal, the trophy of life and all its striving. . . . The unique God is with me even in death" (Cohen 1995, 460–61; 1978, 532). While, as Poma points out, this "guarded argument" links this ultimate redemption "with the meaning of peace as the eternal historical ideal of humanity, . . . this cannot hide its eschatological traits" (Poma 2005, 428). Such traits also seem to be reflected at the very end of the chapter on immortality and resurrection, wherein Cohen explicitly seeks to combat them, writing that "if the soul has not yet found God, it always may: it is immortal" (Cohen 1995, 337; 1978, 392). The chapter's first words, it is important to keep in mind, are "The idea of the immortality of the soul originates in myth" (Cohen 1995, 296; 1978, 344). This might be an unresolved tension within Cohen or a purposeful vacillation. Indeed, writing of repentance, Weiss described Cohen's inability to reach a static conclusion as corresponding "to the dynamic and non-theorizable character of religious concepts" (Weiss 2012, 167). Immortality could very well be a similar concept, namely, one whose treatment does not allow a static finality.

129. Cohen 2004, 164; "Charakteristik der Ethik Maimunis," in 1924, 3:279–80.

130. Cohen 1995, 315; 1978, 366. Still, Liebeschütz somewhat exaggerates when writing that immortality "for Cohen always remained a mythical concept, [which] has no link to the Jewish law" (1968, 30), as Cohen's mature position does allow an ethically delineated immortality, if not more than that (see n. 128 in this chapter). What remains constant, however, is a strong and unfailing attempt at emphasizing Judaism does not in any way promote an understanding of immortality that could be construed as eudaemonistic.

131. Cohen 2004, 169; "Charakteristik der Ethik Maimunis," in 1924, 3:280.

132. "Das 'Gut' des Menschen," Cohen 2004, 164; "Charakteristik der Ethik Maimunis," in 1924 3:279. See also Cohen 1995, 313; 1978, 364.

133. See Cohen 2004, 164; "Charakteristik der Ethik Maimunis," in 1924, 3:279.

134. Cohen 2004, 177; "Charakteristik der Ethik Maimunis," in 1924, 3:283.

135. As Cohen himself put it, "Aristotelian ethics is nothing but his eudaemonia" (Cohen 2004, 124; "Charakteristik der Ethik Maimunis," in 1924, 3:264).

136. Cohen 2004, 61; "Charakteristik der Ethik Maimunis," in 1924, 3:242.

137. Cohen 2004, 125; "Charakteristik der Ethik Maimunis," in 1924, 3:265.

138. See Cohen 2004, 153; "Charakteristik der Ethik Maimunis," in 1924 3:274; and 1995, 313, 315; 1978, 364, 366–67.

139. Cohen 2004, 69; "Charakteristik der Ethik Maimunis," in 1924, 3:246.

140. Rosenzweig 1924, 237; 2021, lx. This quote, incidentally, was characterized by Gershom Scholem as "the most profound statement that an opponent of Zionism ever made about the movement" (Scholem 2012, 69).

141. Cohen 1995, 362; 1978, 421.

142. Cohen 1995, 450; 1978, 520.

143. Cohen 1995, 459; 1978, 529.

144. Cohen 1995, 449; 1978, 518. Obviously, the connection Cohen seeks to draw with the comment about "peace" (*Friede*) between peace, peace of the soul (*Seelenfriede*), and contentment (*Zufriedenheit*) is terminologically more obvious in German than in English.

145. Cohen 1995, 450; 1978, 520.

146. Cohen 1995, 458; 1978, 528–29.

147. Cohen 1995, 457; 1978, 528.

148. Cohen 1995, 459; 1978, 530.

149. Cohen 1995, 453; 1978, 523. In its emphasis on historical progress, Cohen's notion of *Zufriedenheit*, as Poma indicates, significantly differs from Kant's use of it. See Poma 2005, 426–27.

150. As Bruckstein puts it, Cohen's *Ethics of Maimonides* demonstrates "more explicitly than any other text . . . the hermeneutical correlation between Cohen's Platonic philosophy and what he calls Judaism" (Bruckstein 2006, 116).

151. Rosenzweig 2021, 207; 1924, xxxii.

152. Cohen 2002, 50. Cohen repeats this claim in the introduction to *Religion of Reason*, where again he explains that his own *Ethik des Reinen Willens* "elevated the idea of God to its keystone" (Cohen 1995, 20; 1978, 23). Not all commentators, however, agree that Cohen successfully did so. Munk, for example, argues that in spite of his claims to the contrary, Cohen's idea of God, like Kant's conception of God as a postulate of practical reason, "is not anchored in the methodology of ethics and logic but remains hovering in the System. The idea is included ad libitum, instead of serving as a necessary component in ethics" (Munk 2006, 108). Munk does, however, suggests alternatives drawn from Cohen's methodology that might respond to this problem (see 2006, 109–14).

153. Cohen 1995, 35; 1978, 40.

154. Levinas 1990, 178.

155. Cohen 1995, 44; 1978, 51.

156. Cohen 1995, 38; 1978, 45.

157. Cohen 1995, 41; 1978, 48. See also Cohen 2002, 25, 27.

158. Cohen 1995, 45; 1978, 52.

159. Cohen 1995, 44; 1978, 51.

160. Cohen 1995, 46; 1978, 53.

161. Cohen 1995, 185; 1978, 216.

162. We will return to this issue at some length in chapter 5, under "The Unique Value of Religion."

163. Cohen 1928, 336.

164. Ibid., 337.

165. See Poma 1997, 26–27.

166. Cohen 1928, 361.

167. Ibid.

168. Cohen 2005, 6–7. See also Cohen 2004, 7; "Charakteristik der Ethik Maimunis," in 1924 3:223.

169. Cohen 1984, 17–18.

170. For more on his early psychological interpretation of the Platonic idea, which Cohen had evolved from by the time of "Platons Ideenlehere und die Mathematik," see Poma 1997, 21–26. For more on Cohen's evolving interpretation of Plato, See Kajon 2012, 136–41.

171. See Poma 1997, 33.

172. Cohen 1984, 149; or 2002, 36.

173. These thoughts also enable a more contextualized understanding of why Cohen was so enthusiastically advocating a Platonic interpretation of Maimonides. Plato's idealism relates to an idea of the good beyond existence and mere

materiality, which Cohen thinks ensures values liberated from eudaemonism. While the good is an idea and as such is a hypothesis, Cohen points out that for Plato, the idea of the good is an exceptional one, deserving of a preferential terminology, which is why it is also referred to it as an-hypothesis or non-foundation. The significance is that while all other hypotheses are predicated on prior hypotheses, the hypothesis of the good "constitutes its own ultimate ground. . . . The non-foundation must be considered the ultimate, rock-bottom ground of all grounding" (see Cohen 2004, 11; "Charakteristik der Ethik Maimunis," in 1924, 3:226).

174. Cohen 1995, 185; 1978, 216.

175. Cohen, "Die Religiösen Bewegungen der Gegenwart," in 1924, 1:56.

176. See Vatter 2021, 37.

177. A philosophical position Cohen refers to as a "disease [Krankheit]." See Cohen 1995, 110; 1978, 127.

178. Cohen 1995, 66–67; 1978, 76–77.

179. Cohen 1995, 59; 1978, 68.

180. Cohen 1995, 60–61; 1978, 70.

181. Cohen 1995, 65–66; 1978, 76 (emphasis original).

182. Cohen 1995, 68; 1978, 78.

183. By identifying God with nature, Cohen claims, pantheism brings about a logical contradiction in both concepts, which in and of itself already makes this kind of philosophy false and mistaken. See Cohen 2002, 27–28.

184. Cohen 1995, 68; 1978, 79.

185. See "Tonalities: The Case of Spinoza" in chapter 6.

186. Cohen 2015, 11; "Spinoza über Staat un Religion, Judentum und Christentum," in 1924, 3:303.

187. Cohen 1995, 21; 1978, 24. It is of course important to keep in mind that the German word for "scientific," i.e., *Wissenschaftlich*, pertains, as Zank points out, to both the natural and moral sciences, or the humanities, i.e., *Geisteswissenschaften*. The term *scientific*, in this context, therefore, relates to "an ideal of the systematic totality of all knowledge" (Zank 2006, 2–3).

188. See Cohen 2004, 86–87; "Charakteristik der Ethik Maimunis," in 1924, 3:250.

189. This, as Dietrich points out, significantly distances Cohen's position from Kant's postulation of God as "guarantor of an ultimate other-worldly conjunction of personal virtue and happiness." Cohen's God, rather, is conceived of as the "eternal guarantor of that coordination and interaction of the realms of nature and of freedom which it is necessary to postulate if the moral life is to be conducted in the confidence that environing nature is not indifferent or hostile to the task of moral life"(Dietrich 1980, 247).

190. We will analyze this aspect of Cohen's thought in greater depth in chapter 5, under "The Unique Value of Religion."

191. Cohen, "Religiöse Postulate," in 1924, 1:5.

192. Cohen 2002, 51–52.

193. Cohen, "Der Stil der Propheten," 1924, 1:265–66.

194. Cohen, "Die Religiösen Bewegungen der Gegenwart," in 1924, 1:56–57.

195. Cohen,"Einheit oder Einzigkeit Gottes," in 1924, 1:94.

196. Cohen 2002, 139.

197. Ibid., 50–51.

198. Cohen 1995, 35; 1978, 41. The translation in *Religion of Reason* is "essential content." But Cohen uses merely *inhalt* in the original *Religion der Vernunft*. The translation, therefore, does not allow the differentiation of *inhalt* from Cohen's use of *hauptinhalt* in *Der Begriff der Religion*, 32.

199. Cohen 2002, 32.

200. Ibid., 100.

201. Cohen 1995, 64; 1978, 74.

202. Cohen 1995, 67; 1978, 77.

203. Cohen 1995, 86; 1978, 101.

204. Cohen 1995, 71–72; 1978, 83.

205. Cohen 1995, 72; 1978, 83–84 (emphasis original).

206. Cohen 1995, 84; 1978, 97.

207. Cohen 1995, 82; 1978, 95.

208. Cohen 1995, 79; 1978, 92.

209. Cohen 1995, 83; 1978, 96.

210. Wolfson 2012, 671.

211. Cohen 1995, 48; 1978, 55.

212. Cohen 2002, 105.

213. Ibid., 33.

214. Cohen 2021, 161; "Die Bedeutung des Judentums für den Religiösen Fortschritt der Menscheit," in 1924, 1:29.

215. Cohen 2021, 163; "Die Bedeutung des Judentums für den Religiösen Fortschritt der Menscheit," in 1924, 1:32.

216. Cohen, "Die Religiösen Bewegungen der Gegenwart," in 1924, 1:59.

217. Cohen,"Religiöse Postulate," in 1924, 1:9; and "Die Religiösen Bewegungen der Gegenwart," in 1924, 1:60.

218. Cohen 1995, 21; 1978, 24.

219. See Cohen 2002, 105.

220. Cohen, "Die Lyrik der Psalmen," in 1924, 1:251–52.

221. Cohen, "Über den ästhetischen Wert unserer Religiösen Bildung," in 1924, 1:221.

222. Cohen, "Die Lyrik der Psalmen," in 1924, 1:251.

223. Cohen, "Über den ästhetischen Wert unserer Religiösen Bildung," 1924, 1:221–22.

224. Cohen 1995, 447; 1978, 516.

225. Cohen 1995, 453; 1978, 523.

226. Cohen 1995, 453; 1978, 523.

227. Cohen 1995, 460; 1978, 531.

228. Cohen, "Der Heilige Geist," in 1924, 3:184.

229. Cohen 2021, 146; "Innere Beziehungen der Kantischen Philosophie zum Judentum," in 1924, 1:300 (emphasis original).

230. Cohen 2021, 147; "Innere Beziehungen der Kantischen Philosophie zum Judentum," in 1924, 1:302 (emphasis original).

231. Cohen 2002, 33–34.

232. Cohen, "Die Messiasidee," in 1924, 1:116.

233. Cohen 2002, 20.

234. Ibid., 22.

235. Ibid., 23.

236. Cohen 1995, 96; 1978, 111.

237. Cohen 2002, 33–34.

238. Cohen 1995, 249; 1978, 291. Cohen here echoes ideas he developed in his systematic philosophy. See Fiorato 2005, 147–48.

5. MESSIANIC HUMANITY

1. Kant 1914, 372; see also Cohen 2001, 350.

2. Cohen 2001, 350.

3. Ibid., 352.

4. Ibid., 368.

5. Ibid., 475.

6. Ibid., 476.

7. Cohen 1995, 13; 1978, 15 (emphasis original).

8. Cohen 1995, 178; 1978, 208–9.

9. Cohen 1995, 16; 1978, 18.

10. Hollander 2021, 29.

11. Vatter 2021, 62.

12. To quote Hollander, "For Cohen, ethics is directed at overcoming 'particularity,'" and accordingly, "The state can be ethically significant only if it conceived as a generation of allheit and a transcending of particularity" (2021, 44).

13. Hollander 2021, 47–48. See Hollander 2021, chapter 1, for a comprehensive analysis of Cohen's understanding of the legal person and its significance for Cohen's ethical thought.

14. Cohen 1995, 15; 1978, 18.

15. Cohen 1995, 20; 1978, 23.

16. See Cohen 1995, 167–68; 1978, 194–96.

17. Cohen 1995, 195; 1978, 228.

18. Cohen 1995, 183; 1978, 214.

19. Cohen 1995, 185; 1978, 216.

20. Cohen 1995; 1978, 216.

21. Cohen 1995, 189; 1978, 220.

22. Cohen 1995, 193; 1978, 225.

23. Cohen 1995, 198; 1978, 232.

24. See "Cohen's Unique God" in chapter 4.

25. Cohen 1995, 20; 1978, 23.

26. Cohen 1995, 117; 1978, 135.

27. Cohen 1995, 190; 1978, 222.

28. See Kierkegaard 1983, 56; and Golomb 1992, 78.

29. See Introduction, n. 3.

30. Christian Garve criticized Kant in 1798 for, among other things, reuniting virtue and happiness in seeming contradiction to his own theory. Grave points at this philosophical weakness but, unlike Cohen, does not do so out of an inherent dislike for eudaemonism. His own thought, in fact, is characterized by an empiricist, eudaemonistic sensitivity (see Kant 1999a, 552, n. 1; and Ludwig 2007, 184–90). Kant's response to Garve is discussed by Cohen and was mentioned in the last chapter. See Cohen 2001, 352; and "Cohen Contra Kant" in chapter 4 of the present volume.

31. Hegel remained unconvinced by Kant's notion of the highest good, arguing, among other things, that "Kant's theory systematically occludes, if not excludes, the happiness (or at least the pleasure) that might result from successful moral action" (Westphal 1991, 146), as well as that Kant's *summum bonum* assumes an impossibly sharp differentiation of motives as causes of action and the ends of actions (see Westphal 1991, 147). Sidgwick too found this aspect of Kant lacking. In his lectures on Kant, he states that the notion of practical reason demands a connection between morality and happiness and so too a future life where it could be realized, stating that this notion illustrates well "both the ingenuity of Kant and what I may perhaps be allowed to call his naïveté" (Sidgwick 1905, 19). More generally, Wood argues that Kant's moral arguments for God, immortality, and the highest good do not provide reasons to believe in these postulates, but rather show beliefs to be "very desirable for a moral agent to have, since [they] would rescue such an agent from a practical paradox" (Wood 1970, 404).

32. Cohen 1995, 21; 1978, 24.

33. Cohen 1995, 21; 1978, 24.

34. While Kant's kingdom of ends does not quite include the theological weight Cohen ascribes to his messianic future, he also still did clearly find it appealing, if not necessary, to express his moral view in religious language. See, for example, Kant 2015, 165. This passage in Kant's *Critique of Practical Reason*, as well as others wherein he discusses his moral notion of the highest good in terms of the "kingdom of God," are at the heart of Habermas's analysis of the significance of Kant's religious language and complex attitude towards his ancestral religious heritage (see Habermas 2008a, chapter 8). Habermas suggests that this assimilation of the "semantic legacy of religious traditions" was undertaken by Kant because "he wants to rescue the contents of faith and the religious commitment that can be justified within the bounds of reason alone" (Habermas 2008a, 211). This, according to Habermas, is an astute philosophical gesture as "without the historical credit advanced by positive religion, with its store of suggestive and inspiring images, practical reason would lack the epistemic stimulus to generate the postulates with which it attempts to recuperate a need articulated in religious terms within the horizon of rational reflection" (Habermas 2008a, 223). These thoughts reflect Habermas's own concern, namely, to rely on such recuperation of religious language to better manage what he has termed our "post-secular society" (see 2008b). To quote him once again, "Pure practical reason can no longer be so confident in its ability to counteract a modernization spinning out of control armed solely with the insights of a theory of justice. The latter lacks the creativity of linguistic world-disclosure that a normative consciousness afflicted with accelerating decline requires in order to regenerate itself" (2008a, 211).

35. Habermas 2008; Cohen 1995, 245; 1978, 286.

36. Rosenzweig 2021, 224; 1924, xlviii.

37. Rosenzweig 2021, 223; 1924, xlvii.

38. Rosenzweig 2021,225; 1924, xlviii–xlix.

39. Bergman 1961, 30, 44.

40. Altmann 1962, 378.

41. Ibid., 379. The term *logic* here, Altmann clarifies, does not designate formal logic, but rather Cohen's own "Logic of Origin [Logik der Ursprungs]," at the heart of which stands Cohen's interpretation of the Platonic hypothesis (Altmann 1962, 380).

42. Altmann 1962, 379.

43. Ibid., 397. Altmann is here quoting from Cohen's *Begriff der Religion* (see Cohen 2002, 137).

44. Zank 2000, 176.

45. Ibid., 173.

46. Ibid., 175.

47. Ibid., 36–37.

48. Weiss 2012, 5–10.

49. Ibid., 8.

50. Ibid., 3.

51. Kluback 1984, 3.

52. Cohen 1987, xxi.

53. Cohen 2002, 51. This shift is further emphasized by the fact that Cohen did address the question of the I/You already in 1907 (see Hollander 2012, 50), though as shown above clearly felt by the time he wrote *Religion of Reason* that it cannot be addressed fully without the religious contribution.

54. To quote Kluback, "from 1907 to 1918 a Weltanschauung, dominated by Kant, was surpassed by one which embodied faith in the truth of Israel's monotheism" (Kluback 1984, 1). While Kluback's interpretation accords with my analysis in so far as it too emphasizes some lasting continuities maintained in spite of this shift, as will be shown below, I suggest a slightly different emphasis in terms of the timing of the shift in question. Indeed, I will be arguing that in 1907 the significant axiological shift here explored had not yet occurred and that it most likely occurred after 1912.

55. Cohen 2001, 482.

56. Ibid., 478.

57. Ibid., 479.

58. Ibid., 478.

59. Ibid., 481.

60. Ibid., 482.

61. Cohen 1981, 586–87.

62. See Poma 1997, 81; and Zank 2000, 165–66. It is important to keep in mind as well that from the mid-1870s on, Cohen had been witnessing a rise in antisemitism, the effects of which became deeply personal by the time he left Marburg, as exemplified by the slight of his colleagues in Germany, who did not invite him, as was the norm, to another university and ignored his status as a central Kantian scholar by not inviting him or a representative of his school to join the work on a comprehensive edition of Kant's work. See Liebeschütz 1960, 16–20.

63. Bergman 1961, 43–44.

64. Weiss 2012, 14.

65. Cohen 2002, 42.

66. See, for example, Hermann's *The Communion of the Christian with God*, wherein he discusses Lutheran teachings and writes that "God communes with every individual soul in a special way . . . God enters into a personal relationship

with every individual" and that "the chief end of every real religion is to secure God's communion with each individual soul" (Hermann 1906, 146–47, 153).

67. Cohen 2002, 80.

68. Cohen 1995, 51; 1978, 59.

69. Weiss 2012, 28.

70. Weiss suggests a different reading of the matter, claiming that Cohen dissociates the messianic future from finite actuality and suggests instead that the prophets' messianic future is a "non-actual actuality" we are continually called to promote (Weiss 2012, 206). Weiss relates this paradoxical notion to an "infinitesimal gap" between actuality and the future that is both retained as well as, at least potentially, narrowed. A gap, as he put it, that is both "something" and so maintains the ethical task, as well as "nothing," which allows for "the gap to be closed and the infinite task fulfilled" (2012, 208). For reasons elaborated below, I ascribe to Cohen a more bluntly paradoxical treatment of this problem where the messianic actuality will simply trump current actuality. According to this reading, Cohen allows the religious realm a blunt overcoming of the ethical tensions raised by the actualizing of the infinite task.

71. Cohen 1995, 207; 1978, 242. Interestingly, Kant used the image of "the hopeless effort of rolling the stone of Sisyphus uphill in order to let it roll back down again" (Kant 1979a, 147) in a passage addressing whether "the human race [is] constantly progressing" (1979a, 141). Cohen himself discusses and quotes this passage in his work on Kant. See Cohen 2001, 551.

72. Cohen 1995, 21; 1978, 24.

73. Cohen 1995, 21; 1978, 24–25.

74. As Kierkegaard puts it, "it is great to give up one's desire, but it is greater to hold fast to it after having given it up" (Kierkegaard 1983, 18). Accordingly, when faced with the terrible sacrifice, "Abraham had faith and did not doubt; he believed the preposterous" (Kierkegaard 1983, 20).

75. Cohen 1995, 2; 1978, 3.

76. Cohen 1995, 5; 1978, 5–6.

77. Cohen 1995, 3–4; 1978, 3.

78. Cohen 1995, 3; 1978, 3.

79. Cohen 1995, 3; 1978, 4. In seeking a criterion, Cohen of course again echoes the Platonic, or in this case Socratic, methodology, centered on the quest of a criterion. Geach demarcated two assumptions at the heart of Socrates's effort, assumptions very similar to Cohen's: "(A) that if you know you are correctly predicating a given term 'T' you must 'know what is to be T,' in the sense of being able to give a general criterion for a thing's being T; (B) that it is no use to try and arrive at the meaning of what 'T' is by giving examples of things that are T" (Geach 1966, 371). In a much-debated claim, Geach termed this way of

thinking "the Socratic fallacy, for its locus classicus is the Socratic dialogues," arguing it clearly is a fallacy because "we know heaps of things without being able to define the terms in which we express our knowledge. Formal definitions are only one way of elucidating terms; a set of examples may in a given case be more useful than a formal definition" (1966, 371). While it would be interesting to assess the degree to which Cohen's Platonic, but post-Kantian, approach to Judaism is sufficiently similar to the Socratic methodology, for it to be tainted by that fallacy, if indeed it is one, would demand a comparative effort that cannot be undertaken here. What is clear, however, is that Cohen's methodology, like Plato's (see "The End of Aristotelian Hierarchies" in chapter 1 in the present volume), leads to an essentialist conception of the hypothesized or idealized phenomenon, in this case, Judaism. We will return to Cohen's and Mendelssohn's essentialism in chapter 6.

80. Cohen, "Antwort auf das Offene Schreiben des Herrn Dr. Martin Buber as Hermann Cohen," in 1924, 2:335.

81. Cohen, "Religion und Zionismus," in 1924, 2:323.

82. Cohen 1995, 7–8; 1978, 8–9 (italics original).

83. Cohen 1995, 8; 1978, 9–10 (emphasis original).

84. Cohen 1995, 34; 1978, 39 (emphasis original).

85. Cohen 1995, 34; 1978, 40.

86. Poma 2007, 92.

87. Cohen, "Die Liebe zur Religion," in 1924, 2:142–43.

88. The rising importance of actualization had already been reflected in the development of Cohen's work on Kant. Indeed, Cohen added to his *Kants Begründung der Ethik* when it was published again in 1910 a fourth part dealing directly with the application of ethical principles and the reality of morality in history, a question Cohen had come to realize needed to be asked more sharply in order to complete his analysis of Kant's ethics. See 2001, 373, 563–64.

89. Cohen, "Religiöse Postulate," in 1924, 1:7–8.

90. Ibid.

91. Cohen 1995, 252; 1978, 294.

92. Cohen, "Der Stil der Propheten," in 1924, 1:275.

93. Cohen, "Religion und Zionismus," in 1924, 2:335.

94. Cohen, "Religiöse Postulate," in 1924, 1:8.

95. Cohen 1995, 254; 1978, 296.

96. Wiedebach 2012, xiii. Wiedebach further points out that the differentiation of nation from nationality is a late development in Cohen and that a precise definition of nationality as a "plurality unified in a nation based on a political state can only be found in Cohen's later works" (2012, 2).

97. Cohen, "Antwort auf das Offene Schreiben des Herrn Dr. Martin Buber as Hermann Cohen," in 1924, 2:338.

98. Cohen 1995, 264; 1978, 308.

99. Cohen 1995, 268; 1978, 313.

100. See Cohen 1995, 267, 268; 1978, 311, 313.

101. Cohen 1995, 286; 1978, 333–34.

102. Cohen, "Der Stil der Propheten," in 1924, 1:275.

103. Cohen 1995, 234; 1978, 273.

104. Cohen 1995, 284; 1978, 330.

105. Cohen 1995, 260; 1978, 303 (emphasis original).

106. Cohen 1995, 274; 1978, 319.

107. Cohen, "Die Messiasidee," in 1924, 1:116.

108. To such a degree, in fact, that even some of the prophets themselves, like Jeremiah, had not yet completely freed themselves from "the one sidedness of patriotism." See Cohen 1995, 27; 1978, 31.

109. See "Universal Jewish Morality" in chapter 5.

110. Cohen, "Zum Prioritätsstreit über das Gebot der Nächstenliebe," in 1924, 1:176.

111. Cohen 1995, 280; 1978, 326.

112. Cohen, "Der Stil der Propheten," in 1924, 1:274.

113. Cohen, "Der Nächste," in 1924, 1:183.

114. Cohen 1995, 29; 1978, 338.

115. Cohen 2021, 116; "Das Soziale Ideal bei Platon und den Propheten," in 1924, 1:318.

116. Cohen, "Der Stil der Propheten," in 1924, 1:277.

117. This equality, Cohen seeks to emphasize, includes both sexes. Indeed, according to Cohen, the Bible celebrates the glory of all humans, men as well as women, the dignity of whom is repeatedly lauded in the text (Cohen, "Über den äesthetischen Wert unserer religiösen Bildung," in 1924, 1:222). So Cohen emphasizes the significance of the praise of women at the end of Solomon's proverbs, which he argues shows how "the woman in Jewish antiquity stands in the midst of public life and at the height of general culture" (1924, 223). Other examples Cohen provides for the "equality [Ebenbürtigkeit]" (1924, 223) of women in the Biblical universe include the high status accorded to Moses's sister, the figure of Deborah and the significance of her song, the heroism of Jael, and the story of Ruth and the Shulamite, the protagonist of the Song of Songs (1924, 223–25).

118. Cohen, "Zum Prioritätsstreit über das Gebot der Nächstenliebe," in 1924, 1:176.

119. Cohen, "Die Nächstenliebe im Talmud," in 1924, 1:148.

120. Cohen, "Die Nächste," in 1924, 1:186.

121. Cohen, "Die Nächstenliebe im Talmud," in 1924, 1:148. Delitzsch, Cohen writes, "always saw it as a duty of German theology to defend an ancient religious document whose ties with the Christian universe are undeniable" (1924, 1:148). Franz Delitzsch (1812–1890) was known for his wide erudition in Jewish sources, his significant scholarly contribution to the study of Judaism, and his robust defense of the Jewish sources in light of increasingly virulent antisemitic attacks. He was also an enthusiastic missionary to the Jews who, among other activities, translated the New Testament into Hebrew (see A. Levenson 2002, 383–86). Part of the argument Cohen advances in his "Die Nächstenliebe im Talmud" is that Delitzsch is wrong in various aspects of his depiction of the Talmud in spite of his philosemitic tendencies (in so far, of course, as missionaries can be construed as philosemitic; see A. Levenson 2002, 387). In fact, in the passage here discussed, Cohen quotes, in order to argue against Delitzsch interpretation of *rea*, the latter's *Rohling's Talmudjude Beleuchtet*. While Delitzsche does indeed identify *rea* with *Volksgenosse* (Delitzsch 1881, 13), the work as a whole is a strong reaction against the Catholic theologian August Rohling's profoundly antisemitic *Talmudjude*, which was written in 1871 and presented a thoroughly disparaging depiction of Jewish religious practice, including the ritual murder of Christian children during Passover. See H. W. Smith 1994, 321.

122. Leviticus 19:18

123. Accordingly, rather than *Volksgenosse*, Cohen designates the proper conception for *rea*, or *Nächste*, as *nebenmensch* (e.g., "Die Nächstenliebe im Talmud," in 1924, 1:148), *der Mitmensch*, (e.g., "Der Nachste," in 1924, 1:193), or *der Andere* ("the other," e.g., "Der Nächste," in 1924, 1:186, 193)

124. Cohen, "Die Nächstenliebe im Talmud," in 1924, 1:148.

125. Ibid., 1:150.

126. Cohen, "Die Nächste," in 1924, 1:188.

127. Ibid., 1:194.

128. Cohen, "Die Nächstenliebe im Talmud," in 1924, 1:159.

129. Ibid., 160. I follow Hollander in translating *sittliche person* as "person in the moral sense." See Hollander 2009, 244.

130. Cohen, "Die Nächstenliebe im Talmud," in 1924, 1:160–61.

131. See Hollander 2012, 86.

132. Ibid., 112.

133. See ibid., 98.

134. See ibid., 112.

135. Cohen 2015, 38; "Spinoza über Staat und Religion, Judentum und Christendum," in 1924, 3:345–46 (emphasis original).

136. Cohen, "Was Einigt die Konfessionen?," in 1924, in 1:68.

137. Cohen 2015, 40–41; "Spinoza über Staat und Religion, Judentum und Christendum," in 1924, 3:348–49 (emphasis original).

138. Cohen 2015, 39; "Spinoza über Staat und Religion, Judentum und Christendum," in 1924, 3:346.

139. Cohen 2015, 43; "Spinoza über Staat und Religion, Judentum und Christendum," in 1924, 3:351.

140. Cohen 2015, 52; "Spinoza über Staat und Religion, Judentum und Christendum," in 1924, 3:364. We shall return to the personal aspect of Cohen's critique of Spinoza in chapter 6.

141. Cohen 2015, 59; "Spinoza über Staat und Religion, Judentum und Christendum," in 1924, 3:372.

142. Cohen 1995, 16; 1978, 18–19.

143. Cohen 1995, 17; 1978, 19.

144. Cohen 1995, 19; 1978, 22.

145. Cohen 1995, 114; 1978, 133.

146. ohen, "Was Einigt die Konfessioned?," in 1924, 1:85.

147. Cohen 1995, 34; 1978, 39.

148. So Poma writes that Christianity was the only faith Cohen "did not ignore, apart from Judaism, in his research" (Poma 2006, 125), Again, though not far from being right, Cohen does, even if rarely and arguably rather superficially, address Islam. Interestingly, Cohen's philosophical activity took place from 1833 to 1933, when, as Heschel claims, "Jews were among the finest scholars and greatest admirers of Islam in Europe" (Heschel 2012, 93). In some cases, such as with Gustav Weil for example, they even presented Islam as superior to both Judaism and Christianity (Heschel 2012, 96).

149. Cohen 2015, 48; "Spinoza über Staat und Religion, Judentum und Christendum," in 1924, 3:359.

150. Cohen, "Das Problem der jüdischen Sittenlehre," in 1924, 3:11.

151. Cohen 1995, 239; 1978, 280.

152. Cohen, "Was Einigt die Konfessionen?," in 1924, 1:79.

153. Cohen, "Religion und Sittlichkeit," in 1924, 3:132.

154. Cohen 1995, 61; 1978, 70.

155. Cohen 1995, 92; 1978, 107–8. See also Heschel 2012, 101.

156. Cohen 2004, 183–84; "Charakteristik der Ethik Maimunis," in 1924, 285.

157. See Myers 2001, 203.

158. Treitschke 1880, 1, 2–3.

159. Ibid., 2, 4. For more on Treitschke's attack and its historical context, see Meyer 1966.

160. Cohen, "Ein Bekenntnis in der Judenfrage," in 1924, 2:75.

161. Kant 1999c, 336. Quoted in Cohen, "Ein Bekenntnis in der Judenfrage," in 1924, 2:75.

162. Cohen, "Ein Bekenntnis in der Judenfrage," in 1924, 2:75.

163. Cohen 1924, 2:76–77.

164. Myers 2001, 203.

165. Cohen, "Die Nächstenliebe im Talmud," in 1924, 1:162.

166. See Palmer 2006, 51–52. The so-called Marburg Antisemitism Trial occurred in 1888 and was instigated by Ferdinand Fenner, a schoolteacher who had turned to antisemitism, apparently out of spite that his heavily indebted paternal estate had been bought by a Jew (Sieg 1993, 228). His continued antisemitic propaganda led to the children of his school repeatedly insulting and harassing the children at the Jewish school, leading to a complaint filed by the chief rabbi of Marburg, Leo Munk (Sieg 1993, 229). Munk was outraged at Fenner's activities, which included a public speech during which he had proclaimed that "a good Jew does what the Talmud tells him to do; he is then a scoundrel in our eyes. If he does not do what the Talmud tells him to, he is a scoundrel in the eyes of the Jews. He is, at any rate, a scoundrel in all cases" (Sieg 1993, 229). Fenner was eventually tried for abusing a state-protected religion. Scholarly expertise was sought to argue the opposing positions; Cohen defended the Talmud's universal credentials while the Orientalist and virulent antisemite Paul de Lagarde attacked it (Sieg 1993, 229, 230). Cohen's testimony was deemed more trustworthy, and Fenner was eventually sentenced to a prison sentence of two weeks as well as obliged to pay the costs of litigation (Sieg 1993, 229, 240). Cohen published his defense as "Die Nächstenliebe im Talmud."

167. Cohen, "Deutschtum und Judentum (I)," in 1924, 2:244, translated in Myers 2001, 210.

168. Cohen 1995, 17; 1978, 19.

169. Cohen, "Die Liebe Zur Religion," in 1924, 2:144.

170. Ibid., 2:143–44.

171. Erlewine 2016, 1.

172. Cohen 1995, 338; 1978, 393.

173. Cohen 1995, 49; 1978, 56–57.

174. See Erlewine 2016, 36–37. See also "Cohen's Unique God" in chapter 4.

175. Cohen 1995, 48; 1978, 55–56.

176. Cohen 1995, 54; 1978, 63.

177. Cohen 1995, 54; 1978, 63.

178. Cohen 1995, 344; 1978, 400.

179. Cohen 1995, 171; 1978, 199.

180. Cohen 1995, 17; 1978, 19.

181. Erlewine 2016, 43.

182. Ibid., 49.

183. Cohen 1995, 264; 1978, 308 (emphasis original).

184. Cohen 1995, 264; 1978, 309.

185. See "Cohen's Unique God" in chapter 4.

186. Cohen 1981, 1.

187. Cohen 2021, 105; "Das Soziale Ideal bei Platon und den Propheten," in 1924, 1:306.

188. Cohen 2021, 129; "Das Soziale Ideal bei Platon und den Propheten," in 1924, 1:330.

189. Cohen 2021, 114–15; "Das Soziale Ideal bei Platon und den Propheten," in 1924, 1:316.

190. Cohen 2021, 113; "Das Soziale Ideal bei Platon und den Propheten," in 1924, 314.

191. Cohen 1995, 251; 1978, 293.

192. Cohen, "Das Soziale Ideal bei Platon und den Propheten," in 1924, 1:313. Interestingly, Cohen makes this claim in spite of the fact he here uses the term *cosmopolitanism* (*Kosmopolitismus*), which is of course itself Greek, and was, according to Diogenes Laertius, first used by Diogenes of Sinope to describe himself (see Diogenes Laertius 1925, 2:64). This could be an awkward phrasing, or, given that Cohen often uses the Germanic term *Weltbürgertum* and its derivatives to describe aspects of the prophetic ethos (see, e.g., Cohen, "Die Bedeutung des Judentums für den Religiösen Fortschritt der Menscheit," in 1924, 1:35), a conscious choice to make a somewhat ironical point about the difference between the etymological origin of terms versus their contextual origin.

193. Cohen 1995, 250; 1978, 292.

194. Cohen 1995, 249; 1978, 291.

195. Cohen 1995, 169; 1978, 196.

196. Cohen 1995, 169; 1978, 196.

197. Cohen 1995, 169–70; 1978, 197–98.

198. Derrida 1991, 54–55.

199. Cohen, "Antwort auf das Offene Schreiben des Herrn Dr. Martin Buber as Hermann Cohen," in 1924, 2:336.

200. Indeed, he was all too aware also of towering figures within German culture that did not stand for the kind of ideals his idealized Germanism stood for. So, for example, Cohen points out that Germany did not only produce Kant and Goethe but also Schopenhauer and Nietzsche, not only Mozart and Bach but also Wagner, adding that "it must be generally understood, that these names are divorced from the basic concepts of the German Aesthetic" (Cohen, "Deutschtum un Judentum (I)," in 1924, 2:284).

201. Schwarzchild 1979, 138.

202. Ibid., 141.

203. Ibid., 150.

204. Cohen, "Deutschtum un Judentum (I)," in 1924, 2:242.

205. Ibid., 278, 287. The clearly primordial value of the German cultural contribution is such in Cohen's eyes that it makes him wonder about the then current "ingratitude of the peoples" (1924, 184).

206. Cohen 1924, 2:274. Indeed, in a similar spirit, Cohen claims that the rights Jews have gained in Germany, even if limited, are "of a higher value for religious survival than that apparent absolute equality of the Jews abroad" (Cohen 1924, 2:280).

207. Indeed, it is the case, as pointed out in chapter 3, that Mendelssohn believes that there can be no progress of the whole of humanity, that each nation finds itself in different stages of progress in different eras, and that progress can only apply to the individual (1983, 96; 1971–, 8:162–63). This would of course completely undermine Cohen's understanding of the crucial messianic task, which demands of us precisely to actively lift the whole of humanity and is backed by a divine promise that this effort will not be in vain. Still, it is not the case that Mendelssohn disavows all versions of Messianism. So, for example, while emphasizing the concordance of the Unitarian articles of faith and those of Judaism, Mendelssohn writes that a remaining difference is that "we still await a future Messiah who will be called to restore our nation and free it from all political oppression, and that all nations will then unite in worshipping the one true God" (Mendelssohn 2011, 26; 1971–, 7:102). While this statement does not necessarily contradict his view about human progress given in *Jerusalem* (as the progress brought by the Messiah could very well be radically different from the kind of human-led progress Mendelssohn denies in *Jerusalem*), it seems likely Mendelssohn's position in *Jerusalem* evolved slightly from the phrasing here quoted, formulated in 1770, thirteen years before *Jerusalem*. Indeed, as we saw in chapter 3, at the end of *Jerusalem*, Mendelssohn explicitly states that a "union of faiths is not tolerance" and accordingly that "diversity is evidently the plan and purpose of Providence" (Mendelssohn 1983, 138; 1971–, 8:202). One could also argue that diversity is the plan of providence until the Messiah comes or that the different religions can conceivably unite in worshipping the one true God in diverse ways. Still, while Mendelssohn did not forsake messianic belief completely, and in fact his notion of there being no progress in human history until the arrival of the Messiah does very much cohere with central tenets of the Jewish tradition (see Raz-Krakotzin 2007, 534–37), it remains the case that Messianism, however the notion is interpreted, is far less emphasized in Mendelssohn than in Cohen.

208. Cohen, "Deutschtum und Judentum (I)," in 1924, 2:267.

209. Cohen, "Deutschtum und Judentum (II)," in 1924, 2:316.

210. Cohen, "Religiöse Postulate," in 1924, 1:9–10.

211. Cohen, "Die Liebe zur Religion," in 1924, 2:142.

212. Cohen 2002, 4–5.

213. To be clear, Cohen does not exclude these cultures inherently but rather because he estimates they have not undergone the necessary process of idealization or "reached the stage of articulation displayed in scientific culture" that demarcates Cohen's universalistic religion of reason (Cohen 1995, 8; 1978, 9). Presumably, were they to reach such a stage, they would gain a stake in the religion of reason. It remains the case, however, that this is a significant exclusion, as the concrete ways in which Cohen characterizes that process of idealization would demand these cultures let go of the historical "cult" that particularizes them and adhere to cultural forms promoted by Cohen. Indeed, if Cohen does not even allow the use of the term *religion* for Chinese, Indian, Babylonian, or Greek "cults," presumably these "cults" would therefore have to be abandoned for the cultures from which they arose to reach the relevant stage of "scientific culture."

214. Cohen 1995, 233; 1978, 272.

215. Cohen 1995, 52; 1978, 60.

216. Cohen 1995, 52; 1978, 60.

217. Cohen 1995, 52–53; 1978, 61. Cohen adds that this does not mean the prophets failed to "recognize the humanity of men as such" (Cohen 1995, 53; 1978, 61). This suggests that the killing of human beings, conceived as religiously and morally necessitated, does not necessarily mean disregard for their humanity. We shall return to this point in the next chapter.

218. See Freudenthal 2015, 220–21. Freudenthal, in fact, goes further, arguing that Mendelssohn denies the very possibility of actual idolaters, suggesting instead that for Mendelssohn, all religious practitioners are on a scale between the ideal type of idolatry and the one of enlightened religion (see Freudenthal 2015, 222–23). The phrasing used above reflects the weaker claim necessary for our comparative point, that is, the great reluctance Mendelssohn has in pointing at idolatry, one certainly not shared by Cohen in the quoted passages.

219. See Mendelssohn 1983, 129–30; 1971–, 8:194–95.

220. Cohen 1995, 120; 1978, 139.

221. Cohen 1995, 9; 1978, 8.

222. Cohen, "Der Nächste," in 1924, 1:195.

223. Cohen 1995, 52–53; 1978, 61.

24. See Zank 2000, 266.

225. Cohen 1995, 252; 1978, 295.

226. Cohen 1995, 252–53; 1978, 295 (emphasis original).

227. Cohen 1995, 22, 281; 1978, 26, 327–28. See also, "Die Messiasidee," in 1924, 1:117.

228. Buber 1967, 108–9.

229. Cohen to Dr. Leo Munk, March 27, 1907, in Cohen 1939, 77.

230. Bergman 1961, 41.

231. Cohen, "Die Nächstenliebe im Talmud," in 1924, 1:145.

232. Gordon 1999, 34.

233. Cohen 2021, 134; "Innere Beziehungen der Kantischen Philosophie zum Judentum," in 1924, 1:289.

234. Cohen, "Die Nächstenliebe im Talmud," in 1924, 1:158.

235. Ibid., 1:158.

236. Cohen 1995, 338; 1978, 394.

237. Cohen 1995, 339–40; 1978, 395.

238. Cohen 1995, 339–40; 1978, 396.

239. Cohen 1995, 341; 1978, 397.

240. Cohen 1995, 345; 1978, 401.

241. Cohen 1995, 346; 1978, 403.

242. Cohen 1995, 366; 1978, 425.

243. Cohen 1995; 1978, 426.

244. Cohen 1995; 1978, 426.

245. Cohen 1995, 368; 1978, 427.

246. The encounter, supposedly, occurred while Cohen was still in Marburg. See Bergson 1961, 41.

247. Liebeschütz adds that "the distinction between the centre, which could be described in the terms of idealism, and the periphery, the ritual accompanying daily life, remained, but the same emotional atmosphere comprised both" (Liebeschütz 1968, 30).

6. JEWISH UNIVERSALISMS

1. Mendelssohn 1971–, 3.2:66; 15.2: 23–24. See also Gottlieb 2011, 44.

2. Mendelssohn 1997e, 153; 1971–, 2:407.

3. Mendelssohn 1997e, 153; 1971–, 2:407.

4. To quote yet another eloquent and particularly vivid passage to that effect from Mendelssohn's Phädon, "What is more terrifying to the human soul than annihilation? And what is more wretched than a man who sees annihilation closing in on him, and in hopeless fear, awaits it and believes it to be at hand. In prosperity, the horrific thought of non-existence slinks in between the most cheerful images, like a serpent between flowers, and poisons the enjoyment of life; and in misfortune it strikes man totally hopeless to the ground, while it

wears away the only comfort for him which can sweeten his misery, the hope for a better future" (Mendelssohn 2007, 136; 1971–, 3.1: 115).

5. Rotenstreich 1996, 92.

6. Compare Mendelssohn 1983, 97; 1971–, 8:164; with Spinoza 2016b, 270. See also Guttman 1981, 365–67.

7. Luzzato 1969, 3.

8. Of course, that does not mean that some religions aren't less commonsensical than others. But given that common sense is construed by Mendelssohn as universally "common," the tendency is for religions to be construed as truthful rather than mistaken.

9. Cohen, "Der Stil der Propheten," in 1924, 1:264, 265; 1995, 22; 1978, 26.

10. Cohen, "Zum Prioritätsstreit über das Gebot der Nächstenliebe," in 1924, 1:176.

11. Cohen 2002, 4–5.

12. Cohen 1995, 233; 1978, 272.

13. Nietzsche 2002, 164. See also note 17 in the introduction to this volume.

14. Mendelssohn 1983, 102; 1971–, 8:169.

15. See Mendelssohn 2012b, 157; 1971–, 3.2: 197.

16. Mendelssohn 2012b, 156; 1971–, 3.2:196.

17. Mendelssohn 2011, 30; 1971–, 7:106. See "Mendelssohn's Pluralism" in chapter 3.

18. Having quoted the *Rig-Veda* (1.164.46), "The wise speak of what is One in many ways," Doniger notes that "right from the beginning, Hindu texts and practices tell of the simultaneous existence of polytheism and a broader belief in the ultimate oneness of the divine—not exactly monotheism, but a unitary substratum supporting a vigorous polytheism. And yet there has been from time to time an angry debate, in which some Hindus find it insulting to be called polytheists" (Doniger 2014, 10). So, Vedantic monists "acknowledged the reality of the gods of the pantheon but accorded them a secondary, illusory status in comparison with the enduring, real status of the underlying monistic being" (Doniger 2014, 14), and, significantly, the monistic view of the universal Brahman eventually developed a universalism according to which "all religions were essentially the same" (Doniger 2014, 15). This certainly is not a uniform position within the Hindu traditions or among the Hindu people (see Dandekar 1968, 424). However, the very existence of such strands would at the very least provide grounds for Mendelssohn to argue for the universality of his beloved natural religion and presumably make a case that unacceptably polytheistic strands within Hinduism, if there are any, are unfortunate deteriorations of an original common understanding of the one God.

19. Of course, this is not to say that Mendelssohn was right with regards to the Indian religion or any other tradition he seeks to put under the umbrella of his natural religion, only that his case is not utterly naïve and that there might still be grounds for likeminded thinkers to make it.

20. So Mendelssohn, while discussing the significance of the ceremonial law, makes the point it would remain necessary "as long as polytheism, anthropomorphism and religious usurpation dominate the globe," terming all three "pests of reason [Plagegeister der Vernunft]." Mendelssohn to Herz Homberg, September 22, 1783, in Mendelssohn 1971–, 13:134.

21. Exodus 20:3

22. Mendelssohn 2011, 223; 1971–, 16:186. As Gottlieb points out, Mendelssohn here follows Nachmanides in claiming that the commandment does not apply to gentiles, who are "permitted to worship angels, heavenly bodies, demons or human beings, and even sensible representations of these beings as long as the worshippers recognize the supreme authority of God" (Gottlieb 2006, 220).

23. Mendelssohn 2011, 223; 1971–, 16:186.

24. Mendelssohn 2011, 224; 1971–, 16:186.

25. Mendelssohn 1983, 102; 1971–, 8:169.

26. See, for example, Altmann 1987, 247; Eisen 1990, 242; Guttman 1981, 375–76; or Schonfeld 2016, 367.

27. See "Appraising Mendelssohn's Jewish Values" in chapter 3.

28. Mendelssohn 1983, 131; 1971–, 8:196.

29. Mendelssohn 1983, 95; 1971–, 8:162.

30. Again, this is in complete contrast with Mendelssohn, whose very assumptions about language, to quote Rosenstock, break "with the Enlightenment ideal of linguistic accuracy measured by a scientific regime of truth" (Rosenstock 2010, 59).

31. Berlin 1980, 145. The significance of the *Volksgeist* for Cohen relates particularly to the critical significance of *Völkerpsychologie* in his intellectual development. As Beiser notes, the young Cohen was a "champion of the new science of Völkerpsychologie," and though he eventually distanced himself from it to some degree, he never repudiated it "and integrated important elements of it into his later philosophy" (Beiser 2018, 22).

32. Levinger 2000, 48.

33. Schmidt 1956, 407.

34. Cassirer 1951, 233.

35. Dussel 1993, 70.

36. Ibid., 73.

37. Hegel 1956, 341.

38. Bentley 2007, 22.

39. See Beiser 2014, 4.0. So Wiedebach writes that Cohen "could not avoid the kind of mystification that is concomitant with national fundamentalism" (Wiedebach 2012, xiv). Wiedebach also points out that the "grand mystification" to which he subjects Deutschtum leads to its conception as "an infallible cultural knowledge about universal lawfulness" (2012, 247). It is, however, at the very least debatable whether this universal sensitivity in any way abets the problematic nature of Cohen's fervent nationalism amidst the violent madness of a terrible world war.

41. It is, in this context, important too to take note of Cohen's precarious position as a Jew in the era of German nationalism. Mendelssohn sought to argue against the perceived particularism of Judaism in the age of cosmopolitanism, one far less nationalistically inclined. Cohen of course, as we have seen throughout, sought to make the universalistic argument against the accusations of Jewish particularism as well but, given the times he was living in, had to also defend Judaism from a different charge, namely, that Jews were somehow overly "international" and as such unable to show true patriotism to the nation in which they lived. So, for example, when Fenner (see chapter 5, n. 166 in the present volume) was brought in front of the local school committee in the early stages of what became the Marburg antisemitism trial, he claimed there was grave danger in positing "the equality of international Judaism and homegrown Germanism" (quoted in Sieg 1993, 206). Cohen had, in other words, to respond to a basic European antisemitic trope that had become particularly virulent in his time. As Horkheimer and Adorno put it, "all the great achievements of their prominent members were not enough to allow Jews to be admitted to the peoples of Europe; having been prevented from putting down roots they were then criticized as rootless" (Horkheimer and Adorno 2002, 143). The Jew, therefore, as Bonefeld puts it, "is seen to personify abstract values" and is opposed to the "Volksgenosse [who] portrays himself as rooted in blood and ancestral tradition" (Bonefeld 2005, 159).

42. Cohen 1995, 52; 1978, 60–61.

43. Cohen 1995, 74; 1978, 86.

44. Erlewine 2010, 149.

45. Ibid., 154.

46. Cohen 1995, 121; 1978, 140.

47. Erlewine 2010, 132.

48. Ibid., 155.

49. Cohen 1995, 52–53; 1978, 60–61 (emphasis original).

50. "The literal, superficial view of the source of great divine ideas," Cohen wrote, "was and is repugnant to me" (Cohen, "Ein Gruβ der Pietät," in 1924,

2:423). Beiser refers to this passage when explaining that Cohen left the Jewish Theological Seminary of Breslau and broke off his rabbinic career primarily because he feared such literal readings would restraint his intellectual freedom. See, Beiser 2018, 15.

51. Cohen 1995, 22, 281; 1978, 26, 327–28. See also "Morally Required Intolerance" in chapter 5.

52. Cohen 1995, 121; 1978, 140.

53. Cohen 1995, 53; 1978, 61.

54. See Cohen 1995, 339, 397; 1978, 394, 461.

55. For a succinct summary of some of the main relevant arguments to that effect, see Tricoire 2017, 4.

56. Cohen 2015, 4; "Spinoza über Staat und Religion, Judentum und Christendum," in 1924, 3:293 (emphasis original).

57. Cohen 2015, 37; "Spinoza über Staat und Religion, Judentum und Christendum," in 1924, 3:344.

58. Cohen 2015, 27; "Spinoza über Staat und Religion, Judentum und Christendum," in 1924, 3:329.

59. Cohen 2015, 51; "Spinoza über Staat und Religion, Judentum und Christendum," in 1924, 3:362.

60. Cohen 2015, 56; "Spinoza über Staat und Religion, Judentum und Christendum," in 1924, 3:368.

61. Cohen 2015, 58–57; "Spinoza über Staat und Religion, Judentum und Christendum," in 1924, 3:371.

62. Cohen 2001, 467. Beiser argues that the recognition of Spinoza's "noxious influence on Kant" was particularly significant in turning Cohen against a philosopher he had previously admired. See Beiser 2018, 274.

63. Cohen 2015, 58; "Spinoza über Staat und Religion, Judentum und Christendum," in 1924, 3:371.

64. Cohen 2015, 51; "Spinoza über Staat und Religion, Judentum und Christendum," in 1924, 3:363.

65. Cohen 2015, 52; "Spinoza über Staat und Religion, Judentum und Christendum," in 1924, 3:364 (emphasis original).

66. Cohen 2015, 30; "Spinoza über Staat und Religion, Judentum und Christendum," in 1924, 3:333.

67. Cohen 2015, 49; "Spinoza über Staat und Religion, Judentum und Christendum," in 1924, 3:360.

68. Indeed, Cohen further seeks to undermine Spinoza's credibility by repeating claims he received a pension from de Witt. Cohen 2015, 2; "Spinoza über Staat und Religion, Judentum und Christendum," in 1924, 3:291.

69. Cohen 2015, 2–5; "Spinoza über Staat und Religion, Judentum und Christentum," 290–95.

70. One made explicit once more in Cohen's critique of Spinoza's misinterpretation of Maimonides, which is not merely a philological mistake, but rather a "psychological enigma" that allows us to "peer into his soul" (Cohen 2015, 39, 43; 1924, 3:346, 351).

71. Hans Liebeschütz 1960, 225.

72. Cohen 2015, 58; "Spinoza über Staat und Religion, Judentum und Christendum," in 1924, 3:371.

73. To quote Strauss, "to Mendelssohn, his critique of 'purified' Spinozism comes down not so much to the actuality of things outside God, as to the actuality of man qua I outside God . . . what for him is the decisive objection against Spinozism, 'purified' as well as authentic, more exactly, what for him is the decisive objection against Spinozism because for him it is a self-evident presupposition, is not so much God's transcendence as it is the archetypal substantiality of the I as a 'closed-off' awareness, in the sense that even God's thoughts of the finite I are simply images of the archetype" (Strauss 2012a, 123).

74. See Altmann 1973, 739.

75. Guttman 1981, 362.

76. Mendelssohn 1997c, 106; 1971–, 1:14

77. Mendelssohn 2012a, 93–94; 1971–, 3.2:106.

78. See Mendelssohn 2012a, 109; 1971–, 3.2:123.

79. Mendelssohn 1983, 73–75; 1971–, 8:140–42.

80. So Altmann suggests it is Spinoza that Mendelssohn is thinking about when describing the effects of excommunication on a religiously inclined person (see Altmann 1981a, 173). If this is indeed the case, then the difference here between Cohen's justification of Spinoza's excommunication and Mendelssohn's condemnation of it serves as a clear example of how different axiological prioritizations underpin different practical stances towards a given issue. This, however, does not mean that Mendelssohn and Cohen will always have different ethical principles or practical stances. As mentioned in the introduction, the axiological question, What is valuable? is different from the ethical one, What ought to be done? Different axiological prioritizations could therefore still yield at times similar ethical principles or pragmatic stances. Even in such cases, however, the analysis of the axiological difference is relevant to understanding the structure upon which similar ethical principles or pragmatic stances rest.

81. Derrida 1991, 66.

82. Mendelssohn 2012b, 149; 1971–, 3.2:188.

83. As Rosenzweig puts it, the very word *apologetics* is afflicted with "a bad odor." Rosenzweig 2000, 107. See also Kavka 2004, 4.

84. See N. Smith 2008, 8.

85. Nick Smith suggests that the modern use of *apology* "gained momentum around the sixteenth century, when Shakespeare used it in Richard III to imply a kind of regret" (see N. Smith 2008, 8). In more religious contexts, such as Montaigne's use of the word in his *Apology for Raymond Sebond*, the term ought to still carry its etymological origin of defense, as in "the long tradition of defending and reinforcing religious doctrine—particularly Christian beliefs—through argumentation" (see N. Smith 2008, 8). This exercise, however, clearly cannot be construed as only, or even perhaps particularly, Christian, as it is reflected in the works of many, if not most, Jewish philosophers. Still, Nick Smith helpfully clarifies the varying meanings of the term, and the problem, as mentioned, is that these varying meanings seem at times to become somewhat tangled. So Rashkover writes that "traditionally, apologetics has meant the defense of the faith to the nonbeliever," referring to the meaning of a defense in the religious context, but then adds that to apologize "is to admit rather than hold onto a lie," which seems to relate to the modern sense of the term (Rashkover 2012, 421). Similarly, Hughes relates the apologetic effort of finding a "'Jewish' essence and subsequently make it conform to larger set of 'non-Jewish' issues" to "an attempt to apologize for Judaism" (Hughes 2013, 14). My point here is that confusing the classic religio-philosophical apology with the modern, regretful one, connotatively, if not in regards to content, ascribes to apologetic efforts a regretful, reactive, and meek attitude that is very far from anything genuinely reflected by many such efforts.

86. Plato 1997, 36d–37, 32–33.

87. Diogenes Laertius 1925, 1:171. See also Brickhouse and Smith 2004, 167–68.

88. Mendelssohn 1983, 97–98; 1971–, 8:164–65.

89. These remarks raise the question of the degree to which their stances can be construed as having had genuine precedents in previous and traditional Jewish texts and sources. After all, the fact they viewed themselves as faithful to Judaism doesn't necessarily make it so. However, assessing whether either one can convincingly make this claim would demand a comprehensive and exhaustive contextualization of the respective positions of both within the historical Jewish religious and philosophical corpus, one that would be beyond the scope of the current line of argumentation. In addition, even if such a textual and historical contextualization did show their interpretations are in some sense original and new, or reflective of their contemporary sensitivities rather than traditional ones, it would still remain arguably rather difficult to make any con-

clusive judgments about their faithfulness to the constitutive canon of Judaism. After all, they could still claim, for example, that their interpretations reflect the previously misunderstood essence of Judaism.

90. Cohen 2021, 149; "Innere Beziehungen der Kantischen Philosophie zum Judentum," in 1924, 1:304 (emphasis original). See also Poma 2007, 92. As mentioned earlier, it is clear that Cohen's Neo-Platonic conception of the hypothesis would lead to such an essentialism. See chapter 5, n. 79 in the present volume.

91. Mendelssohn 1983, 102; 1971–, 8:168.

92. Mendelssohn 1983, 102; 1971–, 8:168.

93. Goetschel 2004, 164.

94. Poma 2007, 92.

95. As such, it is likely that both Mendelssohn and Cohen would have resisted the notion they were engaged in a radical revaluation in so far as that would involve inserting new values into existing concepts. They could have accepted their engagement in a more moderate kind of revaluative effort in so far as such an effort would involve a reprioritization of values that have at times gone astray, that is, a refocusing on an original essence. Either way, these highly speculative considerations do not undermine the notion that thinking of their efforts as revaluative can be an insightful analytic tool.

96. Geuss 1999, 3–5.

97. Ibid.

BIBLIOGRAPHY

Altmann, Alexander (1962). "Hermann Cohens Begriff Der Korrelation." In *In Zwei Welten: Siegfried Moses zum Fünfundsiebzigsten Geburtstag*, edited by Hans Tramer, 377–99. Tel Aviv: Bitaon.

——— (1973). *Moses Mendelssohn: A Biographical Study*. Philadelphia: The Jewish Publication Society of America.

——— (1974). "The Philosophical Roots of Moses Mendelssohn's Plea for Emancipation." In *Jewish Social Studies* 36, no. 3/4: 191–202.

——— (1981a). "Mendelssohn on Excommunication: The Ecclesiastical Law Background." In *Essays in Jewish Intellectual History*, 119–41. Hannover: University Press of New England.

——— (1981b). "Moses Mendelssohn's Proofs for the Existence of God." In *Essays in Jewish Intellectual History*, 170–89. Hannover: University Press of New England.

——— (1983). "Commentary." In *Jerusalem, or on Religious Power and Judaism*, by Moses Mendelssohn, translated by Allan Arkush, 143–240. Waltham: Brandeis University Press.

——— (1987). "Moses Mendelssohn's Concept of Judaism Reexamined." In *Von der Mittelalterlichen zur Modernen Aufklärung: Studien Zur Jüdischen Geistesgeschichte*, 234–48. Tübingen: Mohr Siebeck.

Aristotle (1993a). *Metaphysics*. Translated by W. D. Ross. In *The Complete Works of Aristotle*, vol. 2, edited by Jonathan Barnes, 1552–728. Princeton: Princeton University Press.

——— (1993b). *Nicomachean Ethics*. Translated by W. D. Ross. In *The Complete Works of Aristotle*, vol. 2, edited by Jonathan Barnes, 1729–867. Princeton: Princeton University Press.

——— (1993c). *Politics*. Translated by Benjamin Jowett. In *The Complete Works of Aristotle*, vol. 2, edited by Jonathan Barnes, 1986–2125. Princeton: Princeton University Press.

Arkush, Allan (1994). *Moses Mendelssohn and the Enlightenment*. Albany, State University of New York Press.

——— (1999). "The Questionable Judaism of Moses Mendelssohn." *New German Critique* 77: 29–44.

Assman, Jan (2010). *The Price of Monotheism*. Translated by Robert Savage. Stanford: Stanford University Press.

Aufderheide, Joachim, and Ralf M. Bader (2015). "Introduction." In *The Highest Good in Aristotle and Kant*, edited by Joachim Aufderheide and Ralf M. Bader, 1–14. Oxford: Oxford University Press.

Augustine (1991). *Confessions*. Translated by Henry Chadwick. Oxford: Oxford University Press.

Bacon, Francis (2000). *The New Organon*. Edited by Lisa Jardin and Michael Silverthorne. Cambridge: Cambridge University Press.

Bader, Ralf M. (2015). "Kant's Theory of the Highest Good." In *The Highest Good in Aristotle and Kant*, edited by Joachim Aufderheide and Ralf M. Bader, 183–213. Oxford: Oxford University Press.

Badiou, Alain (2003). *Saint Paul: The Foundation of Universalism*. Translated by Ray Brassier. Stanford: Stanford University Press.

Barney, Rachel (2015). "The Inner Voice: Kant on Conditionality and God as Cause." In *The Highest Good in Aristotle and Kant*, edited by Joachim Aufderheide and Ralf M. Bader, 158–82. Oxford: Oxford University Press.

Baron, Salo Wittmayer (1928). "Ghetto and Emancipation: Shall We Revise the Traditional View?" *The Menorah Journal* 14, no. 6: 515–26.

Bauer, Bruno (1843). *Die Judenfrage*. Braunschweig: Druck und Verlag von Friedrich Otto.

——— (2002). *An English Edition of Bruno Bauer's 1843 Christianity Exposed: A Recollection of the Eighteenth Century and a Contribution to the Crisis of the Nineteenth Century*. Translated by Esther Ziegler and Jutta Hamm. Edited by Paul Trejo. Lewiston: Edwin Mellen.

Beck, Lewis White (1969). *Early German Philosophy: Kant and His Predecessors*. Cambridge: Harvard University Press.

Becker, Sophie (1884). *Vor Hundert Jahren: Elise von der Reckes Reisen durch Deutschland 1784–86 nach dem Tagebuche Ihrer Beglieterin Sophie Becker*. Edited by G. Karo and M. Geyer. Stuttgart: Spemann.

Beiser, Frederick C. (2014). *The Genesis of Neo-Kantianism, 1796–1880*. Oxford: Oxford University Press.

——— (2018). *Hermann Cohen: An Intellectual Biography*. Oxford: Oxford University Press.

Ben-Amos, Avner (1993). "Monuments and Memory in French Nationalism." *History and Memory* 5, no. 2: 50–81.

Beneke, Chris (2006). *Beyond Toleration: The Religious Origins of American Pluralism*. Oxford: Oxford University Press.

Bentley, Jerry H. (1996). "Cross-Cultural Interaction and Periodization in World History." *The American Historical Review* 101, no. 3: 749–70.
——— (2007). "Early Modern Europe and the Early Modern World." In *Between the Middle Ages and Modernity: Individual and Community in the Early Modern World*, edited by Charles H. Parker and Jerry H. Bentley, 13–31. Lanham: Rowman & Littlefield Publishers.
Bergman, Samuel Hugo (1961). *Faith and Reason: An Introduction to Modern Jewish Thought*. Translated by Alfred Jospe. New York: Schocken Books.
Berkeley, George (1967). *A Treatise Concerning the Principles of Human Knowledge*. In *The Works of George Berkeley Bishop of Cloyne*, vol. 2, edited by T. E. Jessop, 1–114. London: Thomas Nelson and Sons.
Berlin, Isaiah (1980). *Vico and Herder: Two Studies in the History of Ideas*. London: Chatto & Windus.
——— (2001). "My Intellectual Path." In *The Power of Ideas*, edited by Henry Hardy, 1–23. Princeton: Princeton University Press.
Bleeck, Klaus (2008). "J. B. Basedows ethische Grundlegung einer, 'vernünftigen' Lebenspraxis aus dem Geiste der Philosophie, Natürlichen Theologie und des Christentum." In *"Die Stammutter aller guten Schulen": Das Dessauer Philanthropinum und der deutsche Philanthropismus 1774–1793*, edited by Jörn Garber, 99–168. Tübingen: Niemayer.
Bonefeld, Werner (2005). "Nationalism and Anti-Semitism in Anti-globalization Perspective." In *Human Dignity: Social Autonomy and the Critique of Capitalism*, edited by Werner Bonefeld and Kosmas Psychopedis, 147–72. London: Ashgate.
Bourel, Dominique (2004). *Moses Mendelssohn: La Naissance du Judaïsme Moderne*. Paris: Gallimard.
Boyarin, Daniel (1994). *A Radical Jew: Paul and the Politics of Identity*. Berkeley: University of California Press.
Brett, Mark G. (1996). "Interpreting Ethnicity: Method, Hermeneutics, Ethics." In *Ethnicity and the Bible*, edited by Mark G. Brett, 3–24. Leiden: E. J. Brill.
Brickhouse, Thomas C., and Smith, Nicholas D. (2004). *Routledge Philosophy Guidebook to Plato and the Trial of Socrates*. London: Routledge.
Bruckstein, Almut Sh. (2006). "*Hermann Cohen*. Ethics of Maimonides: *Residues of Jewish Philosophy—Traumatized*." In *Hermann Cohen's Ethics*, edited by Robert Gibbs, 115–25. Leiden: Brill.
Buber, Martin (1967). "The Holy Way: A Word to the Jews and to the Nations." In *On Judaism*, edited by Nahum N. Glatzer, 108–48. New York: Schocken Books.

Burnyeat, Myles (1998). "The Sceptic in His Place and Time." In *The Original Sceptics: A Controversy*, edited by Miles Burnyeat and Michael Frede, 92–126. Indianapolis: Hackett Publishing Company.

Cassirer, Ernst (1951). *The Philosophy of the Enlightenment.* Translated by Fritz C. A. Koelln and James P. Pettergrove. Princeton: Princeton University Press.

——— (1981). *Kant's Life and Thought.* Translated by James Haden. New Haven: Yale University Press.

Cavallar, Georg (2014). "Sources of Kant's Cosmopolitanism: Basedow, Rousseau, and Cosmopolitan Education." *Studies in Philosophy and Education* 33, no. 4: 369–89.

Charuty, Giordana (2011). "Les Métamorphoses d'Omai." *Gradhiva: Revue d'anthropologie et d'histoire des arts* 13: 182–203.

Ching, Julia, and Willard G. Oxtoby (1992). *Moral Enlightenment: Leibniz and Wolff on China.* Nettetal: Steyler Verlag.

Cohen, Hermann (1924). *Hermann Cohens Jüdische Schriften.* 3 vols. Edited by Bruno Strauss. Berlin: C. A. Schwetschke & Sohn.

——— (1928). "Platons Ideenlehre und die Mathematik" [1879]. In *Schriften zur Philosophie und Zeitgeschichte*, vol. 1, edited by Albert Görland and Ernst Cassirer, 336–66. Berlin: Akademie Verlag.

——— (1939). *Briefe.* Edited by Bertha and Bruno Strauss. Berlin: Schocken.

——— (1978). *Religion der Vernunft aus den Quellen des Judentums* [1929, 2nd ed.]. Wiesbaden: Fourier Verlag.

——— (1981). *Ethik des Reinen Willens* [1907, 2nd ed.]. In *Werke*, vol. 7. Hildesheim: Georg Olms Verlag.

——— (1984)."Einleitung Mit Kritischen Nachtrag Zur 'Geschichte des Materialismus' von F. A. Lange" [1896]. In *Werke*, vol. 5. Hildesheim: Olms Verlag.

——— (1987). *Kants Theorie der Erfahrung* [1871]. In *Werke*, vol. 1.3. Hildesheim: Olms Verlag.

——— (1995). *Religion of Reason out of the Sources of Judaism.* Translated by Simon Kaplan. Atlanta: Scholars Press.

——— (2001). *Kants Begründung der Ethik.* [1910, 2nd ed.]. In *Werke*, vol. 2. Hildesheim: Georg Olms Verlag.

——— (2002). *Der Begriff der Religion im System der Philosophie* [1915]. In *Werke*, vol. 10. Hildesheim: Georg Olms Verlag.

——— (2004). *Ethics of Maimonides.* Translated by Almut Sh. Bruckstein. Madison: University of Wisconsin Press.

——— (2005). *Logik der Reinen Erkentnnis* [1914, 2nd ed.]. Hildesheim: Georg Olms Verlag.

——— (2015). *Spinoza on State & Religion, Judaism & Christianity*. Translated by Robert S. Schine. Jerusalem: Shalem Press, 2015.

——— (2021). *Writings on Neo-Kantianism & Jewish Philosophy*. Edited by Samuel Moyn and Robert S. Schine. Waltham: Brandeis University Press.

Cohen, William (1969). "Thomas Jefferson and the Problem of Slavery." *The Journal of American History* 56, no. 3: 503–26.

Conley, Tom (2005). "The *Essays* and the New World." In *The Cambridge Companion to Montaigne*, edited by Ullrich Langer, 74–95. Cambridge: Cambridge University Press.

Connaughton, Richard (2005). *Omai: The Prince Who Never Was*. London: Timewell Press.

Cooke, Paul D. (1996). *Hobbes and Christianity: Reassessing the Bible in Leviathan*. Lanham: Rowman & Littlefield.

Cooper, Anthony Ashley (2000). "Sensus Communis, An Essay on the Freedom of Wit and Humour in a Letter to a Friend." In *Characteristics of Men, Manners, Opinions, Times*, edited by Lawrence E. Klein, 29–68. Cambridge: Cambridge University Press.

Craig, Edward (1997). *Hume on Religion*. Shimla: Indian Institute of Advanced Study.

Curley, Edwin M. (1992). "'I Durst Not Write So Boldly' or How to Read Hobbes' Theological-Political Treatise." Online article. https://docs.google.com/document/d/1dZ2hUU_HHcqDB5Hla4DhyZhg5epJ-79U8I8G9LTPBTg/edit (accessed March 10, 2023).

Dandekar, Ramchandra Narayan (1968). "God in Hindu Thought." *Annals of the Bhandarkar Oriental Research Institute* 48: 433–65.

Daston, Lorraine (1994). "Enlightenment Calculations." *Critical Inquiry* 21, no. 1: 182–202.

De Launay, Marc (2000). "Notice." In *Néokantismes et théorie de la connaissance*, translated and edited by Marc de Launay, 13–22. Paris: Vrin.

Deleuze, Gilles (2006). Nietzsche *and Philosophy*. Translated by Hugh Tomlinson. New York: Columbia University Press.

Delitzsch, Franz (1881). *Rohlings Talmudjude Beleuchtet*. Leipzig, Dörffling & Franke.

Demos, Raphael (1937). "Plato's Idea of the Good." *The Philosophical Review* 46, no. 3: 245–75.

Derrida, Jacques (1991). "Interpretations at War: Kant, the Jew, the German." Translated by Moshe Ron. *New Literary History* 22, no. 1: 39–95.

Descartes, René (1996). *Meditations on First Philosophy*. Translated and edited by John Cottingham. Cambridge: Cambridge University Press.

Di Giovanni, George (1989). "From Jacobi's Philosophical Novel to Fichte's Idealism: Some Comments on the 1798–99 'Atheism Dispute.'" *Journal of the History of Philosophy* 27, no. 1: 75–100.

—— (1994). "The Unfinished Philosophy of Friedrich Heinrich Jacobi – Introductory Study." In *The Main Philosophical Writings and the Novel "Allwill,"* by Friedrich Heinrich Jacobi, translated by George Di Giovanni, 1–170. Montreal: McGill-Queen's University Press.

Dietrich, Wendell S. (1980). "The Function of the Idea of Messianic Mankind in Hermann Cohen's Later Thought." *Journal of the American Academy of Religion* 48, no. 2: 245–58.

Diogenes Laertius (1925). *Lives of Eminent Philosophers*. 2 vols. translated by R. D. Hicks. London: William Heinemann.

D'Israeli, Isaac (1798). "A Biographical Sketch of the Jewish Socrates." *Monthly Magazine* 6, no. 2: 38–44.

Doniger, Wendy (2014). *On Hinduism*. Oxford: Oxford University Press.

Dussel, Enrique (1993). "Eurocentrism and Modernity (Introduction to the Frankfurt Lectures)." *Boundary 2* 20, no. 3: 65–76.

Eisen, Arnold (1990). "Divine Legislation as 'Ceremonial Script': Mendelssohn on the Commandments." *AJS Review* 15, no. 2: 239–67.

Eisenstein, Elizabeth L. (1980). *The Printing Press as an Agent of Change*. Vol. 1. Cambridge: Cambridge University Press.

Ellingson, Ter (2001). *The Myth of the Noble Savage*. Berkeley: University of California Press.

Epicurus (1926). *The Extant Remains*. Translated by Cyril Bailey. Oxford: Clarendon Press.

Erlewine, Robert (2010). *Monotheism and Tolerance: Recovering a Religion of Reason*. Bloomington: Indiana University Press.

—— (2014). "Reason within the Bounds of Religion: Assman, Cohen, and the Possibilities of Monotheism." In *Judaism, Liberalism & Political Theology*, edited by Randi Rashkover and Martin Kavka, 269–89 Bloomington: Indiana University Press.

—— (2016). *Judaism and the West: From Hermann Cohen to Joseph Soloveitchik*. Bloomington: Indiana University Press.

Estes, Yolanda, and Curtis Bowman (2010). *J. F. Fichte and the Atheism Dispute (1798–1800)*. Translated by Curtis Bowman. Farnham: Ashgate.

Fackenheim, Emil L. (1996). "Hermann Cohen – After Fifty Years." In *Jewish Philosophers and Jewish Philosophy*, edited by Michael L. Morgan, 41–56. Bloomington: Indiana University Press.

Feiner, Shmuel (2010). *Moses Mendelssohn: Sage of Modernity*. New Haven: Yale University Press.

——— (2011). *The Jewish Enlightenment*. Philadelphia: University of Pennsylvania Press, 2011.

Feldman, Louis H. (1992). "Was Judaism a Missionary Religion in Ancient Times?" In *Jewish Assimilation, Acculturation and Accommodation: Past Traditions, Current Issues and Future Prospects*, edited by Menachem Mor, 24–37. Lanham: University Press of America.

Ferry, Luc (1990). *Political Philosophy 1: Rights—The New Quarrel Between the Ancients and the Moderns*. Vol. 1. Translated by Franklin Philip. Chicago: University of Chicago Press.

Fichte, Johann Gottlieb (2010). "Appeal to the Public." In *J. F. Fichte and the Atheism Dispute (1798–1800)*, translated by Curtis Bowman, edited by Yolanda Estes and Curtis Bowman, 85–126. Farnham: Ashgate.

Findlay, J. N. (1970). *Axiological Ethics*. London: Macmillan & Co.

Fiorate, Pierfrancesco (2005). "Notes on Future and History in Hermann Cohen's Anti-eschatological Messianism." In *Hermann Cohen's Critical Idealism*, edited by Reinier Munk, 133–60. Leiden: Springer.

Fogel, Jeremy (2020). "A Polynesian, a Jew, and a Hindu Walk into Jerusalem: On Mendelssohn's Religious Universalism." *The Journal of Jewish Thought and Philosophy* 28, no. 2: 151–83.

Foot, Philippa (1994). "Nietzsche's Immoralism." In Nietzsche, *Genealogy, Morality: Essays on* Nietzsche*'s Genealogy of Morals*, edited by Richard Schacht, 3–14. Berkeley: University of California Press.

Forster, Greg (2003). "Divine Law and Human Law in Hobbes's *Leviathan*." *History of Political Thought* 24, no. 2: 189–217.

Fox, Marvin (1990). *Interpreting Maimonides: Studies in Methodology, Metaphysics, and Moral Philosophy*. Chicago: The University of Chicago Press, 1990.

Franks, Paul W. "Jewish Philosophy after Kant: The Legacy of Salomon Maimon." In *The Cambridge Companion to Jewish Philosophy*, edited by Michael L. Morgan and Peter Eli Gordon, 53–79. Cambridge: Cambridge University Press, 2007.

Fraser, David (2001). *Frederick the Great: King of Prussia*. New York: Fromm International.

Frederic Roy de Prusse et Electeur de Brandebourg (1760). *Poesies diverses ou oeuvres du philosophe de sans-souci*. Pozdam.

Frederickson, George M. (2002). *Racism: A Short History*. Princeton: Princeton University Press.

Freud, Sigmund (1961). *The Future of an Illusion*. Translated by James Strachey. New York: W. W. Norton & Company.

Freudenthal, Gideon (2012). *No Religion without Idolatry: Mendelssohn's Jewish Enlightenment*. Notre Dame: University of Notre Dame Press.

——— (2015). "Idolatry Everywhere, Idolaters Nowhere." In *Moses Mendelssohn: Enlightenment, Religion, Politics and Nationalism*, edited by Michah Gottlieb and Charles H. Manekin, 205–35. Bethesda: University Press of Maryland.

Friedman, Marilyn (1989). "Feminism and Modern Friendship: Dislocating the Community." *Ethics* 99, no. 2: 275–90.

Funkenstein, Amos (1986). *Theology and the Scientific Imagination: From the Middle Ages to the Seventeenth Century*. Princeton: Princeton University Press.

Geach, Peter T. (1966). "Plato's *Euthyphro*: An Analysis and Commentary." *The Monist* 50, no. 3: 369–82.

Gellner, Ernest (1992). *Reason and Culture: The Historical Role of Rationality and Rationalism*. Oxford: Blackwell Publishers.

Georgi, Dieter (1986). *The Opponents of Paul in Second Corinthians*. Minneapolis: Fortress Press.

Geuss, Raymond (1999). *Morality, Culture, and History: Essays on German Philosophy*. Cambridge: Cambridge University Press.

Goetschel, Willi (2004). *Spinoza's Modernity: Mendelssohn, Lessing, and Heine*. Madison: The University of Wisconsin Press.

Goldenberg, David M. (2013). "It Is Permitted to Marry a Kushite." *AJS Review* 37, no. 1: 29–49.

Golomb, Jacob (1992). "Kierkegaard's Ironic Ladder to Authentic Faith." *International Journal for Philosophy of Religion* 32, no. 2: 65–81.

Gordon, Peter Eli (1999). "Science, Finitude, and Infinity: Neo-Kantianism and the Birth of Existentialism." *Jewish Social Studies* 6, no. 1: 30–53.

Gorski, Philip S. (2003). *The Disciplinary Revolution: Calvinism and the Rise of the State in Early Modern Europe*. Chicago: The University of Chicago Press.

Gottlieb, Michah (2006). "Mendelssohn's Metaphysical Defense of Religious Pluralism." *The Journal of Religion* 86, no. 2: 205–25.

——— (2011). *Faith and Freedom: Moses Mendelssohn's Theological-Political Thought*. Oxford: Oxford University Press.

Gramsci, Antonio (1975). *Prison Notebooks*. 3 vols. Translated and edited by Joseph A. Buttigieg. New York: Columbia University Press.

Grant, Edward (1984). "Were There Significant Differences between Medieval and Early Modern Scholastic Natural Philosophy? The Case for Cosmology." *Noûs* 18, No. 1: 5–14.

Gray, John (2007). *Enlightenment's Wake: Politics and Culture at the Close of the Modern Age*. London: Routledge.

Gullan-Whur, Margaret (1998). *Within Reason: A Life of Spinoza*. London: Jonathan Cape.

Guttman, Julius (1981). "Mendelssohn's *Jerusalem* and Spinoza's *Theologico-Political Treatise*." In *Studies in Jewish Thought: An Anthology of German Jewish Scholarship*, edited by Alfred Jospe, 361–86. Detroit: Wayne State University Press.

Habermas, Jürgen (2008a). *Between Naturalism and Religion*. Translated by Ciaran Cronin. Cambridge: Polity Press.

——— (2008b). "Notes on Post-secular Society." *New Perspectives Quarterly* 25, no. 4: 17–29.

Hägglund, Martin (2019). *This Life: Secular Faith and Spiritual Freedom*. New York: Pantheon Books.

Harrison, Peter (1992). "Descartes on Animals." *The Philosophical Quarterly (1950-)* 42, no. 167: 219–27.

Harvey, Steven (1991). "A New Islamic Source of the Guide of the Perplexed." *Maimonidean Studies* 2: 31–47.

Heath, Malcolm (2008). "Aristotle on Natural Slavery." *Phronesis* 53, no. 3: 243–70.

Hegel, Georg Wilhelm Friedrich (1956). *The Philosophy of History*. Translated by J. Sibree. New York: Dover Publications.

——— (2003). *Elements of the Philosophy of Right*. Translated by H. B. Nisbet. Cambridge: Cambridge University Press.

Heidegger, Martin (2002). "Nietzsche's Word: 'God is Dead.'" In *Off The Beaten Track*, translated and edited by Julian Young and Kenneth Haynes, 157–99. Cambridge: Cambridge University Press.

Heine, Heinrich (2007). *On the History of Religion and Philosophy in Germany*. Translated by Howard Pollack-Milgate. Cambridge: Cambridge University Press.

Helmreich, Christian (2014). "Glück, Glückseligkeit, Seligkeit, Wohlfahrt." In *Dictionary of Untranslatables: A Philosophical Lexicon*, translated by Steven Rendall, Christian Hubert, Jeffrey Mehlman, Nathanael Stein, and Michael Syrotinski, edited by Barbara Cassin, 397–402. Princeton: Princeton University Press.

Hermann, Wilhelm (1906). *The Communion of the Christian with God*. Translated by J. Sandys Stanyon. London: Williams & Norgate.

Heschel, Susannah (2012). "German Jewish Scholarship on Islam as a Tool for De-Orientalizing Judaism." *New German Critique* 39(3), no. 117: 91–107.

Hess, Moses (2005). *The Holy History of Mankind and Other Writings.* Edited by Shlomo Avineri. Cambridge: Cambridge University Press.

Hick, John (1985). "A Philosophy of Religious Pluralism." In *Problems of Religious Pluralism*, 28–45. New York: Palgrave Macmillan.

Hobbes, Thomas (1840). *Considerations upon the Reputation, Loyalty, Manners, and Religion of Thomas Hobbes.* In *The English Works of Thomas Hobbes*, vol. 4, edited by William Molesworth, 409–40. London: John Bohn.

——— (1958). *Leviathan.* Oxford: Oxford University Press.

Hollander, Dana (2009). "Ethical-Political Universality out of the Sources of Judaism: Reading Hermann Cohen's 1888 Affidavit in and out of Context." In *New Directions in Jewish Philosophy*, edited by Aaron Hughes and Elliot Wolfson, 229–49. Bloomington: Indiana University Press.

——— (2012). "Love-of-Neighbor and Ethics out of Law in the Philosophy of Hermann Cohen." In *German-Jewish Thought between Religion and Politics: Festschrift in Honor of Paul Mendes-Flohr on the Occasion of His Seventieth Birthday*, edited by Christian Wiese and Martina Urban, 83–114. Berlin: De Gruyter.

——— (2021). *Ethics out of Law: Hermann Cohen and the "Neighbor."* Toronto: University of Toronto Press.

Holowchak, M. Andrew (2012). "The 'Reluctant' Politician: Thomas Jefferson's Debt to Epicurus." *Eighteenth-Century Studies* 45, no. 2: 277–97.

Holwell, John Zephaniah (1767). *Interesting Historical Events Relative to the Provinces of Bengal and the Empire of Indostan.* 2 vols. London: T. Becket & P. A. De Hondt.

Holzhey, Helmut (2005). "Cohen and the Marburg School in Context." In *Hermann Cohen's Critical Idealism*, edited by Reinier Munk, 3–40. Leiden: Springer.

Horkheimer, Max, and Theodor W. Adorno (2002). *Dialectic of Enlightenment.* Translated by Edmund Jephcott. Edited by Gunzelin Schmid Noerr. Stanford: Stanford University Press, 2002.

Huang, Yong (1995). "Religious Pluralism and Interfaith Dialogue: Beyond Universalism and Particularism." *International Journal for Philosophy of Religion* 37, no. 3: 127–44.

Hubatsch, Walter (1975). *Frederick the Great of Prussia: Absolutism and Administration.* Translated by Patrick Doran. London: Thames and Hudson.

Hughes, Aaron W. (2013). *Rethinking Jewish Philosophy: Beyond Particularism and Universalism.* Oxford: Oxford University Press.

Hume, David (1958). *A Treatise of Human Nature*. Oxford: Clarendon Press.
——— (1969). *The Letters of David Hume*. Vol. 1. Edited by J. Y. T Greig. Oxford: Oxford University Press.
——— (1976). *The Natural History of Religion and Dialogues Concerning Natural Religion*. Edited by A. Wayne Colver and John Valdimir Prince. Oxford: Oxford University Press.
——— (1987). "Of the Dignity or Meanness of Human Nature." In *Essays Moral, Political and Literary*, edited by Eugen F. Miller, 81–88. Indianapolis: Liberty Fund.
——— (2007). *An Enquiry Concerning Human Understanding*. Oxford: Oxford University Press.
——— (2012). "Of National Characters." In *Political Essays*, edited by Knud Haakonssen, 78–92. Cambridge: Cambridge University Press.
Insole, Christopher J. (2016). "Kant on Christianity, Religion and Politics: Three Hopes, Three Limits." *Studies in Christian Ethics* 29, no. 1: 14–33.
Isaac, Benjamin H. (2006). *The Invention of Racism in Classical Antiquity*. Princeton: Princeton University Press.
Iserloh, Erwin (1968). *The Theses Were Not Posted: Luther between Reform and Reformation*. Boston: Beacon Press.
Israel, Jonathan I. (2002). *Radical Enlightenment: Philosophy and the Making of Modernity 1650–1750*. Oxford: Oxford University Press.
Jacobi, Friedrich Heinrich (1916). *Wider Mendelssohns Beschuldigungen in dessen Schreiben an die Freunde Lessings*. In *Die Hauptschriften zum Pantheismusstreit Zwischen Jacobi und Mendelssohn*, edited by Heinrich Scholz, 327–64. Berlin: Verlag von Reughter & Reichard.
——— (1994). *Concerning the Doctrine of Spinoza in Letters to Herr Moses Mendelssohn*. In *The Main Philosophical Writings and The Novel "Allwill,"* translated by George Di Giovanni, 173–253. Montreal: McGill-Queen's University Press.
Jacquette, Dale (1998). "Aristotle's Refutation of the Universal Good." *The Journal of Value Inquiry* 32, no. 3: 301–24.
Janiak, Andrew (2010). *Newton as Philosopher*. Cambridge: Cambridge University Press.
Jefferson, Thomas (1950). *Basic Writings*. Edited by Philip S. Foner. Garden City: Halcyon House.
Joas, Hans (2000). *The Genesis of Values*. Chicago: University of Chicago Press.
Johnson, Monte, and Catherine Wilson (2007). "Lucretius and the History of Science." In *The Cambridge Companion to Lucretius*, edited by Stuart

Gillespie and Philip Hardie, 131–48. Cambridge: Cambridge University Press.

Joppien, Rüdiger (1979). "Philippe Jacques de Loutherbourg's Pantomime 'Omai, or, a Trip round the World,' and the Artists of Captain Cook's Voyages." In *Captain Cook and the South Pacific*, edited by T. C. Mitchell, 81–136. Canberra: Australian National University Press.

Jospe, Alfred (1969). "Introduction." In *Jerusalem and Other Jewish Writings*, by Moses Mendelssohn, translated and edited by Alfred Jospe, 1–9. New York: Schocken Books.

Jospe, Raphael (2007). "Moses Mendelssohn: A Medieval Modernist." In *Sepharad in Ahskenaz: Medieval Knowledge and Eighteenth-Century Enlightened Discourse*, edited by Resianne Fontaine, Andrea Schatz, and Irene Zwiep, 107–40. Amsterdam: Royal Netherlands Academy of the Arts and Sciences.

Justin Martyr (2003). *Dialogue with Trypho*. Translated by Thomas B. Falls. Washington: The Catholic University of America Press.

Kajon, Irene (2012). "The Discovery of the 'True Plato' in Some Twentieth-Century German Jewish Thinkers." In *German-Jewish Thought between Religion and Politics: Festschrift in Honor of Paul Mendes-Flohr on the Occasion of His Seventieth Birthday*, edited by Christian Wiese and Martina Urban, 133–49. Berlin: De Gruyter.

Kant, Immanuel (1902–). *Kants Gesammelte Schriften*. 29 vols. Edited by the Königlich Preussische Akademie der Wissenschaften. Berlin: Reimer/Walter de Gruyter.

——— (1914). *Critique of Judgement*. Translated by J. H. Bernard. London: Macmillan and Co.

——— (1929). *Critique of Pure Reason*. Translated by Norman-Kemp Smith. Hampshire: Palmgrave.

——— (1979a). *The Conflict of the Faculties*. Translated by Mary J. Gregor. New York: Abaris Books.

——— (1979b). *The One Possible Basis for a Demonstration of the Existence of God*. Translated by Gordon Treash. New York: Abaris Books.

——— (1997). *Groundwork of the Metaphysics of Morals*. Translated and edited by Mary Gergor. Cambridge: Cambridge University Press.

——— (1999a). *Correspondence*. Translated and edited by Arnulf Zweig. Cambridge: Cambridge University Press.

——— (1999b). "On the Common Saying: That May Be Correct in Theory, but It Is of No Use in Practice." In *Practical Philosophy*, translated and edited by Mary J. Gregor, 273–310. Cambridge: Cambridge University Press.

——— (1999c). "Towards Perpetual Peace: A Philosophical Sketch." In *Practical Philosophy*, translated and edited by Mary J. Gregor, 311–52. Cambridge: Cambridge University Press.

——— (2007). "Of the Different Races of Human Beings." In *Anthropology, History, and Education*, translated by Holly Wilson and Günter Zöller, edited by Günter Zöller and Robert B. Louden, 82–97. Cambridge: Cambridge University Press.

——— (2012). *Lectures on Anthropology*. Translated by Robert R. Clewis, Robert B. Louden, G. Felicitas Munzel, and Allen W. Wood. Edited by Allen W. Wood and Robert B. Louden. Cambridge: Cambridge University Press.

——— (2015). *Critique of Practical Reason*. Translated and edited by Mary J. Gregor. Cambridge: Cambridge University.

Kaplan, Lawrence (1998). "Maimonides and Mendelssohn on the Origins of Idolatry, the Election of Israel, and the Oral Law." In *Perspectives on Jewish Thought and Mysticism*, edited by Alfred L. Ivry, Elliot R. Wolfson, and Allan Arkush, 423–56. Amsterdam: Harwood Academic Publishers.

Katz, Jacob (1973). *Out of the Ghetto: The Social Background of Jewish Emancipation, 1770–1870*. Syracuse: Syracuse University Press.

——— (1980). *From Prejudice to Destruction: Anti-Semitism, 1700–1933*. Cambridge: Harvard University Press.

Kavka, Martin (2004). *Jewish Messianism and the History of Philosophy*. Cambridge: Cambridge University Press.

Kierkegaard, Søren (1983). *Fear and Trembling/Repetition*. Translated and edited by Howard V. Hong and Edna H. Hong. Princeton: Princeton University Press.

——— (1988). *Stages on Life's Way*. Translated and edited by Howard V. Hong and Edna H. Hong. Princeton: Princeton University Press.

Kleist, Heinrich von (1923). *Sämtliche Werke*. Vol. 4. Edited by Arnold Zweig. Munich: Rösl & Cie.

Kluback, William (1984). *Hermann Cohen: The Challenges of a Religion of Reason*. Chico, CA: Scholars Press.

Köhler, Wolfgang (1938). *The Place of Value in a World of Facts*. New York: Liveright Publishing Corporation.

Koyré, Alexandre (1943). "Galileo and Plato." *Journal of the History of Ideas* 4, no. 4: 400–28.

——— (1957). *From the Closed World to the Infinite Universe*. Baltimore: The John Hopkins University Press.

Lach, Donald F. (1953). "The Sinophilism of Christian Wolff (1679–1754)." *Journal of the History of Ideas* 14, no. 4 (October): 561–74.

Lamm, Norman (1965). "Man's Position in the Universe. A Comparative Study of the Views of Saadia Gaon and Maimonides." *The Jewish Quarterly Review* 55, no. 3: 208–34.

Landry, Stan M. (2011). "From Orthodoxy to Atheism: The Apostasy of Bruno Bauer, 1835–1843." *Journal of Religion and Society* 13: 1–20.

Laursen, J. C. (2016). "Basedow, Johann Bernhard." In *The Bloomsbury Dictionary of Eighteenth-Century Philosophers*, vol. 1, edited by Heiner F. Klemme and Manfred Kuehn, 40–43. London: Bloomsbury.

Leibniz, Gottfried Wilhelm (1951). *Selections*. Edited by Philip P. Winer. New York: Charles Scribner's Sons.

——— (1973). *Discourse on Metaphysics*. In *Discourse on Metaphysics; Correspondence with Arnaud; Monadology*, translated by George R. Montgomery, 1–64. La Salle: The Open Court Publishing Company.

——— (1994). *Writings on China*. Translated by Daniel J. Cook and Henry Rosemont Jr. Chicago: Open Court.

Levenson, Alan (2002). "Missionary Protestants as Defenders and Detractors of Judaism: Franz Delitzsch and Hermann Strack." *The Jewish Quarterly Review* 92, no. 3/4: 383–420.

Levenson, Jon D. (1996). "The Universal Horizon of Biblical Particularism." In *Ethnicity and the Bible*, edited by Mark G. Brett, 143–70. Leiden: E. J. Brill.

Levinas, Emmanuel (1990). "Monotheism and Language." In *Difficult Freedom: Essays on Judaism*, translated by Seán Hand, 178–80. Baltimore: John Hopkins University Press.

Levinger, Matthew (2000). *Enlightened Nationalism: The Transformation of Prussian Political Culture 1806–1848*. Oxford: Oxford University Press.

Liebeschütz, Hans (1960). "Hermann Cohen und Spinoza." *Bulletin des Leo Baeck Instituts* 3, no. 12: 225–38.

——— (1968). "Hermann Cohen and His Historical Background." *The Leo Baeck Institute Year Book* 13, no. 1: 3–33.

Liebmann, Otto (1912). *Kant und die Epigonen*. Berlin: Reuther & Richard.

Locke, John (1985). *An Essay Concerning Human Understanding*. Edited by Peter H. Nidditch. Oxford: Clarendon Press.

——— (2003). *Two Treatises of Government*. Edited by Peter Laslett. Cambridge: Cambridge University Press.

——— (2010a). "A Letter Concerning Toleration." In *Locke on Toleration*, translated by Michael Silverthorne, edited by Richard Vernon, 3–46. Cambridge: Cambridge University Press.

——— (2010b). "A Second Letter Concerning Toleration." In *Locke on Toleration*, edited by Richard Vernon, 67–107. Cambridge: Cambridge University Press.

Lovejoy, Arthur O. (1978). *The Great Chain of Being: A Study of the History of an Idea*. Cambridge: Harvard University Press.

Lorberbaum, Menachem (2007). "Making Space for Leviathan: On Hobbes' Political Theory." *Hebraic Political Studies* 2, no. 1: 78–100.

Louden, Robert B. (2012). "'Not a Slow Reform, but a Swift Revolution': Kant and Basedow on the Need to Transform Education." In *Kant on Education: Interpretations and Commentary*, edited by Klas Roth and Chris W. Surpenant, 39–54. London: Routledge.

Ludwig, Bernd (2007). "Kant, Garve, and the Motives of Moral Action." *Journal of Moral Philosophy* 4, no. 2: 183–93.

Luzzatto, Moshe Chayim (1969). *The Path of the Just*. Translated by Shraga Silverstein. Jerusalem: Feldheim.

MacIntyre, Alasdair (2007). *After Virtue: A Study in Moral Theory*. Notre Dame: University of Notre Dame Press.

Magnis, Nicholas E. (1999). "Thomas Jefferson and Slavery: An Analysis of His Racist Thinking as Revealed by His Writings and Political Behavior." *Journal of Black Studies* 29, no. 4: 491–509.

Maimon, Solomon (2018). *The Autobiography of Solomon Maimon*. Translated by Paul Reitter. Princeton: Princeton University Press.

Maimonides, Moses (1963). *The Guide of the Perplexed*. 2 vols. Translated by Shlomo Pines. Chicago: The University of Chicago Press.

Margolin, Ron (2018). "Moses Hess as a Prophet of Spiritual Zionism: The Origins of Messianic Jewish Humanism." *Modern Judaism* 38, no. 1: 75–95.

Martin, A. Lynn (1973). "The Jesuit Mystique." *The Sixteenth Century Journal* 4, no. 1 (April): 31–40.

Martinich, Aloysius P. (1999). *Hobbes: A Biography*. Cambridge: Cambridge University Press.

——— (2003). *The Two Gods of Leviathan: Thomas Hobbes on Religion and Politics*. Cambridge: Cambridge University Press.

McCarthy, Vincent A. (1986). *Quest for a Philosophical Jesus: Christianity and Philosophy in Rousseau, Kant, Hegel, and Schelling*. Macon: Mercer University Press.

McCormick, Eric H. (2013). *Omai: Pacific Envoy*. Auckland: Auckland University Press.

Mehigan, Timothy J. (2011). *Heinrich von Kleist: Writing After Kant*. Rochester: Camden House.

Melamed, Abraham (2016). "The Greek Theory of Climate in Medieval Jewish Thought: Absorption, Influence and Application." In *The Routledge Handbook of Identity and the Environment in the Classical and Medieval Worlds*, edited by Rebecca Futo Kennedy and Molly Jones-Lewis, 114–30. London: Routledge.

Mendelssohn, Moses (1971–). *Gesammelte Schriften: Jubiläumsausgabe.* 24 vols. Edited by Ismar Elbogen, Julius Guttmann, Eugene Mittwoch, Alexander Altmann, et al. Stuttgardt-Bad Cannstatt: F. Frommann.

——— (1983). *Jerusalem, or on Religious Power and Judaism.* Translated by Allan Arkush. Waltham: Brandeis University Press.

——— (1997a). "Dialogues." In *Philosophical Writings*, translated and edited by Daniel I. Dahlstrom, 96–130. Cambridge: Cambridge University Press.

——— (1997b). "On Evidence in Metaphysical Sciences." In *Philosophical Writings*, translated and edited by Daniel I. Dahlstrom, 251–306. Cambridge: Cambridge University Press.

——— (1997c). "On Probability." In *Philosophical Writings*, translated and edited by Daniel I. Dahlstrom, 233–51. Cambridge: Cambridge University Press.

——— (1997d). "On Sentiments." In *Philosophical Writings*, translated and edited by Daniel I. Dahlstrom, 7–95. Cambridge: Cambridge University Press.

——— (1997e). "Rhapsody or Additions to the Letters on Sentiments." In *Philosophical Writings*, translated and edited by Daniel I. Dahlstrom, 131–68. Cambridge: Cambridge University Press.

——— (2007). *Phädon or on the Immortality of the Soul.* Translated by Patricia Noble. New York: Peter Lang.

——— (2011). *Writings on Judaism, Christianity, & the Bible.* Translated by Curtis Bowman, Elias Sacks, and Allan Arkush. Edited By Michah Gottlieb. Waltham: Brandeis University Press.

——— (2012a). *Morning Hours.* In *Last Works*, translated by Bruce Rosenstock, 1–137. Urbana: University of Illinois Press.

——— (2012b). *To the Friends of Lessing.* In *Last Works*, translated by Bruce Rosenstock, 139–76. Urbana: University of Illinois Press.

Meyer, Michael A. (1966). "Great Debate on Antisemitism: Jewish Reaction to New Hostility in Germany 1879–1881." *The Leo Baeck Institute Yearbook* 11, no. 1: 137–70.

——— (1975). "Where Does the Modern Period of Jewish History Begin?" *Judaism* 24, no. 3: 329–39.

Montaigne, Michel de (1991a). "On the Cannibals." In *The Complete Essays*, translated and edited by M. A. Screech, 228–41. London: Penguin Books.

——— (1991b). "That the Taste of Good and Evil Things Depends in Large Part on the Opinion We Have of Them." In *The Complete Essays*, translated and edited by M. A. Screech, 52–72. London: Penguin Books.

Moore, George Edward (1922). *Principia Ethica*. Cambridge: Cambridge University Press.

Mozi (2010). *The Mozi: A Complete Translation*. Translated and annotated by Ian Johnston. Hong Kong: The Chinese University Press.

Munk, Reinier (2006). "On the Idea of God in Cohen's *Ethik*." In *Hermann Cohen's Ethics*, edited by Robert Gibbs, 105–14. Leiden: Brill.

Myers, David N. (2001). "Hermann Cohen and the Quest for Protestant Judaism." *The Leo Baeck Institute Year Book* 46, no. 1: 195–214.

Nadler, Steven (1999). *Spinoza: A Life*. Cambridge: Cambridge University Press.

Newton, Isaac (1999). *The Principia: Mathematical Principles of Natural Philosophy*. Translated by I. Bernard Cohen and Anne Whitman. Berkeley: University of California Press.

Nietzsche, Friedrich (1967). *Ecce Homo*. In *On the Genealogy of Morals and Ecce Homo*, translated and edited by Walter Kaufmann, 201–338. New York: Vintage Books.

——— (1994). *On The Genealogy of Morality*. Translated by Carol Diethe. Cambridge: Cambridge University Press.

——— (2002). *Beyond Good and Evil*. Translated by Judith Norman. Cambridge: Cambridge University Press.

——— (2005). *The Anti-Christ*. In *The Anti-Christ, Ecce Homo, Twilight of the Idols, and Other Writings*, translated by Judith Norman, 1–67. Cambridge: Cambridge University Press.

——— (2007). *Untimely Meditations*. Translated by R. J. Hollingdale. Edited by Daniel Breazeale. Cambridge: Cambridge University Press.

——— (2008). *The Gay Science*. Translated by Josefine Nauckhoff. Cambridge: Cambridge University Press.

Nordmann, Sophie (2007). *Du singulier à l'universel: Essai sur la philosophie religieuse de Hermann Cohen*. Paris: J. Vrin.

Oakes, Guy (2003). "Max Weber on Value Rationality and Value Spheres." *Journal of Classical Sociology* 3, no. 1: 27–45.

O'Brien, Charles H. (1969). "Ideas of Religious Toleration at the Time of Joseph II. A Study of the Enlightenment among Catholics in Austria." *Transactions of the American Philosophical Society* 59, no. 7: 1–80.

Paine, Thomas (1896). *The Age of Reason*. Edited by Moncure Daniel Conway. New York: G. P. Putnam's Sons.

Palmer, Gesine (2006). "Judaism as 'Method' with Hermann Cohen and Franz Rosenzweig." In *Hermann Cohen's Ethics*, edited by Robert Gibbs, 37–64. Leiden: Brill.

Patterson, Jessica E. M. (2017). "An Eighteenth-Century Account of Sati: John Zephaniah Holwell's 'Religious Tenets of the Gentoos' and 'Voluntary Sacrifice' (1767)." *South Asia: Journal of South Asian Studies* 40, no. 1: 24–39.

Perkins, Franklin (2004). *Leibniz and China: A Commerce of Light.* Cambridge: Cambridge University Press.

Perry, Ralph Barton (1926). *General Theory of Value.* Cambridge: Harvard University Press.

Plato (1997a). *Apology.* Translated by G. M. A. Grube. In *Complete Works*, edited by John M. Cooper, 17–36. Indianapolis: Hacket Publishing Company.

——— (1997b). *Gorgias.* Translated by Donald J. Zeyl. In *Complete Works*, edited by John M. Cooper, 791–869. Indianapolis: Hacket Publishing Company.

——— (1997c). *Philebus.* Translated by Dorothea Frede. In *Complete Works*, edited by John M. Cooper, 398–456. Indianapolis: Hacket Publishing Company.

——— (1997d). *Republic.* Translated by G. M. A. Grube. Revised by C. D. C. Reeve. In *Complete Works*, edited by John M. Cooper, 971–1223. Indianapolis: Hacket Publishing Company.

Pogson Smith, William George (1958). "The Philosophy of Hobbes." In *Leviathan*, by Thomas Hobbes, vii–xxxii. Oxford: Oxford University Press.

Poma, Andrea (1997). *The Critical Philosophy of Hermann Cohen.* Translated by John Denton. Albany: State University of New York Press.

——— (2005). "Suffering and Non-eschatological Messianism in Hermann Cohen." In *Hermann Cohen's Critical Idealism*, edited by Reinier Munk, 413–28. Leiden: Springer.

——— (2006). "Religion of Reason and Judaism in Hermann Cohen." In *Yearning for Form and Other Essays on Hermann Cohen's Thought*, 111–28. Dordrecht: Springer.

——— (2007). "Hermann Cohen: Judaism and Critical Idealism." Translated by John Denton. In *The Cambridge Companion to Jewish Philosophy*, edited by Michael L. Morgan and Peter Eli Gordon, 80–101. Cambridge: Cambridge University Press.

Popkin, Richard (1979). *The History of Scepticism from Erasmus to Spinoza.* Berkeley: University of California Press.

Proast, Jonas (2010). "The Argument of the Letter Concerning Toleration, Briefly Considered and Answered." In *Locke on Toleration*, edited by Richard Vernon, 54–66. Cambridge: Cambridge University Press.

Rashkover, Randi (2012). "Revelation." In *The Cambridge History of Jewish Philosophy*, vol. 2, *The Modern Era*, edited by Martin Kavka, Zachary Braiterman, and David Novak, 399–426. Cambridge: Cambridge University Press.

Raz-Krakotzkin, Amnon (2007). "Jewish Memory between Exile and History." *The Jewish Quarterly Review* 97, no. 4: 530–43.

Reid, Thomas (1983). *An Inquiry into the Human Mind on the Principles of Common Sense*. In *Inquiry and Essays*, edited by Ronald E. Beanblossoms and Keither Lehrer, 1–102. Indianapolis: Hackett.

Revah, Israel Salvator (1959). *Spinoza et le Dr. Juan de Prado*. Paris: Mouton & Co.

——— (1964). "Aux origines de la rupture Spinozienne: Nouveaux documents sur l'incroyance dans la communauté Judéo-Portugaise d'Amsterdam a l'époque de l'excommunication de Spinoza." *Revue des Études Juives* 123: 359–431.

Richards, John F. (2003). *The Unending Frontier: An Environmental History of the Early Modern World*. Berkeley: University of California Press.

Rokéah, David (2002). *Justin Martyr and the Jews*. Leiden: Brill.

Rosenstock, Bruce (2010). *Philosophy and the Jewish Question: Mendelssohn, Rosenzweig, and Beyond*. New York: Fordham University Press.

——— (2012). "Notes." In *Last Works*, by Moses Mendelssohn, translated by Bruce Rosenstock, 178–220. Urbana: University of Illinois Press.

Rosenzweig, Franz (1924). "Einleitung." In *Hermann Cohens Jüdische Schriften*, vol. 1, edited by Bruno Strauss, xiii–lxiv. Berlin: C. A. Schwetschke & Sohn.

——— (2000). "Apologetic Thinking." In *Philosophical and Theological Writing*, translated and edited by Paul W. Franks and Michael L. Morgan, 95–108. Indianapolis: Hackett Publishing Company.

——— (2021). "Introduction to the Jewish Writings of Hermann Cohen." In *Hermann Cohen: Writings on Neo-Kantiansim & Jewish Philosophy*, edited by Samuel Moyn and Robert S. Schine Waltham. Brandeis University Press.

Rotenstreich, Nathan (1996). "Hermann Cohen: Judaism in the Context of German Philosophy." In *Essays in Jewish Philosophy in the Modern Era*, edited by Reinier Munk, 86–101. Amsterdam: J. C. Gieben.

Rousseau, Jean Jacques (1979). *Emile or on Education*. Translated by Allan Bloom. New York: Basic Books.

Routledge, Robin L. (2008). "Death and Afterlife in the Old Testament." *Journal of European Baptist Studies* 9, no. 1: 22–39.

Rowe, Christopher (2007). "The Form of the Good and the Good in Plato's Republic." In *Pursuing the Good: Ethics and Metaphysics in Plato's Republic*, edited by Douglas Cairns, Frits-Gregor Herrman, and Terry Penner, 124–53. Edinburgh: Edinburgh University Press.

Ruderman, David B. (2000). *Jewish Enlightenment in an English Key: Anglo-Jewry's Construction of Modern Jewish Thought*. Princeton: Princeton University Press.

—— (2011). *Early Modern Jewry: A New Cultural History*. Princeton: Princeton University Press.

Ruether, Rosemary (1997). *Faith and Fratricide: The Theological Roots of Anti-Semitism*. Eugene, OR: Wipf & Stock Publishers.

Runesson, Anders (2000). "Particularistic Judaism and Universalistic Christianity? Some Critical Remarks on Terminology and Theology." *Studia Theologica – Nordic Journal of Theology* 54, no. 1: 55–75.

Schäfer, Peter (1997). *Judeophobia: Attitudes toward the Jews in the Ancient World*. Cambridge: Harvard University Press.

Schlereth, Thomas J. (1977). *The Cosmopolitan Ideal in Enlightenment Thought: Its Form and Function in the Ideas of Franklin, Hume, and Voltaire, 1694–1790*. Notre Dame: The University of Notre Dame Press.

Schmidt, Royal J. (1956). "Cultural Nationalism in Herder." *Journal of the History of Ideas* 17, no. 3 (June): 407–17.

Schmitt, Carl (1996). *The Leviathan in the State Theory of Thomas Hobbes*. Translated by George Schwab and Erna Hilfstein. Westport: Greenwood Press.

Scholem, Gershom (2012). *From Berlin to Jerusalem: Memories of My Youth*. Translated by Harry Zohn. Philadelphia: Paul Dry Books.

Schonfeld, Eli (2010), "Living Law: Hermann Cohen Facing St. Paul's Critique of the Law." *Reshit: Studies in Judaism* 2: 80–110 (Hebrew).

—— (2016)"Forsaken God: Moses Mendelssohn and Rabbi Jacob Emden on Chosenness and Universalism." *Daat: A Journal of Jewish Philosophy & Kabbalah* 81: 351–68 (Hebrew).

Schopenhauer, Arthur (2000). "Sketch of a History of the Doctrine of the Ideal and the Real." In *Parerga and Paralipomena: Short Philosophical Essays*, vol.1, translated by E. F. J. Payne, 1–28. Oxford: Oxford University Press.

Schwarzschild, Steven S. (1962a). "Do Noachites Have to Believe in Revelation? (A Passage in Dispute between Maimonides, Spinoza, Mendelssohn and H. Cohen). A Contribution to a Jewish View of

Natural Law: The Textual Question." *The Jewish Quarterly Review* 52, no. 4: 297–308.

——— (1962b). "Do Noachites Have to Believe in Revelation? (Continued)." *The Jewish Quarterly Review* 53, no. 1: 30–65.

——— (1979). "'Germanism and Judaism' – Hermann Cohen's Normative Paradigm of the German-Jewish Symbiosis." In *Jews and Germans from 1860 to 1933: The Problematic Symbiosis*, edited by David Bronsen, 129–72. Heidelberg: Carl Winter.

Schwoerer, Lois G. (1990). "Locke, Lockean Ideas, and the Glorious Revolution." *Journal of the History of Ideas* 51, no. 4: 531–48.

Sedgwick, Sally (2011). "Hegel on the Empty Formalism of Kant's Categorical Imperative." In *A Companion to Hegel*, edited by Stephen Houlgate and Michael Baur, 265–80. Chichester: Willey-Blackwell.

Sedley, David (1991). "Is Aristotle's Teleology Anthropocentric?" *Phronesis: A Journal for Ancient Philosophy* 36, no. 2: 179–96.

Sextus Empiricus (1955). *Outlines of Pyrrhonism*. Translated by R. G. Bury. Cambridge: Harvard University Press.

Shavin, David (2007). "Introduction." In *Phädon or on the Immortality of the Soul*, by Moses Mendelssohn, translated by Patricia Noble, 3–38. New York: Peter Lang.

Shields, C. (2015). "The *Summum Bonum* in Aristotle's Ethics: Fractured Goodness." In *The Highest Good in Aristotle and Kant*, edited by Joachim Auferheide and Ralf M. Bader, 83–111. Oxford: Oxford University Press.

Sidgwick, Henry (1905). *Lectures on the Philosophy of Kant and Other Philosophical Lectures & Essays*. London: Macmillan.

Sieg, Ulrich (1993). "'Der Wissenschaft und dem Leben Tut Dasselbe Not: Ehrfurcht vor der Wahrheit' Hermann Cohens Gutachten im Marburger Antisemitismusprozeß 1888." In *Philosopihsches Denken – Politisches Wirken*, edited by Reihard Brandt and Franz Orlik, 222–49. Hildesheim: Georg Olms Verlag.

Smith, Helmut Walser (1994). "The Learned and the Popular Discourse of Anti-Semitism in the Catholic Milieu of the Kaiserreich." *Central European History* 27, no. 3: 315–28.

Smith, Nick (2008). *I Was Wrong: The Meanings of Apologies*. Cambridge: Cambridge University Press.

Sorkin, David (1994). "The Case for Comparison: Moses Mendelssohn and the Religious Enlightenment." *Modern Judaism* 14, no. 2: 121–38.

——— (2012). *Moses Mendelssohn and the Religious Enlightenment*. London: Peter Halban.

Spinoza, Benedictus de (1985a). *Ethics*. In *The Collected Works of Spinoza*, vol. 1, translated and edited by Edwin Curley, 408–617. Princeton: Princeton University Press.

——— (1985b). *Short Treatise on God, Man, and His Well-Being*. In *The Collected Works of Spinoza*, vol. 1, translated and edited by Edwin Curley, 59–156. Princeton: Princeton University Press.

——— (2016a). *Letters: January 1671–Late 1676*. In *The Collected Works of Spinoza*, vol. 2, translated and edited by Edwin Curley, 374–490. Princeton: Princeton University Press.

——— (2016b). *The Theological-Political Treatise*. In *The Collected Works of Spinoza*, vol. 2, translated and edited by Edwin Curley, 65–354. Princeton: Princeton University Press.

Springborg, Patricia (1996). "Hobbes on Religion." In *The Cambridge Companion to Hobbes*, edited by Tom Sorell, 346–80. Cambridge: Cambridge University Press.

Starn, Randolph (2002). "The Early Modern Muddle." *Journal of Early Modern History* 6, no. 3: 296–307.

Stern, Menahem (1980). *Greek and Latin Authors on Jews and Judaism*. 2 vols. Jerusalem: The Israel Academy of Sciences and Humanities.

Strauss, Leo (1988). *Persecution and the Art of Writing*. Chicago: The University of Chicago Press.

——— (1989). "What Is Political Philosophy?" In *An Introduction to Political Philosophy*, edited by Hilail Gildin, 3–58. Detroit: Wayne State University Press.

——— (2012a). "Introduction to *Morning Hours* and *To the Friends of Lessing*." In *Leo Strauss on Moses Mendelssohn*, translated and edited by Martin D. Yaffe, 59–145. Chicago: Chicago University Press.

——— (2012b) "Introduction to *Phädon*." In *Leo Strauss on Moses Mendelssohn*, translated and edited by Martin D. Yaffe, 29–49. Chicago: The University of Chicago Press.

Sutcliffe, Adam (1998). "Myth, Origins, Identity: Voltairé, The Jews and the Enlightenment Notion of Toleration." *The Eighteenth Century* 39, no. 2: 107–26.

Taylor, Charles (1989). *Sources of the Self: The Making of Modern Identity*. Cambridge: Harvard University Press.

Taylor, Miriam S. (1995). *Anti-Judaism and Early Christian Identity: A Critique of Scholarly Consensus*. Leiden: Brill.

Treitschke, Heinrich von (1880). "Ein Wort über unser Judenthum." Berlin: G. Reimer.

Tricoire, Damien (2017). "Introduction." In *Enligthened Colonialism: Civilization Narratives and Imperial Politics in the Age of Reason*, edited by Damien Tricoire, 1–22. Cham: Palgrave Macmillan.

Vatter, Miguel (2021). *Living Law: Jewish Political Theology from Hermann Cohen to Hannah Arendt*. Oxford: Oxford University Press.

Vernon, Richard (2010). "Introduction." In *Locke on Toleration*, by John Locke, edited by Richard Vernon, viii–xxxii. Cambridge: Cambridge University Press.

Voltaire, François-Marie Arouet (1829). "Defense du mondain ou l'apologie du luxe." In *Oeuvres complètes de Voltaire*, vol. 10, 404–7. Paris: Armand-Aubréé.

——— (1878) "Essai sur les moeurs." In *Oeuvres complètes de Voltaire*, vol. 11, 3–552. Paris: Garnier Fréres.

——— (1971). *Philosophical Dictionary*. Edited and translated by Theodore Besterman. Middlesex: Penguin Books.

——— (2000). *Treatise on Tolerance*. Translated by Brian Masters. Cambridge: Cambridge University Press.

Waldron, Jeremy (2002). *God, Locke, and Equality: Christian Foundations in Locke's Political Thought*. Cambridge: Cambridge University Press.

Walford, David (1992). "General Introduction." In *Theoretical Philosophy, 1755–1770*, by Immanuel Kant, translated and edited by David Walford, xxxv–xlviii. Cambridge: Cambridge University Press.

Weber, Max (1990). *Basic Concepts in Sociology*. Translated by H. P. Secher. New York: Citadel Press.

——— (1991). "Religious Rejections of the World and Their Direction." In *Essays in Sociology*, translated and edited by H. H. Gerth and C. Wright Mills, 323–62. London: Routledge.

——— (2011). "'Objectivity' in Social Science." In *Methodology of the Social Sciences*, translated and edited by Edward A. Shils and Henry A. Finch, 1–49. New Brunswick: Transaction Publishers.

Weiss, Daniel (2012). *Paradox and the Prophet: Hermann Cohen and the Indirect Communication of Religion*. Oxford: Oxford University Press.

Westphal, Kenneth R. (1991). "Hegel's Critique of Kant's Moral World View." *Philosophical Topics* 19, no. 2: 133–76.

Wider, Kathleen (1986). "Women Philosophers in the Ancient Greek World: Donning the Mantle." *Hypatia* 1, no. 1: 21–62.

Wiedebach, Hartwig (2012). *The National Element in Hermann Cohen's Philosophy and Religion*. Translated by William Templer. Leiden: Brill.

Wolfson, Elliot R. (2012). "Imagination and the Theolatrous Impulse: Configuring God in Modern Jewish Thought." In *The Cambridge History of Jewish Philosophy: The Modern Era*, edited by Z. Braiterman, M. Kavka, and D. Novak, 663–703. Cambridge: Cambridge University Press.

Wood, Allan W. (1970). *Kant's Moral Religion*. Ithaca & London: Cornell University Press.

Wright, Rosemary (2013). *Cosmology in Antiquity*. London: Routledge.

Yovel, Yirmiyahu (1991). "The Infinite Mode and Natural Laws in Spinoza." In *God and Nature: Spinoza's Metaphysics*, edited by Yirmiyahu Yovel, 79–96. Leiden: E. J. Brill.

——— (1998). *Dark Riddle: Hegel,* Nietzsche *and the Jews*. Pennsylvania: The Pennsylvania State University Press.

Zank, Michael (2000). *The Idea of Atonement in the Philosophy of Hermann Cohen*. Providence: Brown Judaic Studies.

——— (2006). "The Ethics in Hermann Cohen's Philosophical System." In *Hermann Cohen's Ethics*, edited by Robert Gibbs, 1–15. Leiden: Brill.

Zerubavel, Eviatar (1992). *Terra Cognita: The Mental Discovery of America*. New Brunswick: Rutgers University Press.

INDEX